BERKELEY'S PHILOSOPHICAL

WRITINGS

GEORGE BERKELEY

Berkeley's Philosophical Writings

EDITED WITH AN INTRODUCTION
BY *DAVID M. ARMSTRONG*

COLLIER BOOKS
Macmillan Publishing Company
NEW YORK
COLLIER MACMILLAN PUBLISHERS
LONDON

Macmillan Publishing Company
866 Third Avenue, New York, N.Y. 10022
Collier Macmillan Canada, Inc.

Library of Congress Catalog Card Number: 64-22680

A Collier Books Original

First Edition 1965
11   10   9   8

ISBN 0-02-064170-2

Macmillan books are available at special discounts for
bulk purchases for sales promotions, premiums,
fund-raising, or educational use. For details, contact:

Special Sales Director
Macmillan Publishing Company
866 Third Avenue
New York, New York 10022

Printed in the United States of America

Table of Contents

Chronology

1685 George Berkeley born at Kilkenny, Ireland, March 12

1696 Entered Kilkenny College

1700 Entered Trinity College, Dublin (aged fifteen)

1704 Graduated B.A.; Remained in Trinity

1707 Elected Fellow of Trinity; Writing *Philosophical Commentaries*

1709 Published *Essay on Vision;* Ordained Deacon

1710 Published *Principles of Human Knowledge;* Ordained Priest

1712 Published *Passive Obedience*

1713 First visit to England; Published *Three Dialogues;* Presented at court by Swift; Toured Continent briefly

1716-20 Second Continental tour, as tutor to son of Bishop of Clogher

1721 Published *De Motu;* Returned to Dublin and Trinity College

1722 Appointed to Deanery of Dromore, but unable to gain possession of the sinecure

1724 Appointed Dean of Derry; Resigned from Trinity; To London to press a scheme for a college in the Bermudas

1726 Parliament approved a grant for St. Paul's College, Bermuda

1728 Married Anne Forster; Sailed for America, settled at Newport, Rhode Island

1731 Informed that grant for St. Paul's would not be paid; Returned to London

1732 Published *Alciphron,* an attack on contemporary freethinking

1734 Appointed Bishop of Cloyne; Returned to Ireland, settled at Cloyne

1744 Published *Siris: a chain of Philosophical Reflections and Inquiries concerning the virtues of Tar Water*

1752 Removed to Oxford, where his son, George, became undergraduate at Christ Church

1753 Died at Oxford, January 14, buried in Christ Church chapel

Editor's Introduction

ONE GOOD WAY to study philosophy is to study the systems of the great philosophers. In an English-speaking country, there is much to be said for beginning with Berkeley. His most important works are superlatively well written. They are simple and clear. They are quite brief. What they say may be wrong, but it is never dull. There is interesting argument for even the most incredible assertion.

Berkeley's two main philosophical works are the *Principles of Human Knowledge* and the *Three Dialogues between Hylas and Philonous*. He wrote the *Three Dialogues* after the *Principles* had been received with scorn and incomprehension, hoping that a more informal presentation of the same doctrines would secure him a better hearing. In the *Dialogues,* Philonous ("Mind-lover") represents Berkeley, and he gradually wins over Hylas ("Materialist") to his point of view.

I. *Physical objects cannot exist unperceived*

It is the main object of the *Principles* and the *Dialogues* to defend this strange doctrine. Berkeley does not maintain simply that we can never *know* whether such things as trees exist unperceived. Nor does he maintain even that trees do not, *as a matter of fact,* exist unperceived. He maintains the far more radical thesis that physical objects *cannot* exist unperceived. The notion of the existence of unperceived objects, he holds, *involves a contradiction.* Sometimes he presents his doctrine by saying that physical objects can exist only "in the mind."

BERKELEY'S FIRST ARGUMENT

This argument is to be found in the opening sections of the *Principles* (Secs. 1-7), after the Introduction. The bare bones of the argument may be exhibited thus:

(i) Sensible qualities of objects are nothing but "ideas" in the mind

(ii) Physical objects are nothing more than their sensible qualities

7

So, therefore:

(iii) Physical objects are nothing but "ideas" in the mind.

In order to understand Berkeley's first premise, we must first know what he means by the word "idea." He does not use the word in the sense we give it today. He takes over the term for his great predecessor, John Locke, whose *Essay concerning Human Understanding* was almost the sole starting-point for Berkeley's thinking in the *Principles* and the *Dialogues*. Now Locke uses the word "idea" in an extraordinarily wide way. It covers *at least*: (a) sense-perceptions (sense-impressions); (b) bodily sensations (such things as pains or tickles); (c) mental images; (d) thoughts and concepts. The use of one word to cover this heterogeneous class of things leads Locke into all sorts of errors. In particular, it leads him to ignore the vast differences between these classes of things, and to think that they are more or less alike. Berkeley uses the word in the same portmanteau way, and, as a result, is led into many of the same errors.

But, *in the present argument*, Berkeley is thinking of what are now sometimes called *"sense-impressions."* "Sense-impression" is itself a tricky term, as modern philosophy has found to its cost. But when I look at a book with a blue cover, to take an example, it seems reasonable to say that I have a visual experience of a certain blue shape, an experience that I might possibly have even in the absence of the book. This we may call a sense-impression, or, in Berkeley's less satisfactory terminology, an idea. In the same way, when I hear a train go by I have an auditory experience which we may call an auditory sense-impression, and so on.

We can now re-state the first premise of Berkeley's argument. He is saying that the blueness of a book's surface, the noise of a train, the roundness of a pond, the roughness of a piece of cloth, all the properties of objects that we perceive by our senses, are simply sense-impressions. And sense-impressions, of course, demand a perceiver to have them.

But Berkeley has made a serious mistake here. If a book has the sensible quality of blueness, then we can say "The book *is blue*." But if the book "presents me with blue sense-impressions" we can say no more than "The book *looks blue to me*." Now, "is blue" and "looks blue to me" do not mean the same thing. A thing can *be* blue without looking blue to me, and *look blue to me* without being blue. So Berkeley is wrong to identify sensible qualities and sense-impressions, which means that the first premise of the argument is false.

In the *Principles,* Berkeley does not argue for, but simply assumes, the truth of this premise. But the first half of the *First Dialogue* (pp. 137-158) is devoted to an attempt to establish it. Unfortunately, although this portion of the dialogue contains some very interesting material, as argument for this premise it is a failure. For, again and again, Berkeley fails to distinguish between (i) a thing's having a certain quality, and (ii) the thing seeming to a perceiver to have a certain quality; which means that the extended argument is really an elaborate begging of the question.

As an example, consider his argument (pp. 139-142) to prove that *heat* is nothing but pain or pleasure, and so does not exist except "in the mind." When Hylas very reasonably suggests that heat is simply the *cause* of pain in us, Philonous retorts that when we put our hand near a fire we do not get one sensation of heat, and a second sensation of pain, but only "one simple uniform sensation." Now, even if we grant this dubious contention, Berkeley is begging the question by identifying *the heat* with any sensation. The most he could say is that *the feeling of heat* is nothing but a pain. But then his labor is wasted, because there is no need to prove that *feelings* of heat are pains in order to prove they are "in the mind." *Feelings* of heat must be "in the mind." But this does nothing to prove that *heat* is in the mind.

At this point, one might be tempted to defend Berkeley by saying: "But how can you prove that there is anything more than feelings of heat? Perhaps the ordinary distinction between heat and feelings of heat is incorrect." This misses the point. Berkeley is here trying to *prove* that all sensible qualities are "in the mind," and it is no good retorting "How do you *disprove* Berkeley's contention?" He is not arguing that his position is a possible one, but that it must be true. So it seems that Berkeley fails to establish the first premise of his argument, which invalidates the whole line of argument.

BERKELEY'S SECOND ARGUMENT

This argument, which is even less satisfactory, is to be found in the *Principles,* Sec. 23, and in the *First Dialogue* (pp. 163-164).

It is a proof by *reductio ad absurdum.* Suppose I try to imagine physical objects, for instance books or trees, existing unperceived. The attempt is necessarily a failure, Berkeley argues, because "you yourself perceive or think of them all the while."

Notice that this argument cannot really be expected to prove that physical objects cannot exist *unperceived*. The best it can prove is that physical objects cannot exist un-thought of—un*con*ceived. Berkeley slips between "perceiving" and "thinking." There are two reasons why this is easy for him. In the first place, although Berkeley is never very explicit on the matter, he seems to hold an Image theory of thinking. That is to say, he seems to believe that to think is to have a train of mental images passing through the mind—the picture theory of thinking. In the second place, he makes no very sharp distinction between mental images on the one hand, and sense-impressions on the other. They are lumped together under the blanket-word "idea." The result is that he slides easily from thinking to the having of images, and from the having of images to the having of sense-impressions, and so fails to distinguish clearly between thinking and perceiving.

So the argument must be that we cannot think of objects existing *unthought* of, because to try to do so *is* to think of them. But it is clear that there must be something wrong with the argument because, if it were valid, it would establish the truth of patent absurdities. For I can use the same method of argument to prove that the existence of anything, past, present or future that is unthought of *by me* is inconceivable. For suppose I try to think of such a thing. I fail, because I am thinking of it. So only the things I think of can exist!

What is wrong with the argument? The first point to notice is that the sense of "thought of" in which Berkeley is claiming that nothing can exist is an incredibly empty one. It means only "a reference of any sort at all." Even if I speak of "things that have never been thought of before," that phrase is to count as a reference to those things: it is to count as thinking of them. So perhaps we can admit to Berkeley that, when we speak of things existing that have never been thought of, there is a trivial sense in which, in speaking of them, we are thinking of them. But in every other sense except this trivial one, things can exist unthought of.

But even this is too great a concession to Berkeley's argument. Berkeley is maintaining that the notion of an unthought-of thing involves a contradiction. But this is false. Suppose I say out loud "There is nobody speaking in this room now." The remark is absurd, but the statement involves no actual *contradiction*. It is not like saying "There is a round square in the room." It is only the *speaking of the statement* that involves any absurdity: it is the fact that I make the statement out loud that entails that it is false.

Now, equally, there is no contradiction in the statement "There are things that nobody has thought of." It is only *the making of the statement* that involves absurdity: it is only the fact that it has been put forward that entails that it is false. But if this proposition, "There are things that nobody has thought of" is not self-contradictory, then Berkeley has quite failed to prove that the physical world must be thought of in order to exist.

We have now discussed, and criticized, Berkeley's two official lines of argument for his thesis that physical objects cannot exist unperceived. But there is a more powerful line of argument, closely related to the first official line of argument, which Berkley never states quite clearly because of his confusion between sense-impressions and sensible qualities.

The argument has two steps. The first step is to argue that, when we perceive, the *immediate* object of perception can never be anything but one of our own sense-impressions or "ideas." Everything else that we claim to perceive is an inference (normally perfectly automatic and perfectly instantaneous) based on the perception of our own "ideas."

In order to make the first step, Berkeley must appeal to what has since become known as the Argument from Illusion. It may be presented thus. If we consider any veridical perception, it is always imaginable, at the very least, that it might be non-veridical, although the perceptual experience was exactly the same. Contrariwise, if we consider non-veridical perceptions, such as sensory illusions or hallucinations, it is always imaginable, at the very least, that they might be veridical perceptions.

Now if we consider a non-veridical perception, such as an hallucination, it seems clear that the perception has an object. The pink rat-like shapes in the drunkard's visual field are certainly there. Yet, at the same time, it must be admitted that they are simply sense-impressions or "ideas" in the drunkard's mind. But, as we have seen, it would be possible for the drunkard to have exactly the same perceptual experience and yet be perceiving real, physical, pink rats. So surely we must admit that, even in the case of veridical perception, the *immediate* object of the perception can never be anything but one of our own sense-impressions or "ideas."

This, it seems, is the argument that Berkeley should have advanced. But, because of his confusion between sense-impressions and sensible qualities, he never states it clearly.

Now for the second step of the argument. If we accept the view that the immediate objects of perception must always be our own sense-impressions or "ideas," there seem to be only two views that we can take about the physical world. (i) The natural thing to say is that physical objects are the *causes* of our sense-impressions or "ideas," exist independently of them, and are never anything but *mediately* perceived by means of the immediately perceived "ideas." This is the *Representative* theory of perception, and it was the theory held by Locke and by most of Berkeley's contemporaries and predecessors. (ii) If we reject this view, then there seems nothing to do except identify the physical world with our "ideas" of it, which is Berkeley's position.

So, granted the first step of the argument, that the only possible immediate objects of perception are our own sense-impressions or "ideas," Berkeley has only to disprove the Representative theory to establish his own view of the physical world by default. This explains the importance that he attaches to the attack on Representative theories in general, and Locke's theory in particular. What is more, Berkeley is at his philosophical best in this attack.

CRITICISM OF LOCKE AND THE REPRESENTATIVE THEORY

We may begin by considering arguments directed against Locke's particular version of the Representative theory, and then look at arguments directed against *any* Representative theory.

(i) CRITICISM OF LOCKE'S DISTINCTION BETWEEN PRIMARY AND SECONDARY QUALITIES

Locke's doctrine of primary and secondary qualities is

expounded in his *Essay*, Bk. II, ch. 8, "Some further considerations concerning our simple ideas." Berkeley's criticism is to be found in the *Principles*, Secs. 9-15, and the *First Dialogue* (pp. 151-158). See also Sec. 2 in the selections from the *Philosophical Commentaries* in this volume. There is an important discussion of the topic in Hume's *Treatise of Human Nature*, Bk. I, Part IV, Sec. 4, "Of the Modern Philosophy."

If physical objects are never immediately perceived, but simply cause "ideas" in our mind which are the immediate objects of perception, what are we to say that physical objects are *like*? Do they resemble the ideas they cause? According to Locke, and here he is following Galileo, Descartes, Newton and Boyle, physical objects themselves have only the properties of extension, figure, motion, solidity and number. (Descartes omits solidity.) Following Boyle, Locke calls these the *primary* qualities of objects. But qualities such as colour, sound, taste, smell, heat and cold, are not properties of physical objects at all, but are mere qualities of our "ideas" or sense-impressions, caused in us by the action of the minute parts of physical objects on our senses. Locke calls the powers of physical objects to produce such "ideas" in us the *secondary* qualities of the objects. (Berkeley, in what is an easier usage, calls colours, sounds, tastes and smells themselves the secondary qualities. We shall follow Berkeley.)

This division between primary and secondary qualities had already been propounded by the Greek Atomists. Its revival by Galileo reflected the birth of modern physics. Only those properties of physical objects which physics took seriously were accounted real properties of the objects.

Berkeley's attack on the distinction between the primary and secondary qualities involves some sophistries, but he advances at least two important arguments. In the first place, he argues that it is impossible to conceive of a physical object which has the Lockean primary qualities alone, and no secondary qualities at all. (This argument is worked out in greater detail by Hume in the section of the *Treatise* already mentioned.) The moral Berkeley draws from this is that, since the secondary qualities are confessedly mere "ideas," the primary qualities must be equally "ideas." But the argument could be equally used to try to prove that both sets of properties are objective properties of independent physical objects. The most it *really* proves, if it is valid, is that the allegedly different sorts of qualities have the same status, whatever that status is.

In the second place, he points out that some of the *arguments* that Locke used to try to establish the subjectivity of the secondary qualities, would, if valid, apply equally to the primary qualities. Under different conditions of perception, objects appear to have different colours, emit different sounds, and so on. This was taken to be a proof of the subjectivity of the secondary qualities. But Berkeley points out that we have exactly the same phenomenon in the case of the primary qualities. Thus, an object may look tiny in the distance, or a round pond look elliptical when viewed from an angle. Berkeley again takes the argument to prove that both primary and secondary qualities are subjective; but again the best it can prove is that they must be given the same status, whatever that status is.

It has been objected to Berkeley here that, in the case of the primary qualities, there is a technique—measurement—for sorting out real from apparent properties which is lacking in the case of the secondary qualities. But perhaps Berkeley could reply that in the case of colours, sounds, etc., we do have techniques—of a different sort—for distinguishing real from apparent qualities. If this reply is valid, no significant distinction has been made between primary and secondary qualities.

(ii) CRITICISM OF LOCKE'S DOCTRINE OF SUBSTANCE

Locke's view is expounded in the *Essay*, Bk. II, ch. 23 and ch. 13, Secs. 18-20. Berkeley's criticism is to be found in the *Principles*, Secs. 16-17 (especially), and 68-81; also in the *First Dialogue* (pp. 160-163). See also Section 3 of the selections from the *Philosophical Commentaries* in this volume. Hume takes up the same questions in the *Treatise*, Bk. I, Part I, Sec. 6.

Locke holds that if we consider the real properties of physical objects we find that we have to attribute these properties *to something*. (In fact, of course, Locke holds that the real properties of objects are confined to the primary qualities. But this is irrelevant to his argument here.) This something Locke calls *substance*.

What is the nature of substance? Locke says that we can know nothing of it. It is "something we know not what."

We can conceive it solely as "that which supports properties" or "that in which properties inhere." Locke sometimes speaks carelessly, and speaks of substance as the unknown support of our *ideas*. (See *Essay*, Bk. II, ch. 23, Sec. 1.) This makes it look as if he meant by substance simply physical objects. Berkeley sometimes exploits this confusion for his own ends, "refuting" the view that physical objects exist independently of being perceived simply by refuting the Lockean doctrine of substance. But when Locke speaks accurately, it is clear that he thinks that substance is the unknown factor in physical objects which supports their properties.

Berkeley objects that Locke, in his doctrine of substance, uses words in a meaningless way. Locke says that we have a *relative* notion of substance as "that which supports the properties of things" or "that in which the properties of things inhere." But, Berkeley asks, what do these words "support" and "inhere" mean in these formulae? We certainly cannot take them in their *literal* sense, in which pillars support a house, or pins inhere in a pincushion. But if we cannot take them literally, we must take them analogically. What is the analogy involved? Berkeley argues that Locke is unable to find any analogical meaning for the words. The result is, he says, that Locke really uses the words "support" and "inhere" *in a quite empty way*. But, if this is so, Locke has failed to give his doctrine of substance any real content. It is a mere form of words.

Berkeley's criticism here (which is independent of his own theory that physical objects are simply "ideas" in the mind) has found wide-spread acceptance in modern philosophy. But difficulties remain. If we reject Locke's "unknown substratum" what account can we give of the nature of physical objects? Must we say that a thing is simply the collection of its qualities? This leads to serious difficulties. Consider the case of two objects that have exactly the same shape and size. Surely we want to say that each object has its own *instance* of identical properties? But if we are trying to give an account of objects as a collection of qualities, what are we doing talking about *instances*? Two different instances of the same quality do not differ in quality. What then do they differ in? We seem to be forced to talk about something more than mere qualities, and are in danger of falling back into a Lockean account once more. What is needed is an account of physical objects which neither postulates an unknown substratum, nor identifies objects with the collection of their qualities. It would take us too far to try to develop such an account here.

(iii) WE HAVE NO GOOD REASON TO BELIEVE THERE ARE OBJECTS LYING BEYOND OUR "IDEAS"

We pass on to consider those arguments of Berkeley's which are directed against *any* version of the Representative theory of perception. In the first place, Berkeley argues that, if the immediate objects of perception are never anything but our own sense-impressions, then we can never have any *good reason* to believe in the existence of physical objects which cause these sense-impressions. Berkeley develops this argument in the *Principles*, Sec. 18, 20, 86-8; and in the *First Dialogue* (pp. 166-168). See also Section 4 of the selections from the *Philosophical Commentaries* in this volume.

There can be no question of *deducing* the existence of the physical world from the fact that we have certain trains of "ideas" or sense-impressions. Any argument for the existence of physical objects lying beyond the impressions must therefore be based on *experience*. But what experience can we have that would support our belief in the existence of physical objects? By hypothesis, we can never directly perceive the correlation between the having of sense-impressions of a certain sort, and the presence of physical objects of a certain sort. If it is said that the senses corroborate each other, touch confirming sight, for instance, the reply is that this only proves that our visual and tactual impressions are correlated in a certain way. So neither reason nor experience can provide any evidence for the existence of a physical world.

Acceptance of this argument has one embarrassing consequence, of which Berkeley never shows any awareness. Like everybody else, Berkeley believes that there are other minds besides his own. They cannot be immediately perceived: they can only be inferred from what is immediately perceived—according to Berkeley, "ideas" or sense-impressions. Now if Berkeley will not allow that he has any good reason to believe in material objects lying beyond his "ideas," can we not ask him what good reason he has to believe in other minds lying beyond his "ideas?" If his argument was valid in the case of material objects, it ought to be equally valid in the case of other minds. But this reduces Berkeley's position to absurdity.

So we reach the ironical conclusion that, if valid, the argument refutes not only Locke but Berkeley himself.

But is the argument valid? Berkeley is undoubtedly right in pointing out that, if all we ever perceive are our own "ideas," then there can be no *direct* evidence for the existence of a physical world lying beyond them. But might there not be *indirect* evidence? Consider the case of *molecules*. Until very recently, when the electron microscope was invented, there was nothing that approached direct evidence for the existence of molecules. But the hypothesis that they existed was accepted because it was confirmed indirectly in all sorts of ways. Granted the unobserved existence of molecules, all sorts of *other* observations could be successfully predicted. Now, in the same way, a defender of the Representative theory might argue that the existence of the physical world is an hypothesis that is indirectly confirmed by the nature of our sense-experience. (And he could take the same line about other minds.)

Is this reply adequate? Can we accept the view that the existence of the physical world is a postulate which has received endless indirect confirmation, but which can never be directly confirmed? If we can, Berkeley is answered. If not, because of the problem about other minds, both Berkeley and Locke are involved in common ruin.

(iv) THERE CAN BE NO RESEMBLANCE BETWEEN "IDEAS" AND PHYSICAL OBJECTS

The next argument of Berkeley's to be mentioned is extremely ingenious, probably valid, but seldom considered. It is found in the *Principles,* Sec. 8, and in the *First Dialogue* (pp. 169-170). See also Section 5 of the selections from the *Philosophical Commentaries* in this volume.

Suppose we consider any property of any one of our "ideas," for instance, its colour. Since the "idea" is immediately perceived, it follows that colour is an immediately perceivable property. Can a physical object have this property? It cannot, because according to the Representative theory physical objects cannot be immediately perceived, and so cannot have this immediately perceivable property. The same holds for all other properties of our "ideas." It follows that there can be no resemblance at all between "idea" and physical objects. But if this is so, and if all knowledge of the physical world comes from our perception of our "ideas," it follows that we can know literally nothing of the nature of physical objects. But this is a *reductio ad absurdum* of the Representative theory.

(v) PHYSICAL OBJECTS COULD NOT CAUSE "IDEAS" IN US

The last of Berkeley's important arguments against the Representative theory, an argument to which he attaches great importance, turns on his theory of causation. It is discussed in the *Principles*, Secs. 19, 25, 30-2, 51-3, 60-6, 102-8, and in the *Second Dialogue* (pp. 178-180). See also the *Correspondence with Samuel Johnson*, I, 2-3, 5 and II, 1-3; also Section 6 of the selections from the *Philosophical Commentaries* in this volume.

He argues that even if there were physical objects lying beyond our "ideas," they could never be the *cause* of our "ideas," because the only thing that is capable of causing anything is a *spirit*. Suppose we consider a sequence such as that which occurs when one billiard-ball comes in contact with another, and the second ball moves. We would normally say that the first billiard-ball *caused* the second ball to move, or *made* it move. But Berkeley thinks this to be a loose way of speaking. If we scrutinize the sequence we can find no element of *agency* or *making* in it. It is only if we consider the operation of the will, as when we move the limbs of our body, that we find genuine agency. It follows that, even if there were material objects lying beyond our "ideas," they could never do what the Representative theory wants them to do: bring about "ideas" in us.

This enables Berkeley to advance one of his two new proofs of God's existence (*Principles*, Secs. 29-30). Since our sense-impressions are independent of our will, their cause cannot lie in ourselves. It is impossible that they be caused by matter, or by anything that is not a spirit. They must therefore be caused by some other spirit. The "strong, lively and distinct" nature of our sense-impressions, and their "steadiness, order and coherence" sufficiently testify the power, wisdom and benevolence of their author.

Why, then, do we *speak* of one billiard-ball *making* the other move? According to Berkeley, when we speak of causes in nature we are simply referring to *observed regularities in our sense-experience*, regularities which are the effect of the goodness of God, enabling us to anticipate the course of experience, and steer our lives accordingly. This means that the business of *natural science* is simply to seek out, and give a systematic account of, these regularities in experience.

Now Berkeley is undoubtedly right in saying that there is some difference between the action of one billiard-ball on another, and the action of the will. When I decide to raise my arm, and do so, there seems to be some *rational connection* between my decision and my bodily action. The decision *prefigures* the action, it is directed towards just that action, and remains so directed even in cases where the decision cannot be implemented (due, say, to sudden paralysis). There is no such rational connection in mere physical sequences. It merely *happens* that the impact of the first billiard-ball makes the second ball move. We can say that Berkeley draws the moral from this that so-called physical causation is not really causation, because there is no rational connection. But might not the real moral be that causation *need* not involve the rational connection that Berkeley thinks is required? Berkeley's argument is therefore not conclusive.

Hume's theory of causation may be thought of as a sceptical successor to Berkeley's view, although there was probably little direct influence. Hume also noticed that, in such cases as that of the billiard-balls, we can find nothing but regular sequence. But he draws the opposite moral. He concludes that, when we speak of one billiard-ball *making* another billiard-ball move, we *mean* nothing more than that this is an observed regularity. In appropriate circumstances, whenever the first billiard-ball strikes the second one, the second ball moves. (This is a little too simple an account of Hume's view, ignoring, among other things, the psychological element that he thinks present in our concept of causation. But it is not seriously misleading.) Hume goes on to say that *all* causation reduces to mere regular sequence, even the operation of the will. But, in the case of the will, Hume simply overlooks the difficulty of his position. There is some more intimate connection between my decision to move my arm, and the movement of my arm, than there is between the motions of the two billiard-balls. Can a Humean theory explain this?

If we accept Berkeley's view that the only possible immediate objects of perception are our own "ideas" or sense-impressions, and if we also accept as valid his rejection of the Representative theory of perception, then it seems that we must accept his thesis that physical things are mere congeries of "ideas," that is, that physical objects can exist only when perceived.

But, as Berkeley is well aware, this view of his is exposed to a number of objections. The most important difficulties that Berkeley considers, and tries to dispose of, are those concerning (i) Unobserved objects; (ii) The distinction between appearances and realities; (iii) The nature of mind or spirit.

DIFFICULTIES FOR BERKELEY'S VIEW OF THE PHYSICAL WORLD

1. UNOBSERVED OBJECTS

Everybody believes that physical objects continue to exist when nobody is perceiving them. And even if one became doubtful of the truth of this belief, one would still have to admit that it was perfectly *possible* for physical objects to exist unperceived. But if physical objects are nothing but "ideas," and "ideas" can exist only when perceived, it seems that Berkeley is forced to say that it is *impossible* for physical objects to exist unperceived. Yet this would be a *reductio ad absurdum* of his position.

Berkeley's solution, or rather solutions, to the problem are found in the *Principles,* Secs. 3, 45, 48 and in the *Second* and *Third Dialogues* (pp. 174-176 and 193, 213-217). See also the *Correspondence with Samuel Johnson,* I, 7-9; III, 1, and IV, 1; also Section 7 of the selections from the *Philosophical Commentaries* in this volume.

The solution of the problem which he emphasizes most is the appeal to the "perceptions" of God. What it comes to is this: When we talk about "unperceived objects" we do not really mean "objects unperceived *by any mind at all.*" The *Infinite* spirit, God, still perceives the object. So to talk of "unperceived objects" is a short, and inaccurate, way of talking of "objects unperceived by any finite mind, but perceived by the Infinite one."

This manoeuvre even enables Berkeley to produce an entirely original argument for the existence of God. (It is not prominent in the *Principles,* but is given an important place in the *Dialogues.*) For, given Berkeley's account of the physical world, and given that physical objects can exist unperceived by any finite mind, there *must* be an Infinite mind to perceive them on these occasions.

Berkeley's solution here implies that, when an atheist talks about unperceived objects, he is really talking about God, and so contradicting his atheism. This incredible conclusion would seem enough in itself to cast doubt on his solution. But there are also further difficulties.

What is the *nature* of these "unperceived objects" that God goes on perceiving all the time? It seems that, like perceived objects, they must also be "ideas," but in this case "ideas" of God. We are thus led to the concept of a great realm of the "ideas" of God of which the "ideas" of finite perceivers are a mere fragmentary copy. And this explains Berkeley's occasional and tantalizing references, in the *Principles* and *Dialogues*, to "archetypes" of our "ideas." God's "ideas" are the archetypes of our "ideas," and it is to them we are referring when we speak of "unperceived objects."

But now it seems that Berkeley has landed himself with a version of the Representative theory of perception. Behind the fragmentary realm of our own "ideas" lies the great realm of the "ideas" of God, and the former copies the latter. Yet, since "ideas" are causally inactive, according to Berkeley, the second realm has no value in explaining why we have the "ideas" we do. For our "ideas" are produced in us directly by God. So there seems no reason to postulate such a realm except as an *ad hoc* device to solve Berkeley's problem about unobserved objects. Instead of postulating three things: our own "ideas," the archetypal realm and God; why not simply postulate our own "ideas" and God?

This problem leads Berkeley, when he faces up to the issue, to try to play down the realm of "archetypes." His most explicit treatment of the problem is found in the very important discussion of the account of the Creation in Genesis, at the end of the *Third Dialogue* (pp. 213-217). Hylas raises the question of what Philonous can understand by the creation of the world *before* the creation of finite spirits. The obvious answer seems to be: God brought the archetypal realm of "ideas" into existence before he created finite spirits and gave them "ideas." But Berkeley does not say this. For it now turns out that the "archetypal realm" cannot be created, because it is not in time. It "existed from everlasting in the mind of God."

So the "archetypal realm" has contracted into nothing but God's foreknowledge of the course of the world. Such foreknowledge Christian thinkers generally concede to God, although they have some difficulty in reconciling it with a belief in man's free-will.

The "archetypal realm" then ceases to be a third object poised between our "ideas" and God. But now the *original* difficulty about unperceived objects re-appears. On p. 193 of the same *Dialogue*, for instance, Berkeley had written of unperceived objects:

> There is therefore some other mind [i.e. God's mind] wherein they exist during the intervals between the times of my perceiving them, as likewise they did before my birth, and would do after my supposed annihilation.

But these are unperceived physical objects *in time,* things that can be created or destroyed. The *eternal* archetypal realm is useless here. So the problem returns: what do we mean by the existence of unperceived objects in time?

It is at this point that Berkeley turns to his second solution of the problem about unobserved objects, a solution which is much more inconspicuous in his writings than the appeal to God, but destined to be much more important historically. Speaking of the Creation in the *Third Dialogue,* he says:

> May we not understand it to have been entirely in respect of finite spirits; so that things, with regard to us, may properly be said to begin their existence, or be created, when God decreed *they should become perceptible* to intelligent creatures. . . ? (pp. 215-216, my italics.)

This is not unambiguous, but it seems to be the same line of thought as that of the *Principles,* Sec. 3, where Berkeley says that one thing we might mean by saying the table in the study exists unperceived is that *if* somebody were to go into the study, he *would* perceive the table. According to this view, to talk about unperceived objects is to talk about *unfulfilled* possibilities of having "ideas."

Statements about unfulfilled possibilities are well known to modern philosophy under the name of "contrary-to-fact conditional statements" or "counter-factuals." Consider the statement "If I had ignited this gunpowder, it would have exploded." Although I did nothing of the kind, we can still say that the statement is *true.* In the same way, it is true that if I had gone into the study, I would have seen the table. Berkeley is simply suggesting that to talk about unperceived objects really *means* nothing more than the assertion of a counter-factual statement about "ideas."

This is the solution of the problem of unobserved objects that has commended itself to Berkeley's philosophical descendants: the Phenomenalists. Phenomenalism might be called "Berkeley without God," and John Stuart Mill, who was a Phenomenalist, spoke of physical objects as mere "permanent possibilities of sensation." (See his classical exposition of Phenomenalism in *An Examination of Sir William Hamilton's Philosophy*, chs. XI and XII, and the Appendix to these chapters, *Sixth Edition*, 1889.)

Modern philosophy has seen an incredibly complicated and difficult controversy over the question whether all statements about unperceived objects can be translated into counter-factual statements. Many difficulties have emerged. There is, however, one very simple and obvious criticism of the Phenomenalist program. A Phenomenalist is forced to maintain that to assert the existence of a perceived object, and to assert the existence of an unperceived object, is to employ two different senses of the word "existence." For the existence of a perceived object involves the *actual* having of sense-impressions, but the "existence" of an unperceived object involves only the *unfulfilled possibility* of having sense-impressions. Yet, surely, when in ordinary speech we assert the existence of unperceived objects, do we not think that they exist *in exactly the same sense that perceived objects exist?* Yet this Phenomenalism cannot allow.

It seems probable, therefore, that Berkeley can give no satisfactory solution to his problem about unobserved objects.

2. APPEARANCE AND REALITY

If all our sense-experience is a matter of having "ideas," and there is no question of these "ideas" corresponding, or failing to correspond, to physical reality, what becomes of our ordinary distinction between really perceiving something, and being under sensory illusion? Does not Berkeley's theory obliterate this distinction? Berkeley deals with this problem in the *Principles*, Secs. 30, 33, 36 and in the *Second* and *Third Dialogues* (pp. 178, 197 and 200-201). See also Section 8 of the selections from the *Philosophical Commentaries* in this volume.

What we call real things, he says, are the "ideas" perceived by sense. They are to be contrasted with the "ideas" formed in the imagination. The two classes of "ideas" may be distinguished by three marks. (i) The "ideas" of sense are more vivid and clear than the "ideas" of the imagination; (ii) the "ideas" of sense, being caused in us by God, are not under the control of our will, while the "ideas" of the imagination are; (iii) the "ideas" of sense come to us in an orderly and coherent way, while the "ideas" of the imagination do not.

The distinction Berkeley is trying to draw here is between what we should now call *sense-impressions,* on the one hand, and *mental images,* on the other. (Berkeley makes his task easier by failing to mention *memory*-images, which presumably should be classed with mental images.) Berkeley's blanket-term shows its misleadingness here, by tempting us to make the confusion between sense-impressions and mental images in the first place.

But whether or not Berkeley has given a correct account of the distinction, he is quite wrong to think that it coincides with the distinction between real things and things that are not real in the field of perception. Agreed that we do not think of our mental images as perceptions of real things, still we want to say that many of our sense-impressions quite fail to correspond with reality, that is, that they are not perceptions of real things either. When an oar is plunged half into the water, we want to say that *it looks bent to us,* but that it is not really bent. We have appearance, not reality. Yet we have "ideas of sense."

Berkeley takes this point up in only one place: in the *Third Dialogue* (pp. 200-201). There he says that the mistake made by anybody who is deceived by the "bent oar," lies not in the sense-impression, but simply in the expectation that it will be accompanied by certain further sense-experiences. The oar will not feel bent, or continue to look bent when taken out of the water. The appearance is, as a modern philosopher was to put it, a *wild* sense-impression (even if not as completely wild as, say, an hallucinatory one); it fails to cohere and fit in with the rest of our experience. An illusory "idea of sense" is a disorderly "idea of sense." In fact, the mark Berkeley uses to distingush veridical from illusory sense-impressions, is the same as his third mark of distinction between sense-impressions and mental images.

Is Berkeley's distinction between veridical perception and sensory illusion satisfactory? We do often use the test of coherence with our other perceptions when we are in doubt whether our perceptions correspond to physical reality or not. But do we think that the incoherence of an impression is *what we mean* by calling a perception illusory? Since, for Berkeley, there is no question of a physical reality to which our impressions correspond, he has to say that incoherence is the very essence of sensory illusion. This has some strange consequences. If all our impressions were "wild," that is to say, if they were such that no coherent and orderly patterns of experiences existed, Berkeley would be forced to say, not merely that we could not *tell* which perceptions were veridical, but that the whole distinction between appearance and reality in the field of sense-experience quite lacked application. Again, let us suppose it were possible to find two equally orderly and coherent systems for the organizing of our sense-impressions, yet each system treated different perceptions as illusory ones, and treated the illusory perceptions of the other system as veridical. Then Berkeley would be forced to say that it was a completely arbitrary question which system was the system of "physical reality." These strange consequences at least raise doubts whether Berkeley can give a satisfactory account of the distinction between appearance and reality in the field of sense-perception.

3. THE NATURE OF MIND OR SPIRIT

For Berkeley, the world contains nothing besides spirits and their "ideas," a community presided over by the master-spirit, God. He discusses spirits in the *Principles*, Secs. 2, 27, 49, 89, 135-48 and in the *Third Dialogue* (pp. 193-196 and 211-212). See also the *Correspondence with Samuel Johnson*, I, 10-11; III, 3; IV, 3; also Section 10 of the selections from the *Philosophical Commentaries* in this volume.

From the point of view of Berkeley's theory of the physical world, the all-important question is that of the *relationship* between "ideas" and spirits. Now Berkeley is always speaking of "ideas" being "in the mind." This suggests that he thinks that they are in some way parts of the mind, or states of the mind. But at other times this suggestion is repudiated by Berkeley. He then says that to speak of "ideas" being "in" the mind is simply to say that they are *perceived* by the mind, and that the mind or spirit itself is a simple, indivisible, spiritual substance quite distinct from its "ideas."

But this leads to problems. If the mind and its "ideas" are

really "distinct existences" (in Hume's useful phrase), then it seems to follow that it must be at least a meaningful conception that one should exist without the other, and that, in particular, "ideas" should be capable of existing outside any mind. Yet, in fact, it seems to be meaningless to talk of sense-impressions, sensations or mental images existing outside minds. The conclusion must be that they are not, after all, distinct from the mind.

The reaction of many of Berkeley's philosophical descendants to this difficulty was to take the bold step of *identifying* the mind with its "ideas." The mind is just a bundle of "ideas." And it is interesting to notice that this position tempted Berkeley himself, as a famous entry in the *Philosophical Commentaries* shows (Entry 580, see Section 10 of the selections in this volume). On this view, later to be called Neutral Monism, Berkeley's "ideas" are thought of as a neutral stuff, and minds and bodies are simply different ways of grouping the stuff.

This view is open to a number of objections. One of the most serious is that the notion of a bundle, collection or group of objects implies the logical possibility that the objects bundled, collected or grouped should exist outside the bundle. (The sticks in a bundle of sticks do not *have* to come in bundles.) But this implies, once again, that it should be meaningful to speak of single "ideas" existing outside any mind. This seems to be a *reductio ad absurdum* of Neutral Monism.

But if, alternatively, like Berkeley we hold fast to the notion of the mind as a spiritual substance, then it seems that we must admit that "ideas" are, after all, some sort of qualification or affection of that substance. This, too, leads to very difficult problems, which have not been much explored, either by Berkeley, or by his successors. Exactly how are "ideas" related to the spiritual substance? What is a spiritual substance anyway? Is the notion any less mysterious than the unknowable substratum that Locke finds in material objects? Such questions are hard to answer, yet it is difficult to see how Berkeley, or a philosophical descendant of his, could adopt any other theory of mind except Neutral Monism or a doctrine of spiritual substance.

One difficulty, already urged by Samuel Johnson (*Correspondence*, I, 10), is the question of what makes two different spirits *two*? As Johnson sees, it cannot be difference of place, because space, for Berkeley, reduces to mere "ideas." It cannot be qualitative differences among spirits, for we can imagine two spirits with identical spiritual history. So what is the principle of differentiation between spiritual substances?

We see, then, that Berkeley's case for saying that physical objects do not exist except when perceived depends, when correctly stated, on the validity of two steps: (i) the Argument from Illusion, which is supposed to establish that the immediate objects of perception cannot be anything but "ideas"; (ii) refutation of the Representative theory of perception, which holds that these "ideas" are caused in us by external physical objects. If the position to which Berkeley is then led is unsatisfactory—and we have seen that his replies to certain objections are unsatisfactory—then there must be something wrong with the line of argument by which he reaches his position. Some philosophers have tried to rehabilitate the Representative theory of perception, the most recent attempt being R. J. Hirst's *The Problems of Perception* (George Allen and Unwin, 1959). But modern philosophers who disagree with Berkeley have been more inclined to question the Argument from Illusion. The late John Austin's *Sense and Sensibilia* (Oxford University Press, 1962) is a systematic attack on the argument. I myself have proposed an analysis of sensory illusion which evades Berkeley's conclusions in *Perception and the Physical World* (Routledge and Kegan Paul, 1961).

II. *Berkeley's criticism of Abstract Ideas*

In attacking the doctrine of Abstract Ideas, Berkeley is once again criticizing Locke. Locke's discussion is to be found in his *Essay*, Bk. II, ch. 11, Secs. 9-11; Bk. III, ch. 3, Secs. 1-14; Bk. IV, ch. 7, Sec. 9. Berkeley criticizes Locke in the *Introduction* to the *Principles*, Secs. 6-25. See also Section 11 in the selections from the *Philosophical Commentaries* in this volume. Hume supports Berkeley in the *Treatise*, Bk. I, Part I, Sec. 7. For a modern discussion, see G. J. Warnock, *Berkeley* (Pelican book), ch. 4.

One important way that Locke arrives at his doctrine of Abstract Ideas is by thinking about those words that are applied to whole classes of objects. What does a word like man *stand for?* It does not stand for any individual man, as the word "Peter" does, nor is it the name for the whole class lumped together, as the word "men" seems to be. Locke concludes that it must stand for *an object in the user's mind*. (Plato, following a similar line of argument, was led to think that such words stood for objects in the Platonic realm of Forms.) The mind makes this object by mentally abstracting from the particular men it perceives everything that is common and peculiar to men, and nothing more. Thus it forms the Abstract Idea of man. The mind can then *use* this mental object to see whether new particulars come up to the specifications required to apply the word "man" to them, in much the same way that an architect can use a plan to see whether a particular house fits certain specifications.

Berkeley interprets Locke as holding that Abstract Ideas are a special sort of *mental image*. He has been criticized for this interpretation, but it has at least this much justification: if Locke is not talking about mental images it is hard to know what sort of mental object he is referring to. Berkeley goes on to point out that it would be quite impossible to have a mental image which would do justice to what was common and peculiar to such classes as the class of men. If we try to meet Locke's specifications, the Abstract Idea of man could have no particular colour, shape, size, posture or any other quality, which means that it would be no image at all.

It is true that Berkeley overplays his hand a little. He argues that an image must be *perfectly determinate* in character, a thing that is quite obviously not true of many mental images. It is perfectly possible, for example, to have a mental image of a piece of crimson cloth *of no particular shade of crimson*. In his discussion of images (indeed, in his discussion of "ideas" generally), Berkeley seems secretly dominated by the model of *physical objects*. A physical object must be perfectly determinate in all its characteristics, but it does not follow that this is true of mental images or sense-impressions. Nevertheless, it is clear that mental images could not have the incredible degree of indeterminacy that Locke's theory of general words demands.

If there are no Abstract Ideas, what do general words stand for? It is here that Berkeley makes his really important contribution. He attacks the notion that general words have to stand for some *one* thing, whether in the mind or outside it, as if they were a strange sort of proper name. A word or an "idea" (image) becomes general simply by the fact that it is properly applied, not to a single object, but to *any* member of a particular class of things. Once we grasp this obvious point, then we see that Locke's Abstract Ideas are unnecessary and useless. The meaning of a general word is not a *thing*, but a *fact* about the word: the fact that the word is applied to any member of a certain class of things.

It is true that Berkeley is still not completely clear about the point. This comes out, for example, in Sec. 18 of the *Introduction*, where he attacks the notion that all words have "one only precise and settled signification" by arguing that this cannot be the case with general words which "signify indifferently" a whole class of objects. Now if "signification" means "meaning" here, as it seems to do, then what Berkeley is saying is absurd. A general word like "man" or "triangle" may have one and only one perfectly precise *meaning*. What Berkeley should have said is that general words can be *applied* to more than one object. The trouble is that he still has the lurking idea that all words are *names*. And so, when he sees that a general word is applied to any member of a whole class of objects, he concludes that it is the *name* of all the objects in the class, and then concludes that the word has many meanings.

What is Berkeley's interest in this question? Why does he preface the *Principles* by an attack on Abstract Ideas? The answer is that he believes that it is the attempt to separate in thought what cannot be separated in reality, the attempt involved in Locke's doctrine, that has led previous thinkers to deny his view that physical objects can exist only when perceived. To try to distinguish physical existence from being perceived is to be guilty of false abstraction, just as much as it is to form an "idea" of a triangle with no particular size and shape. It must be said, however, that Berkeley is not really advancing any *argument* here, because he admits that there can be legitimate abstraction, where the objects abstracted from each other are capable of independent existence (cf. *Introduction*, Sec. 10). The whole question, then, is whether or not the abstraction of physical existence from being perceived is vicious.

III. *Berkeley's Theory of Vision*

Berkeley's *Essay towards a New Theory of Vision* was the first work that he published. Its contentions are briefly touched on in the *Principles*, Secs. 43-4; and in the *First Dialogue* (pp. 165-166). Berkeley defended his theory of vision again in a pamphlet of some importance *The Theory of Vision Vindicated* (not published in these selections).

The *Essay* divides into four parts (i) Secs. 2-51; (ii) Secs. 52-87; (iii) Secs. 88-120; (iv) Secs. 121-159. The main themes are all introduced in the first part: the last three parts take up matters of comparative detail. Even within the first part, the student is advised to omit, at least on first reading, the discussion of the complex Barrovian case: Secs. 29-40. It has no particular *philosophical* interest. The centre of the *Essay* is therefore Secs. 2-28 and 41-51. The argument here may be further subdivided into four steps.

1. (Sec. 2) Berkeley argues (as was generally argued by students of vision in his day) that distance out from the eye cannot be immediately perceived by sight, but is only *suggested* to the mind by "cues" given to sight. His argument, not original to him, may be put by saying that since objects produce a merely *two-dimensional* picture on the retina, there can be no question of an *immediate* visual perception of three dimensions.

This argument appears to assume something that is completely false, viz. that the image on the retina is the immediate object of sight. In fact the image is simply one intermediate link in the causal chain from object to brain which eventually produces, not perception of any part of the chain, but perception of the object where the chain began. It is true that this may be conceded, yet it may still be argued that the two-dimensional nature of the retinal image makes it impossible to conceive of a *mechanism* that would produce anything more than immediate perception of two dimensions. But to this it may be replied, as J. J. Gibson does, that:

> The qualities of solidity and depth . . . do not have any replica in the two-dimensional retinal image but they may very well prove to have correlates there. (*The Perception of the Visual World,* 1950, p. 8)

2. (Secs. 3-15) If we cannot perceive distance by the eye immediately, then how do we judge distance by the eye? Berkeley first sets out the received view of the way we manage to do this (Secs. 3-7), and then gives reasons for rejecting them (Secs. 8-15). According to the then orthodox view, we judge of distances by an unconscious trigonometry. The most important suggestion was that we judged the *angle*

that our eyes made at the object seen, an angle whose size necessarily got smaller as the distance got greater, and so judged distance. Now Berkeley saw clearly that this was silly. For in order to use such angles as visual cues to depth, we would need to see them immediately. But how can one see such angles immediately, *without seeing depth immediately?* Somebody who takes seriously the idea that distance is not immediately perceived cannot use such cues.

3. (Secs. 16-28) The result is that Berkeley has to look for a set of visual cues to depth which will not presuppose that depth is immediately perceived, which will have a merely contingent connection with the distance of objects, and which will be learnt by experience. This is the business of Secs. 16-28, but the particular cues that Berkeley finds to be involved in the visual perception of depth are of no great *philosophical* interest.

4. (Secs. 41-51) These sections are the real heart of the *Essay,* and Berkeley proceeds to draw from his earlier argument two conclusions of great importance.

The first is that the immediate objects of sight are "in the mind." The *New Theory of Vision* thus becomes a curtain-raiser for the *Principles;* the doctrine that is eventually to be put forward about *all* immediate objects of perception is here proved for one case only.

Unfortunately, however, there is nothing in Berkeley's argument in the *Essay* to give the slightest warrant for this conclusion. Why should the fact, if it is a fact, that we cannot perceive distance immediately by sight show that what we do perceive immediately by sight is "in the mind"? Berkeley says that to a man born blind, on first being made to see, all objects seen would seem to be "in his eye, or rather in his mind" (Sec. 41). His correction of himself here shows how he has been misled. He is unconsciously thinking of the *retina* as the immediate object of sight. This means that the immediate objects of sight are "in us" in the sense of "in our *body.*" He then makes a further unconscious transition from this sense of "in us" to the sense where it means "in our *mind.*"

Berkeley's conclusion would of course follow if he proved what in fact he simply assumes: that the immediate objects of sight are "ideas." But then the question of the immediate visual perception of *distance* would become irrelevant, for visual "ideas," that is, visual sense-impressions, would be in the mind whether they were two- or three-dimensional in nature.

But Berkeley's second conclusion is a much more cogent piece of reasoning. If all original visual experience is two-dimensional only, where do we get our concept of three-dimensional objects from? In default of some theory of innate ideas, it seems that the concept must derive from some other sort of sense-experience. Berkeley therefore argues that the immediate perception of distance is to be found in tactual and bodily perception. In ordinary speech, we speak of seeing and feeling the very same thing. But, he argues, this cannot be an accurate way of expressing ourselves. The immediate objects of sight and touch may be correlated with each other in all sorts of ways, but they cannot be identical. And, indeed, if the immediate objects of sight are two-dimensional, while the immediate objects of touch are three-dimensional, it seems that we must agree with Berkeley. The apparently valid conclusion of his argument is therefore that the general structure of the world revealed to sight and touch is very different from that which is uncritically adopted by common sense.

Nevertheless, even if his argument is valid, Berkeley's conclusion is only as good as his original premise: that distance cannot be immediately perceived. If we reject this, that is, if we allow that distance is immediately perceived by sight, we can go back to the view that we see and touch the very same thing.

IV. *Berkeley's Philosophy of Science*

Berkeley's views on what we should now call the Philosophy of Science are to be found in the *Principles*, Secs. 97-8, 101-117; and in *De Motu*. See also the *Correspondence with Samuel Johnson, passim,* on Cause, Space and Time; also Sections 6, 12, and 13 of the selections from the *Philosophical Commentaries* in this volume.

Since, as we have already seen, Berkeley will allow no efficient cause but *spirit*, it follows that in studying the laws of nature, natural philosophers (that is to say, scientists) are simply discovering regularities in those trains of "ideas" (sense-impressions) that God is pleased to send us.

But although scientists *test* their theories by reference to observation, these theories frequently contain terms which do not seem to refer to observables at all. Thus, Isaac Newton had talked of *force,* of *gravitation,* and of *absolute space* and *time,* none of which seemed to be objects that can be directly observed. Modern science has multiplied unobservables recklessly. Atomic physicists talk of physical objects as made up of unobservable particles, such as electrons, protons, and neutrons. Cosmologists talk of such things as curvature of space. How can this be reconciled with Berkeley's thesis that the physical world is nothing but "ideas"?

Berkeley's answer is that, when we talk about space, force and gravitation, we are not really talking about *objects* at all.

> *Force, gravity, attraction,* and terms of this sort are useful for reasonings and reckonings about motion and bodies in motion, but not for understanding the simple nature of motion itself or for indicating so many distinct qualities. (*De Motu,* Sec. 17)

They are mere *conceptual devices* which help us to organize known phenomena, and predict new phenomena, but they do not correspond to anything in reality. Thus, to talk about Space and Time is not to talk about mysterious and unobservable universal containers of the physical world, but is simply to speak about the network of spatial and temporal *relations* that are observed to hold between observed things. To talk about gravity is not to talk about a mysterious and unobservable influence, but is a convenient way of talking about the observable motions of objects, bringing many different motions under the one formula.

Berkeley's doctrine here is of especial interest because it does not depend on his doctrine of the physical world. Even if he is wrong in saying that physical objects are simply "ideas," it may still be true that some, or even all, the unobserved entities spoken of by science are mere conceptual devices. Thus it has been maintained in modern times that to speak of physical objects as "composed" of such "objects" as electrons, protons and neutrons is a mere *manner of speaking.* Talk about such "objects" is really just a convenient way of organizing and predicting the behaviour of *observable* objects in certain experimental situations. Yet taking this line does not necessarily involve accepting a Berkeleyan Phenomenalism. One could hold that the physical world existed independently of persons, and yet still say that many, or even all, "scientific entities" were mere "manners of speaking." So whether Berkeley's doctrine of scientific unobservables is true or not, it is at least a line of thought that must be seriously considered by any philosopher of science.

DAVID M. ARMSTRONG

A Note on the Text

THE TEXT of the *Principles of Human Knowledge,* the *Three Dialogues,* and the *New Theory of Vision* is based on Fraser's 1901 edition of *The Works of George Berkeley.* It has, however, been revised to remove all important divergences between Fraser's text and the final editions supervised by Berkeley. Passages from earlier editions that Berkeley omitted in his final edition have not generally been included, nor have passages that he inserted been noted as such. However, in a few cases where deletions and insertions seem of especial interest, a note has been made.

The translation of *De Motu,* by A. A. Luce is reprinted from Vol. 4 of the Luce and Jessop edition of Berkeley's writings, and the selections from the *Philosophical Commentaries* are based on the text given by Luce in Vol. 1 of the same edition. Both are printed here by kind permission of Thomas Nelson and Sons Ltd.

The Correspondence with Samuel Johnson is taken from *Samuel Johnson, President of King's College, His Career and Writings,* edited by H. and C. Schneider, 4 vols., New York, 1929, and is reprinted here by kind permission of Columbia University Press.

The text of the Epistles of Marcus Aurelius, the Three Dialogues and further reading of Reason is based on Falkner's 1901 edition of The Works of George Berkeley. In this book there have been reprinted, famous and important, *Principles* and *Three Dialogues* and the final edition superseded the Berkeley edition ... in the final edition have not generally been included, nor have cases where material been noted as such. However in a few cases where deletions and insertions were of special interest, a note has been made.

The translation of *De Motu* alone is by A. Luce, is reprinted from Vol. 4 of the *Works*, and this publication of Berkeley's writings and the selections from the *Philosophical Commentaries* are reprinted in the text given by Luce in Vol. 1 of the same edition. Both are printed here by kind permission of Thomas Nelson and Son, Ltd.

The *Curriculum* issue with *Samuel Johnson* is taken from *Samuel Johnson: A Selection of King's College, the Career and Writings* edited by H. and K. Schneider, 2 vols., New York, 1929, and reprinted here by kind permission of Columbia University Press.

1933.

Johnston, G. A., *The Development of Berkeley's Philosophy*, London, 1923.

Selected Bibliography

Works by Berkeley

Philosophical Commentaries, first published by A. C. Fraser, 1871, under the title of *Commonplace Book*, 1707-08.
An Essay towards a New Theory of Vision, 1709.
A Treatise concerning the Principles of Human Knowledge, 1710.
Passive Obedience, 1712.
Three Dialogues between Hylas and Philonous, 1713.
De Motu, 1721.
Alciphron: or the Minute Philosopher, 1732.
The Theory of Vision Vindicated and Explained, 1733.
The Analyst, 1734.
The Querist, 1735-37.
Siris, 1744.

The standard edition of Berkeley's writings is *The Works of George Berkeley, Bishop of Cloyne*, ed. by A. A. Luce and T. E. Jessop, 9 vols. Edinburgh, 1948-1957. Uniform with this edition is the standard life of Berkeley, *The Life of George Berkeley*, by A. A. Luce, Edinburgh, 1949.

Works About Berkeley

Barnes, Winston, "Did Berkeley misunderstand Locke?," *Mind*, Vol. XLIX, Jan. 1940.
Beardsley, Monroe C., "Berkeley on Abstract Ideas," *Mind*, Vol. LII, April 1943.
"George Berkeley; Lectures on the Bi-Centenary of his Death." *University of California publications in Philosophy*, Vol. 29.
Broad, C. D., "Berkeley's argument about Material Substance," *Proceedings of the British Academy*, Vol. 28, 1942.
Hicks, G. Dawes, *Berkeley*, London, 1932.
"Homage to George Berkeley," *Hermathena*, No. 82, Dublin, 1953.
Johnston, G. A., *The Development of Berkeley's Philosophy*, London, 1923.

Luce, A. A., *Berkeley and Malebranche*, Oxford, 1934.

Luce, A. A., *Berkeley's Immaterialism*, London, 1945.

Mabbott, J. D., "The Place of God in Berkeley's Philosophy," *Journal of Philosophical Studies*, Vol. VI, Jan. 1931.

Morris, C. R., *Locke, Berkeley, Hume*, Oxford, 1931.

Sillem, E. A., *George Berkeley and the Proofs for the Existence of God*, London and New York, 1957.

Warnock, G. J., *Berkeley*, Pelican Books, 1953.

On Berkeley's Theory of Vision

Abbott, T. K., *Sight and Touch*, London, 1864.

Armstrong, D. M., *Berkeley's Theory of Vision*, Melbourne, 1961.

"George Berkeley Bicentenary," *British Journal for the Philosophy of Science*, Vol. IV, May 1953.

Mill, John Stuart, *Dissertations and Discussions*, Vol. I: *Bailey on Berkeley's Theory of Vision*, London, 1875.

On Berkeley's Philosophy of Science

"George Berkeley Bicentenary," *British Journal for the Philosophy of Science*, Vol. IV, May 1953.

On Berkeley's Philosophical Commentaries

Johnston, G. A., *Berkeley's Commonplace Book*, London, 1930.

Luce, A. A., *Berkeley's Philosophical Commentaries*, London, 1944.

Berkeley's Philosophical Writings

The Principles of Human Knowledge

The Principles of Human Knowledge was published in Dublin in 1710. Berkeley brought out a second edition in 1734. It is Berkeley's most important work in philosophy, containing almost all his main doctrines, but concerned chiefly to argue for his view that physical things exist only when perceived. The long Introduction, with its attack on the doctrine of Abstract Ideas, is probably not as important for his main theme as Berkeley believed it to be. The student who prefers a more informal presentation of Berkeley's views might preface his reading of the *Principles* by the *Three Dialogues*. But Berkeley writes so clearly in both works that it is a matter of taste which is read first. The *First Dialogue* contains extended argument for the reduction of sensible qualities to "ideas," which is not found in the *Principles*, but the *Dialogues* omit any long discussion of Abstract Ideas and say little about natural science and mathematics.

A Treatise

Concerning the

Principles of Human Knowledge

[PART I] [1]

Wherein the Chief Causes of Error and Difficulty in the Sciences, with the Grounds of Scepticism, Atheism, and Irreligion, Are Inquired Into

---

[1] [Berkeley never published any further part.—Ed.]

To the Right Honourable [1]
Thomas, Earl of Pembroke, &c.

Knight of the Most Noble Order of the Garter, and One of
the Lords of Her Majesty's Most Honourable Privy Council

MY LORD,

YOU will perhaps wonder that an obscure person, who has
not the honour to be known to your lordship, should presume to address you in this manner. But that a man who has
written something with a design to promote Useful Knowledge
and Religion in the world should make choice of your lordship for his patron, will not be thought strange by any one
that is not altogether unacquainted with the present state of
the church and learning, and consequently ignorant how great
an ornament and support you are to both. Yet, nothing could
have induced me to make you this present of my poor endeavours, were I not encouraged by that candour and native
goodness which is so bright a part in your lordship's character. I might add, my lord, that the extraordinary favour and
bounty you have been pleased to shew towards our Society [2]
gave me hopes you would not be unwilling to countenance
the studies of one of its members. These considerations determined me to lay this treatise at your lordship's feet, and
the rather because I was ambitious to have it known that I
am with the truest and most profound respect, on account of
that learning and virtue which the world so justly admires in
your lordship,

My Lord,
Your lordship's most humble
and most devoted servant,
GEORGE BERKELEY.

The Preface[1]

WHAT I here make public has, a long and scrupulous inquiry, seemed to me evidently true and not unuseful to be known; particularly to those who are tainted with Scepticism, or want a demonstration of the existence and immateriality of God, or the natural immortality of the Soul. Whether it be so or no I am content the reader should impartially examine; since I do not think myself any farther concerned for the success of what I have written than as it is agreeable to truth. But, to the end this may not suffer, I make it my request that the reader suspend his judgment till he has once at least read the whole through, with that degree of attention and thought which the subject-matter shall seem to deserve. For, as there are some passages that, taken by themselves, are very liable (nor could it be remedied) to gross misinterpretation, and to be charged with most absurd consequences, which, nevertheless, upon an entire perusal will appear not to follow from them; so likewise, though the whole should be read over, yet, if this be done transiently, it is very probable my sense may be mistaken: but to a thinking reader, I flatter myself it will be throughout clear and obvious.

As for the characters of novelty and singularity which some of the following notions may seem to bear, it is, I hope, needless to make any apology on that account. He must surely be either very weak, or very little acquainted with the sciences, who shall reject a truth that is capable of demonstration, for no other reason but because it is newly known, and contrary to the prejudices of mankind.

Thus much I thought fit to premise, in order to prevent, if possible, the hasty censures of a sort of men who are too apt to condemn an opinion before they rightly comprehend it.

[1] [Omitted from the second edition.—Ed.]

Introduction

1. PHILOSOPHY being nothing else but the study of Wisdom and Truth, it may with reason be expected that those who have spent most time and pains in it should enjoy a greater calm and serenity of mind, a greater clearness and evidence of knowledge, and be less disturbed with doubts and difficulties than other men. Yet, so it is, we see the illiterate bulk of mankind, that walk the highroad of plain common sense, and are governed by the dictates of nature, for the most part easy and undisturbed. To them nothing that is familiar appears unaccountable or difficult to comprehend. They complain not of any want of evidence in their senses, and are out of all danger of becoming Sceptics. But no sooner do we depart from sense and instinct to follow the light of a superior principle—to reason, meditate, and reflect on the nature of things, but a thousand scruples spring up in our minds, concerning those things which before we seemed fully to comprehend. Prejudices and errors of sense do from all parts discover themselves to our view; and, endeavouring to correct these by reason, we are insensibly drawn into uncouth paradoxes, difficulties, and inconsistencies, which multiply and grow upon us as we advance in speculation; till at length, having wandered through many intricate mazes, we find ourselves just where we were, or, which is worse, sit down in a forlorn Scepticism.

2. The cause of this is thought to be the obscurity of things, or the natural weakness and imperfection of our understandings. It is said the faculties we have are few, and those designed by nature for the support and comfort of life, and not to penetrate into the inward essence and constitution of things: besides, the mind of man being finite, when it treats of things which partake of Infinity, it is not to be wondered at if it run into absurdities and contradictions, out of which it is impossible it should ever extricate itself; it being of the nature of the Infinite not to be comprehended by that which is finite.

3. But, perhaps, we may be too partial to ourselves in placing the fault originally in our faculties, and not rather in the wrong use we make of them. It is a hard thing to suppose that right deductions from true principles should ever

45

end in consequences which cannot be maintained or made consistent. We should believe that God has dealt more bountifully with the sons of men than to give them a strong desire for that knowledge which he had placed quite out of their reach. This were not agreeable to the wonted indulgent methods of Providence, which, whatever appetites it may have implanted in the creatures, doth usually furnish them with such means as, if rightly made use of, will not fail to satisfy them. Upon the whole, I am inclined to think that the far greater part, if not all, of those difficulties which have hitherto amused philosophers, and blocked up the way to knowledge, are entirely owing to ourselves. We have first raised a dust, and then complain we cannot see.

4. My purpose therefore is, to try if I can discover what those Principles are which have introduced all that doubtfulness and uncertainty, those absurdities and contradictions, into the several sects of philosophy; insomuch that the wisest men have thought our ignorance incurable, conceiving it to arise from the natural dullness and limitation of our faculties. And surely it is a work well deserving our pains to make a strict inquiry concerning the First Principles of Human Knowledge; to sift and examine them on all sides: especially since there may be some grounds to suspect that those lets and difficulties, which stay and embarrass the mind in its search after truth, do not spring from any darkness and intricacy in the objects, or natural defect in the understanding, so much as from false Principles which have been insisted on, and might have been avoided.

5. How difficult and discouraging soever this attempt may seem, when I consider what a number of very great and extraordinary men have gone before me in the like designs, yet I am not without some hopes; upon the consideration that the largest views are not always the clearest, and that he who is short-sighted will be obliged to draw the object nearer, and may, perhaps, by a close and narrow survey, discern that which had escaped far better eyes.

6. In order to prepare the mind of the reader for the easier conceiving what follows, it is proper to premise somewhat, by way of Introduction, concerning the nature and abuse of Language. But the unravelling this matter leads me in some measure to anticipate my design, by taking notice of what seems to have had a chief part in rendering speculation in-

tricate and perplexed, and to have occasioned innumerable errors and difficulties in almost all parts of knowledge. And that is the opinion that the mind hath a power of framing *abstract* ideas or notions of things. He who is not a perfect stranger to the writings and disputes of philosophers must needs acknowledge that no small part of them are spent about abstract ideas. These are in a more especial manner thought to be the object of those sciences which go by the name of logic and metaphysics, and of all that which passes under the notion of the most abstracted and sublime learning; in all which one shall scarce find any question handled in such a manner as does not suppose their existence in the mind, and that it is well acquainted with them.

7. It is agreed on all hands that the *qualities* or *modes* of things do never really exist each of them apart by itself, and separated from all others, but are mixed, as it were, and blended together, several in the same object. But, we are told, the mind, being able to consider each quality singly, or abstracted from those other qualities with which it is united, does by that means frame to itself *abstract ideas*. For example, there is conceived by sight an object extended, coloured, and moved: this mixed or compound idea the mind resolving into its simple, constituent parts, and viewing each by itself, exclusive of the rest, does frame the abstract ideas of extension, colour, and motion. Not that it is possible for colour or motion to exist without extension; but only that the mind can frame to itself by abstraction the idea of colour exclusive of extension, and of motion exclusive of both colour and extension.

8. Again, the mind having observed that in the particular extensions perceived by sense there is something common and alike in all, and some other things peculiar, as this or that figure or magnitude, which distinguish them one from another, it considers apart, or singles out by itself, that which is common; making thereof a most abstract idea of extension; which is neither line, surface, nor solid, nor has any figure or magnitude, but is an idea entirely prescinded from all these. So likewise the mind, by leaving out of the particular colours perceived by sense that which distinguishes them one from another, and retaining that only which is common to all, makes an idea of colour in abstract; which is neither red, nor blue, nor white, nor any other determinate colour. And,

in like manner, by considering motion abstractedly, not only from the body moved, but likewise from the figure it describes, and all particular directions and velocities, the abstract idea of motion is framed; which equally corresponds to all particular motions whatsoever that may be perceived by sense.

9. And as the mind frames to itself abstract ideas of *qualities* or *modes*, so does it, by the same precision, or mental separation, attain abstract ideas of the more compounded *beings* which include several co-existent qualities. For example, the mind having observed that Peter, James, and John resemble each other in certain common agreements of shape and other qualities, leaves out of the complex or compound idea it has of Peter, James, and any other particular man, that which is peculiar to each, retaining only what is common to all, and so makes an abstract idea, wherein all the particulars equally partake; abstracting entirely from and cutting off all those circumstances and differences which might determine it to any particular existence. And after this manner it is said we come by the abstract idea of *man*, or, if you please, humanity, or human nature; wherein it is true there is included colour, because there is no man but has some colour, but then it can be neither white, nor black, nor any particular colour, because there is no one particular colour wherein all men partake. So likewise there is included stature, but then it is neither tall stature, nor low stature, nor yet middle stature, but something abstracted from all these. And so of the rest. Moreover, there being a great variety of other creatures that partake in some parts, but not all, of the complex idea of man, the mind, leaving out those parts which are peculiar to men, and retaining those only which are common to all the living creatures, frames the idea of *animal;* which abstracts not only from all particular men, but also all birds, beasts, fishes, and insects. The constituent parts of the abstract idea of animal are body, life, sense, and spontaneous motion. By *body* is meant body without any particular shape or figure, there being no one shape or figure common to all animals; without covering, either of hair, or feathers, or scales, &c., nor yet naked: hair, feathers, scales, and nakedness being the distinguishing properties of particular animals, and for that reason left out of the abstract idea. Upon the same account, the spontaneous motion must be neither walking, nor flying, nor creeping; it is nevertheless a motion, but what that motion is it is not easy to conceive.

10. Whether others have this wonderful faculty of abstracting their ideas, they best can tell. For myself, I find indeed I have a faculty of imagining, or representing to myself, the ideas of those particular things I have perceived, and of variously compounding and dividing them. I can imagine a man with two heads; or the upper parts of a man joined to the body of a horse. I can consider the hand, the eye, the nose, each by itself abstracted or separated from the rest of the body. But then whatever hand or eye I imagine, it must have some particular shape and colour. Likewise the idea of man that I frame to myself must be either of a white, or a black, or a tawny, a straight, or a crooked, a tall, or a low, or a middle-sized man. I cannot by any effort of thought conceive the abstract idea above described. And it is equally impossible for me to form the abstract idea of motion distinct from the body moving, and which is neither swift nor slow, curvilinear nor rectilinear; and the like may be said of all other abstract general ideas whatsoever. To be plain, I own myself able to abstract in one sense, as when I consider some particular parts or qualities separated from others, with which, though they are united in some object, yet it is possible they may really exist without them. But I deny that I can abstract from one another, or conceive separately, those qualities which it is impossible should exist so separated; or that I can frame a general notion, by abstracting from particulars in the manner aforesaid—which last are the two proper acceptations of *abstraction*. And there is ground to think most men will acknowledge themselves to be in my case. The generality of men which are simple and illiterate never pretend to abstract notions. It is said they are difficult and not to be attained without pains and study. We may therefore reasonably conclude that, if such there be, they are confined only to the learned.

11. I proceed to examine what can be alleged in defence of the doctrine of abstraction, and try if I can discover what it is that inclines the men of speculation to embrace an opinion so remote from common sense as that seems to be. There has been a late deservedly esteemed philosopher [2], who, no doubt, has given it very much countenance, by seeming to think the having abstract general ideas is what puts the widest

difference in point of understanding betwixt man and beast. "The having of general ideas," saith he, "is that which puts a perfect distinction betwixt man and brutes, and is an excellency which the faculties of brutes do by no means attain unto. For it is evident we observe no foot-steps in them of making use of general signs for universal ideas; from which we have reason to imagine that they have not the faculty of abstracting, or making general ideas, since they have no use of words, or any other general signs." And a little after:— "Therefore, I think, we may suppose, that it is in this that the species of brutes are discriminated from man: and it is that proper difference wherein they are wholly separated, and which at last widens to so wide a distance. For if they have any ideas at all, and are not bare machines (as some would have them[3]), we cannot deny them to have some reason. It seems as evident to me that they do, some of them, in certain instances, reason, as that they have sense; but it is only in particular ideas, just as they receive them from their senses. They are the best of them tied up within those narrow bounds, and have not (as I think) the faculty to enlarge them by any kind of abstraction."—*Essay on Human Understanding*, B. II. ch. 11. § 10 and 11. I readily agree with this learned author, that the faculties of brutes can by no means attain to abstraction. But then if this be made the distinguishing property of that sort of animals, I fear a great many of those that pass for men must be reckoned into their number. The reason that is here assigned, why we have no grounds to think brutes have abstract general ideas, is, that we observe in them no use of words, or any other general signs; which is built on this supposition, to wit, that the making use of words implies having general ideas. From which it follows that men who use language are able to abstract or generalize their ideas. That this is the sense and arguing of the author will further appear by his answering the question he in another place puts: "Since all things that exist are only particulars, how come we by general terms?" His answer is: "Words become general by being made the signs of general ideas."—*Essay on Human Understanding*, B. III. ch. 3. § 6. But it seems that a word becomes general by being made the sign, not of an abstract general idea, but of several particular ideas, any one of which it

[3] [Descartes.—Ed.]

indifferently suggests to the mind. For example, when it is said "the change of motion is proportional to the impressed force," or that "whatever has extension is divisible," these propositions are to be understood of motion and extension in general; and nevertheless it will not follow that they suggest to my thoughts an *idea* of motion without a body moved, or any determinate direction and velocity; or that I must conceive an *abstract general idea* of extension, which is neither line, surface, nor solid, neither great nor small, black, white, nor red, nor of any other determinate colour. It is only implied that whatever particular motion I consider, whether it be swift or slow, perpendicular, horizontal, or oblique, or in whatever object, the axiom concerning it holds equally true. As does the other of every particular extension; it matters not whether line, surface, or solid, whether of this or that magnitude or figure.

12. By observing how ideas become general, we may the better judge how words are made so. And here it is to be noted that I do not deny absolutely there are *general ideas*, but only that there are any *abstract general ideas*. For, in the passages we have quoted wherein there is mention of general ideas, it is always supposed that they are formed by abstraction, after the manner set forth in sections 8 and 9. Now, if we will annex a meaning to our words, and speak only of what we can conceive, I believe we shall acknowledge that an idea, which considered in itself is particular, becomes general, by being made to represent or stand for all other particular ideas of the same sort. To make this plain by an example. Suppose a geometrician is demonstrating the method of cutting a line in two equal parts. He draws, for instance, a black line of an inch in length: this, which in itself is a particular line, is nevertheless *with regard to its signification* general; since, as it is there used, it represents all particular lines whatsoever; so that what is demonstrated of it is demonstrated of all lines, or, in other words, of a line in general. And, as *that particular line* becomes general by being made a sign, so the *name* line, which taken absolutely is particular, by being a sign, is made general. And as the former owes its generality, not to its being the sign of an abstract or general line, but of all particular right lines that may possibly exist, so the latter must be thought to derive its generality from the same cause, namely, the various particular lines which it indifferently denotes.

13. To give the reader a yet clearer view of the nature of abstract ideas, and the uses they are thought necessary to, I shall add one more passage out of the *Essay on Human Understanding*, which is as follows:—"Abstract ideas are not so obvious or easy to children, or the yet unexercised mind, as particular ones. If they seem so to grown men, it is only because by constant and familiar use they are made so. For, when we nicely reflect upon them, we shall find that general ideas are fictions and contrivances of the mind, that carry difficulty with them, and do not so easily offer themselves as we are apt to imagine. For example, does it not require some pains and skill to form the general idea of a triangle (which is yet none of the most abstract, comprehensive, and difficult); for it must be neither oblique nor rectangle, neither equilateral, equicrural, nor scalenon; but all and none of these at once? In effect, it is something imperfect, that cannot exist; an idea wherein some parts of several different and inconsistent ideas are put together. It is true the mind, in this imperfect state, has need of such ideas, and makes all the haste to them it can, for the conveniency of communication and enlargement of knowledge; to both which it is naturally very much inclined. But yet one has reason to suspect such ideas are marks of our imperfection. At least this is enough to shew that the most abstract and general ideas are not those that the mind is first and most easily acquainted with, nor such as its earliest knowledge is conversant about."—B. IV. ch. 7. § 9. If any man has the faculty of framing in his mind such an idea of a triangle as is here described, it is in vain to pretend to dispute him out of it, nor would I go about it. All I desire is that the reader would fully and certainly inform himself whether he has such an idea or no. And this, methinks, can be no hard task for any one to perform. What more easy than for any one to look a little into his own thoughts, and there try whether he has, or can attain to have, an idea that shall correspond with the description that is here given of the general idea of a triangle—which is neither oblique nor rectangle, equilateral, equicrural nor scalenon, but all and none of these at once?

14. Much is here said of the difficulty that abstract ideas carry with them, and the pains and skill requisite to the forming them. And it is on all hands agreed that there is need of great toil and labour of the mind, to emancipate our thoughts from particular objects, and raise them to those

sublime speculations that are conversant about abstract ideas. From all which the natural consequence should seem to be, that so difficult a thing as the forming abstract ideas was not necessary for *communication,* which is so easy and familiar to all sorts of men. But, we are told, if they seem obvious and easy to grown men, it is only because by constant and familiar use they are made so. Now, I would fain know at what time it is men are employed in surmounting that difficulty, and furnishing themselves with those necessary helps for discourse. It cannot be when they are grown up; for then it seems they are not conscious of any such painstaking. It remains therefore to be the business of their childhood. And surely the great and multiplied labour of framing abstract notions will be found a hard task for that tender age. Is it not a hard thing to imagine that a couple of children cannot prate together of their sugar-plums and rattles and the rest of their little trinkets, till they have first tacked together numberless inconsistencies, and so framed in their minds abstract general ideas, and annexed them to every common name they make use of?

15. Nor do I think them a whit more needful for the *enlargement of knowledge* than for communication. It is, I know, a point much insisted on, that all knowledge and demonstration are about universal notions, to which I fully agree. But then it does not appear to me that those notions are formed by abstraction in the manner premised—*universality,* so far as I can comprehend, not consisting in the absolute, positive nature or conception of anything, but in the relation it bears to the particulars signified or represented by it; by virtue whereof it is that things, names, or notions, being in their own nature *particular,* are *rendered universal.* Thus, when I demonstrate any proposition concerning triangles, it is supposed that I have in view the universal idea of a triangle: which ought not to be understood as if I could frame an *idea* of a triangle which was neither equilateral, nor scalenon, nor equicrural; but only that the particular triangle I consider, whether of this or that sort it matters not, doth equally stand for and represent all rectilinear triangles whatsoever, and is in that sense universal. All which seems very plain and not to include any difficulty in it.

16. But here it will be demanded, how we can know any proposition to be true of all particular triangles, except we have first seen it demonstrated of the abstract idea of a

triangle which equally agrees to all? For, because a property may be demonstrated to agree to some one particular triangle, it will not thence follow that it equally belongs to any other triangle which in all respects is not the same with it. For example, having demonstrated that the three angles of an isosceles rectangular triangle are equal to two right ones, I cannot therefore conclude this affection agrees to all other triangles which have neither a right angle nor two equal sides. It seems therefore, that, to be certain this proposition is universally true, we must either make a particular demonstration for every particular triangle, which is impossible; or once for all demonstrate it of the abstract idea of a triangle, in which all the particulars do indifferently partake, and by which they are all equally represented. To which I answer, that, though the idea I have in view whilst I make the demonstration be, for instance, that of an isosceles rectangular triangle whose sides are of a determinate length, I may nevertheless be certain it extends to all other rectilinear triangles, of what sort or bigness soever. And that because neither the right angle, nor the equality, nor determinate length of the sides are at all concerned in the demonstration. It is true the diagram I have in view includes all these particulars; but then there is not the least mention made of *them* in the proof of the proposition. It is not said the three angles are equal to two right ones, because one of them is a right angle, or because the sides comprehending it are of the same length. Which sufficiently shews that the right angle might have been oblique, and the sides unequal, and for all that the demonstration have held good. And for this reason it is that I conclude that to be true of any obliquangular or scalenon which I had demonstrated of a particular right-angled equicrural triangle, and not because I demonstrated the proposition of the abstract idea of a triangle. [And here it must be acknowledged that a man may *consider* a figure merely as triangular; without attending to the particular qualities of the angles, or relations of the sides. *So far he may abstract.* But this will never prove that he can frame an abstract, general, inconsistent *idea* of a triangle. In like manner we may consider Peter so far forth as man, or so far forth as animal, without framing the forementioned abstract idea, either of man or of animal; inasmuch as all that is perceived is not considered.] [4]

---

[4] [Added in the second edition.—Ed.]

17. It were an endless as well as an useless thing to trace the Schoolmen, those great masters of abstraction, through all the manifold inextricable labyrinths of error and dispute which their doctrine of abstract natures and notions seems to have led them into. What bickerings and controversies, and what a learned dust have been raised about those matters, and what mighty advantage has been from thence derived to mankind, are things at this day too clearly known to need being insisted on. And it had been well if the ill effects of that doctrine were confined to those only who make the most avowed profession of it. When men consider the great pains, industry, and parts that have for so many ages been laid out on the cultivation and advancement of the sciences, and that notwithstanding all this the far greater part of them remain full of darkness and uncertainty, and disputes that are like never to have an end; and even those that are thought to be supported by the most clear and cogent demonstrations contain in them paradoxes which are perfectly irreconcilable to the understandings of men; and that, taking all together, a small portion of them does supply any real benefit to mankind, otherwise than by being an innocent diversion and amusement—I say, the consideration of all this is apt to throw them into a despondency and perfect contempt of all study. But this may perhaps cease upon a view of the false Principles that have obtained in the world; amongst all which there is none, methinks, hath a more wide influence over the thoughts of speculative men than this of *abstract general ideas*.

18. I come now to consider the *source* of this prevailing notion, and that seems to me to be *language*. And surely nothing of less extent than reason itself could have been the source of an opinion so universally received. The truth of this appears as from other reasons so also from the plain confession of the ablest patrons of abstract ideas, who acknowledge that they are made in order to naming; from which it is clear consequence that if there had been no such thing as speech or universal signs, there never had been any thought of abstraction. See B. III. ch. 6. § 39, and elsewhere of the *Essay on Human Understanding*.

Let us examine the manner wherein Words have contributed to the origin of that mistake.—First then, it is thought that every name has, or ought to have, one only precise and settled signification; which inclines men to think there are certain abstract determinate ideas that constitute the true and only immediate signification of each general name; and that it is by the mediation of these abstract ideas that a general name comes to signify any particular thing. Whereas, in truth, there is no such thing as one precise and definite signification annexed to any general name, they all signifying indifferently a great number of particular ideas. All which does evidently follow from what has been already said, and will clearly appear to any one by a little reflexion. To this it will be objected that every name that has a definition is thereby restrained to one certain signification. For example, a triangle is defined to be "a plain surface comprehended by three right lines"; by which that name is limited to denote one certain idea and no other. To which I answer, that in the definition it is not said whether the surface be great or small, black or white, nor whether the sides are long or short, equal or unequal, nor with what angles they are inclined to each other; in all which there may be great variety, and consequently there is no one settled idea which limits the signification of the word triangle. It is one thing for to keep a name constantly to the same *definition*, and another to make it stand everywhere for the same *idea*: the one is necessary, the other useless and impracticable.

19. But, to give a farther account how words came to produce the doctrine of abstract ideas, it must be observed that it is a received opinion that language has no other end but the communicating ideas, and that every significant name stands for an idea. This being so, and it being withal certain that names which yet are not thought altogether insignificant do not always mark out particular conceivable ideas, it is straightway concluded that they stand for abstract notions. That there are many names in use amongst speculative men which do not always suggest to others determinate, particular ideas is what nobody will deny. And a little attention will discover that it is not necessary (even in the strictest reasonings) that significant names which stand for ideas should, every time they are used, excite in the understanding the ideas they are made to stand for: in reading and discoursing, names being for the most part used as letters are in Algebra, in which, though a particular quantity be marked by each letter, yet to proceed right it is not requisite that in every

step each letter suggest to your thoughts that particular quantity it was appointed to stand for.

20. Besides, the communicating of ideas marked by words is not the chief and only end of language, as is commonly supposed. There are other ends, as the raising of some passion, the exciting to or deterring from an action, the putting the mind in some particular disposition; to which the former is in many cases barely subservient, and sometimes entirely omitted, when these can be obtained without it, as I think doth not unfrequently happen in the familiar use of language. I entreat the reader to reflect with himself, and see if it doth not often happen, either in hearing or reading a discourse, that the passions of fear, love, hatred, admiration, and disdain, and the like, arise immediately in his mind upon the perception of certain words, without any ideas coming between. At first, indeed, the words might have occasioned ideas that were fitting to produce those emotions; but, if I mistake not, it will be found that, when language is once grown familiar, the hearing of the sounds or sight of the characters is oft immediately attended with those passions which at first were wont to be produced by the intervention of ideas that are now quite omitted. May we not, for example, be affected with the promise of a *good thing*, though we have not an idea of what it is? Or is not the being threatened with danger sufficient to excite a dread, though we think not of any particular evil likely to befall us, nor yet frame to ourselves an idea of danger in abstract? If any one shall join ever so little reflection of his own to what has been said, I believe that it will evidently appear to him that general names are often used in the propriety of language without the speakers designing them for marks of ideas in his own, which he would have them raise in the mind of the hearer. Even proper names themselves do not seem always spoken with a design to bring into our view the ideas of those individuals that are supposed to be marked by them. For example, when a schoolman tells me "Aristotle hath said it," all I conceive he means by it is to dispose me to embrace his opinion with the deference and submission which custom has annexed to that name. And this effect may be so instantly produced in the minds of those who are accustomed to resign their judgment to authority of that philosopher, as it is impossible any idea either of his person, writings, or repu-

tation should go before. [So close and immediate a connexion may custom establish betwixt the very word Aristotle and the motions of assent and reverence in the minds of some men.] [5] Innumerable examples of this kind may be given, but why should I insist on those things which every one's experience will, I doubt not, plentifully suggest unto him?

21. We have, I think, shewn the impossibility of Abstract Ideas. We have considered what has been said for them by their ablest patrons; and endeavoured to shew they are of no use for those ends to which they are thought necessary. And lastly, we have traced them to the source from whence they flow, which appears evidently to be Language.

It cannot be denied that words are of excellent use, in that by their means all that stock of knowledge which has been purchased by the joint labours of inquisitive men in all ages and nations may be drawn into the view and made the possession of one single person. But at the same time it must be owned that most parts of knowledge have been strangely perplexed and darkened by the abuse of words, and general ways of speech wherein they are delivered. Since therefore words are so apt to impose on the understanding, whatever ideas I consider, I shall endeavour to take them bare and naked into my view; keeping out of my thoughts, so far as I am able, those names which long and constant use hath so strictly united with them. From which I may expect to derive the following advantages:—

22. *First,* I shall be sure to get clear of all controversies purely verbal, the springing up of which weeds in almost all the sciences has been a main hindrance to the growth of true and sound knowledge. *Secondly,* this seems to be a sure way to extricate myself out of that fine and subtle net of abstract ideas, which has so miserably perplexed and entangled the minds of men; and that with this peculiar circumstance, that by how much the finer and more curious was the wit of any man, by so much the deeper was he likely to be ensnared and faster held therein. *Thirdly,* so long as I confine my thoughts to my own ideas, divested of words, I do not see how I can easily be mistaken. The objects I consider, I clearly and adequately know. I cannot be deceived in thinking I have an idea which I have not. It is not possible

[5] [Omitted in the second edition.—Ed.]

for me to imagine that any of my own ideas are alike or unlike that are not truly so. To discern the agreements or disagreements there are between my ideas, to see what ideas are included in my compound idea and what not, there is nothing more requisite than an attentive perception of what passes in my own understanding.

23. But the attainment of all these advantages does presuppose an entire deliverance from the deception of words; which I dare hardly promise myself, so difficult a thing it is to dissolve an union so early begun, and confirmed by so long a habit as that betwixt words and ideas. Which difficulty seems to have been very much increased by the doctrine of *abstraction*. For, so long as men thought *abstract* ideas were annexed to their words, it does not seem strange that they should use words for ideas; it being found an impracticable thing to lay aside the word, and retain the *abstract* idea in the mind; which in itself was perfectly inconceivable. This seems to me the principle cause why those who have so emphatically recommended to others the laying aside all use of words in their meditations, and contemplating their bare ideas, have yet failed to perform it themselves. Of late many have been very sensible of the absurd opinions and significant disputes which grow out of the abuse of words. And, in order to remedy these evils, they advise well, that we attend to the ideas signified, and draw off our attention from the words which signify them. But, how good soever this advice may be they have given others, it is plain they could not have a due regard to it themselves, so long as they thought the only immediate use of words was to signify ideas, and that the immediate signification of every general name was a determinate abstract idea.

24. But these being known to be mistakes, a man may with greater ease prevent his being imposed on by words. He that knows he has no other than *particular* ideas, will not puzzle himself in vain to find out and conceive the *abstract* idea annexed to any name. And he that knows names do not always stand for ideas will spare himself the labour of looking for ideas where there are none to be had. It were, therefore, to be wished that every one would use his utmost endeavours to obtain a clear view of the ideas he would consider; separating from them all that dress and incumbrance of words which so much contribute to blind the judgment and divide the attention. In vain do we extend our view

into the heavens and pry into the entrails of the earth, in vain do we consult the writings of learned men and trace the dark footsteps of antiquity. We need only draw the curtain of words, to behold the fairest tree of knowledge, whose fruit is excellent, and within the reach of our hand.

25. Unless we take care to clear the First Principles of Knowledge from the embarras and delusion of Words, we may make infinite reasonings upon them to no purpose; we may draw consequences from consequences, and be never the wiser. The farther we go, we shall only lose ourselves the more irrecoverably, and be the deeper entangled to difficulties and mistakes. Whoever therefore designs to read the following sheets, I entreat him that he would make my words the occasion of his own thinking, and endeavour to attain the same train of thoughts in reading that I had in writing them. By this means it will be easy for him to discover the truth or falsity of what I say. He will be out of all danger of being deceived by my words. And I do not see how he can be led into an error by considering his own naked, undisguised ideas.

Of the

Principles

of

Human Knowledge

1. It is evident to any one who takes a survey of the *objects of human knowledge*, that they are either *ideas* actually imprinted on the senses; or else such as are perceived by attending to the passions and operations of the mind; or lastly, *ideas* formed by help of memory and imagination—either compounding, dividing, or barely representing those originally perceived in the aforesaid ways. By sight I have the ideas of light and colours, with their several degrees and variations. By touch I perceive hard and soft, heat and cold, motion and resistance; and of all these more and less either as to quantity or degree. Smelling furnishes me with odours; the palate with tastes; and hearing conveys sounds to the mind in all their variety of tone and composition.

And as several of these are observed to accompany each other, they come to be marked by one name, and so to be reputed as one *thing.* Thus, for example, a certain colour, taste, smell, figure and consistence having been observed to go together, are accounted one distinct thing, signified by the name apple; other collections of ideas constitute a stone, a tree, a book, and the like sensible things; which as they are pleasing or disagreeable excite the passions of love, hatred, joy, grief, and so forth.

2. But, besides all that endless variety of ideas or objects of knowledge, there is likewise Something which knows or perceives them; and exercises divers operations, as willing, imagining, remembering, about them. This perceiving, active being is what I call *mind, spirit, soul,* or *myself.* By which words I do not denote any one of my ideas, but a thing entirely distinct from them, wherein they exist, or, which is

the same thing, whereby they are perceived; for the existence of an idea consists in being perceived.

3. That neither our thoughts, nor passions, nor ideas formed by the imagination, exist without the mind is what everybody will allow. And to me it seems no less evident that the various sensations or ideas imprinted on the Sense, however blended or combined together (that is, whatever objects they compose), cannot exist otherwise than in a mind perceiving them. I think an intuitive knowledge may be obtained of this, by any one that shall attend to what is meant by the term *exist* when applied to sensible things. The table I write on I say exists; that is, I see and feel it: and if I were out of my study I should say it existed; meaning thereby that if I was in my study I might perceive it, or that some other spirit actually does perceive it. There was an odour, that is, it was smelt; there was a sound, that is, it was heard; a colour or figure, and it was perceived by sight or touch. This is all that I can understand by these and the like expressions. For as to what is said of the *absolute* existence of unthinking things, without any relation to their being perceived, that is to me perfectly unintelligible. Their *esse* is *percipi*; nor is it possible they should have any existence out of the minds or thinking things which perceive them.

4. It is indeed an opinion strangely prevailing amongst men, that houses, mountains, rivers, and in a word all sensible objects, have an existence, natural or real, distinct from their being perceived by the understanding. But, with how great an assurance and acquiescence soever this Principle may be entertained in the world, yet whoever shall find in his heart to call it in question may, if I mistake not, perceive it to involve a manifest contradiction. For, what are the forementioned objects but the things we perceive by sense? and what do we perceive besides our own ideas or sensations? and is it not plainly repugnant that any one of these, or any combination of them, should exist unperceived?

5. If we thoroughly examine this tenet it will, perhaps, be found at bottom to depend on the doctrine of *abstract ideas*. For can there be a nicer strain of abstraction than to distinguish the existence of sensible objects from their being perceived, so as to conceive them existing unperceived? Light and colours, heat and cold, extension and figures—in a word the things we see and feel—what are they but so many sensa-

tions, notions, ideas, or impressions on the sense? and is it possible to separate, even in thought, any of these from perception? For my part, I might as easily divide a thing from itself. I may, indeed, divide in my thoughts, or conceive apart from each other, those things which perhaps I never perceived by sense so divided. Thus, I imagine the trunk of a human body without the limbs, or conceive the smell of a rose without thinking on the rose itself. So far, I will not deny, I can abstract; if that may properly be called *abstraction* which extends only to the conceiving separately such objects as it is possible may really exist or be actually perceived asunder. But my conceiving or imagining power does not extend beyond the possibility of real existence or perception. Hence, as it is impossible for me to see or feel anything without an actual sensation of that thing, so is it impossible for me to conceive in my thoughts any sensible thing or object distinct from the sensation or perception of it.

6. Some truths there are so near and obvious to the mind that a man need only open his eyes to see them. Such I take this important one to be, viz. that all the choir of heaven and furniture of the earth, in a word all those bodies which compose the mighty frame of the world, have not any subsistence without a mind; that their *being* is to be perceived or known; that consequently so long as they are not actually perceived by me, or do not exist in my mind, or that of any other created spirit, they must either have no existence at all, or else subsist in the mind of some Eternal Spirit: it being perfectly unintelligible, and involving all the absurdity of abstraction, to attribute to any single part of them an existence independent of a spirit. To be convinced of which, the reader need only reflect, and try to separate in his own thoughts the *being* of a sensible thing from its *being perceived*.

7. From what has been said it is evident there is not any other Substance than *Spirit*, or that which perceives. But, for the fuller proof of this point, let it be considered the sensible qualities are colour, figure, motion, smell, taste, and such like, that is, the ideas perceived by sense. Now, for an idea to exist in an unperceiving thing is a manifest contradiction; for to have an idea is all one as to perceive: that therefore wherein colour, figure, and the like qualities exist must perceive them. Hence it is clear there can be no unthinking substance or *substratum* of those ideas.

8. But, say you, though the ideas themselves do not exist without the mind, yet there may be things like them, whereof they are copies or resemblances; which things exist without the mind, in an unthinking substance. I answer, an idea can be like nothing but an idea; a colour or figure can be like nothing but another colour or figure. If we look but never so little into our thoughts, we shall find it impossible for us to conceive a likeness except only between our ideas. Again, I ask whether those supposed *originals*, or external things, of which our ideas are the pictures or representations, be themselves perceivable or no? If they are, then *they* are ideas, and we have gained our point: but if you say they are not, I appeal to any one whether it be sense to assert a colour is like something which is invisible; hard or soft, like something which is intangible; and so of the rest.

9. Some there are who make a distinction betwixt *primary* and *secondary* qualities. By the former they mean extension, figure, motion, rest, solidity or impenetrability, and number; by the latter they denote all other sensible qualities, as colours, sounds, tastes, and so forth. The ideas we have of these last they acknowledge not to be the resemblances of anything existing without the mind, or unperceived; but they will have our ideas of the *primary qualities* to be patterns or images of things which exist without the mind, in an unthinking substance which they call Matter. By Matter, therefore, we are to understand an inert, senseless substance, in which extension, figure, and motion do actually subsist. But it is evident, from what we have already shewn, that extension, figure and motion are only ideas existing in the mind, and that an idea can be like nothing but another idea; and that consequently neither they nor their archetypes can exist in an unperceiving substance. Hence, it is plain that the very notion of what is called *Matter* or *corporeal substance*, involves a contradiction in it.

10. They who assert that figure, motion, and the rest of the primary or original qualities do exist without the mind, in unthinking substances, do at the same time acknowledge that colours, sounds, heat, cold, and such-like secondary qualities, do not; which they tell us are sensations, existing in the mind alone, that depend on and are occasioned by the different size, texture, and motion of the minute particles of matter. This they take for an undoubted truth, which they

can demonstrate beyond all exception. Now, if it be certain that those *original* qualities are inseparably united with the other sensible qualities, and not, even in thought, capable of being abstracted from them, it plainly follows that *they* exist only in the mind. But I desire any one to reflect, and try whether he can, by any abstraction of thought, conceive the extension and motion of a body without all other sensible qualities. For my own part, I see evidently that it is not in my power to frame an idea of a body extended and moving, but I must withal give it some colour or other sensible quality, which is acknowledged to exist only in the mind. In short, extension, figure, and motion, abstracted from all other qualities, are inconceivable. Where therefore the other sensible qualities are, there must these be also, to wit, in the mind and nowhere else.

11. Again, *great* and *small*, *swift* and *slow*, are allowed to to exist nowhere without the mind; being entirely relative, and changing as the frame or position of the organs of sense varies. The extension therefore which exists without the mind is neither great nor small, the motion neither swift nor slow; that is, they are nothing at all. But, say you, they are extension in general, and motion in general. Thus we see how much the tenet of extended moveable substances existing without the mind depends on that strange doctrine of *abstract ideas*. And here I cannot but remark how nearly the vague and indeterminate description of Matter, or corporeal substance, which the modern philosophers are run into by their own principles, resembles that antiquated and so much ridiculed notion of *materia prima*, to be met with in Aristotle and his followers. Without extension solidity cannot be conceived: since therefore it has been shewn that extension exists not in an unthinking substance, the same must also be true of solidity.

12. That *number* is entirely the creature of the mind, even though the other qualities be allowed to exist without, will be evident to whoever considers that the same thing bears a different denomination of number as the mind views it with different respects. Thus, the same extension is one, or three, or thirty-six, according as the mind considers it with reference to a yard, a foot, or an inch. Number is so visibly relative, and dependent on men's understanding, that it is strange to think how any one should give it an absolute existence without the mind. We say one book, one page, one line, &c.; all these

are equally units, though some contain several of the others. And in each instance, it is plain, the unit relates to some particular combination of ideas *arbitrarily* put together by the mind.

13. Unity I know some will have to be a simple or uncompounded idea, accompanying all other ideas in the mind.[1] That I have any such idea answering the word *unity* I do not find; and if I had, methinks I could not miss finding it; on the contrary, it should be the most familiar to my understanding, since it is said to accompany all other ideas, and to be perceived by all the ways of sensation and reflexion. To say no more, it is an *abstract idea*.

14. I shall farther add, that, after the same manner as modern philosophers prove certain sensible qualities to have no existence in Matter, or without the mind, the same thing may be likewise proved of all other sensible qualities whatsoever. Thus, for instance, it is said that heat and cold are affections only of the mind, and not at all patterns of real beings, existing in the corporeal substances which excite them; for that the same body which appears cold to one hand seems warm to another. Now, why may we not as well argue that figure and extension are not patterns or resemblances of qualities existing in Matter; because to the same eye at different stations, or eyes of a different texture at the same station, they appear various, and cannot therefore be the images of anything settled and determinate without the mind? Again, it is proved that sweetness is not really in the sapid thing; because the thing remaining unaltered the sweetness is changed into bitter, as in case of a fever or otherwise vitiated palate. Is it not as reasonable to say that motion is not without the mind; since if the succession of ideas in the mind become swifter, the motion, it is acknowledged, shall appear slower, without any alteration in any external object?

15. In short, let any one consider those arguments which are thought manifestly to prove that colours and tastes exist only in the mind, and he shall find they may with equal force be brought to prove the same thing of extension, figure, and motion. Though it must be confessed this method of arguing does not so much prove that there is no extension or colour in an outward object, as that we do not know by sense which is the true extension or colour of the object. But

---

[1] [Locke, *Essay*, Bk. II, ch. 7. Sec. 7. and ch. 16. Sec. 1.—Ed.]

the arguments foregoing plainly shew it to be impossible that any colour or extension at all, or other sensible quality whatsoever, should exist in an unthinking subject without the mind, or in truth that there should be any such thing as an outward object.

16. But let us examine a little the received opinion. It is said extension is a *mode* or *accident* of Matter, and that Matter is the *substratum* that supports it. Now I desire that you would explain to me what is meant by Matter's *supporting* extension. Say you, I have no idea of Matter; and therefore cannot explain it. I answer, though you have no positive, yet, if you have any meaning at all, you must at least have a relative idea of Matter; though you know not what it is, yet you must be supposed to know what relation it bears to accidents, and what is meant by its supporting them. It is evident *support* cannot here be taken in its usual or literal sense, as when we say that pillars support a building. In what sense therefore must it be taken?

17. If we inquire into what the most accurate philosophers declare themselves to mean by *material substance*, we shall find them acknowledge they have no other meaning annexed to those sounds but the idea of Being in general, together with the relative notion of its supporting accidents. The general idea of Being appeareth to me the most abstract and incomprehensible of all other; and as for its supporting accidents, this, as we have just now observed, cannot be understood in the common sense of those words: it must therefore be taken in some other sense, but what that is they do not explain. So that when I consider the two parts or branches which make the signification of the words *material substance*, I am convinced there is no distinct meaning annexed to them. But why should we trouble ourselves any farther, in discussing this material *substratum* or support of figure and motion and other sensible qualities? Does it not suppose they have an existence without the mind? And is not this a direct repugnancy, and altogether inconceivable?

18. But, though it were possible that solid, figured, moveable substances may exist without the mind, corresponding to the ideas we have of bodies, yet how is it possible for us to know this? Either we must know it by Sense or by Reason. As for our senses, by them we have the knowledge only of our sensations, ideas, or those things that are immediately perceived by sense, call them what you will: but they do not

inform us that things exist without the mind, or unperceived, like to those which are perceived. This the materialists themselves acknowledge.—It remains therefore that if we have any knowledge at all of external things, it must be by reason inferring their existence from what is immediately perceived by sense. But what reason can induce us to believe the existence of bodies without the mind, from what we perceive, since the very patrons of Matter themselves do not pretend there is any necessary connexion betwixt them and our ideas? I say it is granted on all hands (and what happens in dreams, frensies, and the like, puts it beyond dispute) that it is possible we might be affected with all the ideas we have now, though no bodies existed without resembling them. Hence it is evident the supposition of external bodies is not necessary for the producing our ideas; since it is granted they are produced sometimes, and might possibly be produced always, in the same order we see them in at present, without their concurrence.

19. But, though we might possibly have all our sensations without them, yet perhaps it may be thought easier to conceive and explain the manner of their production, by supposing external bodies in their likeness rather than otherwise; and so it might be at least probable there are such things as bodies that excite their ideas in our minds. But neither can this be said. For, though we give the materialists their external bodies, they by their own confession are never the nearer knowing how our ideas are produced; since they own themselves unable to comprehend in what manner body can act upon spirit, or how it is possible it should imprint any idea in the mind. Hence it is evident the production of ideas or sensations in our minds, can be no reason why we should suppose Matter or corporeal substances; since that is acknowledged to remain equally inexplicable with or without this supposition. If therefore it were possible for bodies to exist without the mind, yet to hold they do so must needs be a very precarious opinion; since it is to suppose, without any reason at all, that God has created innumerable beings that are entirely useless, and serve to no manner of purpose.

20. In short, if there were external bodies, it is impossible we should ever come to know it; and if there were not, we might have the very same reasons to think there were that we have now. Suppose—what no one can deny possible—an intelligence, without the help of external bodies, to be af-

fected with the same train of sensations or ideas that you are, imprinted in the same order and with like vividness in his mind. I ask whether that intelligence hath not all the reason to believe the existence of Corporeal Substances, represented by his ideas, and exciting them in his mind, that you can possibly have for believing the same thing? Of this there can be no question. Which one consideration were enough to make any reasonable person suspect the strength of whatever arguments he may think himself to have, for the existence of bodies without the mind.

21. Were it necessary to add any farther proof against the existence of Matter, after what has been said, I could instance several of those errors and difficulties (not to mention impieties) which have sprung from that tenet. It has occasioned numberless controversies and disputes in philosophy, and not a few of far greater moment in religion. But I shall not enter into the detail of them in this place, as well because I think arguments *a posteriori* are unnecessary for confirming what has been, if I mistake not, sufficiently demonstrated *a priori*, as because I shall hereafter find occasion to speak somewhat of them.

22. I am afraid I have given cause to think I am needlessly prolix in handling this subject. For, to what purpose is it to dilate on that which may be demonstrated with the utmost evidence in a line or two, to any one that is capable of the least reflexion? It is but looking into your own thoughts, and so trying whether you can conceive it possible for a sound, or figure, or motion, or colour to exist without the mind or unperceived. This easy trial may perhaps make you see that what you contend for is a downright contradiction. Insomuch that I am content to put the whole upon this issue:—If you can but conceive it possible for one extended moveable substance, or in general for any one idea, or anything like an idea, to exist otherwise than in a mind perceiving it, I shall readily give up the cause. And, as for all that compages of external bodies you contend for, I shall grant you its existence, though you cannot either give me any reason why you believe it exists, or assign any use to it when it is supposed to exist. I say, the bare possibility of your opinions being true shall pass for an argument that it is so.

23. But, say you, surely there is nothing easier than for me to imagine trees, for instance, in a park, or books existing

in a closet, and nobody by to perceive them. I answer, you may so, there is no difficulty in it. But what is all this, I beseech you, more than framing in your mind certain ideas which you call *books* and *trees*, and at the same time omitting to frame the idea of any one that may perceive them? But do not you yourself perceive or think of them all the while? This therefore is nothing to the purpose: it only shews you have the power of imagining, or forming ideas in your mind; but it does not shew that you can conceive it possible the objects of your thought may exist without the mind. To make out this, it is necessary that you conceive them existing unconceived or unthought of; which is a manifest repugnancy. When we do our utmost to conceive the existence of external bodies, we are all the while only contemplating our own ideas. But the mind, taking no notice of itself, is deluded to think it can and does conceive bodies existing unthought of, or without the mind, though at the same time they are apprehended by, or exist in, itself. A little attention will discover to any one the truth and evidence of what is here said, and make it unnecessary to insist on any other proofs against the existence of *material substance*.

24. It is very obvious, upon the least inquiry into our own thoughts, to know whether it be possible for us to understand what is meant by the *absolute existence of sensible objects in themselves*, or *without the mind*. To me it is evident those words mark out either a direct contradiction, or else nothing at all. And to convince others of this, I know no readier or fairer way than to entreat they would calmly attend to their own thoughts; and if by this attention the emptiness or repugnancy of those expressions does appear, surely nothing more is requisite for their conviction. It is on this therefore that I insist, to wit, that the *absolute existence of unthinking things* are words without a meaning, or which include a contradiction. This is what I repeat and inculcate, and earnestly recommend to the attentive thoughts of the reader.

25. All our ideas, sensations, or the things which we perceive, by whatsoever names they may be distinguished, are visibly inactive: there is nothing of power or agency included in them. So that one idea or object of thought cannot produce or make any alteration in another. To be satisfied of the truth of this, there is nothing else requisite but a bare observation

of our ideas. For, since they and every part of them exist only in the mind, it follows that there is nothing in them but what is perceived: but whoever shall attend to his ideas, whether of sense or reflexion, will not perceive in them any power or activity; there is, therefore, no such thing contained in them. A little attention will discover to us that the very being of an idea implies passiveness and inertness in it; insomuch that it is impossible for an idea to do anything, or, strictly speaking, to be the cause of anything: neither can it be the resemblance or pattern of any active being, as is evident from sect. 8. Whence it plainly follows that extension, figure, and motion cannot be the cause of our sensations. To say, therefore, that these are the effects of powers resulting from the configuration, number, motion, and size of corpuscles, must certainly be false.

26. We perceive a continual succession of ideas; some are anew excited, others are changed or totally disappear. There is therefore, *some* cause of these ideas, whereon they depend, and which produces and changes them. That this cause cannot be any quality or idea or combination of *ideas*, is clear from the preceding section. It must therefore be a *substance*; but it has been shewn that there is no corporeal or material substance: it remains therefore that the cause of ideas is an incorporeal active substance or Spirit.

27. A Spirit is one simple, undivided, active being—as it perceives ideas it is called the *understanding*, and as it produces or otherwise operates about them it is called the *will*. Hence there can be no *idea* formed of a soul or spirit; for all ideas whatever, being passive and inert (vid. sect. 25), they cannot represent unto us, by way of image or likeness, that which acts. A little attention will make it plain to any one, that to have an idea which shall be *like* that active Principle of motion and change of ideas is absolutely impossible. Such is the nature of Spirit, or that which acts, that it cannot be of itself perceived, but only by the effects which it produceth. If any man shall doubt of the truth of what is here delivered, let him but reflect and try if he can frame the idea of any power or active being; and whether he has ideas of two principal powers, marked by the names *will* and *understanding*, distinct from each other, as well as from a third idea of Substance or Being in general, with a relative notion of its supporting or being the subject of the aforesaid powers—

which is signified by the name *soul* or *spirit*. This is what some hold; but, so far as I can see, the words *will, soul, spirit*, do not stand for different ideas, or, in truth, for any idea at all, but for something which is very different from ideas, and which, being an agent, cannot be like unto, or represented by, any idea whatsoever. [Though it must be owned at the same time that we have some *notion* of soul, spirit, and the operations of the mind, such as willing, loving, hating—inasmuch as we know or understand the meaning of these words.] [2]

28. I find I can excite ideas in my mind at pleasure, and vary and shift the scene as oft as I think fit. It is no more than *willing*, and straightway this or that idea arises in my fancy; and by the same power it is obliterated and makes way for another. This making and unmaking of ideas doth very properly denominate the mind active. Thus much is certain and grounded on experience: but when we talk of unthinking agents, or of exciting ideas exclusive of volition, we only amuse ourselves with words.

29. But, whatever power I may have over my own thoughts, I find the ideas actually perceived by Sense have not a like dependence of *my* will. When in broad daylight I open my eyes, it is not in my power to choose whether I shall see or no, or to determine what particular objects shall present themselves to my view: and so likewise as to the hearing and other senses; the ideas imprinted on them are not creatures of *my* will. There is therefore some other Will or Spirit that produces them.

30. The ideas of Sense are more strong, lively, and distinct than those of the Imagination; they have likewise a steadiness, order, and coherence, and are not excited at random, as those which are the effects of human wills often are, but in a regular train or series—the admirable connexion whereof sufficiently testifies the wisdom and benevolence of its Author. Now the set rules, or established methods, wherein the Mind we depend on excites in us the ideas of Sense, are called *the laws of nature*; and these we learn by experience, which teaches us that such and such ideas are attended with such and such other ideas, in the ordinary course of things.

[2] [Added in the second edition.—Ed.]

31. This gives us a sort of foresight, which enables us to regulate our actions for the benefit of life. And without this we should be eternally at a loss: we could not know how to act anything that might procure us the least pleasure, or remove the least pain of sense. That food nourishes, sleep refreshes, and fire warms us; that to sow in the seed-time is the way to reap in the harvest; and in general that to obtain such or such ends, such or such means are conducive—all this we know, not by discovering any *necessary connexion* between our ideas, but only by the observation of the *settled laws* of nature; without which we should be all in uncertainty and confusion, and a grown man no more know how to manage himself in the affairs of life than an infant just born.

32. And yet this consistent uniform working, which so evidently displays the Goodness and Wisdom of that Governing Spirit whose Will constitutes the laws of nature, is so far from leading our thoughts to Him, that it rather sends them wandering after second causes. For, when we perceive certain ideas of Sense constantly followed by other ideas, and we know this is not of our own doing, we forthwith attribute power and agency to the ideas themselves, and make one the cause of another, than which nothing can be more absurd and unintelligible. Thus, for example, having observed that when we perceive by sight a certain round luminous figure, we at the same time perceive by touch the idea or sensation called heat, we do from thence conclude the sun to be the *cause* of heat. And in like manner perceiving the motion and collision of bodies to be attended with sound, we are inclined to think the latter the *effect* of the former.

33. The ideas imprinted on the Senses by the Author of nature are called *real things*: and those excited in the imagination, being less regular, vivid, and constant, are more properly termed *ideas* or *images of* things, which they copy and represent. But then our *sensations*, be they never so vivid and distinct, are nevertheless ideas: that is, they exist in the mind, or are perceived by it, as truly as the ideas of its own framing. The ideas of Sense are allowed to have more reality in them, that is, to be more strong, orderly, and coherent than the creatures of the mind; but this is no argument that they exist without the mind. They are also less dependent on the spirit or thinking substance which perceives them, in that they are excited by the will of another and more powerful

Spirit: yet still they are *ideas*: and certainly no idea, whether faint or strong, can exist otherwise than in a mind perceiving it.

34. Before we proceed any farther it is necessary we spend some time in answering Objections which may probably be made against the Principles we have hitherto laid down. In doing of which, if I seem too prolix to those of quick apprehensions, I desire I may be excused, since all men do not equally apprehend things of this nature; and I am willing to be understood by every one.

First, then, it will be objected that by the foregoing principles all that is real and substantial in nature is banished out of the world, and instead thereof a chimerical scheme of *ideas* takes place. All things that exist exist only in the mind; that is, they are purely notional. What therefore becomes of the sun, moon, and stars? What must we think of houses, rivers, mountains, trees, stones; nay, even of our own bodies? Are all these but so many chimeras and illusions on the fancy?— To all which, and whatever else of the same sort may be objected, I answer, that by the Principles premised we are not deprived of any one thing in nature. Whatever we see, feel, hear, or any wise conceive or understand, remains as secure as ever, and is as real as ever. There is a *rerum natura*, and the distinction between realities and chimeras retains its full force. This is evident from sect. 29, 30, and 33, where we have shewn what is meant by *real things*, in opposition to *chimeras* or *ideas of our own framing*; but then they both equally exist in the mind, and in that sense are alike *ideas*.

35. I do not argue against the existence of any one thing that we can apprehend, either by sense or reflection. That the things I see with my eyes and touch with my hands do exist, really exist, I make not the least question. The only thing whose existence we deny is that which *philosophers* call Matter or corporeal substance. And in doing of this there is no damage done to the rest of mankind, who, I dare say, will never miss it. The Atheist indeed will want the colour of an empty name to support his impiety; and the Philosophers may possibly find they have lost a great handle for trifling and disputation.

36. If any man thinks this detracts from the existence or reality of things, he is very far from understanding what hath

been premised in the plainest terms I could think of. Take here an abstract of what has been said:—There are spiritual substances, minds, or human souls, which will or excite ideas in themselves at pleasure; but these are faint, weak, and unsteady in respect of others they perceive by sense: which, being impressed upon them according to certain rules or laws of nature, speak themselves the effects of a Mind more powerful and wise than human spirits. These latter are said to have *more reality* in them than the former;—by which is meant that they are more affecting, orderly, and distinct, and that they are not fictions of the mind perceiving them. And in this sense the sun that I see by day is the real sun, and that which I imagine by night is the idea of the former. In the sense here given of *reality*, it is evident that every vegetable, star, mineral, and in general each part of the mundane system, is as much a *real being* by our principles as by any other. Whether others mean anything by the term *reality* different from what I do, I entreat them to look into their own thoughts and see.

37. It will be urged that thus much at least is true, to wit, that we take away all *corporeal substances.* To this my answer is, that if the word *substance* be taken in the vulgar sense, for a *combination* of sensible qualities, such as extension, solidity, weight, and the like—this we cannot be accused of taking away: but if it be taken in a philosophic sense, for the support of accidents or qualities without the mind—then indeed I acknowledge that we take it away, if one may be said to take away that which never had any existence, not even in the imagination.

38. But after all, say you, it sounds very harsh to say we eat and drink ideas, and are clothed with ideas. I acknowledge it does so—the word *idea* not being used in common discourse to signify the several combinations of sensible qualities which are called *things*; and it is certain that any expression which varies from the familiar use of language will seem harsh and ridiculous. But this doth not concern the truth of the proposition, which in other words is no more than to say, we are fed and clothed with those things which we perceive immediately by our senses. The hardness or softness, the colour, taste, warmth, figure, and suchlike qualities, which combined together constitute the several sorts of victuals and apparel, have been shewn to exist only in the mind that perceives them: and this is all that is meant by calling them *ideas*;

which word, if it was as ordinarily used as *thing*, would sound no harsher nor more ridiculous than it. I am not for disputing about the propriety, but the truth of the expression. If therefore you agree with me that we eat and drink and are clad with the immediate objects of sense, which cannot exist unperceived or without the mind, I shall readily grant it is more proper or conformable to custom that they should be called *things* rather than *ideas*.

39. If it be demanded why I make use of the word *idea*, and do not rather in compliance with custom call them *things*; I answer, I do it for two reasons:—First, because the term *thing*, in contradistinction to *idea*, is generally supposed to denote somewhat existing without the mind: Secondly, because *thing* hath a more comprehensive signification than *idea*, including spirits, or thinking things, as well as ideas. Since therefore the objects of sense exist only in the mind, and are withal thoughtless and inactive, I chose to mark them by the word *idea*; which implies those properties.

40. But, say what we can, some one perhaps may be apt to reply, he will still believe his senses, and never suffer any arguments, how plausible soever, to prevail over the certainty of them. Be it so; assert the evidence of sense as high as you please, we are willing to do the same. That what I see, hear, and feel doth exist, that is to say, is perceived by me, I no more doubt than I do of my own being. But I do not see how the testimony of sense can be alleged as a proof for the existence of anything which is *not* perceived by sense. We are not for having any man turn sceptic and disbelieve his senses; on the contrary, we give them all the stress and assurance imaginable; nor are there any principles more opposite to Scepticism than those we have laid down, as shall be hereafter clearly shewn.

41. *Secondly*, it will be objected that there is a great difference betwixt real fire for instance, and the idea of fire, betwixt dreaming or imagining oneself burnt, and actually being so. This and the like may be urged in opposition to our tenets.—To all which the answer is evident from what hath been already said; and I shall only add in this place, that if real fire be very different from the idea of fire, so also is the real pain that it occasions very different from the idea of the same pain, and yet nobody will pretend that real pain either is, or can possibly be, in an unperceiving thing, or without the mind, any more than its idea.

42. *Thirdly*, it will be objected that we see things actually without or at a distance from us, and which consequently do not exist in the mind; it being absurd that those things which are seen at the distance of several miles should be as near to us as our own thoughts.—In answer to this, I desire it may be considered that in a dream we do oft perceive things as existing at a great distance off, and yet for all that, those things are acknowledged to have their existence only in the mind.

43. But, for the fuller clearing of this point, it may be worth while to consider how it is that we perceive distance, and things placed at a distance, by sight. For, that we should in truth *see* external space, and bodies actually existing in it, some nearer, others farther off, seems to carry with it some opposition to what hath been said of their existing nowhere without the mind. The consideration of this difficulty it was that gave birth to my *Essay towards a New Theory of Vision*, which was published not long since. Wherein it is shewn that distance or outness is neither immediately of itself perceived by sight, nor yet apprehended or judged of by lines and angles, or anything that hath a necessary connexion with it; but that it is only suggested to our thoughts by certain visible ideas, and sensations attending vision, which in their own nature have no manner of similitude or relation either with distance or things placed at a distance; but, by a connexion taught us by experience, they come to signify and suggest them to us, after the same manner that words of any language suggest the ideas they are made to stand for. Insomuch that a man born blind, and afterwards made to see, would not, at first sight, think the things he saw to be without his mind, or at any distance from him. See sec. 41 of the forementioned treatise.

44. The ideas of sight and touch make two species entirely distinct and heterogeneous. The former are marks and prognostics of the latter. That the proper objects of sight neither exist without the mind, nor are the images of external things, was shewn even in that treatise. Though throughout the same the contrary be supposed true of *tangible objects;*—not that to suppose that vulgar error was necessary for establishing the notion therein laid down, but because it was beside my purpose to examine and refute it, in a discourse concerning *Vision*. So that in strict truth the ideas of sight, when we apprehend by them distance, and things placed at a distance,

do not suggest or mark out to us things actually existing at a distance, but only admonish us what ideas of touch will be imprinted in our minds at such and such distances of time, and in consequence of such or such actions. It is, I say, evident, from what has been said in the foregoing parts of this Treatise, and in sect. 147 and elsewhere of the Essay concerning Vision, that visible ideas are the Language whereby the Governing Spirit on whom we depend informs us what tangible ideas he is about to imprint upon us, in case we excite this or that motion in our own bodies. But for a fuller information in this point I refer to the Essay itself.

45. *Fourthly*, it will be objected that from the foregoing principles it follows things are every moment annihilated and created anew. The objects of sense exist only when they are perceived: the trees therefore are in the garden, or the chairs in the parlour, no longer than while there is somebody by to perceive them. Upon shutting my eyes all the furniture in the room is reduced to nothing, and barely upon opening them it is again created.—In answer to all which, I refer the reader to what has been said in sect. 3, 4, &c.; and desire he will consider whether he means anything by the actual existence of an idea distinct from its being perceived. For my part, after the nicest inquiry I could make, I am not able to discover that anything else is meant by those words; and I once more entreat the reader to sound his own thoughts, and not suffer himself to be imposed on by words. If he can conceive it possible either for his ideas or their archetypes to exist without being perceived, then I give up the cause. But if he cannot, he will acknowledge it is unreasonable for him to stand up in defence of he knows not what, and pretend to charge on me as an absurdity, the not assenting to those propositions which at bottom have no meaning in them.

46. It will not be amiss to observe how far the received principles of philosophy are themselves chargeable with those pretended absurdities. It is thought strangely absurd that upon closing my eyelids all the visible objects around me should be reduced to nothing; and yet is not this what philosophers commonly acknowledge, when they agree on all hands that light and colours, which alone are the proper and immediate objects of sight, are mere sensations that exist no longer than they are perceived? Again, it may to some perhaps seem very incredible that things should be every moment

creating; yet this very notion is commonly taught in the schools. For the Schoolmen, though they acknowledge the existence of Matter, and that the whole mundane fabric is framed out of it, are nevertheless of opinion that it cannot subsist without the divine conservation; which by them is expounded to be a continual creation.

47. Farther, a little thought will discover to us that, though we allow the existence of Matter or corporeal substance, yet it will unavoidably follow, from the principles which are now generally admitted, that the particular bodies, of what kind soever, do none of them exist whilst they are not perceived. For, it is evident, from sect. 11 and the following sections, that the Matter philosophers contend for is an incomprehensible Somewhat, which hath none of those particular qualities whereby the bodies falling under our senses are distinguished one from another. But, to make this more plain, it must be remarked that the infinite divisibility of Matter is now universally allowed, at least by the most approved and considerable philosophers, who on the received principles demonstrate it beyond all exception. Hence, it follows there is an infinite number of parts in each particle of Matter which are not perceived by sense. The reason therefore that any particular body seems to be of a finite magnitude, or exhibits only a finite number of parts to sense, is, not because it contains no more, since in itself it contains an infinite number of parts, but because the sense is not acute enough to discern them. In proportion therefore as the sense is rendered more acute, it perceives a greater number of parts in the object, that is, the object appears greater; and its figure varies, those parts in its extremities which were before unperceivable appearing now to bound it in very different lines and angles from those perceived by an obtuser sense. And at length, after various changes of size and shape, when the sense becomes infinitely acute, the body shall seem infinite. During all which there is no alteration in the body, but only in the sense. Each body therefore, considered in itself, is infinitely extended, and consequently void of all shape and figure. From which it follows that, though we should grant the existence of Matter to be never so certain, yet it is withal as certain, the materialists themselves are by their own principles forced to acknowledge, that neither the particular bodies perceived by sense, nor anything like them, exists without the mind. Matter, I say, and each

particle thereof, is according to them infinite and shapeless; and it is the mind that frames all that variety of bodies which compose the visible world, any one whereof does not exist longer than it is perceived.

48. But, after all, if we consider it, the objection proposed in sect. 45 will not be found reasonably charged on the Principles we have premised, so as in truth to make any objection at all against our notions. For, though we hold indeed the objects of sense to be nothing else but ideas which cannot exist unperceived, yet we may not hence conclude they have no existence except only while they are perceived by *us;* since there may be some other spirit that perceives them though we do not. Wherever bodies are said to have no existence without the mind, I would not be understood to mean this or that particular mind, but all minds whatsoever. It does not therefore follow from the foregoing Principles that bodies are annihilated and created every moment, or exist not at all during the intervals between *our* perception of them.

49. *Fifthly,* it may perhaps be objected that if extension and figure exist only in the mind, it follows that the mind is extended and figured; since extension is a mode or attribute which (to speak with the Schools) is predicated of the subject in which it exists.—I answer, those qualities are in the mind only as they are perceived by it;—that is, not by way of *mode* or *attribute,* but only by way of *idea.* And it no more follows the soul or mind is extended, because extension exists in it alone, than it does that it is red or blue, because those colours are on all hands acknowledged to exist in it, and nowhere else. As to what philosophers say of subject and mode, that seems very groundless and unintelligible. For instance, in this proposition "a die is hard, extended, and square," they will have it that the word *die* denotes a subject or substance, distinct from the hardness, extension, and figure which are predicated of it, and in which they exist. This I cannot comprehend: to me a die seems to be nothing distinct from those things which are termed its modes or accidents. And, to say a die is hard, extended, and square is not to attribute those qualities to a subject distinct from and supporting them, but only an explication of the meaning of the word *die.*

50. *Sixthly,* you will say there have been a great many

things explained by matter and motion; take away these and you destroy the whole corpuscular philosophy, and undermine those mechanical principles which have been applied with so much success to account for the phenomena. In short, whatever advances have been made, either by accident or modern philosophers, in the study of nature do all proceed on the supposition that corporeal substance or Matter doth really exist.—To this I answer that there is not any one phenomenon explained on that supposition which may not as well be explained without it, as might easily be made appear by an induction of particulars. To explain the phenomena, is all one as to shew why, upon such and such occasions, we are affected with such and such ideas. But how Matter should operate on a Spirit, or produce any idea in it, is what no philosopher will pretend to explain; it is therefore evident there can be no use of Matter in natural philosophy. Besides, they who attempt to account for things do it, not by corporeal substance, but by figure, motion, and other qualities; which are in truth no more than mere ideas, and therefore cannot be the cause of anything, as hath been already shewn. See sect. 25.

51. *Seventhly*, it will upon this be demanded whether it does not seem absurd to take away natural causes, and ascribe everything to the immediate operation of spirits? We must no longer say upon these principles that fire heats, or water cools, but that a spirit heats, and so forth. Would not a man be deservedly laughed at, who should talk after this manner?— I answer, he would so: in such things we ought to think with the learned, and speak with the vulgar. They who to demonstration are convinced of the truth of the Copernican system do nevertheless say "the sun rises," "the sun sets," or "comes to the meridian"; and if they affected a contrary style in common talk it would without doubt appear very ridiculous. A little reflection on what is here said will make it manifest that the common use of language would receive no manner of alteration or disturbance from the admission of our tenets.

52. In the ordinary affairs of life, any phrases may be retained, so long as they excite in us proper sentiments, or dispositions to act in such a manner as is necessary for our well-being, how false soever they may be if taken in a strict and speculative sense. Nay, this is unavoidable, since, propriety being regulated by custom, language is suited to the received opinions, which are not always the truest. Hence it is impos-

sible—even in the most rigid, philosophic reasonings—so far to alter the bent and genius of the tongue we speak as never to give a handle for cavillers to pretend difficulties and inconsistencies. But, a fair and ingenuous reader will collect the sense from the scope and tenor and connexion of a discourse, making allowances for those inaccurate modes of speech which use has made inevitable.

53. As to the opinion that there are no corporeal causes, this has been heretofore maintained by some of the Schoolmen, as it is of late by others among the modern philosophers; who though they allow Matter to exist, yet will have God alone to be the immediate efficient cause of all things. These men saw that amongst all the objects of sense there was none which had any power or activity included in it; and that by consequence this was likewise true of whatever bodies they supposed to exist without the mind, like unto the immediate objects of sense. But then, that they should suppose an innumerable multitude of created beings, which they acknowledge are not capable of producing any one effect in nature, and which therefore are made to no manner of purpose, since God might have done everything as well without them—this I say, though we should allow it possible, must yet be a very unaccountable and extravagant supposition.

54. In the *eighth* place, the universal concurrent assent of mankind may be thought by some an invincible argument in behalf of Matter, or the existence of external things. Must we suppose the whole world to be mistaken? And if so, what cause can be assigned of so widespread and predominant an error?—I answer, first, that, upon a narrow inquiry, it will not perhaps be found so many as is imagined do really believe the existence of Matter or things without the mind. Strictly speaking, to believe that which involves a contradiction, or has no meaning in it, is impossible; and whether the foregoing expressions are not of that sort, I refer it to the impartial examination of the reader. In one sense, indeed, men may be said to believe that Matter exists; that is, they act as if the immediate cause of their sensations, which affects them every moment, and is so nearly present to them, were some senseless unthinking being. But, that they should clearly apprehend any meaning marked by those words, and form thereof a settled speculative opinion, is what I am not able to conceive. This is not the only instance wherein men impose

upon themselves, by imagining they believe those propositions which they have often heard, though at bottom they have no meaning in them.

55. But secondly, though we should grant a notion to be ever so universally and steadfastly adhered to, yet this is but a weak argument of its truth to whoever considers what a vast number of prejudices and false opinions are everywhere embraced with the utmost tenaciousness, by the unreflecting (which are the far greater) part of minkind. There was a time when the antipodes and motion of the earth were looked upon as monstrous absurdities even by men of learning: and if it be considered what a small proportion they bear to the rest of mankind, we shall find that at this day those notions have gained but a very inconsiderable footing in the world.

56. But it is demanded that we assign a cause of this prejudice, and account for its obtaining in the world. To this I answer, that men knowing they perceived several ideas, whereof they themselves were not the authors, as not being excited from within, nor depending on the operation of their wills, this made them maintain *those* ideas or objects of perception, had an existence independent of and without the mind, without ever dreaming that a contradiction was involved in those words. But, philosophers having plainly seen that the immediate objects of perception do not exist without the mind, they in some degree corrected the mistake of the vulgar; but at the same time run into another, which seems no less absurd, to wit, that there are certain objects really existing without the mind, or having a subsistence distinct from being perceived, of which our ideas are only images or resemblances, imprinted by those objects on the mind. And this notion of the philosophers owes its origin to the same cause with the former, namely, their being conscious that *they* were not the authors of their own sensations; which they evidently knew were imprinted from without, and which therefore must have *some* cause, distinct from the minds on which they are imprinted.

57. But why they should suppose the ideas of sense to be excited in us by things in their likeness, and not rather have recourse to *Spirit*, which alone can act, may be accounted for. First, because they were not aware of the repugnancy there is, as well in supposing things like unto our ideas existing without, as in attributing to them power or activity. Secondly, because the Supreme Spirit which

excites those ideas in our minds, is not marked out and limited to our view by any particular finite collection of sensible ideas, as human agents are by their size, complexion, limbs, and motions. And thirdly, because His operations are regular and uniform. Whenever the course of nature is interrupted by a miracle, men are ready to own the presence of a Superior Agent. But, when we see things go on in the ordinary course, they do not excite in us any reflexion; their order and concatenation, though it be an argument of the greatest wisdom, power, and goodness in their Creator, is yet so constant and familiar to us, that we do not think them the immediate effects of a *Free Spirit;* especially since inconsistency and mutability in acting, though it be an imperfection, is looked on as a mark of *freedom.*

58. *Tenthly,* it will be objected that the notions we advance are inconsistent with several sound truths in philosophy and mathematics. For example, the motion of the earth is now universally admitted by astronomers as a truth grounded on the clearest and most convincing reasons. But, on the foregoing Principles, there can be no such thing. For, motion being only an idea, it follows that if it be not perceived it exists not: but the motion of the earth is not perceived by sense.—I answer, That tenet, if rightly understood, will be found to agree with the Principles we have premised: for, the question whether the earth moves or no amounts in reality to no more than this, to wit, whether we have reason to conclude, from what has been observed by astronomers, that if we were placed in such and such circumstances, and such or such a position and distance both from the earth and sun, we should perceive the former to move among the choir of the planets, and appearing in all respects like one of them: and this, by the established rules of nature, which we have no reason to mistrust, is reasonably collected from the phenomena.

59. We may, from the experience we have had of the train and succession of ideas in our minds, often make, I will not say uncertain conjectures, but sure and well-grounded predictions concerning the ideas we shall be affected with pursuant to a great train of actions; and be enabled to pass a right judgment of what would have appeared to us, in case we were placed in circumstances very different from those we are in at present. Herein consists the knowledge of nature,

which may preserve its use and certainty very consistently with what hath been said. It will be easy to apply this to whatever objections of the like sort may be drawn from the magnitude of the stars, or any other discoveries in astronomy or nature.

60. In the *eleventh* place, it will be demanded to what purpose serves that curious organization of plants, and the animal mechanism in the parts of animals. Might not vegetables grow, and shoot forth leaves and blossoms, and animals perform all their motions, as well without as with all that variety of internal parts so elegantly contrived and put together;—which, being ideas, have nothing powerful or operative in them, nor have any *necessary* connexion with the effects ascribed to them? If it be a Spirit that immediately produces every effect by a *fiat*, or act of his will, we must think all that is fine and artificial in the works, whether of man or nature, to be made in vain. By this doctrine, though an artist hath made the spring and wheels, and every movement of a watch, and adjusted them in such a manner as he knew would produce the motions he designed; yet he must think all this done to no purpose, and that it is an Intelligence which directs the index, and points to the hour of the day. If so, why may not the Intelligence do it, without *his* being at the pains of making the movements and putting them together? Why does not an empty case serve as well as another? And how comes it to pass, that whenever there is any fault in the going of a watch, there is some corresponding disorder to be found in the movements, which being mended by a skilful hand all is right again? The like may be said of all the Clockwork of Nature, great part whereof is so wonderfully fine and subtle as scarce to be discerned by the best microscope. In short, it will be asked, how, upon our Principles, any tolerable account can be given, or any final cause assigned of an innumerable multitude of bodies and machines, framed with the most exquisite art, which in the common philosophy have very opposite uses assigned them, and serve to explain abundance of phenomena?

61. To all which I answer, first, that though there were some difficulties relating to the administration of Providence, and the uses by it assigned to the several parts of nature, which I could not solve by the foregoing Principles, yet this objection could be of small weight against the truth and

certainty of those things which may be proved *a priori,* with the utmost evidence. Secondly, but neither are the received principles free from the like difficulties; for, it may still be demanded to what end God should take those roundabout methods of effecting things by instruments and machines, which no one can deny might have been effected by the mere command of His will, without all that *apparatus.* Nay, if we narrowly consider it, we shall find the objection may be retorted with greater force on those who hold the existence of those machines without the mind; for it has been made evident that solidity, bulk, figure, motion, and the like have no *activity* or *efficacy* in them, so as to be capable of producing any one effect in nature. See sect. 25. Whoever therefore supposes them to exist (allowing the supposition possible) when they are not perceived does it manifestly to no purpose; since the only use that is assigned to them, as they exist unperceived, is that they produce those perceivable effects which in truth cannot be ascribed to anything but Spirit.

62. But, to come nigher the difficulty, it must be observed that though the fabrication of all those parts and organs be not absolutely necessary to the producing any effect, yet it is necessary to the producing of things in a constant regular way, according to the laws of nature. There are certain general laws that run through the whole chain of natural effects: these are learned by the observation and study of nature, and are by men applied, as well to the framing artificial things for the use and ornament of life as to the explaining the various phenomena. Which explication consists only in shewing the conformity any particular phenomenon hath to the general laws of nature, or, which is the same thing, in discovering the *uniformity* there is in the production of natural effects; as will be evident to whoever shall attend to the several instances wherein philosophers pretend to account for appearances. That there is a great and conspicuous *use* in these regular constant methods of working observed by the Supreme Agent hath been shewn in sect. 31. And it is no less visible that a particular size, figure, motion, and disposition of parts are necessary, though not absolutely to the producing any effect, yet to the producing it according to the standing mechanical laws of nature. Thus, for instance, it cannot be denied that God, or the Intelligence that sustains and rules the ordinary course of things, might if

He were minded to produce a miracle, cause all the motions on the dial-plate of a watch, though nobody had ever made the movements and put them in it. But yet, if He will act agreeably to the rules of mechanism, by Him for wise ends established and maintained in the creation, it is necessary that those actions of the watchmaker, whereby *he* makes the movements and rightly adjusts them, precede the production of the aforesaid motions; as also that any disorder in them be attended with the perception of some corresponding disorder in the movements, which being once corrected all is right again.

63. It may indeed on some occasions be necessary that the Author of nature display His overruling power in producing some appearance out of the ordinary series of things. Such exceptions from the general rules of nature are proper to surprise and awe men into an acknowledgment of the Divine Being; but then they are to be used but seldom, otherwise there is a plain reason why they should fail of that effect. Besides, God seems to choose the convincing our reason of His attributes by the works of nature, which discover so much harmony and contrivance in their make, and are such plain indications of wisdom and beneficence in their Author, rather than to astonish us into a belief of His Being by anomalous and surprising events.

64. To set this matter in a yet clearer light, I shall observe that what has been objected in sect. 60 amounts in reality to no more than this:—*ideas* are not anyhow and at random produced, there being a certain order and connexion between them, like to that of cause and effect: there are also several combinations of them, made in a very regular and artificial manner, which seem like so many instruments in the hand of nature that, being hid as it were behind the scenes, have a secret operation in producing those appearances which are seen on the theatre of the world, being themselves discernible only to the curious eye of the philosopher. But, since one idea cannot be the cause of another, to what purpose is that connexion? And since those instruments, being barely *inefficacious* perceptions in the mind, are not subservient to the production of natural effects, it is demanded why they are made; or, in other words, what reason can be assigned why God should make us, upon a close inspection into His works, behold so great variety of ideas, so artfully laid together, and so much according to rule; it not being credible that He

would be at the expense (if one may so speak) of all that art and regularity to no purpose?

65. To all which my answer is, first, that the connexion of ideas does not imply the relation of *cause* and *effect*, but only of a mark or *sign* with the *thing signified*. The fire which I see is not the cause of the pain I suffer upon my approaching it, but the mark that forewarns me of it. In like manner the noise that I hear is not the effect of this or that motion or collision of the ambient bodies, but the sign thereof. Secondly, the reason why ideas are formed into machines, that is, artificial and regular combinations, is the same with that for combining letters into words. That a few original ideas may be made to signify a great number of effects and actions, it is necessary they be variously combined together. And to the end their use be permanent and universal, these combinations must be made by *rule*, and with *wise contrivance*. By this means abundance of information is conveyed unto us, concerning what we are to expect from such and such actions, and what methods are proper to be taken for the exciting such and such ideas. Which in effect is all that I conceive to be distinctly meant when it is said that, by discerning the figure, texture, and mechanism of the inward parts of bodies, whether natural or artificial, we may attain to know the several uses and properties depending thereon, or the nature of the thing.

66. Hence, it is evident that those things which, under the notion of a cause co-operating or concurring to the production of effects, are altogether inexplicable and run us into great absurdities, may be very naturally explained, and have a proper and obvious use assigned to them, when they are considered only as marks or signs for *our* information. And it is the searching after and endeavouring to understand [those signs instituted by the Author of Nature,] [3] that ought to be the employment of the natural philosopher; and not the pretending to explain things by *corporeal* causes; which doctrine seems to have too much estranged the minds of men from that Active Principle, that supreme and wise Spirit "in whom we live, move, and have our being."

67. In the *twelfth* place, it may perhaps be objected that—though it be clear from what has been said that there can

[3] [The first edition has "this language (if I may so call it) of the Author of Nature, . . ."—Ed.]

be no such thing as an inert, senseless, extended, solid, figured, moveable Substance, existing without the mind, such as philosophers describe Matter; yet, if any man shall leave out of his idea of Matter the positive ideas of extension, figure, solidity and motion, and say that he means only by that word an inert, senseless substance, that exists without the mind, or unperceived, which is the *occasion* of our ideas, or at the presence whereof God is pleased to excite ideas in us—it doth not appear but that Matter taken in this sense may possibly exist.—In answer to which I say, first, that it seems no less absurd to suppose a substance without accidents, than it is to suppose accidents without a substance. But secondly, though we should grant this unknown substance may possibly exist, yet where can it be supposed to be? That it exists not in the mind is agreed; and that it exists not in place is no less certain, since all extension exists only in the mind, as hath been already proved. It remains therefore that it exists nowhere at all.

68. Let us examine a little the description that is here given us of Matter. It neither acts, nor perceives, nor is perceived: for this is all that is meant by saying it is an inert, senseless, unknown substance; which is a definition entirely made up of negatives, excepting only the relative notion of its standing under or supporting. But then it must be observed that it supports nothing at all, and how nearly this comes to the description of a *nonentity* I desire may be considered. But, say you, it is the *unknown occasion*, at the presence of which ideas are excited in us by the will of God. Now, I would fain know how anything can be present to us, which is neither perceivable by sense nor reflexion, nor capable of producing any idea in our minds, nor is at all extended, nor hath any form, nor exists in any place. The words "to be present," when thus applied, must needs be taken in some abstract and strange meaning, and which I am not able to comprehend.

69. Again, let us examine what is meant by *occasion*. So far as I can gather from the common use of language, that word signifies either the agent which produces any effect, or else something that is observed to accompany or go before it, in the ordinary course of things. But, when it is applied to Matter, as above described, it can be taken in neither of those senses; for Matter is said to be passive and inert, and so cannot be an agent or efficient cause. It is also unperceiv-

able, as being devoid of all sensible qualities, and so cannot be the occasion of our perceptions in the latter sense; as when the burning my finger is said to be the occasion of the pain that attends it. What therefore can be meant by calling *Matter* an *occasion?* This term is either used in no sense at all, or else in some sense very distant from its received signification.

70. You will perhaps say that Matter, though it be not perceived by us, is nevertheless perceived by God, to whom it is the occasion of exciting ideas in our minds. For, say you, since we observe our sensations to be imprinted in an orderly and constant manner, it is but reasonable to suppose there are certain constant and regular occasions of their being produced. That is to say, that there are certain permanent and distinct parcels of Matter, corresponding to our ideas, which, though they do not excite them in our minds, or anywise immediately affect us, as being altogether passive, and unperceivable to us, they are nevertheless to God, by whom they *are* perceived, as it were so many occasions to remind Him when and what ideas to imprint on our minds: that so things may go on in a constant uniform manner.

71. In answer to this, I observe that, as the notion of Matter is here stated, the question is no longer concerning the existence of a thing distinct from *Spirit* and *idea*, from perceiving and being perceived; but whether there are not certain Ideas (of I know not what sort) in the mind of God, which are so many marks or notes that direct Him how to produce sensations in our minds in a constant and regular method: much after the same manner as a musician is directed by the notes of music to produce that harmonious train and composition of sound which is called a tune; though they who hear the music do not perceive the notes, and may be entirely ignorant of them. But this notion of Matter seems too extravagant to deserve a confutation. Besides, it is in effect no objection against what we have advanced, viz. that there is no senseless unperceived substance.

72. If we follow the light of reason, we shall, from the constant uniform method of our sensations, collect the goodness and wisdom of the Spirit who excites them in our minds; but this is all that I can see reasonably concluded from thence. To me, I say, it is evident that the being of a Spirit—infinitely wise, good, and powerful—is abundantly sufficient to explain all the appearances of nature. But, as for *inert, senseless Matter*, nothing that I perceive has any the least

connexion with it, or leads to the thoughts of it. And I would fain see any one explain any the meanest phenomenon in nature by it, or shew any manner of reason, though in the lowest rank of probability, that he can have for its existence; or even make any tolerable sense or meaning of that supposition. For, as to its being an occasion, we have, I think, evidently shewn that with regard to us it is no occasion. It remains therefore that it must be, if at all, the occasion to God of exciting ideas in us; and what this amounts to we have just now seen.

73. It is worth while to reflect a little on the motives which induced men to suppose the existence of *material substance;* that so having observed the gradual ceasing and expiration of those motives or reasons, we may proportionably withdraw the assent that was grounded on them. First, therefore, it was thought that colour, figure, motion, and the rest of the sensible qualities or accident did really exist without the mind; and for this reason it seemed needful to suppose some unthinking *substratum* or substance wherein they did exist, since they could not be conceived to exist by themselves. Afterwards, in process of time, men being convinced that colours, sounds, and the rest of the sensible, secondary qualities had no existence without the mind, they stripped this *substratum* or material substance of *those* qualities, leaving only the primary ones, figure, motion, and such-like; which they still conceived to exist without the mind, and consequently to stand in need of a material support. But, it having been shewn that none even of these can possibly exist otherwise than in a Spirit or Mind which perceives them, it follows that we have no longer any reason to suppose the being of Matter, nay, that it is utterly impossible there should be any such thing;— so long as that word is taken to denote an *unthinking substratum* of qualities or accidents, wherein they exist without the mind.

74. But—though it be allowed by the materialists themselves that Matter was thought of only for the sake of supporting accidents, and, the reason entirely ceasing, one might expect the mind should naturally, and without any reluctance at all, quit the belief of what was solely grounded thereon: yet the prejudice is riveted so deeply in our thoughts that we can scarce tell how to part with it, and are therefore inclined, since the *thing* itself is indefensible, at least to retain the *name;* which we apply to I know not what ab-

stracted and indefinite notions of *being,* or *occasion,* though without any shew of reason, at least so far as I can see. For, what is there on our part, or what do we perceive, amongst all the ideas, sensations, notions which are imprinted on our minds, either by sense or reflexion, from whence may be inferred the existence of an inert, thoughtless, unperceived occasion? and, on the other hand, on the part of an All-sufficient Spirit, what can there be that should make us believe or even suspect He is directed by an inert occasion to excite ideas in our minds?

75. It is a very extraordinary instance of the force of prejudice, and much to be lamented, that the mind of man retains so great a fondness, against all the evidence of reason, for a stupid thoughtless *Somewhat,* by the interposition whereof it would as it were screen itself from the Providence of God, and remove Him farther off from the affairs of the world. But, though we do the utmost we can to secure the belief of Matter; though, when reason forsakes us, we endeavour to support our opinion on the bare possibility of the thing, and though we indulge ourselves in the full scope of an imagination not regulated by reason to make out that poor possibility; yet the upshot of all is—that there are certain *unknown* Ideas in the mind of God; for this, if anything, is all that I conceive to be meant by *occasion* with regard to God. And this at the bottom is no longer contending for the thing, but for the name.

76. Whether therefore there are such Ideas in the mind of God, and whether *they* may be called by the name *Matter,* I shall not dispute. But, if you stick to the notion of an unthinking substance or support of extension, motion, and other sensible qualities, then to me it is most evidently impossible there should be any such thing; since it is a plain repugnancy that those qualities should exist in, or be supported by, an unperceiving substance.

77. But, say you, although it be granted that there is no thoughtless support of extension, and the other qualities or accidents which we perceive, yet there may perhaps be some inert, unperceiving substance or *substratum* of some other qualities, as incomprehensible to us as colours are to a man born blind, because we have not a sense adapted to them. But, if we had a new sense, we should possibly no more doubt of *their* existence than a blind man made to see does of the existence of light and colours.—I answer, first, if what

you mean by the word *Matter* be only the unknown support of unknown qualities, it is no matter whether there is such a thing or no, since it no way concerns us. And I do not see the advantage there is in disputing about what we know not *what*, and we know not why.

78. But, secondly, if we had a new sense, it could only furnish us with new ideas or sensations; and then we should have the same reason against *their* existing in an unperceiving substance that has been already offered with relation to figure, motion, colour, and the like. *Qualities*, as hath been shewn, are nothing else but *sensations* or *ideas*, which exist only in a mind perceiving them; and this is true not only of the ideas we are acquainted with at present, but likewise of all possible ideas whatever.

79. But you will insist, What if I have no reason to believe the existence of Matter? what if I cannot assign any use to it, or explain anything by it, or even conceive what is meant by that word? yet still it is no contradiction to say that Matter *exists*, and that this Matter is *in general a substance*, or *occasion of ideas*; though indeed to go about to unfold the meaning, or adhere to any particular explication of those words may be attended with great difficulties.—I answer, when words are used without a meaning, you may put them together as you please, without danger of running into a contradiction. You may say, for example, that *twice two* is equal to *seven;* so long as you declare you do not take the words of that proposition in their usual acceptation, but for marks of you know not what. And, by the same reason, you may say there is an inert thoughtless substance without accidents, which is the occasion of our ideas. And we shall understand just as much by one proposition as the other.

80. In the *last* place, you will say, What if we give up the cause of material Substance, and stand to it that Matter is an unknown *Somewhat*—neither substance nor accident, spirit nor idea—inert, thoughtless, indivisible, immovable, unextended, existing in no place? For, say you, whatever may be urged against *substance* or *occasion*, or any other positive or relative notion of Matter, hath no place at all, so long as this negative definition of Matter is adhered to.—I answer, You may, if so it shall seem good, use the word *Matter* in the same sense as other men use *nothing*, and so make those

terms convertible in your style. For, after all, this is what appears to me to be the result of that definition; the parts whereof, when I consider with attention, either collectively or separate from each other, I do not find that there is any kind of effect or impression made on my mind, different from what is excited by the term *nothing*.

81. You will reply, perhaps, that in the foresaid definition is included what doth sufficiently distinguish it from nothing— the positive abstract idea of *quiddity, entity,* or *existence.* I own, indeed, that those who pretend to the faculty of framing abstract general ideas do talk as if they had such an idea, which is, say they, the most abstract and general notion of all: that is to me the most incomprehensible of all others. That there are a great variety of spirits of different orders and capacities, whose faculties, both in number and extent, are far exceeding those the Author of my being has bestowed on me, I see no reason to deny. And for me to pretend to determine, by my own few, stinted, narrow inlets of perception, what ideas the inexhaustible power of the Supreme Spirit may imprint upon them, were certainly the utmost folly and presumption. Since there may be, for aught that I know, innumerable sorts of ideas or sensations, as different from one another, and from all that I have perceived, as colours are from sounds. But, how ready soever I may be to acknowledge the scantiness of my comprehension, with regard to the endless variety of spirits and ideas that may possibly exist, yet for any one to pretend to a *notion* of Entity or Existence, *abstracted* from *spirit* and *idea,* from perceived and being perceived, is, I suspect, a downright repugnancy and trifling with words.

It remains that we consider the objections which may possibly be made on the part of Religion.

82. Some there are who think that though the arguments for the real existence of bodies which are drawn from Reason be allowed not to amount to demonstration, yet the Holy Scriptures are so clear in the point, as will sufficiently convince every good Christian, that bodies do really exist, and are something more than mere ideas; there being in Holy Writ innumerable facts related which evidently suppose the reality of timber and stone, mountains and rivers, and cities, and human bodies—To which I answer that no sort of writings whatever, sacred or profane, which use those and

the like words in the vulgar acceptation, or so as to have a meaning in them, are in danger of having their truth called in question by our doctrine. That all those things do really exist; that there are bodies, even corporeal substances, when taken in the vulgar sense, has been shewn to be agreeable to our principles: and the difference betwixt *things* and *ideas*, *realities* and *chimeras*, has been distinctly explained. See sect. 29, 30, 33, 36, &c. And I do not think that either what philosophers call *Matter*, or the existence of objects without the mind, is anywhere mentioned in Scripture.

83. Again, whether there be or be not external things, it is agreed on all hands that the proper use of words is the marking *our* conceptions, or things only as they are known and perceived by us: whence it plainly follows, that in the tenets we have laid down there is nothing inconsistent with the right use and significancy of language, and that discourse, of what kind soever, so far as it is intelligible, remains undisturbed. But all this seems so very manifest, from what has been largely set forth in the premises, that it is needless to insist any farther on it.

84. But, it will be urged that miracles do, at least, lose much of their stress and import by our principles. What must we think of Moses' rod? was it not *really* turned into a serpent? or was there only a change of *ideas* in the minds of the spectators? And, can it be supposed that our Saviour did no more at the marriage-feast in Cana than impose on the sight, and smell, and taste of the guests, so as to create in them the appearance or idea only of wine? The same may be said of all other miracles: which, in consequence of the foregoing principles, must be looked upon only as so many cheats, or illusions of fancy.—To this I reply, that the rod was changed into a real serpent, and the water into real wine. That this does not in the least contradict what I have elsewhere said will be evident from sect. 34 and 35. But this business of *real* and *imaginary* has been already so plainly and fully explained, and so often referred to, and the difficulties about it are so easily answered from what has gone before, that it were an affront to the reader's understanding to resume the explication of it in this place. I shall only observe that if at table all who were present should see, and smell, and taste, and drink wine, and find the effects of it, with me there could be no doubt of its reality. So that at bottom the scruple concerning real miracles has no place at

all on ours, but only on the received principles, and consequently makes rather for than against what has been said.

85. Having done with the Objections, which I endeavoured to propose in the clearest light, and gave them all the force and weight I could, we proceed in the next place to take a view of our tenets in their Consequences. Some of these appear at first sight—as that several difficult and obscure questions, on which abundance of speculation has been thrown away, are entirely banished from philosophy. Whether corporeal substance can think? Whether Matter be infinitely divisible? And how it operates on spirit?—these and the like inquiries have given infinite amusement to philosophers in all ages. But, depending on the existence of Matter, they have no longer any place on our Principles. Many other advantages there are, as well with regard to religion as the sciences, which it is easy for any one to deduce from what has been premised. But this will appear more plainly in the sequel.

86. From the Principles we have laid down it follows human knowledge may naturally be reduced to two heads —that of *ideas* and that of *Spirits*. Of each of these I shall treat in order.

And First as to *ideas,* or *unthinking things.* Our knowledge of these has been very much obscured and confounded, and we have been led into very dangerous errors, by supposing a two-fold existence of sense—the one *intelligible* or in the mind, the other *real* and without the mind. Whereby unthinking things are thought to have a natural subsistence of their own, distinct from being perceived by spirits. This, which, if I mistake not, hath been shewn to be a most groundless and absurd notion, is the very root of Scepticism; for, so long as men thought that real things subsisted without the mind, and that their knowledge was only so far forth *real* as it was *conformable to real things,* it follows they could not be certain that they had any real knowledge at all. For how can it be known that the things which are perceived are conformable to those which are not perceived, or exist without the mind?

87. Colour, figure, motion, extension, and the like, considered only as so many *sensations* in the mind, are perfectly

known; there being nothing in them which is not perceived. But, if they are looked on as notes or images, referred to *things* or *archetypes existing without the mind*, then are we involved all in scepticism. We see only the appearances, and not the real qualities of things. What may be the extension, figure, or motion of anything really and absolutely, or in itself, it is impossible for us to know, but only the proportion or relation they bear to our senses. Things remaining the same, our ideas vary; and which of them, or even whether any of them at all, represent the true quality really existing in the thing, it is out of our reach to determine. So that, for aught we know, all we see, hear, and feel, may be only phantom and vain chimera, and not at all agree with the real things existing in *rerum natura*. All this scepticism follows from our supposing a difference between *things* and *ideas,* and that the former have a subsistence without the mind, or unperceived. It were easy to dilate on this subject, and shew how the arguments urged by sceptics in all ages depend on the supposition of external objects.

88. So long as we attribute a real existence to unthinking things, distinct from their being perceived, it is not only impossible for us to know with evidence the nature of any real unthinking being, but even that it exists. Hence it is that we see philosophers distrust their senses, and doubt of the existence of heaven and earth, of everything they see or feel, even of their own bodies. And after all their labour and struggle of thought, they are forced to own we cannot attain to any self-evident or demonstrative knowledge of the existence of sensible things. But, all this doubtfulness, which so bewilders and confounds the mind and makes philosophy ridiculous in the eyes of the world, vanishes if we annex a meaning to our words, and do not amuse ourselves with the terms *absolute, external, exist,* and such like, signifying we know not what. I can as well doubt of my own being as of the being of those things which I actually perceive by sense: it being a manifest contradiction that any sensible object should be immediately perceived by sight or touch, and at the same time have no existence in nature; since the very existence of an *unthinking being* consists in *being perceived.*

89. Nothing seems of more importance towards erecting a firm system of sound and real knowledge, which may be proof against the assault of Scepticism, than to lay the beginning in a distinct explication of *what is meant* by *thing,*

reality, existence; for in vain shall we dispute concerning the real existence of things, or pretend to any knowledge thereof, so long as we have not fixed the meaning of those words. *Thing* or *being* is the most general name of all: it comprehends under it two kinds, entirely distinct and heterogeneous, and which have nothing common but the name, viz. *spirits* and *ideas.* The former are active, indivisible, substances: the latter are inert, fleeting, dependent beings; which subsist not by themselves, but are supported by, or exist in, minds or spiritual substances.

[We comprehend our own existence by inward feeling or reflection, and that of other spirits by reason. We may be said to have some knowledge or *notion* of our own minds, of spirits and active beings; whereof in a strict sense we have not *ideas.* In like manner, we know and have a *notion* of relations between things or ideas; which relations are distinct from the ideas or things related, inasmuch as the latter may be perceived by us without our perceiving the former. To me it seems that *ideas, spirits,* and *relations* are all in their respective kinds the object of human knowledge and subject of discourse; and that the term *idea* would be improperly extended to signify *everything* we know or have any notion of.] [4]

90. Ideas imprinted on the senses are *real* things, or do really exist: this we do not deny; but we deny they *can* subsist without the minds which perceive them, or that they are resemblances of any archetypes existing without the mind; since the very being of a sensation or idea consists in being perceived, and an idea can be like nothing but an idea. Again, the things perceived by sense may be termed *external,* with regard to their origin; in that they are not generated from within by the mind itself, but imprinted by a Spirit distinct from that which perceives them. Sensible objects may likewise be said to be "without the mind" in another sense, namely when they exist in some other mind. Thus, when I shut my eyes, the things I saw may still exist; but it must be in another mind.

91. It were a mistake to think that what is here said derogates in the least from the reality of things. It is acknowledged, on the received principles, that extension, motion, and in a word all sensible qualities, have need of a support, as

[4] [Added in second edition.—Ed.]

not being able to subsist by themselves. But the objects perceived by sense are allowed to be nothing but combinations of those qualities, and consequently cannot subsist by themselves. Thus far it is agreed on all hands. So that in denying the things perceived by sense an existence independent of a substance or support wherein they may exist, we detract nothing from the received opinion of their *reality*, and are guilty of no innovation in that respect. All the difference is that, according to us, the unthinking beings perceived by sense have no existence distinct from being perceived, and cannot therefore exist in any other substance than those unextended indivisible substances, or *spirits*, which act, and think and perceive them. Whereas philosophers vulgarly hold that the sensible qualities exist in an inert, extended, unperceiving Substance, which they call *Matter*, to which they attribute a natural subsistence, exterior to all thinking beings, or distinct from being perceived by any mind whatsoever, even the Eternal Mind of the Creator; wherein they suppose only Ideas of the corporeal substances created by Him: if indeed they allow them to be at all *created*.

92. For, as we have shewn the doctrine of Matter or Corporeal Substance to have been the main pillar and support of Scepticism, so likewise upon the same foundation have been raised all the impious schemes of Atheism and Irreligion. Nay, so great a difficulty has it been thought to conceive Matter produced out of nothing, that the most celebrated among the ancient philosophers, even of those who maintained the being of a God, have thought Matter to be uncreated and co-eternal with Him. How great a friend *material substance* has been to Atheists in all ages were needless to relate. All their monstrous systems have so visible and necessary a dependence on it, that when this cornerstone is once removed, the whole fabric cannot choose but fall to the ground; insomuch that it is no longer worth while to bestow a particular consideration on the absurdities of every wretched sect of Atheists.

93. That impious and profane persons should readily fall in with those systems which favour their inclinations, by deriding *immaterial substance*, and supposing the soul to be divisible, and subject to corruption as the body; which exclude all freedom, intelligence, and design from the formation of things, and instead thereof make a self-existent, stupid, unthinking substance the root and origin of all beings; that they

should hearken to those who deny a Providence, or inspection of a Superior Mind, over the affairs of the world, attributing the whole series of events either to blind chance or fatal necessity, arising from the impulse of one body on another—all this is very natural. And, on the other hand, when men of better principles observe the enemies of religion lay so great a stress on *unthinking Matter*, and all of them use so much industry and artifice to reduce everything to it; methinks they should rejoice to see them deprived of their grand support, and driven from that only fortress, without which your Epicureans, Hobbists, and the like, have not even the shadow of a pretence, but become the most cheap and easy triumph in the world.

94. The existence of Matter, or bodies unperceived, has not only been the main support of Atheists and Fatalists, but on the same principle doth Idolatry likewise in all its various forms depend. Did men but consider that the sun, moon, and stars, and every other object of the senses, are only so many sensations in their minds, which have no other existence but barely being perceived, doubtless they would never fall down and worship *their own ideas;* but rather address their homage to that Eternal Invisible Mind which produces and sustains all things.

95. The same absurd principle, by mingling itself with the articles of our faith, hath occasioned no small difficulties to Christians. For example, about the Resurrection, how many scruples and objections have been raised by Socinians and others? But do not the most plausible of them depend on the supposition that a body is denominated the *same*, with regard not to the form, or that which is perceived by sense, but the material substance, which remains the same under several forms? Take away this *material substance*—about the identity whereof all the dispute is—and mean by *body* what every plain ordinary person means by that word, to wit, that which is immediately seen and felt, which is only a combination of sensible qualities or ideas: and then their most unanswerable objections come to nothing.

96. Matter being once expelled out of nature drags with it so many sceptical and impious notions, such an incredible number of disputes and puzzling questions, which have been thorns in the sides of divines as well as philosophers, and made so much fruitless work for mankind, that if the arguments we have produced against it are not found equal to demon-

stration (as to me they evidently seem), yet I am sure all friends to knowledge, peace, and religion have reason to wish they were.

97. Beside the external existence of the objects of perception, another great source of errors and difficulties with regard to ideal knowledge is the doctrine of *abstract ideas*, such as it hath been set forth in the Introduction. The plainest things in the world, those we are most intimately acquainted with and perfectly know, when they are considered in an abstract way, appear strangely difficult and incomprehensible. Time, place, and motion, taken in particular or concrete, are what everybody knows; but, having passed through the hands of a metaphysician, they become too abstract and fine to be apprehended by men of ordinary sense. Bid your servant meet you at such a *time*, in such a *place*, and he shall never stay to deliberate on the meaning of those words. In conceiving that particular time and place, or the motion by which he is to get thither, he finds not the least difficulty. But if *time* be taken exclusive of all those particular actions and ideas that diversify the day, merely for the continuation of existence or duration in abstract, then it will perhaps gravel even a philosopher to comprehend it.

98. For my own part, whenever I attempt to frame a simple idea of *time*, abstracted from the succession of ideas in my mind, which flows uniformly, and is participated by all beings, I am lost and embrangled in inextricable difficulties. I have no notion of it at all: only I hear others say it is infinitely divisible, and speak of it in such a manner as leads me to harbour odd thoughts of my existence: since that doctrine lays one under an absolute necessity of thinking, either that he passes away innumerable ages without a thought, or else that he is annihilated every moment of his life: both which seem equally absurd. Time therefore being nothing, abstracted from the succession of ideas in our minds, it follows that the duration of any finite spirit must be estimated by the number of ideas or actions succeeding each other in that same spirit of mind. Hence, it is a plain consequence that the soul always thinks. And in truth whoever shall go about to divide in his thoughts or abstract the *existence* of a spirit from its *cogitation*, will, I believe, find it no easy task.

99. So likewise when we attempt to abstract *extension* and *motion* from all other qualities, and consider them by them-

selves, we presently lose sight of them, and run into great extravagances. [Hence spring those odd paradoxes, that the fire is not hot, nor the wall white; or that heat and colour are in the objects nothing but figure and motion.] [5] All which depend on a twofold abstraction: first, it is supposed that extension, for example, may be abstracted from all other sensible qualties; and, secondly, that the entity of extension may be abstracted from its being perceived. But, whoever shall reflect, and take care to understand what he says, will, if I mistake not, acknowledge that all sensible qualities are alike *sensations,* and alike *real;* that where the extension is, there is the colour too, to wit, in his mind, and that their archetypes can exist only in some other *mind:* and that the objects of sense are nothing but those sensations, combined, blended, or (if one may so speak) concreted together; none of all which can be supposed to exist unperceived. [And that consequently the wall is as truly white as it is extended, and in the same sense.] [6]

100. What it is for a man to be happy, or an object good, every one may think he knows. But to frame an abstract idea of happiness, prescinded from all particular pleasure, or of goodness from everything that is good, this is what few can pretend to. So likewise a man may be just and virtuous without having precise ideas of justice and virtue. The opinion that those and the like words stand for general notions, abstracted from all particular persons and actions, seems to have rendered morality difficult, and the study thereof of less use to mankind. And in effect the doctrine of *abstraction* has not a little contributed towards spoiling the most useful parts of knowledge.

101. The two great provinces of speculative science conversant about ideas received from sense and their relations, are Natural Philosophy and Mathematics. With regard to each of these I shall make some observations.

And first I shall say somewhat of Natural Philosophy. On this subject it is that the sceptics triumph. All that stock of arguments they produce to depreciate our faculties and make mankind appear ignorant and low, are drawn principally from

[5] [Omitted in the second edition.—Ed.]
[6] [Omitted in the second edition.—Ed.]

The Principles of Human Knowledge / 103

this head, namely, that we are under an invincible blindness as to the *true* and *real* nature of things. This they exaggerate, and love to enlarge on. We are miserably bantered, say they, by our senses, and amused only with the outside and shew of things. The real essence, the internal qualities and constitution of even the meanest object, is hid from our view: something there is in every drop of water, every grain of sand, which it is beyond the power of human understanding to fathom or comprehend. But, it is evident from what has been shewn that all this complaint is groundless, and that we are influenced by false principles to that degree as to mistrust our senses, and think we know nothing of those things which we perfectly comprehend.

102. One great inducement to our pronouncing ourselves ignorant of the nature of things is, the current opinion that every thing includes *within itself* the cause of its properties: or that there is in each object an inward essence, which is the source whence its discernible qualities flow, and whereon they depend. Some have pretended to account for appearances by occult qualities; but of late they are mostly resolved into mechanical causes, to wit, the figure, motion, weight, and suchlike qualities, of insensible particles: whereas, in truth, there is no other agent or efficient cause than *spirit* it being evident that motion, as well as all other *ideas*, is perfectly inert. See sect. 25. Hence, to endeavour to explain the production of colours or sounds, by figure, motion, magnitude, and the like, must needs be labour in vain. And accordingly we see the attempts of that kind are not at all satisfactory. Which may be said in general of those instances wherein one idea or quality is assigned for the cause of another. I need not say how many hypotheses and speculations are left out, and how much the study of nature is abridged by this doctrine.

103. The great mechanical principle now in vogue is *attraction*. That a stone falls to the earth, or the sea swells towards the moon, may to some appear sufficiently explained thereby. But how are we enlightened by being told this is done by attraction? Is it that that word signifies the manner of the tendency, and that it is by the mutual drawing of bodies instead of their being impelled or protruded towards each other? But nothing is determined of the manner or action, and it may as truly (for aught we know) be termed *impulse,* or *protrusion,* as *attraction*. Again, the parts of steel we see

cohere firmly together, and this also is accounted for by attraction; but, in this, as in the other instances, I do not perceive that anything is signified besides the effect itself; for as to the manner of the action whereby it is produced, or the cause which produces it, these are not so much as aimed at.

104. Indeed, if we take a view of the several phenomena, and compare them together, we may observe some likeness and conformity between them. For example, in the falling of a stone to the ground, in the rising of the sea towards the moon, in cohesion and crystallization, there is something alike; namely, an union or mutual approach of bodies. So that any one of these or the like phenomena may not seem strange or surprising to a man who has nicely observed and compared the effects of nature. For that only is thought so which is uncommon, or a thing by itself, and out of the ordinary course of our observation. That bodies should tend towards the centre of the earth is not thought strange, because it is what we perceive every moment of our lives. But that they should have a like gravitation towards the centre of the moon may seem odd and unaccountable to most men, because it is discerned only in the tides. But a philosopher, whose thoughts take in a larger compass of nature, having observed a certain similitude of appearances, as well in the heavens as the earth, that argue innumerable bodies to have a mutual tendency towards each other, which he denotes by the general name *attraction*, whatever can be reduced to that, he thinks justly accounted for. Thus he explains the tides by the attraction of the terraqueous globe towards the moon; which to him doth not appear odd or anomalous, but only a particular example of a general rule or law of nature.

105. If therefore we consider the difference there is betwixt natural philosophers and other men, with regard to their knowledge of the phenomena, we shall find it consists, not in an exacter knowledge of the efficient cause that produces them—for that can be no other than the *will of a spirit*—but only in a greater largeness of comprehension, whereby analogies, harmonies, and agreements are discovered in the works of nature, and the particular effects explained, that is, reduced to general rules, see sect. 62: which rules, grounded on the analogy and uniformness observed in the production of natural effects, are most agreeable and sought after by the mind; for that they extend our prospect beyond what is present and near to us, and enable us to make very

probable conjectures touching things that may have happened at very great distances of time and place, as well as to predict things to come: which sort of endeavour towards Omniscience is much affected by the mind.

106. But we should proceed warily in such things: for we are apt to lay too great a stress on analogies, and, to the prejudice of truth, humour that eagerness of the mind, whereby it is carried to extend its knowledge into general theorems. For example, gravitation or mutual attraction, because it appears in many instances, some are straightway for pronouncing *universal;* and that to attract and be attracted by every other body is an essential quality inherent in all bodies whatsoever. Whereas it appears the fixed stars have no such tendency towards each other; and, so far is that gravitation from being *essential* to bodies that in some instances a quite contrary principle seems to shew itself; as in the perpendicular growth of plants, and the elasticity of the air. There is nothing necessary or essential in the case; but it depends entirely on the will of the Governing Spirit, who causes certain bodies to cleave together or tend towards each other according to various laws, whilst He keeps others at a fixed distance; and to some He gives a quite contrary tendency to fly asunder, just as He sees convenient.

107. After what has been premised, I think we may lay down the following conclusions. First, it is plain philosophers amuse themselves in vain, when they enquire for any natural efficient cause, distinct from a *mind* or *spirit.* Secondly, considering the whole creation is the workmanship of a *wise and good Agent,* it should seem to become philosophers to employ their thoughts (contrary to what some hold) about the final causes of things. And I must confess I see no reason why pointing out the various ends to which natural things are adapted, and for which they were originally with unspeakable wisdom contrived, should not be thought one good way of accounting for them, and altogether worthy a philosopher. Thirdly, from what has been premised, no reason can be drawn why the history of nature should not still be studied, and observations and experiments made; which, that they are of use to mankind, and enable us to draw any general conclusions, is not the result of any immutable habitudes or relations between things themselves, but only of God's goodness and kindness to men in the administration of the world. See sects. 30 and 31. Fourthly, by a diligent observation of

the phenomena within our view, we may discover the general laws of nature, and from them deduce other phenomena. I do not say *demonstrate;* for all deductions of that kind depend on a supposition that the Author of Nature always operates uniformly, and in a constant observance of those rules *we* take for principles, which we cannot evidently know.

108. [It appears from sect. 66, &c. that the steady consistent methods of nature may not unfitly be styled the Language of its Author, whereby He discovers His attributes to our view and directs us how to act for the convenience and felicity of life.] [7] Those men who frame general rules from the phenomena, and afterwards derive the phenomena from those rules, seem to consider signs rather than causes. A man may well understand natural signs without knowing their analogy, or being able to say by what rule a thing is so or so. And, as it is very possible to write improperly, through too strict an observance of general grammar-rules; so, in arguing from general rules of nature, it is not impossible we may extend the analogy too far, and by that means run into mistakes.

109. As in reading other books a wise man will choose to fix his thoughts on the sense and apply it to use, rather than lay them out in grammatical remarks on the language; so, in perusing the volume of nature, methinks it is beneath the dignity of the mind to affect an exactness in reducing each particular phenomenon to general rules, or shewing how it follows from them. We should propose to ourselves nobler views, such as to recreate and exalt the mind with a prospect of the beauty, order, extent, and variety of natural things: hence, by proper inferences, to enlarge our notions of the grandeur, wisdom, and beneficence of the Creator: and lastly, to make the several parts of the creation, so far as in us lies, subservient to the ends they were designed for—God's glory, and the sustentation and comfort of ourselves and fellow-creatures.

110. The best key for the aforesaid analogy, or natural Science, will be easily acknowledged to be a certain celebrated Treatise of *Mechanics.* [8] In the entrance of which justly admired treatise, Time, Space, and Motion are distinguished into *absolute* and *relative, true* and *apparent, mathematical*

---

[7] [Omitted in the second edition.—Ed.]
[8] [Newton's *Principia.*—Ed.]

and *vulgar:* which distinction, as it is at large explained by the author, does suppose those quantities to have an existence without the mind: and that they are ordinarily conceived with relation to sensible things, to which nevertheless in their own nature they bear no relation at all.

111. As for *Time,* as it is there taken in an absolute, or abstracted sense, for the duration or perseverance of the existence of things, I have nothing more to add concerning it after what has been already said on that subject. Sects. 97 and 98. For the rest, this celebrated author holds there is an *absolute Space,* which, being unperceivable to sense, remains in itself similar and immovable; and relative space to be the measure thereof, which, being moveable and defined by its situation in respect of sensible bodies, is vulgarly taken for immoveable space. *Place* he defines to be that part of space which is occupied by any body: and according as the space is absolute or relative so also is the place. *Absolute Motion* is said to be the translation of a body from absolute place to absolute place, as relative motion is from one relative place to another. And because the parts of absolute space do not fall under our senses, instead of them we are obliged to use their sensible measures; and so define both place and motion with respect to bodies which we regard as immoveable. But it is said, in philosophical matters we must abstract from our senses; since it may be that none of those bodies which seem to be quiescent are truly so; and the same thing which is moved relatively may be really at rest. As likewise one and the same body may be in relative rest and motion, or even moved with contrary relative motions at the same time, according as its place is variously defined. All which ambiguity is to be found in the apparent motions; but not at all in the true or absolute, which should therefore be alone regarded in philosophy. And the true we are told are distinguished from apparent or relative motions by the following properties. First, in true or absolute motion, all parts which preserve the same position with respect of the whole, partake of the motions of the whole. Secondly, the place being moved, that which is placed therein is also moved: so that a body moving in a place which is in motion doth participate the motion of its place. Thirdly, true motion is never generated or changed otherwise than by force impressed on the body itself. Fourthly, true motion is always changed by force impressed on the body moved. Fifthly, in circular motion, barely

relative, there is no centrifugal force, which nevertheless, in that which is true or absolute, is proportional to the quantity of motion.

112. But, notwithstanding what hath been said, I must confess it does not appear to me that there can be any motion other than *relative:* so that to conceive motion there must be conceived at least two bodies; whereof the distance or position in regard to each other is varied. Hence, if there was one only body in being it could not possibly be moved. This seems evident, in that the idea I have of motion doth necessarily include relation.

113. But, though in every motion it be necessary to conceive more bodies than one, yet it may be that one only is moved, namely, that on which the force causing the change in the distance or situation of the bodies is impressed, or in other words, that to which the action is applied. For, however some may define relative motion, so as to term that body *moved* which changes its distance from some other body whether the force or action causing that change were impressed on it or no, yet, as relative motion is that which is perceived by sense, and regarded in the ordinary affairs of life, it follows that every man of common sense knows what it is as well as the best philosopher. Now, I ask any one whether, in his sense of motion as he walks along the streets, the stones he passes over may be said to *move,* because they change distance with his feet? To me it appears that though motion includes a relation of one thing to another, yet it is not necessary that each term of the relation be denominated from it. As a man may think of somewhat which does not think, so a body may be moved to or from another body which is not therefore itself in motion.

114. As the place happens to be variously defined, the motion which is related to it varies. A man in a ship may be said to be quiescent with relation to the sides of the vessel, and yet move with relation to the land. Or he may move eastward in respect of the one, and westward in respect of the other. In the common affairs of life, men never go beyond the Earth to define the place of any body; and what is quiescent in respect of *that* is accounted *absolutely* to be so. But philosophers, who have a greater extent of thought, and juster notions of the system of things, discover even the Earth itself to be moved. In order therefore to fix their notions, they seem to conceive the Corporeal World as finite, and the

utmost unmoved walls or shell thereof to be the place whereby they estimate true motions. If we sound our own conceptions, I believe we may find all the absolute motion we can frame an idea of to be at bottom no other than relative motion thus defined. For, as has been already observed, absolute motion, exclusive of *all* external relation, is incomprehensible: and to this kind of relative motion all the above-mentioned properties, causes, and effects ascribed to absolute motion will, if I mistake not, be found to agree. As to what is said of the centrifugal force, that it does not at all belong to circular relative motion, I do not see how this follows from the experiment which is brought to prove it. See Newton's *Philosophiae Naturalis Principia Mathematica, in Schol. Def. VIII.* For the water in the vessel, at that time wherein it is said to have the greatest relative circular motion, hath, I think, no motion at all: as is plain from the foregoing section.

115. For, to denominate a body *moved*, it is requisite, first, that it change its distance or situation with regard to some other body: and secondly, that the force or action occasioning that change be applied to it. If either of these be wanting, I do not think that, agreeably to the sense of mankind, or the propriety of language, a body can be said to be in motion. I grant indeed that it is possible for us to think a body, which we see change its distance from some other, to be moved, though it have no force applied to it (in which sense there may be apparent motion); but then it is because the force causing the change of distance is imagined by us to be applied or impressed on that body thought to move. Which indeed shews we are capable of mistaking a thing to be in motion which is not, and that is all.

116. From what has been said, it follows that the philosophic consideration of motion doth not imply the being of an *absolute Space*, distinct from that which is perceived by sense, and related to bodies: which that it cannot exist without the mind is clear upon the same principles that demonstrate the like of all other objects of sense. And perhaps, if we inquire narrowly, we shall find we cannot even frame an idea of *pure Space exclusive of all body*. This I must confess seems impossible, as being a most abstract idea. When I excite a motion in some part of my body, if it be free or without resistance, I say there is *Space*. But if I find a resistance, then I say there is *Body*: and in proportion as the resistance to motion is lesser or greater, I say the space is

more or less *pure*. So that when I speak of pure or empty space, it is not to be supposed that the word *space* stands for an idea distinct from, or conceivable without, body and motion. Though indeed we are apt to think every noun substantive stands for a distinct idea that may be separated from all others; which hath occasioned infinite mistakes. When, therefore, supposing all the world to be annihilated besides my own body, I say there still remains *pure Space;* thereby nothing else is meant but only that I conceive it possible for the limbs of my body to be moved on all sides without the least resistance: but if that too were annihilated then there could be no motion, and consequently no Space. Some, perhaps, may think the sense of seeing doth furnish them with the idea of pure space; but it is plain from what we have elsewhere shewn, that the ideas of space and distance are not obtained by that sense. See the *Essay concerning Vision*.

117. What is here laid down seems to put an end to all those disputes and difficulties that have sprung up amongst the learned concerning the nature of *pure Space*. But the chief advantage arising from it is that we are freed from that dangerous dilemma, to which several who have employed their thoughts on this subject imagine themselves reduced, viz. of thinking either that Real Space is God, or else that there is something beside God which is eternal, uncreated, infinite, indivisible, immutable. Both which may justly be thought pernicious and absurd notions. It is certain that not a few divines, as well as philosophers of great note, have, from the difficulty they found in conceiving either limits or annihilation of space, concluded it must be *divine*. And some of late have set themselves particularly to shew that the incommunicable attributes of God agree to it. Which doctrine, how unworthy soever it may seem of the Divine Nature, yet I must confess I do not see how we can get clear of it, so long as we adhere to the received opinions.

118. Hitherto of Natural Philosophy. We come now to make some inquiry concerning that other great branch of speculative knowledge, to wit, Mathematics. These, how celebrated soever they may be for their clearness and certainty of demonstration, which is hardly anywhere else to be found, cannot nevertheless be supposed altogether free from mistakes, if in their principles there lurks some secret error which is common to the professors of those sciences with the

rest of mankind. Mathematicians, though they deduce their theorems from a great height of evidence, yet their first principles are limited by the consideration of Quantity. And they do not ascend into any inquiry concerning those transcendental maxims which influence all the particular sciences; each part whereof, Mathematics not excepted, doth consequently participate of the errors involved in them. That the principles laid down by mathematicians are true, and their way of deduction from those principles clear and incontestible, we do not deny. But we hold there may be certain erroneous maxims of greater extent than the object of Mathematics, and for that reason not expressly mentioned, though tacitly supposed, throughout the whole progress of that science; and that the ill effects of those secret unexamined errors are diffused through all the branches thereof. To be plain, we suspect the mathematicians are no less deeply concerned than other men in the errors arising from the doctrine of abstract general ideas, and the existence of objects without the mind.

119. Arithmetic hath been thought to have for its object abstract ideas of *number*. Of which to understand the properties and mutual habitudes, is supposed no mean part of speculative knowledge. The opinion of the pure and intellectual nature of numbers in abstract has made them in esteem with those philosophers who seem to have affected an uncommon fineness and elevation of thought. It hath set a price on the most trifling numerical speculations, which in practice are of no use, but serve only for amusement; and hath heretofore so far infected the minds of some, that they have dreamed of mighty *mysteries* involved in numbers, and attempted the explication of natural things by them. But, if we narrowly inquire into our own thoughts, and consider what has been premised, we may perhaps entertain a low opinion of those high flights and abstractions, and look on all inquiries about numbers only as so many *difficiles nugae*, so far as they are not subservient to practice, and promote the benefit of life.

120. Unity in abstract we have before considered in sect. 13; from which, and what has been said in the Introduction, it plainly follows there is not any such idea. But, number being defined a *collection of units*, we may conclude that, if there be no such thing as unity, or unit in abstract, there are no *ideas* of number in abstract, denoted by the numeral names and figures. The theories therefore in Arithmetic, if

they are abstracted from the names and figures, as likewise from all use and practice, as well as from the particular things numbered, can be supposed to have nothing at all for their object. Hence we may see how entirely the science of numbers is subordinate to practice, and how jejune and trifling it becomes when considered as a matter of mere speculation.

121. However, since there may be some who, deluded by the specious show of discovering abstracted verities, waste their time in arithmetical theorems and problems which have not any use, it will not be amiss if we more fully consider and expose the vanity of that pretence. And this will plainly appear by taking a view of Arithmetic in its infancy, and observing what it was that originally put men on the study of that science, and to what scope they directed it. It is natural to think that at first, men, for ease of memory and help of computation, made use of counters, or in writing of single strokes, points, or the like, each whereof was made to signify an unit, *i.e.* some one thing of whatever kind they had occasion to reckon. Afterwards they found out the more compendious ways of making one character stand in place of several strokes or points. And, lastly, the notation of the Arabians or Indians came into use; wherein, by the repetition of a few characters or figures, and varying the signification of each figure according to the place it obtains, all numbers may be most aptly expressed. Which seems to have been done in imitation of language, so that an exact analogy is observed betwixt the notation by figures and names, the nine simple figures answering the nine first numeral names and places in the former, corresponding to denominations in the latter. And agreeably to those conditions of the simple and local value of figures, were contrived methods of finding, from the given figures or marks of the parts, what figures and how placed are proper to denote the whole, or *vice versa*. And having found the sought figures, the same rule or analogy being observed throughout, it is easy to read them into words; and so the number becomes perfectly known. For then the number of any particular things is said to be known, when we know the name or figures (with their due arrangement) that according to the standing analogy belong to them. For, these signs being known, we can by the operations of arithmetic know the signs of any part of the particular sums signified by them; and thus computing in signs, (because of

the connexion established betwixt them and the distinct multitudes of things, whereof one is taken for an unit), we may be able rightly to sum up, divide, and proportion the things themselves that we intend to number.

122. In Arithmetic, therefore, we regard not the *things* but the *signs;* which nevertheless are not regarded for their own sake, but because they direct us how to act with relation to things, and dispose rightly of them. Now, agreeably to what we have before observed of Words in general (sect. 19, Introd.), it happens here likewise, that abstract ideas are thought to be signified by numeral names or characters, while they do not suggest ideas of particular things to our minds. I shall not at present enter into a more particular dissertation on this subject; but only observe that it is evident from what has been said, those things which pass for abstract truths and theorems concerning numbers, are in reality conversant about no object distinct from particular numerable things; except only names and characters, which originally came to be considered on no other account but their being *signs,* or capable to represent aptly whatever particular things men had need to compute. Whence it follows that to study them for their own sake would be just as wise, and to as good purpose, as if a man, neglecting the true use or original intention and subserviency of language, should spend his time in impertinent criticisms upon words, or reasonings and controversies purely verbal.

123. From numbers we proceed to speak of *extension,* which, considered as relative, is the object of Geometry. The *infinite* divisibility of *finite* extension, though it is not expressly laid down either as an axiom or theorem in the elements of that science, yet is throughout the same everywhere supposed, and thought to have so inseparable and essential a connexion with the principles and demonstrations in Geometry that mathematicians never admit it into doubt, or make the least question of it. And as this notion is the source from whence do spring all those amusing geometrical paradoxes which have such a direct repugnancy to the plain common sense of mankind, and are admitted with so much reluctance into a mind not yet debauched by learning; so is it the principal occasion of all that nice and extreme subtilty, which renders the study of Mathematics so very difficult and tedious. Hence, if we can make it appear that no *finite* extension contains innumerable parts, or is infinitely divisible, it follows

that we shall at once clear the science of Geometry from a great number of difficulties and contradictions which have ever been esteemed a reproach to human reason, and withal make the attainment thereof a business of much less time and pains than it hitherto hath been.

124. Every particular finite extension which may possibly be the object of our thought is an *idea* existing only in the mind; and consequently each part thereof must be perceived. If, therefore, I cannot *perceive* innumerable parts in any finite extension that I consider, it is certain they are not contained in it. But it is evident that I cannot distinguish innumerable parts in any particular line, surface, or solid, which I either perceive by sense, or figure to myself in my mind. Wherefore I conclude they are not contained in it. Nothing can be plainer to me than that the extensions I have in view are no other than my own ideas; and it is no less plain that I cannot resolve any one of my ideas into an infinite number of other ideas; that is, that they are not infinitely divisible. If by *finite extension* be meant something distinct from a finite idea, I declare I do not know what that is, and so cannot affirm or deny anything of it. But if the terms *extension, parts,* and the like, are taken in any sense conceivable—that is, for *ideas,*—then to say a finite quantity or extension consists of parts infinite in number is so manifest and glaring a contradiction, that every one at first sight acknowledges it to be so. And it is impossible it should ever gain the assent of any reasonable creature who is not brought to it by gentle and slow degrees, as a converted Gentile to the belief of transubstantiation. Ancient and rooted prejudices do often pass into principles. And those propositions which once obtain the force and credit of a *principle,* are not only themselves, but likewise whatever is deducible from them, thought privileged from all examination. And there is no absurdity so gross, which, by this means, the mind of man may not be prepared to swallow.

125. He whose understanding is prepossessed with the doctrine of abstract general ideas may be persuaded that (whatever be thought of the ideas of sense) *extension in abstract* is infinitely divisible. And one who thinks the objects of sense exist without the mind will perhaps, in virtue thereof, be brought to admit that a line but an inch long may contain innumerable parts really existing, though too small to be discerned. These errors are grafted as well in the minds of

geometricians as of other men, and have a like influence on their reasonings; and it were no difficult thing to shew how the arguments from Geometry made use of to support the infinite divisibility of extension are bottomed on them. At present we shall only observe in general whence it is the mathematicians are all so fond and tenacious of that doctrine.

126. It has been observed in another place that the theorems and demonstrations in Geometry are conversant about universal ideas (sect. 15, Introd.): where it is explained in what sense this ought to be understood, to wit, the particular lines and figures included in the diagram are supposed to stand for innumerable others of different sizes; or, in other words, the geometer considers them abstracting from their magnitude: which doth not imply that he forms an abstract idea, but only that he cares not what the particular magnitude is, whether great or small, but looks on that as a thing indifferent to the demonstration. Hence it follows that a line in the scheme but an inch long must be spoken of as though it contained ten thousand parts, since it is regarded not in itself, but as it is universal; and it is universal only in its signification, whereby it *represents* innumerable lines greater than itself, in which may be distinguished ten thousand parts or more, though there may not be above an inch in *it*. After this manner, the properties of the lines signified are (by a very usual figure) transferred to the sign; and thence, through mistake, thought to appertain to it considered in its own nature.

127. Because there is no number of parts so great but it is possible there may be a line containing more, the inch-line is said to contain parts more than any assignable number; which is true, not of the inch taken absolutely, but only for the things signified by it. But men, not retaining that distinction in their thoughts, slide into a belief that the small particular line described on paper contains in itself parts innumerable. There is no such thing as the ten thousandth part of an inch; but there is of a mile or diameter of the earth, which may be signified by that inch. When therefore I delineate a triangle on paper, and take one side, not above an inch for example in length, to be the radius, this I consider as divided into 10,000 or 100,000 parts, or more. For, though the ten thousandth part of that line considered in itself, is nothing at all, and consequently may be neglected without any error or inconveniency, yet these described lines, being

only marks standing for greater quantities, whereof it may be the ten thousandth part is very considerable, it follows that, to prevent notable errors in practice, the radius must be taken of 10,000 parts, or more.

128. From what has been said the reason is plain why, to the end any theorem may become universal in its use, it is necessary we speak of the lines described on paper as though they contained parts which really they do not. In doing of which, if we examine the matter thoroughly, we shall perhaps discover that we cannot conceive an inch itself as consisting of, or being divisible into, a thousand parts, but only some other line which is far greater than an inch, and represented by it; and that when we say a line is *infinitely divisible*, we must mean *a line which is infinitely great*. What we have here observed seems to be the chief cause, why to suppose the *infinite* divisibility of *finite extension* has been thought necessary in Geometry.

129. The several absurdities and contradictions which flowed from this false principle might, one would think, have been esteemed so many demonstrations against it. But, by I know not what logic, it is held that proofs *a posteriori* are not to be admitted against propositions relating to Infinity. As though it were not impossible even for an Infinite Mind to reconcile contradictions; or as if anything absurd and repugnant could have a necessary connexion with truth, or flow from it. But whoever considers the weakness of this pretence, will think it was contrived on purpose to humor the laziness of the mind, which had rather acquiesce in an indolent scepticism than be at the pains to go through with a severe examination of those principles it has ever embraced for true.

130. Of late the speculations about Infinites have run so high, and grown to such strange notions, as have occasioned no small scruples and disputes among the geometers of the present age. Some there are of great note who, not content with holding that finite lines may be divided into an infinite number of parts, do yet farther maintain, that each of those Infinitesimals is itself subdivisible into an infinity of other parts, or Infinitesimals of a second order, and so on *ad infinitum*. These, I say, assert there are Infinitesimals of Infinitesimals of Infinitesimals, without ever coming to an end. So that according to them an inch does not barely contain an infinite number of parts, but an infinity of an infinity *ad*

infinitum of parts. Others there be who hold all orders of Infinitesimals below the first to be nothing at all; thinking it with good reason absurd to imagine there is any positive quantity or part of extension which, though multiplied infinitely, can ever equal the smallest given extension. And yet on the other hand it seems no less absurd to think the square, cube, or other power of a positive real root, should itself be nothing at all; which they who hold Infinitesimals of the first order, denying all of the subsequent orders, are obliged to maintain.

131. Have we not therefore reason to conclude they are *both* in the wrong, and that there is in effect no such thing as parts infinitely small, or an infinite number of parts contained in any finite quantity? But you will say that if this doctrine obtains it will follow the very foundations of Geometry are destroyed, and those great men who have raised that science to so astonishing a height, have been all the while building a castle in the air. To this it may be replied, that whatever is useful in Geometry, and promotes the benefit of human life, does still remain firm and unshaken on our Principles; that science considered as practical will rather receive advantage than any prejudice from what has been said. But to set this in a due light, may be the subject of a distinct inquiry. For the rest, though it should follow that some of the more intricate and subtle parts of Speculative Mathematics may be pared off without any prejudice to truth, yet I do not see what damage will be thence derived to mankind. On the contrary, I think it were highly to be wished that men of great abilities and obstinate application would draw off their thoughts from those amusements, and employ them in the study of such things as lie nearer the concerns of life, or have a more direct influence on the manners.

132. If it be said that several theorems, undoubtedly true, are discovered by methods in which Infinitesimals are made use of, which could never have been if their existence included a contradiction in it:—I answer that upon a thorough examination it will not be found that in any instance it is necessary to make use of or conceive *infinitesimal* parts of *finite* lines, or even quantities less than the *minimum sensible*: nay, it will be evident this is never done, it being impossible.

133. By what we have hitherto said, it is plain that very numerous and important errors have taken their rise from

those false Principles which were impugned in the foregoing parts of this Treatise; and the opposites of those erroneous tenets at the same time appear to be most fruitful Principles, from whence do flow innumerable consequences, highly advantageous to true philosophy as well as to religion. Particularly *Matter*, or *the absolute existence of corporeal objects*, hath been shewn to be that wherein the most avowed and pernicious enemies of all knowledge, whether human or divine, have ever placed their chief strength and confidence. And surely if by distinguishing the real existence of unthinking things from their being perceived, and allowing them a subsistence of their own, out of the minds of spirits, no one thing is explained in nature, but on the contrary a great many inexplicable difficulties arise; if the supposition of Matter is barely precarious, as not being grounded on so much as one single reason; if its consequences cannot endure the light of examination and free inquiry, but screen themselves under the dark and general pretence of *infinites being incomprehensible*; if withal the removal of *this* Matter be not attended with the least evil consequence; if it be not even missed in the world, but everything as well, nay much easier conceived without it; if, lastly, both Sceptics and Atheists are for ever silenced upon supposing only spirits and ideas, and this scheme of things is perfectly agreeable both to Reason and Religion: methinks we may expect it should be admitted and firmly embraced, though it were proposed only as an *hypothesis*, and the existence of Matter had been allowed possible: which yet I think we have evidently demonstrated that it is not.

134. True it is that, in consequence of the foregoing Principles, several disputes and speculations which are esteemed no mean parts of learning are rejected as useless. But how great a prejudice soever against our notions this may give to those who have already been deeply engaged, and made large advances in studies of that nature, yet by others we hope it will not be thought any just ground of dislike to the principles and tenets herein laid down, that they abridge the labour of study, and make human sciences more clear, compendious, and attainable than they were before.

135. Having despatched what we intended to say concerning the knowledge of *ideas*, the method we proposed leads us in the next place to treat of *spirits*; with regard to which,

perhaps, human knowledge is not so deficient as is vulgarly imagined. The great reason that is assigned for our being thought ignorant of the nature of Spirits is our not having an *idea* of it. But, surely it ought not to be looked on as a defect in a human understanding that it does not perceive the idea of Spirit, if it is manifestly impossible there should be any such idea. And this if I mistake not has been demonstrated in section 27. To which I shall here add that a Spirit has been shewn to be the only substance or support wherein unthinking beings or ideas can exist: but that this *substance* which supports or perceives ideas should itself be an idea, or like an idea, is evidently absurd.

136. It will perhaps be said that we want a *sense* (as some have imagined) proper to know substances withal; which, if we had, we might know our own soul as we do a triangle. To this I answer, that in case we had a new sense bestowed upon us, we could only receive thereby some new *sensations* or *ideas of sense*. But I believe nobody will say that what he means by the terms *soul* and *substance* is only some particular sort of idea or sensation. We may therefore infer that, all things duly considered, it is not more reasonable to think our faculties defective, in that they do not furnish us with an *idea* of Spirit, or active thinking substance, than it would be if we should blame them for not being able to comprehend a *round square*.

137. From the opinion that Spirits are to be known after the manner of an idea or sensation have risen many absurd and heterodox tenets, and much scepticism about the nature of the soul. It is even probable that this opinion may have produced a doubt in some whether they had any soul at all distinct from their body; since upon inquiry they could not find they had an idea of it. That an *idea*, which is inactive, and the existence whereof consists in being perceived, should be the image or likeness of an agent subsisting by itself, seems to need no other refutation than barely attending to what is meant by those words. But perhaps you will say that though an idea cannot resemble a Spirit in its thinking, acting, or subsisting by itself, yet it may in some other respects; and it is not necessary that an idea or image be in all respects like the original.

138. I answer, If it does not in those mentioned, it is impossible it should represent it in any other thing. Do but leave out the power of willing, thinking, and perceiving ideas,

and there remains nothing else wherein the idea can be like a spirit. For, by the word *spirit* we mean only that which thinks, wills, and perceives; this, and this alone, constitutes the signification of that term. If therefore it is impossible that any degree of those powers should be represented in an idea, it is evident there can be no idea of a Spirit.

139. But it will be objected that, if there is no *idea* signified by the terms, *soul*, *spirit*, and *substance*, they are wholly insignificant, or have no meaning in them. I answer, those words do mean or signify a real thing; which is neither an idea nor like an idea, but that which perceives ideas, and wills, and reasons about them. What I am *myself*, that which I denote by the term *I*, is the same with what is meant by *soul*, or *spiritual substance*. If it be said that this is only quarrelling at a word, and that, since the immediate significations of other names are by common consent called *ideas*, no reason can be assigned why that which is signified by the name *spirit* or *soul* may not partake in the same appellation. I answer, all the unthinking objects of the mind agree in that they are entirely passive, and their existence consists only in being perceived: whereas a *soul* or *spirit* is an active being, whose existence consists, not in being perceived, but in perceiving ideas and thinking. It is therefore necessary, in order to prevent equivocation and confounding natures perfectly disagreeing and unlike, that we distinguish between *spirit* and *idea*. See sect. 27.

140. In a large sense indeed, we may be said to have an idea [or rather a notion] [9] of *spirit*. That is, we understand the meaning of the word, otherwise we could not affirm or deny anything of it. Moreover, as we conceive the ideas that are in the minds of other spirits by means of our own, which we suppose to be resemblances of them, so we know other spirits by means of our own soul: which in that sense is the image or idea of them; it having a like respect to other spirits that blueness or heat by me perceived has to those ideas perceived by another.

141. It must not be supposed that they who assert the natural immortality of the soul are of opinion that it is absolutely incapable of annihilation even by the infinite power of the Creator who first gave it being, but only that it is not liable to be broken or dissolved by the ordinary laws of nature

[9] [Added in the second edition.—Ed.]

or motion. They indeed who hold the soul of man to be only a thin vital flame, or system of animal spirits, make it perishing and corruptible as the body; since there is nothing more easily dissipated than such a being, which it is naturally impossible should survive the ruin of the tabernacle wherein it is inclosed. And this notion hath been greedily embraced and cherished by the worst part of mankind, as the most effectual antidote against all impressions of virtue and religion. But it hath been made evident that bodies, of what frame or texture soever, are barely passive ideas in the mind, which is more distant and heterogeneous from them than light is from darkness. We have shewn that the soul is indivisible, incorporeal, unextended; and it is consequently incorruptible. Nothing can be plainer than that the motions, changes, decays, and dissolutions which we hourly see befall natural bodies (and which is what we mean by the *course of nature*) cannot possibly affect an active, simple, uncompounded substance: such a being therefore is indissoluble by the force of nature; that is to say, *the soul of man is naturally immortal.*

142. After what has been said, it is, I suppose, plain that our souls are not to be known in the same manner as senseless, inactive objects, or by way of *idea*. Spirits and *ideas* are things so wholly different, that when we say "they exist," "they are known," or the like, these words must not be thought to signify anything common to both natures. There is nothing alike or common in them; and to expect that by any multiplication or enlargement of our faculties, we may be enabled to know a spirit as we do a triangle, seems as absurd as if we should hope to *see a sound*. This is inculcated because I imagine it may be of moment towards clearing several important questions, and preventing some very dangerous errors concerning the nature of the soul.

[We may not, I think, strictly be said to have an *idea* of an active being, or of an action; although we may be said to have a *notion* of them. I have some knowledge or notion of *my mind*, and its acts about ideas; inasmuch as I know or understand what is meant by these words. What I know, that I have some notion of. I will not say that the terms *idea* and *notion* may not be used convertibly, if the world will have it so. But yet it conduceth to clearness and propriety, that we distinguish things very different by different names. It is also to be remarked that, all *relations* including an act of the mind, we cannot so properly be said to have an idea, but rather a notion, of the relations and habitudes between things. But if, in the modern way, the word *idea* is extended to *spirits*, and *relations*, and *acts*, this is, after all, an affair of verbal concern.] [10]

143. It will not be amiss to add, that the doctrine of *abstract ideas* has had no small share in rendering those sciences intricate and obscure which are particularly conversant about spiritual things. Men have imagined they could frame abstract notions of the *powers* and *acts* of the mind, and consider them prescinded as well from the mind or spirit itself, as from their respective objects and effects. Hence a great number of dark and ambiguous terms, presumed to stand for abstract notions, have been introduced into metaphysics and morality; and from these have grown infinite distractions and disputes amongst the learned.

144. But, nothing seems more to have contributed towards engaging men in controversies and mistakes with regard to the nature and operations of the mind, than the being used to speak of those things in terms borrowed from sensible ideas. For example, the will is termed the *motion* of the soul: this infuses a belief that the mind of man is as a ball in motion, impelled and determined by the objects of sense, as necessarily as that is by the stroke of a racket. Hence arise endless scruples and errors of dangerous consequence in morality. All which, I doubt not, may be cleared, and truth appear plain, uniform, and consistent, could but philosophers be prevailed on to retire into themselves, and attentively consider their own meaning.

145. From what hath been said, it is plain that we cannot know the existence of *other spirits* otherwise than by their operations, or the ideas by them, excited in us. I perceive several motions, changes, and combinations of ideas, that inform me there are certain particular agents, like myself, which accompany them, and concur in their production. Hence, the knowledge I have of other spirits is not immediate, as is the knowledge of my ideas; but depending on the intervention of ideas, by me referred to agents or spirits distinct from myself, as effects or concomitant signs.

146. But, though there be some things which convince us

---

[10] [Added in the second edition.—Ed.]

human agents are concerned in producing them, yet it is evident to every one that those things which are called the Works of Nature, that is, the far greater part of the ideas or sensations perceived by us, are *not* produced by, or dependent on, the wills of *men*. There is therefore some other Spirit that causes them; since it is repugnant that they should subsist by themselves. See sect. 29. But, if we attentively consider the constant regularity, order, and concatenation of natural things, the surprising magnificence, beauty and perfection of the larger, and the exquisite contrivance of the smaller parts of the creation, together with the exact harmony and correspondence of the whole, but above all the never-enough-admired laws of pain and pleasure, and the instincts or natural inclinations, appetites, and passions of animals;—I say if we consider all these things, and at the same time attend to the meaning and import of the attributes One, Eternal, Infinitely Wise, Good, and Perfect, we shall clearly perceive that they belong to the aforesaid Spirit, "who works all in all" and "by whom all things consist."

147. Hence, it is evident that God is known as certainly and immediately as any other mind or spirit whatsoever, distinct from ourselves. We may even assert that the existence of God is far more evidently perceived than the existence of men; because the effects of Nature are infinitely more numerous and considerable than those ascribed to human agents. There is not any one mark that denotes a man, or effect produced by him, which does not more strongly evince the being of that Spirit who is the Author of Nature. For it is evident that, in affecting other persons, the will of man hath no other object than barely the motion of the limbs of his body; but that such a motion should be attended by, or excite any idea in the mind of another, depends wholly on the will of the Creator. He alone it is who, "upholding all things by the word of His power," maintains that intercourse between spirits whereby they are able to perceive the existence of each other. And yet this pure and clear Light which enlightens everyone is itself invisible.

148. It seems to be a general pretence of the unthinking herd that they cannot *see* God. Could we but see Him, say they, as we see a man, we should believe that He is, and believing obey His commands. But alas, we need only open our eyes to see the Sovereign Lord of all things, with a *more* full and clear view than we do any one of our fellow-crea-

tures. Not that I imagine we see God (as some will have it) by a direct and immediate view; or see corporeal things, not by themselves, but by seeing that which represents them in the essence of God; which doctrine is, I must confess, to me incomprehensible.[11] But I shall explain my meaning. A human spirit or person is not perceived by sense, as not being an idea. When therefore we see the colour, size, figure, and motions of a man, we perceive only certain sensations or ideas excited in our own minds; and these being exhibited to our view in sundry distinct collections, serve to mark out unto us the existence of finite and created spirits like ourselves. Hence it is plain we do not see a man, if by *man* is meant, that which lives, moves, perceives, and thinks as we do: but only such a certain collection of ideas, as directs us to think there is a distinct principle of thought and motion, like to ourselves, accompanying and represented by it. And after the same manner we see God: all the difference is that, whereas some one finite and narrow assemblage of ideas denotes a particular human mind, whithersoever we direct our view we do at all times and in all places perceive manifest tokens of the Divinity; everything we see, hear, feel, or anywise perceive by sense, being a sign or affect of the power of God; as is our perception of those very motions which are produced by men.

149. It is therefore plain that nothing can be more evident to any one that is capable of the least reflexion than the existence of God, or a Spirit who is intimately present to our minds, producing in them all that variety of ideas or sensations which continually affect us, on whom we have an absolute and entire dependence, in short "in whom we live, and move, and have our being." That the discovery of this great truth, which lies so near and obvious to the mind, should be attained to by the reason of so very few, is a sad instance of the stupidity and inattention of men, who, though they are surrounded with such clear manifestations of the Deity, are yet so little affected by them that they seem, as it were, blinded with excess of light.

150. But you will say—Hath Nature no share in the production of natural things, and must they be all ascribed to the immediate and sole operation of God? I answer, If by *Nature* is meant only the *visible series* of effects or sensations

[11] [Malebranche is meant.—Ed.]

imprinted on our minds according to certain fixed and general laws, then it is plain that Nature, taken in this sense, cannot produce anything at all. But if by *Nature* is meant some being distinct from God, as well as from the laws of nature and things perceived by sense, I must confess that word is to me an empty sound, without any intelligible meaning annexed to it. Nature, in this acceptation, is a vain chimera, introduced by those heathens who had not just notions of the omnipresence and infinite perfection of God. But it is more unaccountable that it should be received among Christians, professing belief in the Holy Scriptures, which constantly ascribe those effects to the immediate hand of God that heathen philosophers are wont to impute to Nature. "The Lord, He causeth the vapours to ascend; He maketh lightnings with rain; He bringeth forth the wind out of His treasures." Jerem. x. 13. "He turneth the shadow of death into the morning, and maketh the day dark with night." Amos. v. 8. "He visiteth the earth, and maketh it soft with showers: He blesseth the springing thereof, and crowneth the year with His goodness; so that the pastures are clothed with flocks, and the valleys are covered over with corn." See Psal. 1xv. But, notwithstanding that this is the constant language of Scripture, yet we have I know not what aversion from believing that God concerns Himself so nearly in our affairs. Fain would we suppose Him at a great distance off, and substitute some blind, unthinking deputy in His stead; though (if we may believe Saint Paul) "He be not far from every one of us."

151. It will, I doubt not, be objected that the slow, gradual, and roundabout methods observed in the production of natural things do not seem to have for their cause the *immediate* hand of an Almighty Agent: besides, monsters, untimely births, fruits blasted in the blossom, rains falling in desert places, miseries incident to human life, and the like, are so many arguments that the whole frame of nature is not immediately actuated and superintended by a Spirit of infinite wisdom and goodness. But the answer to this objection is in a good measure plain from sect. 62; it being visible that the aforesaid methods of nature are absolutely necessary in order to working by the most simple and general rules, and after a steady and consistent manner; which argues both the wisdom and goodness of God. Such is the artificial contrivance of this mighty machine of Nature that, whilst its

motions and various phenomena strike on our senses, the Hand which actuates the whole is itself unperceivable to men of flesh and blood. "Verily" (saith the prophet) "thou art a God that hidest thyself." Isaiah xlv. 15. But, though the Lord conceal Himself from the eyes of the sensual and lazy, who will not be at the least expense of thought, yet to an unbiassed and attentive mind, nothing can be more plainly legible than the intimate presence of an All-wise Spirit, who fashions, regulates, and sustains the whole system of Being. It is clear, from what we have elsewhere observed, that the operating according to general and stated laws is so necessary for our guidance in the affairs of life, and letting us into the secret of nature, that without it all reach and compass of thought, all human sagacity and design, could serve to no manner of purpose. It were even impossible there should be any such faculties or powers in the mind. See sect. 31. Which one consideration abundantly outbalances whatever particular inconveniences may thence arise.

152. We should further consider, that the very blemishes and defects of nature are not without their use, in that they make an agreeable sort of variety, and augment the beauty of the rest of the creation, as shades in a picture serve to set off the brighter and more enlightened parts. We would likewise do well to examine, whether our taxing the waste of seeds and embryos, and accidental destruction of plants and animals before they come to full maturity, as an imprudence in the Author of nature, be not the effect of prejudice contracted by our familiarity with impotent and saving mortals. In *man* indeed a thrifty management of those things which he cannot procure without much pains and industry may be esteemed wisdom. But we must not imagine that the inexplicably fine machine of an animal or vegetable costs the great Creator any more pains or trouble in its production than a pebble does; nothing being more evident than that an Omnipotent Spirit can indifferently produce everything by a mere *fiat* or act of his will. Hence it is plain that the splendid profusion of natural things should not be interpreted weakness or prodigality in the Agent who produces them, but rather be looked on as an argument of the riches of His power.

153. As for the mixture of pain or uneasiness which is in the world, pursuant to the general laws of Nature, and the actions of finite, imperfect Spirits, this, in the state we are in at present, is indispensably necessary to our well-being. But

our prospects are too narrow. We take, for instance, the idea of some one particular pain into our thoughts, and account it *evil*. Whereas, if we enlarge our view, so as to comprehend the various ends, connexions, and dependencies of things, on what occasions and in what proportions we are affected with pain and pleasure, the nature of human freedom, and the design with which we are put into the world; we shall be forced to acknowledge that those particular things which, considered in themselves, appear to be evil, have the nature of good, when considered as linked with the whole system of beings.

154. From what hath been said, it will be manifest to any considering person, that it is merely for want of attention and comprehensiveness of mind that there are any favourers of Atheism or the Manichean Heresy to be found. Little and unreflecting souls may indeed burlesque the works of Providence; the beauty and order whereof they have not capacity, or will not be at the pains, to comprehend. But those who are masters of any justness and extent of thought, and are withal used to reflect, can never sufficiently admire the divine traces of Wisdom and Goodness that shine throughout the economy of Nature. But what truth is there which glares so strongly on the mind that, by an aversion of thought, a wilful shutting of the eyes, we may not escape seeing it? Is it therefore to be wondered at, if the generality of men, who are ever intent on business or pleasure, and little used to fix or open the eye of their mind, should not have all that conviction and evidence of the Being of God which might be expected in reasonable creatures?

155. We should rather wonder that men can be found so stupid as to neglect, than that neglecting they should be unconvinced of such an evident and momentous truth. And yet it is to be feared that too many of parts and leisure, who live in Christian countries, are, merely through a supine and dreadful negligence, sunk into a sort of Atheism. Since it is downright impossible that a soul pierced and enlightened with a thorough sense of the omnipresence, holiness, and justice of that Almighty Spirit, should persist in a remorseless violation of His laws. We ought, therefore, earnestly to meditate and dwell on those important points; that so we may attain conviction without all scruple "that the eyes of the Lord are in every place, beholding the evil and the good; that He is with us and keepeth us in all places whither we go, and

giveth us bread to eat and raiment to put on"; that He is present and conscious to our innermost thoughts; and, that we have a most absolute and immediate dependence on Him. A clear view of which great truths cannot choose but fill our hearts with an awful circumspection and holy fear, which is the strongest incentive to Virtue, and the best guard against Vice.

156. For, after all, what deserves the first place in our studies is, the consideration of GOD and our DUTY; which to promote, as it was the main drift and design of my labours, so shall I esteem them altogether useless and ineffectual if, by what I have said, I cannot inspire my readers with a pious sense of the Presence of God; and, having shewn the falseness or vanity of those barren speculations which make the chief employment of learned men, the better dispose them to reverence and embrace the salutary truths of the Gospel; which to know and to practise is the highest perfection of human nature.

Three Dialogues Between Hylas and Philonous

Berkeley published the *Three Dialogues* in 1713, in an endeavor to overcome the scorn and incomprehension with which the *Principles of Human Knowledge* had been received three years earlier. Written with the highest art, the *Dialogues* are an ideal introduction to Berkeley's thought, being concerned solely to argue for, expound, and defend against objections, his great central principle: that physical objects cannot exist except when perceived. But, like the *Principles*, the *Dialogues* failed to win immediate converts, or even to provoke serious replies from other philosophers.

Three Dialogues

Between

Hylas and Philonous

The Design of which Is Plainly to Demonstrate
the Reality and Perfection of

Human Knowledge

The Incorporeal Nature of the

Soul

And the Immediate Providence of a

Deity

in Opposition to

Sceptics and Atheists

Also to Open a Method for Rendering the Sciences more
Easy, Useful, and Compendious

To the Right Honourable [1]

The Lord Berkeley of Stratton,

Master of the Rolls in the Kingdom of Ireland, Chancellor of
the Duchy of Lancaster, and One of the Lords of
Her Majesty's Most Honourable Privy Council.

MY LORD,

THE virtue, learning, and good sense which are acknowledged
to distinguish your character, would tempt me to indulge
myself the pleasure men naturally take in giving applause to
those whom they esteem and honour: and it should seem of
importance to the subjects of Great Britain that they knew the
eminent share you enjoy in the favour of your sovereign, and
the honours she has conferred upon you, have not been owing
to any application from your lordship, but entirely to her
majesty's own thought, arising from a sense of your personal
merit, and an inclination to reward it. But, as your name is
prefixed to this treatise with an intention to do honour to
myself alone, I shall only say that I am encouraged by the
favour you have treated me with to address these papers to
your lordship. And I was the more ambitious of doing this,
because a Philosophical Treatise could not so properly be
addressed to any one as to a person of your lordship's character, who, to your other valuable distinctions, have added the
knowledge and relish of Philosophy.

I am, with the greatest respect,
My Lord,
Your lordship's most obedient and
most humble servant,
GEORGE BERKELEY.

[1] [Omitted in the final edition.—Ed.]

The Preface[1]

THOUGH it seems the general opinion of the world, no less than the design of nature and Providence, that the end of speculation be Practice, or the improvement and regulation of our lives and actions; yet those who are most addicted to speculative studies, seem as generally of another mind. And indeed if we consider the pains that have been taken to perplex the plainest things, that distrust of the senses, those doubts and scruples, those abstractions and refinements that occur in the very entrance of the sciences; it will not seem strange that men of leisure and curiosity should lay themselves out in fruitless disquisitions, without descending to the practical parts of life, or informing themselves in the more necessary and important parts of knowledge.

Upon the common principles of philosophers, we are not assured of the existence of things from their being perceived. And we are taught to distinguish their *real* nature from that which falls under our senses. Hence arise scepticism and paradoxes. It is not enough that we see and feel, that we taste and smell a thing: its true nature, its absolute external entity, is still concealed. For, though it be the fiction of our own brain, we have made it inaccessible to all our faculties. Sense is fallacious, reason defective. We spend our lives in doubting of those things which other men evidently know, and believing those things which they laugh at and despise.

In order, therefore, to divert the busy mind of man from vain researches, it seemed necessary to inquire into the source of its perplexities; and, if possible, to lay down such Principles as, by an easy solution of them, together with their own native evidence, may at once recommend themselves for genuine to the mind, and rescue it from those endless pursuits it is engaged in. Which, with a plain demonstration of the Immediate Providence of an all-seeing God, and the natural Immortality of the soul, should seem the readiest preparation, as well as the strongest motive, to the study and practice of virtue.

This design I proposed in the First Part of a treatise con-

---

[1] [Omitted in the final edition.—Ed.]

cerning the *Principles of Human Knowledge*, published in the year 1710. But, before I proceed to publish the Second Part,[2] I thought it requisite to treat more clearly and fully of certain Principles laid down in the First, and to place them in a new light. Which is the business of the following *Dialogues*.

In this Treatise, which does not presuppose in the reader any knowledge of what was contained in the former, it has been my aim to introduce the notions I advance into the mind in the most easy and familiar manner; especially because they carry with them a great opposition to the prejudices of philosophers, which have so far prevailed against the common sense and natural notions of mankind.

If the Principles which I here endeavour to propagate are admitted for true, the consequences which, I think, evidently flow from thence are, that Atheism and Scepticism will be utterly destroyed, many intricate points made plain, great difficulties solved, several useless parts of science retrenched, speculation referred to practice, and men reduced from paradoxes to common sense.

And although it may, perhaps, seem an uneasy reflexion to some, that when they have taken a circuit through so many refined and unvulgar notions, they should at last come to think like other men; yet, methinks, this return to the simple dictates of nature, after having wandered through the wild mazes of philosophy, is not unpleasant. It is like coming home from a long voyage: a man reflects with pleasure on the many difficulties and perplexities he has passed through, sets his heart at ease, and enjoys himself with more satisfaction for the future.

As it was my intention to convince Sceptics and Infidels by reason, so it has been my endeavour strictly to observe the most rigid laws of reasoning. And, to an impartial reader, I hope it will be manifest that the sublime notion of a God, and the comfortable expectation of Immortality, do naturally arise from a close and methodical application of thought: whatever may be the result of that loose, rambling way, not altogether improperly termed Free-thinking by certain libertines in thought, who can no more endure the restraints of logic than those of religion or government.

It will perhaps be objected to my design that, so far as it tends to ease the mind of difficult and useless inquiries, it can

---

[2] [Never written.—Ed.]

affect only a few speculative persons. But if, by their speculations rightly placed, the study of morality and the law of nature were brought more into fashion among men of parts and genius, the discouragements that draw to Scepticism removed, the measures of right and wrong accurately defined, and the principles of Natural Religion reduced into regular systems, as artfully disposed and clearly connected as those of some other sciences; there are grounds to think these effects would not only have a gradual influence in repairing the too much defaced sense of virtue in the world, but also, by shewing that such parts of revelation as lie within the reach of human inquiry are most agreeable to right reason, would dispose all prudent, unprejudiced persons to a modest and wary treatment of those sacred mysteries which are above the comprehension of our faculties.

It remains that I desire the reader to withhold his censure of these *Dialogues* till he has read them through. Otherwise, he may lay them aside in a mistake of their design, or on account of difficulties or objections which he would find answered in the sequel. A Treatise of this nature would require to be once read over coherently, in order to comprehend its design, the proofs, solution of difficulties, and the connexion and disposition of its parts. If it be thought to deserve a second reading, this, I imagine, will make the entire scheme very plain. Especially if recourse be had to an Essay I wrote some years since upon *Vision*, and the Treatise concerning the *Principles of Human Knowledge;* wherein divers notions advanced in these *Dialogues* are farther pursued, or placed in different lights, and other points handled which naturally tend to confirm and illustrate them.

The First Dialogue

Philonous. Good morrow, Hylas: I did not expect to find you abroad so early.

Hylas. It is indeed something unusual; but my thoughts were so taken up with a subject I was discoursing of last night, that finding I could not sleep, I resolved to rise and take a turn in the garden.

Phil. It happened well, to let you see what innocent and agreeable pleasures you lose every morning. Can there be a pleasanter time of the day, or a more delightful season of the year? That purple sky, those wild but sweet notes of birds, the fragrant bloom upon the trees and flowers, the gentle influence of the rising sun, these and a thousand nameless beauties of nature inspire the soul with secret transports; its faculties too being at this time fresh and lively, are fit for those meditations, which the solitude of a garden and tranquillity of the morning naturally dispose us to. But I am afraid I interrupt your thoughts: for you seemed very intent on something.

Hyl. It is true, I was, and shall be obliged to you if you will permit me to go on in the same vein; not that I would by any means deprive myself of your company, for my thoughts always flow more easily in conversation with a friend, than when I am alone: but my request is, that you would suffer me to impart my reflexions to you.

Phil. With all my heart, it is what I should have requested myself if you had not prevented me.

Hyl. I was considering the odd fate of those men who have in all ages, through an affectation of being distinguished from the vulgar, or some unaccountable turn of thought, pretended either to believe nothing at all, or to believe the most extravagant things in the world. This however might be borne, if their paradoxes and scepticism did not draw after them some consequences of general disadvantage to mankind. But the mischief lieth here; that when men of less leisure see them who are supposed to have spent their whole time in the pursuits of knowledge professing an entire ignorance of all things, or advancing such notions as are repugnant to plain and commonly received principles, they will be tempted to entertain suspicions concerning the most important truths, which they had hitherto held sacred and unquestionable.

Phil. I entirely agree with you, as to the ill tendency of the affected doubts of some philosophers, and fantastical conceits of others. I am even so far gone of late in this way of thinking, that I have quitted several of the sublime notions I had got in their schools for vulgar opinions. And I give it you on my word; since this revolt from metaphysical notions to the plain dictates of nature and common sense, I find my understanding strangely enlightened, so that I can now easily comprehend a great many things which before were all mystery and riddle.

Hyl. I am glad to find there was nothing in the accounts I heard of you.

Phil. Pray, what were those?

Hyl. You were represented, in last night's conversation, as one who maintained the most extravagant opinion that ever entered into the mind of man, to wit, that there is no such thing as *material substance* in the world.

Phil. That there is no such thing as what *philosophers* call *material substance,* I am seriously persuaded: but, if I were made to see anything absurd or sceptical in this, I should then have the same reason to renounce this that I imagine I have now to reject the contrary opinion.

Hyl. What! can anything be more fantastical, more repugnant to Common Sense, or a more manifest piece of Scepticism, than to believe there is no such thing as *matter?*

Phil. Softly, good Hylas. What if it should prove that you, who hold there is, are, by virtue of that opinion, a greater sceptic, and maintain more paradoxes and repugnances to Common Sense, than I who believe no such thing?

Hyl. You may as soon persuade me, the part is greater than the whole, as that, in order to avoid absurdity and Scepticism, I should ever be obliged to give up my opinion in this point.

Phil. Well then, are you content to admit that opinion for true, which upon examination shall appear most agreeable to Common Sense, and remote from Scepticism?

Hyl. With all my heart. Since you are for raising disputes about the plainest things in nature, I am content for once to hear what you have to say.

Phil. Pray, Hylas, what do you mean by a *sceptic?*

Hyl. I mean what all men mean—one that doubts of everything.

Phil. He then who entertains no doubt concerning some particular point, with regard to that point cannot be thought a sceptic.

Hyl. I agree with you.

Phil. Whether doth doubting consist in embracing the affirmative or negative side of a question?

Hyl. In neither; for whoever understands English cannot but know that *doubting* signifies a suspense between both.

Phil. He then that denies any point, can no more be said to doubt of it, than he who affirmeth it with the same degree of assurance.

Hyl. True.

Phil. And, consequently, for such his denial is no more to be esteemed a sceptic than the other.

Hyl. I acknowledge it.

Phil. How cometh it to pass then, Hylas, that you pronounce me a *sceptic*, because I deny what you affirm, to wit, the existence of Matter? Since, for aught you can tell, I am as peremptory in my denial, as you in your affirmation.

Hyl. Hold, Philonous, I have been a little out in my definition; but every false step a man makes in discourse is not to be insisted on. I said indeed that a *sceptic* was one who doubted of everything; but I should have added, or who denies the reality and truth of things.

Phil. What things? Do you mean the principles and theorems of sciences? But these you know are universal intellectual notions, and consequently independent of Matter. The denial therefore of this doth not imply the denying them.

Hyl. I grant it. But are there no other things? What think you of distrusting the senses, of denying the real existence of sensible things, or pretending to know nothing of them. Is not this sufficient to denominate a man a *sceptic*?

Phil. Shall we therefore examine which of us it is that denies the reality of sensible things, or professes the greatest ignorance of them; since, if I take you rightly, he is to be esteemed the greatest *sceptic*?

Hyl. That is what I desire.

Phil. What mean you by Sensible Things?

Hyl. Those things which are perceived by the senses. Can you imagine that I mean anything else?

Phil. Pardon me, Hylas, if I am desirous clearly to apprehend your notions, since this may much shorten our inquiry. Suffer me then to ask you this farther question. Are those things only perceived by the senses which are perceived immediately? Or, may those things properly be said to be *sensible* which are perceived mediately, or not without the intervention of others?

Hyl. I do not sufficiently understand you.

Phil. In reading a book, what I immediately perceive are the letters; but mediately, or by means of these, are suggested to my mind the notions of God, virtue, truth, &c. Now, that the letters are truly sensible things, or perceived by sense, there is no doubt: but I would know whether you take the things suggested by them to be so too.

Hyl. No, certainly: it were absurd to think *God* or *virtue* sensible things; though they may be signified and suggested to the mind by sensible marks, with which they have an arbitrary connexion.

Phil. It seems then, that by *sensible things* you mean those only which can be perceived *immediately* by sense?

Hyl. Right.

Phil. Doth it not follow from this, that though I see one part of the sky red, and another blue, and that my reason doth thence evidently conclude there must be some cause of that diversity of colours, yet that cause cannot be said to be a sensible thing, or perceived by the sense of seeing?

Hyl. It doth.

Phil. In like manner, though I hear variety of sounds, yet I cannot be said to hear the causes of those sounds?

Hyl. You cannot.

Phil. And when by my touch I perceive a thing to be hot and heavy, I cannot say, with any truth or propriety, that I feel the cause of its heat or weight?

Hyl. To prevent any more questions of this kind, I tell you once for all, that by *sensible things* I mean those only which are perceived by sense; and that in truth the senses perceive nothing which they do not perceive *immediately:* for they make no inferences. The deducing therefore of causes or occasions from effects and appearances, which alone are perceived by sense, entirely relates to reason.

Phil. This point then is agreed between us—That *sensible things are those only which are immediately perceived by sense.* You will farther inform me, whether we immediately perceive by sight anything beside light, and colours, and figures; or by hearing, anything but sounds; by the palate, anything beside taste; by the smell, beside odours; or by the touch, more than tangible qualities.

Hyl. We do not.

Phil. It seems, therefore, that if you take away all sensible qualities, there remains nothing sensible?

Hyl. I grant it.

Phil. Sensible things therefore are nothing else but so many sensible qualities, or combinations of sensible qualities?

Hyl. Nothing else.

Phil. Heat then is a sensible thing?

Hyl. Certainly.

Phil. Doth the *reality* of sensible things consist in being perceived? or, is it something distinct from their being perceived, and that bears no relation to the mind?

Hyl. To *exist* is one thing, and to be *perceived* is another.

Phil. I speak with regard to sensible things only. And of these I ask, whether by their real existence you mean a subsistence exterior to the mind, and distinct from their being perceived?

Hyl. I mean a real absolute being, distinct from, and without any relation to, their being perceived.

Phil. Heat therefore, if it be allowed a real being, must exist without the mind?

Hyl. It must.

Phil. Tell me, Hylas, is this real existence equally compatible to all degrees of heat, which we perceive; or is there any reason why we should attribute it to some, and deny it to others? And if there be, pray let me know that reason.

Hyl. Whatever degree of heat we perceive by sense, we may be sure the same exists in the object that occasions it.

Phil. What! the greatest as well as the least?

Hyl. I tell you, the reason is plainly the same in respect of both. They are both perceived by sense; nay, the greater degree of heat is more sensibly perceived; and consequently, if there is any difference, we are more certain of its real existence than we can be of the reality of a lesser degree.

Phil. But is not the most vehement and intense degree of heat a very great pain?

Hyl. No one can deny it.

Phil. And is any unperceiving thing capable of pain or pleasure?

Hyl. No, certainly.

Phil. Is your material substance a senseless being, or a being endowed with sense and perception?

Hyl. It is senseless without doubt.

Phil. It cannot therefore be the subject of pain?

Hyl. By no means.

Phil. Nor consequently of the greatest heat perceived by sense, since you acknowledge this to be no small pain?

Hyl. I grant it.

Phil. What shall we say then of your external object; is it a material Substance, or no?

Hyl. It is a material substance with the sensible qualities inhering in it.

Phil. How then can a great heat exist in it, since you own it cannot in a material substance? I desire you would clear this point.

Hyl. Hold, Philonous, I fear I was out in yielding intense heat to be a pain. It should seem rather, that pain is something distinct from heat, and the consequence or effect of it.

Phil. Upon putting your hand near the fire, do you perceive one simple uniform sensation, or two distinct sensations?

Hyl. But one simple sensation.

Phil. Is not the heat immediately perceived?

Hyl. It is.

Phil. And the pain?

Hyl. True.

Phil. Seeing therefore they are both immediately perceived at the same time, and the fire affects you only with one simple or uncompounded idea, it follows that this same simple idea is both the intense heat immediately perceived, and the pain; and, consequently, that the intense heat immediately perceived is nothing distinct from a particular sort of pain.

Hyl. It seems so.

Phil. Again, try in your thoughts, Hylas, if you can conceive a vehement sensation to be without pain or pleasure.

Hyl. I cannot.

Phil. Or can you frame to yourself an idea of sensible pain or pleasure in general, abstracted from every particular idea of heat, cold, tastes, smells, &c.?

Hyl. I do not find that I can.

Phil. Doth it not therefore follow, that sensible pain is

nothing distinct from those sensations or ideas, in an intense degree?

Hyl. It is undeniable; and, to speak the truth, I begin to suspect a very great heat cannot exist but in a mind perceiving it.

Phil. What! are you then in that sceptical state of suspense, between affirming and denying?

Hyl. I think I may be positive in the point. A very violent and painful heat cannot exist without the mind.

Phil. It hath not therefore, according to you, any *real* being?

Hyl. I own it.

Phil. Is it therefore certain, that there is no body in nature really hot?

Hyl. I have not denied there is any real heat in bodies. I only say, there is no such thing as an intense real heat.

Phil. But, did you not say before that all degrees of heat were equally real; or, if there was any difference, that the greater were more undoubtedly real than the lesser?

Hyl. True: but it was because I did not then consider the ground there is for distinguishing between them, which I now plainly see. And it is this: because intense heat is nothing else but a particular kind of painful sensation; and pain cannot exist but in a perceiving being; it follows that no intense heat can really exist in an unperceiving corporeal substance. But this is no reason why we should deny heat in an inferior degree to exist in such a substance.

Phil. But how shall we be able to discern those degrees of heat which exist only in the mind from those which exist without it?

Hyl. That is no difficult matter. You know the least pain cannot exist unperceived; whatever, therefore, degree of heat is a pain exists only in the mind. But, as for all other degrees of heat, nothing obliges us to think the same of them.

Phil. I think you granted before that no unperceiving being was capable of pleasure, any more than of pain.

Hyl. I did.

Phil. And is not warmth, or a more gentle degree of heat than what causes uneasiness, a pleasure?

Hyl. What then?

Phil. Consequently, it cannot exist without the mind in an unperceiving substance, or body.

Hyl. So it seems.

Phil. Since, therefore, as well those degrees of heat that are not painful, as those that are, can exist only in a thinking substance; may we not conclude that external bodies are absolutely incapable of any degree of heat whatsoever?

Hyl. On second thoughts, I do not think it so evident that warmth is a pleasure as that a great degree of heat is a pain.

Phil. I do not pretend that warmth is as great a pleasure as heat is a pain. But, if you grant it to be even a small pleasure, it serves to make good my conclusion.

Hyl. I could rather call it an *indolence*. It seems to be nothing more than a privation of both pain and pleasure. And that such a quality or state as this may agree to an un-thinking substance, I hope you will not deny.

Phil. If you are resolved to maintain that warmth, or a gentle degree of heat, is no pleasure, I know not how to convince you otherwise than by appealing to your own sense. But what think you of cold?

Hyl. The same that I do of heat. An intense degree of cold is a pain; for to feel a very great cold, is to perceive a great uneasiness: it cannot therefore exist without the mind; but a lesser degree of cold may, as well as a lesser degree of heat.

Phil. Those bodies, therefore, upon whose application to our own, we perceive a moderate degree of heat, must be concluded to have a moderate degree of heat or warmth in them; and those, upon whose application we feel a like degree of cold, must be thought to have cold in them.

Hyl. They must.

Phil. Can any doctrine be true that necessarily leads a man into an absurdity?

Hyl. Without doubt it cannot.

Phil. Is it not an absurdity to think that the same thing should be at the same time both cold and warm?

Hyl. It is.

Phil. Suppose now one of your hands hot, and the other cold, and that they are both at once put into the same vessel of water, in an intermediate state; will not the water seem cold to one hand, and warm to the other?

Hyl. It will.

Phil. Ought we not therefore, by your principles, to conclude it is really both cold and warm at the same time, that is, according to your concession, to believe an absurdity?

Hyl. I confess it seems so.

Phil. Consequently, the principles themselves are false, since you have granted that no true principle leads to an absurdity.

Hyl. But, after all, can anything be more absurd than to say, *there is no heat in the fire?*

Phil. To make the point still clearer; tell me whether, in two cases exactly alike, we ought not to make the same judgment?

Hyl. We ought.

Phil. When a pin pricks your finger, doth it not rend and divide the fibres of your flesh?

Hyl. It doth.

Phil. And when a coal burns your finger, doth it any more?

Hyl. It doth not.

Phil. Since, therefore, you neither judge the sensation itself occasioned by the pin, nor anything like it to be in the pin; you should not, conformably to what you have now granted, judge the sensation occasioned by the fire, or anything like it, to be in the fire.

Hyl. Well, since it must be so, I am content to yield this point, and acknowledge that heat and cold are only sensations existing in our minds. But there still remain qualities enough to secure the reality of external things.

Phil. But what will you say, Hylas, if it shall appear that the case is the same with regard to all other sensible qualities, and that they can no more be supposed to exist without the mind, than heat and cold?

Hyl. Then indeed you will have done something to the purpose; but that is what I despair of seeing proved.

Phil. Let us examine them in order. What think you of *tastes*—do they exist without the mind, or no?

Hyl. Can any man in his senses doubt whether sugar is sweet, or wormwood bitter?

Phil. Inform me, Hylas. Is a sweet taste a particular kind of pleasure or pleasant sensation, or is it not?

Hyl. It is.

Phil. And is not bitterness some kind of uneasiness or pain?

Hyl. I grant it.

Phil. If therefore sugar and wormwood are unthinking corporeal substances existing without the mind, how can sweetness and bitterness, that is, pleasure and pain, agree to them?

Hyl. Hold, Philonous, I now see what it was deluded me all this time. You asked whether heat and cold, sweetness and bitterness, were not particular sorts of pleasure and pain; to which I answered simply, that they were. Whereas I should have thus distinguished:—those qualities, as perceived by us, are pleasures or pains; but not as existing in the external objects. We must not therefore conclude absolutely, that there is no heat in the fire, or sweetness in the sugar, but only that heat or sweetness, as perceived by us, are not in the fire or sugar. What say you to this?

Phil. I say it is nothing to the purpose. Our discourse proceeded altogether concerning sensible things, which you defined to be, *the things we immediately perceive by our senses.* Whatever other qualities, therefore, you speak of, as distinct from these, I know nothing of them, neither do they at all belong to the point in dispute. You may, indeed, pretend to have discovered certain qualities which you do not perceive, and assert those insensible qualities exist in fire and sugar. But what use can be made of this to your present purpose, I am at a loss to conceive. Tell me then once more, do you acknowledge that heat and cold, sweetness and bitterness (meaning those qualities which are perceived by the senses), do not exist without the mind?

Hyl. I see it is to no purpose to hold out, so I give up the cause as to those mentioned qualities. Though I profess it sounds oddly, to say that sugar is not sweet.

Phil. But, for your farther satisfaction, take this along with you: that which at other times seems sweet, shall, to a distempered palate, appear bitter. And, nothing can be plainer than that divers persons perceive different tastes in the same food; since that which one man delights in, another abhors. And how could this be, if the taste was something really inherent in the food?

Hyl. I acknowledge I know not how.

Phil. In the next place, *odours* are to be considered. And with regard to these, I would fain know whether what hath been said of tastes doth not exactly agree to them? Are they not so many pleasing or displeasing sensations?

Hyl. They are.

Phil. Can you then conceive it possible that they should exist in an unperceiving thing?

Hyl. I cannot.

Phil. Or, can you imagine that filth and ordure affect those brute animals that feed on them out of choice, with the same smells which we perceive in them?

Hyl. By no means.

Phil. May we not therefore conclude of smells, as of the other forementioned qualities, that they cannot exist in any but a perceiving substance or mind?

Hyl. I think so.

Phil. Then as to *sounds,* what must we think of them: are they accidents really inherent in external bodies, or not?

Hyl. That they inhere not in the sonorous bodies is plain from hence: because a bell struck in the exhausted receiver of an air-pump sends forth no sound. The air, therefore, must be thought the subject of sound.

Phil. What reason is there for that, Hylas?

Hyl. Because, when any motion is raised in the air, we perceive a sound greater or lesser, according to the air's motion; but without some motion in the air, we never hear any sound at all.

Phil. And granting that we never hear a sound but when some motion is produced in the air, yet I do not see how you can infer from thence, that the sound itself is in the air.

Hyl. It is this very motion in the external air that produces in the mind the sensation of *sound.* For, striking on the drum of the ear, it causeth a vibration, which by the auditory nerves being communicated to the brain, the soul is thereupon affected with the sensation called *sound.*

Phil. What! is sound then a sensation?

Hyl. I tell you, as perceived by us, it is a particular sensation in the mind.

Phil. And can any sensation exist without the mind?

Hyl. No, certainly.

Phil. How then can sound, being a sensation, exist in the air, if by the *air* you mean a senseless substance existing without the mind?

Hyl. You must distinguish, Philonous, between sound as it is perceived by us, and as it is in itself; or (which is the same thing) between the sound we immediately perceive, and that which exists without us. The former, indeed, is a particular kind of sensation, but the latter is merely a vibrative or undulatory motion in the air.

Phil. I thought I had already obviated that distinction, by the answer I gave when you were applying it in a like case before. But, to say no more of that, are you sure then that sound is really nothing but motion?

Hyl. I am.

Phil. Whatever therefore agrees to real sound, may with truth be attributed to motion?

Hyl. It may.

Phil. It is then good sense to speak of *motion* as of a thing that is *loud, sweet, acute, or grave.*

Hyl. I see you are resolved not to understand me. Is it not evident those accidents or modes belong only to sensible sound, or *sound* in the common acceptation of the word, but not to *sound* in the real and philosophic sense; which, as I just now told you, is nothing but a certain motion of the air?

Phil. It seems then there are two sorts of sound—the one vulgar, or that which is heard, the other philosophical and real?

Hyl. Even so.

Phil. And the latter consists in motion?

Hyl. I told you so before.

Phil. Tell me, Hylas, to which of the senses, think you, the idea of motion belongs? to the hearing?

Hyl. No, certainly; but to the sight and touch.

Phil. It should follow then, that, according to you, real sounds may possibly be *seen* or *felt,* but never *heard.*

Hyl. Look you, Philonous, you may, if you please, make a jest of my opinion, but that will not alter the truth of things. I own, indeed, the inferences you draw me into sound something oddly; but common language, you know, is framed by, and for the use of the vulgar: we must not therefore wonder if expressions adapted to exact philosophic notions seem uncouth and out of the way.

Phil. Is it come to that? I assure you, I imagine myself to have gained no small point, since you make so light of departing from common phrases and opinions; it being a main part of our inquiry, to examine whose notions are widest of the common road, and most repugnant to the general sense of the world. But, can you think it no more than a philosophical paradox, to say that *real sounds are never heard,* and that the idea of them is obtained by some other sense? And is there nothing in this contrary to nature and the truth of things?

Hyl. To deal ingenuously, I do not like it. And, after

the concessions already made, I had as well grant that sounds too have no real being without the mind.

Phil. And I hope you will make no difficulty to acknowledge the same of *colours*.

Hyl. Pardon me: the case of colours is very different. Can anything be plainer than that we see them on the objects?

Phil. The objects you speak of are, I suppose, corporeal Substances existing without the mind?

Hyl. They are.

Phil. And have true and real colours inhering in them?

Hyl. Each visible object hath that colour which we see in it.

Phil. How! is there anything visible but what we perceive by sight?

Hyl. There is not.

Phil. And, do we perceive anything by sense which we do not perceive immediately?

Hyl. How often must I be obliged to repeat the same thing? I tell you, we do not.

Phil. Have patience, good Hylas; and tell me once more, whether there is anything immediately perceived by the senses, except sensible qualities. I know you asserted there was not; but I would now be informed, whether you still persist in the same opinion.

Hyl. I do.

Phil. Pray, is your corporeal substance either a sensible quality, or made up of sensible qualities?

Hyl. What a question that is! who ever thought it was?

Phil. My reason for asking was, because in saying, *each visible object hath that colour which we see in it,* you make visible objects to be corporeal substances; which implies either that corporeal substances are sensible qualities, or else that there is something beside sensible qualities perceived by sight: but, as this point was formerly agreed between us, and is still maintained by you, it is a clear consequence, that your *corporeal substance* is nothing distinct from *sensible qualities.*

Hyl. You may draw as many absurd consequences as you please, and endeavour to perplex the plainest things; but you shall never persuade me out of my senses. I clearly understand my own meaning.

Phil. I wish you would make me understand it too. But, since you are unwilling to have your notion of corporeal substance examined, I shall urge that point no farther. Only be pleased to let me know, whether the same colours which we see exist in external bodies, or some other.

Hyl. The very same.

Phil. What! are then the beautiful red and purple we see on yonder clouds really in them? Or do you imagine they have in themselves any other form than that of a dark mist or vapour?

Hyl. I must own, Philonous, those colours are not really in the clouds as they seem to be at this distance. They are only apparent colours.

Phil. Apparent call you them? how shall we distinguish these apparent colours from real?

Hyl. Very easily. Those are to be thought apparent which, appearing only at a distance, vanish upon a nearer approach.

Phil. And those, I suppose, are to be thought real which are discovered by the most near and exact survey.

Hyl. Right.

Phil. Is the nearest and exactest survey made by the help of a microscope, or by the naked eye?

Hyl. By a microscope, doubtless.

Phil. But a microscope often discovers colours in an object different from those perceived by the unassisted sight. And, in case we had microscopes magnifying to any assigned degree, it is certain that no object whatever, viewed through them, would appear in the same colour which it exhibits to the naked eye.

Hyl. And what will you conclude from all this? You cannot argue that there are really and naturally no colours on objects: because by artificial managements they may be altered, or made to vanish.

Phil. I think it may evidently be concluded from your own concessions, that all the colours we see with our naked eyes are only apparent as those on the clouds, since they vanish upon a more close and accurate inspection which is afforded us by a microscope. Then, as to what you say by way of prevention: I ask you whether the real and natural state of an object is better discovered by a very sharp and piercing sight, or by one which is less sharp?

Hyl. By the former without doubt.

Phil. Is it not plain from *Dioptrics* that microscopes make the sight more penetrating, and represent objects as they would appear to the eye in case it were naturally endowed with a most exquisite sharpness?

Hyl. It is.

Phil. Consequently the microscopical representation is to be thought that which best sets forth the real nature of the thing, or what it is in itself. The colours, therefore, by it perceived are more genuine and real than those perceived otherwise.

Hyl. I confess there is something in what you say.

Phil. Besides, it is not only possible but manifest, that there actually are animals whose eyes are by nature framed to perceive those things which by reason of there minuteness escape our sight. What think you of those inconceivably small animals perceived by glasses? must we suppose they are all stark blind? Or, in case they see, can it be imagined their sight hath not the same use in preserving their bodies from injuries, which appears in that of all other animals? And if it hath, is it not evident they must see particles less than their own bodies; which will present them with a far different view in each object from that which strikes our senses? Even our own eyes do not always represent objects to us after the same manner. In the jaundice every one knows that all things seem yellow. Is it not therefore highly probably those animals in whose eyes we discern a very different texture from that of ours, and whose bodies abound with different humours, do not see the same colours in every object that we do? From all which, should it not seem to follow that all colours are equally apparent, and that none of those which we perceive are really inherent in any outward object?

Hyl. It should.

Phil. The point will be past all doubt, if you consider that, in case colours were real properties or affections inherent in external bodies, they could admit of no alteration without some change wrought in the very bodies themselves: but, is it not evident from what hath been said that, upon the use of microscopes, upon a change happening in the humours of the eye, or a variation of distance, without any manner of real alteration in the thing itself, the colours of any object are either changed, or totally disappear? Nay, all other circumstances remaining the same, change but the situation of some objects, and they shall present different colours to the eye. The same thing happens upon viewing an object in various degrees of light. And what is more known than that the same bodies appear differently coloured by candlelight from what they do in the open day? Add to these the experiment of a prism which, separating the heterogeneous rays of light, alters the colour of any object, and will cause the whitest to appear of a deep blue or red to the naked eye. And now tell me whether you are still of opinion that every body hath its true real colour inhering in it; and, if you think it hath, I would fain know farther from you, what certain distance and position of the object, what peculiar texture and formation of the eye, what degree or kind of light is necessary for ascertaining that true colour, and distinguishing it from apparent ones.

Hyl. I own myself entirely satisfied, that they are all equally apparent, and that there is no such thing as colour really inhering in external bodies, but that it is altogether in the light. And what confirms me in this opinion is, that in proportion to the light colours are still more or less vivid; and if there be no light, then are there no colours perceived. Beside, allowing there are colours on external objects, yet, how is it possible for us to perceive them? For no external body affects the mind, unless it acts first on our organs of sense. But the only action of bodies is motion; and motion cannot be communicated otherwise than by impulse. A distant object therefore cannot act on the eye; nor consequently make itself or its properites perceivable to the soul. Whence it plainly follows that it is immediately some contiguous substance, which, operating on the eye, occasions a perception of colours: and such is light.

Phil. How! is light then a substance?

Hyl. I tell you, Philonous, external light is nothing but a thin fluid substance, whose minute particles being agitated with a brisk motion, and in various manners reflected from the different surfaces of outward objects to the eyes, communicate different motions to the optic nerves; which, being propagated to the brain, cause therein various impressions; and these are attended with the sensations of red, blue, yellow, &c.

Phil. It seems then the light doth no more than shake the optic nerves.

Hyl. Nothing else.

Phil. And consequent to each particular motion of the nerves, the mind is affected with a sensation, which is some particular colour.

Hyl. Right.

Phil. And these sensations have no existence without the mind.

Hyl. They have not.

Phil. How then do you affirm that colours are in the light; since by *light* you understand a corporeal substance external to the mind?

Hyl. Light and colours, as immediately perceived by us, I grant cannot exist without the mind. But in themselves they are only the motions and configurations of certain insensible particles of matter.

Phil. Colours then, in the vulgar sense, or taken for the immediate objects of sight, cannot agree to any but a perceiving substance.

Hyl. That is what I say.

Phil. Well then, since you give up the point as to those sensible qualities which are alone thought colours by all mankind beside, you may hold what you please with regard to those invisible ones of the philosophers. It is not my business to dispute about *them;* only I would advise you to bethink yourself, whether, considering the inquiry we are upon, it be prudent for you to affirm—*the red and blue which we see are not real colours, but certain unknown motions and figures which no man ever did or can see are truly so.* Are not these shocking notions, and are not they subject to as many ridiculous inferences, as those you were obliged to renounce before in the case of sounds?

Hyl. I frankly own, Philonous, that it is in vain to stand out any longer. Colours, sounds, tastes, in a word all those termed *secondary qualities,* have certainly no existence without the mind. But by this acknowledgement I must not be supposed to derogate anything from the reality of Matter, or external objects; seeing it is no more than several philosophers maintain, who nevertheless are the farthest imaginable from denying Matter. For the clearer understanding of this, you must know sensible qualities are by philosophers divided into *Primary* and *Secondary*. The former are Extension, Figure, Solidity, Gravity, Motion, and Rest; and these they hold exist really in bodies. The latter are those above enumerated; or, briefly, *all sensible qualities beside the Primary;* which they assert are only so many sensations or ideas existing nowhere but in the mind. But all this, I doubt not, you are apprised of.

For my part, I have been a long time sensible there was such an opinion current among philosophers, but was never thoroughly convinced of its truth until now.

Phil. You are still then of opinion that *extension* and *figures* are inherent in external unthinking substances?

Hyl. I am.

Phil. But what if the same arguments which are brought against Secondary Qualities will hold good against these also?

Hyl. Why then I shall be obliged to think, they too exist only in the mind.

Phil. Is it your opinion the very figure and extension which you perceive by sense exist in the outward object or material substance?

Hyl. It is.

Phil. Have all other animals as good grounds to think the same of the figure and extension which they see and feel?

Hyl. Without doubt, if they have any thought at all.

Phil. Answer me, Hylas. Think you the senses were bestowed upon all animals for their preservation and well-being in life? or were they given to men alone for this end?

Hyl. I make no question but they have the same use in all other animals.

Phil. If so, is it not necessary they should be enabled by them to perceive their own limbs, and those bodies which are capable of harming them?

Hyl. Certainly.

Phil. A mite therefore must be supposed to see his own foot, and things equal or even less than it, as bodies of some considerable dimension; though at the same time they appear to you scarce discernible, or at best as so many visible points?

Hyl. I cannot deny it.

Phil. And to creatures less than the mite they will seem yet larger?

Hyl. They will.

Phil. Insomuch that what you can hardly discern will to another extremely minute animal appear as some huge mountain?

Hyl. All this I grant.

Phil. Can one and the same thing be at the same time in itself of different dimensions?

Hyl. That were absurd to imagine.

Phil. But, from what you have laid down it follows that both the extension by you perceived, and that perceived by the mite itself, as likewise all those perceived by lesser animals, are each of them the true extension of the mite's foot; that is to say, by your own principles you are led into an absurdity.

Hyl. There seems to be some difficulty in the point.

Phil. Again, have you not acknowledged that no real inherent property of any object can be changed without some change in the thing itself?

Hyl. I have.

Phil. But, as we approach to or recede from an object, the visible extension varies, being at one distance ten or a hundred times greater than at another. Doth it not therefore follow from hence likewise that it is not really inherent in the object?

Hyl. I own I am at a loss what to think.

Phil. Your judgment will soon be determined, if you will venture to think as freely concerning this quality as you have done concerning the rest. Was it not admitted as a good argument, that neither heat nor cold was in the water, because it seemed warm to one hand and cold to the other?

Hyl. It was.

Phil. Is it not the very same reasoning to conclude, there is no extension or figure in an object, because to one eye it shall seem little, smooth, and round, when at the same time it appears to the other, great, uneven, and angular?

Hyl. The very same. But does this latter fact ever happen?

Phil. You may at any time make the experiment, by looking with one eye bare, and with the other through a microscope.

Hyl. I know not how to maintain it; and yet I am loath to give up *extension*, I see so many odd consequences following upon such a concession.

Phil. Odd, say you? After the concessions already made, I hope you will stick at nothing for its oddness. But, on the other hand, should it not seem very odd, if the general reasoning which includes all other sensible qualities did not also include extension? If it be allowed that no idea, nor anything like an idea, can exist in an unperceiving substance, then surely it follows that no figure, or mode of extension, which we can either perceive, or imagine, or have any idea of, can be really inherent in Matter; not to mention the peculiar difficulty there must be in conceiving a material substance, prior to and distinct from extension, to be the *substratum* of extension. Be the sensible quality what it will—figure, or sound, or colour, it seems alike impossible it should subsist in that which doth not perceive it.

Hyl. I give up the point for the present, reserving still a right to retract my opinion, in case I shall hereafter discover any false step in my progress to it.

Phil. That is a right you cannot be denied. Figures and extension being despatched, we proceed next to *motion*. Can a real motion in any external body be at the same time both very swift and very slow?

Hyl. It cannot.

Phil. Is not the motion of a body swift in a reciprocal proportion to the time it takes up in describing any given space? Thus a body that describes a mile in an hour moves three times faster than it would in case it described only a mile in three hours.

Hyl. I agree with you.

Phil. And is not time measured by the succession of ideas in our minds?

Hyl. It is.

Phil. And is it not possible ideas should succeeed one another twice as fast in your mind as they do in mine, or in that of some spirit of another kind?

Hyl. I own it.

Phil. Consequently the same body may to another seem to perform its motion over any space in half the time that it doth to you. And the same reasoning will hold as to any other proportion: that is to say, according to your principles (since the motions perceived are both really in the object) it is possible one and the same body shall be really moved the same way at once, both very swift and very slow. How is this consistent either with common sense, or with what you just now granted?

Hyl. I have nothing to say to it.

Phil. Then as for *solidity*; either you do not mean any sensible quality by that word, and so it is beside our inquiry: or if you do, it must be either hardness or resistance. But both the one and the other are plainly relative to our senses: it being evident that what seems hard to one animal may appear soft to another, who hath greater force and firmness of limbs. Nor is it less plain that the resistance I feel is not in the body.

Hyl. I own the very *sensation* of resistance, which is all you immediately perceive, is not in the body; but the *cause* of that sensation is.

Phil. But the causes of our sensations are not things immediately perceived, and therefore are not sensible. This point I thought had been already determined.

Hyl. I own it was; but you will pardon me if I seem a little embarrassed: I know not how to quit my old notions.

Phil. To help you out, do but consider that if *extension* be once acknowledged to have no existence without the mind, the same must necessarily be granted of motion, solidity, and gravity; since they all evidently suppose extension. It is therefore superfluous, to inquire particularly concerning each of them. In denying extension, you have denied them all to have any real existence.

Hyl. I wonder, Philonous, if what you say be true, why those philosophers who deny the Secondary Qualities any real existence should yet attribute it to the Primary. If there is no difference between them, how can this be accounted for?

Phil. It is not my business to account for every opinion of the philosophers. But, among other reasons which may be assigned for this, it seems probable that pleasure and pain being rather annexed to the former than the latter may be one. Heat and cold, tastes and smells, have something more vividly pleasing or disagreeable than the ideas of extension, figure, and motion affect us with. And, it being too visibly absurd to hold that pain or pleasure can be in an unperceiving Subtance, men are more easily weaned from believing the external existence of the Secondary than the Primary Qualities. You will be satisfied there is something in this, if you recollect the difference you made between an intense and more moderate degree of heat; allowing the one a real existence, while you denied it to the other. But, after all, there is no rational ground for that distinction; for, surely an indifferent sensation is as truly *a sensation* as one more pleasing or painful; and consequently should not any more than they be supposed to exist in an unthinking subject.

Hyl. It is just come into my head, Philonous, that I have somewhere heard of a distinction between absolute and sensible extension. Now, though it be acknowledged that *great* and *small,* consisting merely in the relation which other extended beings have to the parts of our own bodies, do not really inhere in the substances themselves; yet nothing obliges us to hold the same with regard to *absolute extension,* which is something abstracted from *great* and *small,* from this or that particular magnitude or figure. So likewise as to motion; *swift* and *slow* are altogether relative to the succession of ideas in our own minds. But, it doth not follow, because those modifications of motion exist not without the mind, that therefore absolute motion abstracted from them doth not.

Phil. Pray what is it that distinguishes one motion, or one part of extension, from another? Is it not something sensible, as some degree of swiftness or slowness, some certain magnitude or figure peculiar to each?

Hyl. I think so.

Phil. These qualities, therefore, stripped of all sensible properties, are without all specific and numerical differences, as the schools call them.

Hyl. They are.

Phil. That is to say, they are extension in general, and motion in general.

Hyl. Let it be so.

Phil. But it is a universally received maxim that *Everything which exists is particular.* How then can motion in general, or extension in general, exist in any corporeal substance?

Hyl. I will take time to solve your difficulty.

Phil. But I think the point may be speedily decided. Without doubt you can tell whether you are able to frame this or that idea. Now I am content to put our dispute on this issue. If you can frame in your thoughts a distinct *abstract idea* of motion or extension, divested of all those sensible modes, as swift and slow, great and small, round and square, and the like, which are acknowledged to exist only in the mind, I will then yield the point you contend for. But if you cannot, it will be unreasonable on your side to insist any longer upon what you have no notion of.

Hyl. To confess ingenuously, I cannot.

Phil. Can you even separate the ideas of extension and motion from the ideas of all those qualities which they who make the distinction term *secondary?*

Hyl. What! is it not an easy matter to consider extension and motion by themselves, abstracted from all other sensible qualities? Pray how do the mathematicians treat of them?

Phil. I acknowledge, Hylas, it is not difficult to form general propositions and reasonings about those qualities, without mentioning any other; and, in this sense, to consider or treat of them abstractedly. But, how doth it follow that, because I can pronounce the word *motion* by itself, I can form the idea of it in my mind exclusive of body? or, because theorems may be great of extension and figures, without any mention of *great* or *small*, or any other sensible mode or quality, that therefore it is possible such an abstract idea of extension, without any particular size or figure, or sensible quality, should be distinctly formed, and apprehended by the mind? Mathematicians treat of quantity, without regarding what other sensible qualities it is attended with, as being altogether indifferent to their demonstrations. But, when laying aside the words, they contemplate the bare ideas, I believe you will find, they are not the pure abstracted ideas of extension.

Hyl. But what say you to *pure intellect?* May not abstracted ideas be framed by that faculty?

Phil. Since I cannot frame abstract ideas at all, it is plain I cannot frame them by the help of *pure intellect,* whatsoever faculty you understand by those words. Besides, not to inquire into the nature of pure intellect and its spiritual objects, as *virtue, reason, God,* or the like, thus much seems manifest —that sensible things are only to be perceived by sense, or represented by the imagination. Figures, therefore, and extension, being originally perceived by sense, do not belong to pure intellect: but, for your farther satisfaction, try if you can frame the idea of any figure, abstracted from all particularities of size, or even from other sensible qualities.

Hyl. Let me think a little—I do not find that I can.

Phil. And can you think it possible that should really exist in nature which implies a repugnancy in its conception?

Hyl. By no means.

Phil. Since therefore it is impossible even for the mind to disunite the ideas of extension and motion from all other sensible qualities, doth it not follow, that where the one exist there necessarily the other exist likewise?

Hyl. It should seem so.

Phil. Consequently, the very same arguments which you admitted as conclusive against the Secondary Qualities are, without any farther application of force, against the Primary too. Besides, if you will trust your senses, is it not plain all sensible qualities coexist, or to them appear as being in the same place? Do they ever represent a motion, or figure, as being divested of all other visible and tangible qualities?

Hyl. You need say no more on this head. I am free to own, if there be no secret error or oversight in our proceedings hitherto, that *all* sensible qualities are alike to be denied existence without the mind. But, my fear is that I have been too liberal in my former concessions, or overlooked some fallacy or other. In short, I did not take time to think.

Phil. For that matter, Hylas, you may take what time you please in reviewing the progress of our inquiry. You are at liberty to recover any slips you might have made, or offer whatever you have omitted which makes for your first opinion.

Hyl. One great oversight I take to be this—that I did not sufficiently distinguish the *object* from the *sensation*. Now, though this latter may not exist without the mind, yet it will not thence follow that the former cannot.

Phil. What object do you mean? the object of the senses?

Hyl. The same.

Phil. It is then immediately perceived?

Hyl. Right.

Phil. Make me to understand the difference between what is immediately perceived and a sensation.

Hyl. The sensation I take to be an act of the mind perceiving; besides which, there is something perceived; and this I call the *object.* For example, there is red and yellow on that tulip. But then the act of perceiving those colours is in me only, and not in the tulip.

Phil. What tulip do you speak of? Is it that which you see?

Hyl. The same.

Phil. And what do you see beside colour, figure, and extension?

Hyl. Nothing.

Phil. What you would say then is that the red and yellow are coexistent with the extension; is it not?

Hyl. That is not all; I would say they have a real existence without the mind, in some unthinking substance.

Phil. That the colours are really in the tulip which I see is manifest. Neither can it be denied that this tulip may exist independent of your mind or mine; but, that any immediate object of the senses—that is, any idea, or combination of ideas—should exist in an unthinking substance, or exterior to *all* minds, is in itself an evident contradiction. Nor can I imagine how this follows from what you said just now, to wit, that the red and yellow were on the tulip *you saw*, since you do not pretend to *see* that unthinking substance.

Hyl. You have an artful way, Philonous, of diverting our inquiry from the subject.

Phil. I see you have no mind to be pressed that way. To return then to your distinction between *sensation* and *object;* if I take you right, you distinguish in every perception two things, the one an action of the mind, the other not.

Hyl. True.

Phil. And this action cannot exist in, or belong to, any unthinking thing; but, whatever beside is implied in a perception may?

Hyl. That is my meaning.

Phil. So that if there was a perception without any act of the mind, it were possible such a perception should exist in an unthinking substance?

Hyl. I grant it. But it is impossible there should be such a perception.

Phil. When is the mind said to be active?

Hyl. When it produces, puts an end to, or changes, anything.

Phil. Can the mind produce, discontinue, or change anything, but by an act of the will?

Hyl. It cannot.

Phil. The mind therefore is to be accounted *active* in its perceptions so far forth as *volition* is included in them?

Hyl. It is.

Phil. In plucking this flower I am active; because I do it by the motion of my hand, which was consequent upon my volition; so likewise in applying it to my nose. But is either of these smelling?

Hyl. No.

Phil. I act too in drawing the air through my nose; because my breathing so rather than otherwise is the effect of my volition. But neither can this be called *smelling:* for, if it were, I should smell every time I breathed in that manner?

Hyl. True.

Phil. Smelling then is somewhat consequent to all this?

Hyl. It is.

Phil. But I do not find my will concerned any farther. Whatever more there is—as that I perceive such a particular smell, or any smell at all—this is independent of my will, and therein I am altogether passive. Do you find it otherwise with you, Hylas?

Hyl. No, the very same.

Phil. Then, as to seeing, is it not in your power to open your eyes, or keep them shut; to turn them this or that way?

Hyl. Without doubt.

Phil. But, doth it in like manner depend on *your* will that in looking on this flower you perceive *white* rather than any other colour? Or, directing your open eyes towards yonder part of the heaven, can you avoid seeing the sun? Or is light or darkness the effect of your volition?

Hyl. No, certainly.

Phil. You are then in these respects altogether passive?

Hyl. I am.

Phil. Tell me now, whether *seeing* consists in perceiving light and colours, or in opening and turning the eyes?

Hyl. Without doubt, in the former.

Phil. Since therefore you are in the very perception of light and colours altogether passive, what is become of that action you were speaking of as an ingredient in every sensation? And, doth it not follow your own concessions, that the perception of light and colours, including no action in it, may exist in an unperceiving substance? And is not this a plain contradiction?

Hyl. I know not what to think of it.

Phil. Besides, since you distinguish the *active* and *passive* in every perception, you must do it in that of pain. But how is it possible that pain, be it as little active as you please, should exist in an unperceiving substance? In short, do but consider the point, and then confess ingenuously, whether light and colours, tastes, sounds, &c. are not all equally passions or sensations in the soul. You may indeed call them *external objects,* and give them in words what subsistence you please. But, examine your own thoughts, and then tell me whether it be not as I say?

Hyl. I acknowledge, Philonous, that, upon a fair observation of what passes in my mind, I can discover nothing else but that I am a thinking being, affected with variety of sensations; neither is it possible to conceive how a sensation should exist in an unperceiving substance.—But then, on the other hand, when I look on sensible things in a different view, considering them as so many modes and qualities, I find it necessary to suppose a *material substratum,* without which they cannot be conceived to exist.

Phil. Material substratum call you it? Pray, by which of your senses came you acquainted with that being?

Hyl. It is not itself sensible; its modes and qualities only being perceived by the senses.

Phil. I presume then it was by reflexion and reason you obtained the idea of it?

Hyl. I do not pretend to any proper positive *idea* of it. However, I conclude it exists, because qualities cannot be conceived to exist without a support.

Phil. It seems then you have only a relative *notion* of it, or that you conceive it not otherwise than by conceiving the relation it bears to sensible qualities?

Hyl. Right.

Phil. Be pleased therefore to let me know wherein that relation consists.

Hyl. Is it not sufficiently expressed in the term *substratum,* or *substance?*

Phil. If so, the word *substratum* should import that it is spread under the sensible qualities or accidents?

Hyl. True.

Phil. And consequently under extension?

Hyl. I own it.

Phil. It is therefore somewhat in its own nature entirely distinct from extension?

Hyl. I tell you, extension is only a mode, and Matter is something that supports modes. And is it not evident the thing supported is different from the thing supporting?

Phil. So that something distinct from, and exclusive of, extension is supposed to be the *substratum* of extension?

Hyl. Just so.

Phil. Answer me, Hylas. Can a thing be spread without extension? or is not the idea of extension necessarily included in *spreading?*

Hyl. It is.

Phil. Whatsoever therefore you suppose spread under anything must have in itself an extension distinct from the extension of that thing under which it is spread?

Hyl. It must.

Phil. Consequently, every corporeal substance, being the

substratum of extension, must have in itself another extension, by which it is qualified to be a *substratum:* and so on to infinity? And I ask whether this be not absurd in itself, and repugnant to what you granted just now, to wit, that the *substratum* was something distinct from and exclusive of extension?

Hyl. Aye but, Philonous, you take me wrong. I do not mean that Matter is *spread* in a gross literal sense under extension. The word *substratum* is used only to express in general the same thing with *substance.*

Phil. Well then, let us examine the relation implied in the term *substance.* Is it not that it stands under accidents?

Hyl. The very same.

Phil. But, that one thing may stand under or support another, must it not be extended?

Hyl. It must.

Phil. Is not therefore this supposition liable to the same absurdity with the former?

Hyl. You still take things in a strict literal sense. That is not fair, Philonous.

Phil. I am not for imposing any sense on your words: you are at liberty to explain them as you please. Only, I beseech you, make me understand something by them. You tell me Matter supports or stands under accidents. How! is it as your legs support your body?

Hyl. No; that is the literal sense.

Phil. Pray let me know any sense, literal or not literal, that you understand it in.—How long must I wait for an answer, Hylas?

Hyl. I declare I know not what to say. I once thought I understood well enough what was meant by Matter's supporting accidents. But now, the more I think on it the less can I comprehend it: in short I find that I know nothing of it.

Phil. It seems then you have no idea at all, neither relative nor positive, of Matter; you know neither what it is in itself, nor what relation it bears to accidents?

Hyl. I acknowledge it.

Phil. And yet you asserted that you could not conceive how qualities or accidents should really exist, without conceiving at the same time a material support of them?

Hyl. I did.

Phil. That is to say, when you conceive the *real* existence of qualities, you do withal conceive Something which you cannot conceive?

Hyl. It was wrong, I own. But still I fear there is some fallacy or other. Pray what think you of this? It is just come into my head that the ground of all our mistake lies in your treating of each quality by itself. Now, I grant that each quality cannot singly subsist without the mind. Colour cannot without extension, neither can figure without some other sensible quality. But, as the several qualities united or blended together form entire sensible things, nothing hinders why such things may not be supposed to exist without the mind.

Phil. Either, Hylas, you are jesting, or have a very bad memory. Though indeed we went through all the qualities by name one after another, yet my arguments, or rather your concessions, nowhere tend to prove that the Secondary Qualities did not subsist each alone by itself; but, that they were not *at all* without the mind. Indeed, in treating of figure and motion we concluded they could not exist without the mind, because it was impossible even in thought to separate them from all secondary qualities, so as to conceive them existing by themselves. But then this was not the only argument made use of upon that occasion. But (to pass by all that hath been hitherto said, and reckon it for nothing, if you will have it so) I am content to put the whole upon this issue. If you can conceive it possible for any mixture or combination of qualities, or any sensible object whatever, to exist without the mind, then I will grant it actually to be so.

Hyl. If it comes to that the point will soon be decided. What more easy than to conceive a tree or house existing by itself, independent of, and unperceived by, any mind whatsoever? I do at this present time conceive them existing after that manner.

Phil. How say you, Hylas, can you see a thing which is at the same time unseen?

Hyl. No, that were a contradiction.

Phil. Is it not as great a contradiction to talk of *conceiving* a thing which is *unconceived*?

Hyl. It is.

Phil. The tree or house therefore which you think of is conceived by you?

Hyl. How should it be otherwise?

Phil. And what is conceived is surely in the mind?

Hyl. Without question, that which is conceived is in the mind.

Phil. How then came you to say, you conceived a house or tree existing independent and out of all minds whatsoever?

Hyl. That was I own an oversight; but stay, let me consider what led me into it.—It is a pleasant mistake enough. As I was thinking of a tree in a solitary place, where no one was present to see it, methought that was to conceive a tree as existing unperceived or unthought of; not considering that I myself conceived it all the while. But now I plainly see that all I can do is to frame ideas in my own mind. I may indeed conceive in my own thoughts the idea of a tree, or a house, or a mountain, but that is all. And this is far from proving that I can conceive them *existing out of the minds of all Spirits.*

Phil. You acknowledge then that you cannot possibly conceive how any one corporeal sensible thing should exist otherwise than in a mind?

Hyl. I do.

Phil. And yet you will earnestly contend for the truth of that which you cannot so much as conceive?

Hyl. I profess I know not what to think; but still there are some scruples remain with me. Is it not certain I *see things at a distance?* Do we not perceive the stars and moon, for example, to be a great way off? Is not this, I say, manifest to the senses?

Phil. Do you not in a dream too perceive those or the like objects?

Hyl. I do.

Phil. And have they not then the same appearance of being distant?

Hyl. They have.

Phil. But you do not thence conclude the apparitions in a dream to be without the mind?

Hyl. By no means.

Phil. You ought not therefore to conclude that sensible objects are without the mind, from their appearance, or manner wherein they are perceived.

Hyl. I acknowledge it. But doth not my sense deceive me in those cases?

Phil. By no means. The idea or thing which you immediately perceive, neither sense nor reason informs you that *it* actually exists without the mind. By sense you only know that you are affected with such certain sensations of light and colours, &c. And these you will not say are without the mind.

Hyl. True: but, beside all that, do you not think the sight suggests something of *outness* or *distance*?

Phil. Upon approaching a distant object, do the visible size and figure change perpetually, or do they appear the same at all distances?

Hyl. They are in a continual change.

Phil. Sight therefore doth not suggest, or any way inform you, that the visible object you immediately perceive exists at a distance,[1] or will be perceived when you advance farther onward; there being a continued series of visible objects succeeding each other during the whole time of your approach.

Hyl. It doth not; but still I know, upon seeing an object, what object I shall perceive after having passed over a certain distance: no matter whether it be exactly the same or no: there is still something of distance suggested in the case.

Phil. Good Hylas, do but reflect a little on the point, and then tell me whether there be any more in it than this: From the ideas you actually perceive by sight, you have by experience learned to collect what other ideas you will (according to the standing order of nature) be affected with, after such a certain succession of time and motion.

Hyl. Upon the whole, I take it to be nothing else.

Phil. Now, is it not plain that if we suppose a man born blind was on a sudden made to see, he could at first have no experience of what may be *suggested* by sight?

Hyl. It is.

Phil. He would not then, according to you, have any notion of distance annexed to the things he saw; but would take them for a new set of sensations, existing only in his mind?

Hyl. It is undeniable.

Phil. But, to make it still more plain: is not *distance* a line turned endwise to the eye?

Hyl. It is.

Phil. And can a line so situated be perceived by sight?

Hyl. It cannot.

[1] See the *Essay towards a New Theory of Vision*, and its *Vindication*.

Phil. Doth it not therefore follow that distance is not properly and immediately perceived by sight?

Hyl. It should seem so.

Phil. Again, is it your opinion that colours are at a distance?

Hyl. It must be acknowledged they are only in the mind.

Phil. But do not colours appear to the eye as coexisting in the same place with extension and figures?

Hyl. They do.

Phil. How can you then conclude from sight that figures exist without, when you acknowledge colours do not; the sensible appearance being the very same with regard to both?

Hyl. I know not what to answer.

Phil. But, allowing that distance was truly and immediately perceived by the mind, yet it would not thence follow it existed out of the mind. For, whatever is immediately perceived is an idea: and can any idea exist out of the mind?

Hyl. To suppose that were absurd: but, inform me, Philonous, can we perceive or know nothing beside our ideas?

Phil. As for the rational deducing of causes from effects, that is beside our inquiry. And, by the senses you can best tell whether you perceive anything which is not immediately perceived. And I ask you, whether the things immediately perceived are other than your own sensations or ideas? You have indeed more than once, in the course of this conversation, declared yourself on those points; but you seem, by this last question, to have departed from what you then thought.

Hyl. To speak the truth, Philonous, I think there are two kinds of objects:—the one perceived immediately, which are likewise called *ideas;* the other are real things or external objects, perceived by the mediation of ideas, which are their images and representations. Now, I own ideas do not exist without the mind; but the latter sort of objects do. I am sorry I did not think of this distinction sooner; it would probably have cut short your discourse.

Phil. Are those external objects perceived by sense, or by some other faculty?

Hyl. They are perceived by sense.

Phil. How! Is there anything perceived by sense which is not immediately perceived?

Hyl. Yes, Philonous, in some sort there is. For example, when I look on a picture or statue of Julius Cæsar, I may be said after a manner to perceive him (though not immediately) by my senses.

Phil. It seems then you will have our ideas, which alone are immediately perceived, to be pictures of external things: and that these also are perceived by sense, inasmuch as they have a conformity or resemblance to our ideas?

Hyl. That is my meaning.

Phil. And, in the same way that Julius Cæsar, in himself invisible, is nevertheless perceived by sight; real things, in themselves imperceptible, are perceived by sense.

Hyl. In the very same.

Phil. Tell me, Hylas, when you behold the picture of Julius Cæsar, do you see with your eyes any more than some colours and figures, with a certain symmetry and composition of the whole?

Hyl. Nothing else.

Phil. And would not a man who had never known anything of Julius Cæsar see as much?

Hyl. He would.

Phil. Consequently he hath his sight, and the use of it, in as perfect a degree as you?

Hyl. I agree with you.

Phil. Whence comes it then that your thoughts are directed to the Roman emperor, and his are not? This cannot proceed from the sensations or ideas of sense by you then perceived; since you acknowledge you have no advantage over him in that respect. It should seem therefore to proceed from reason and memory: should it not?

Hyl. It should.

Phil. Consequently, it will not follow from that instance that anything is perceived by sense which is not immediately perceived. Though I grant we may, in one acceptation, be said to perceive sensible things mediately by sense: that is, when, from a frequently perceived connexion, the immediate perception of ideas by one sense *suggests* to the mind others, perhaps belonging to another sense, which are wont to be connected with them. For instance, when I hear a coach drive along the streets, immediately I perceive only the sound; but, from the experience I have had that such a sound is connected with a coach, I am said to hear the coach. It is nevertheless evident that, in truth and strictness, nothing can be *heard* but *sound;* and the coach is not then properly perceived by sense, but suggested from experience. So likewise when we are said to see a red-hot bar of iron; the solidity and heat of the iron are not the objects of sight, but suggested to the imagination by the colour and figure which are properly perceived by that sense. In short, those things alone are actually and strictly perceived by any sense, which would have been perceived in case that same sense had then been first conferred on us. As for other things, it is plain they are only suggested to the mind by experience, grounded on former conceptions. But, to return to your comparison of Cæsar's picture, it is plain, if you keep to that, you must hold the real things, or archetypes of our ideas, are not perceived by sense, but by some internal faculty of the soul, as reason or memory. I would therefore fain know what arguments you can draw from reason for the existence of what you call *real things* or *material objects*. Or, whether you remember to have seen them formerly as they are in themselves; or, if you have heard or read of any one that did.

Hyl. I see, Philonous, you are disposed to raillery; but that will never convince me.

Phil. My aim is only to learn from you the way to come at the knowledge of *material beings*. Whatever we perceive is perceived immediately or mediately: by sense, or by reason and reflexion. But, as you have excluded sense, pray shew me what reason you have to believe their existence; or what *medium* you can possibly make use of to prove it, either to mine or your own understanding.

Hyl. To deal ingenuously, Philonous, now I consider the point, I do not find I can give you any good reason for it. But, thus much seems pretty plain, that it is at least possible such things may really exist. And, as long as there is no absurdity in supposing them, I am resolved to believe as I did, till you bring good reasons to the contrary.

Phil. What! Is it come to this, that you only *believe* the existence of material objects, and that your belief is founded barely on the possibility of its being true? Then you will have me bring reasons against it: though another would think it reasonable the proof should lie on him who holds the affirmative. And, after all, this very point which you are now resolved to maintain, without any reason, is in effect what you have more than once during this discourse seen good reason to give up. But, to pass over all this; if I understand you rightly, you say our ideas do not exist without the mind, but that they are copies, images, or representations, of certain originals that do?

Hyl. You take me right.

Phil. They are then like external things?

Hyl. They are.

Phil. Have those things a stable and permanent nature, independent of our senses; or are they in a perpetual change, upon our producing any motions in our bodies—suspending, exerting, or altering, our faculties or organs of sense?

Hyl. Real things, it is plain, have a fixed and real nature, which remains the same notwithstanding any change in our senses, or in the posture and motion of our bodies; which indeed may affect the ideas in our minds; but it were absurd to think they had the same effect on things existing without the mind.

Phil. How then is it possible that things perpetually fleeting and variable as our ideas should be copies or images of anything fixed and constant? Or, in other words, since all sensible qualities, as size, figure, colour, &c., that is, our ideas, are continually changing, upon every alteration in the distance, medium, or instruments of sensation; how can any determinate material objects be properly represented or painted forth by several distinct things, each of which is so different from and unlike the rest? Or, if you say it resembles some one only of our ideas, how shall we be able to distinguish the true copy from all the false ones?

Hyl. I profess, Philonous, I am at a loss. I know not what to say to this.

Phil. But neither is this all. Which are material objects in themselves—perceptible or imperceptible?

Hyl. Properly and immediately nothing can be perceived but ideas. All material things, therefore, are in themselves insensible, and to be perceived only by our ideas.

Phil. Ideas then are sensible, and their archetypes or originals insensible?

Hyl. Right.

Phil. But how can that which is sensible be *like* that which is insensible? Can a real thing, in itself *invisible*, be like a *colour;* or a real thing, which is not *audible*, be like a *sound?* In a word, can anything be like a sensation or idea, but another sensation or idea?

Hyl. I must own, I think not.

Phil. Is it possible there should be any doubt on the point? Do you not perfectly know your own ideas?

Hyl. I know them perfectly; since what I do not perceive or know can be no part of my idea.

Phil. Consider, therefore, and examine them, and then tell me if there be anything in them which can exist without the mind: or if you can conceive anything like them existing without the mind.

Hyl. Upon inquiry, I find it is impossible for me to conceive or understand how anything but an idea can be like an idea. And it is most evident that *no idea can exist without the mind.*

Phil. You are therefore, by your principles, forced to deny the *reality* of sensible things; since you made it to consist in an absolute existence exterior to the mind. That is to say, you are a downright sceptic. So I have gained my point, which was to shew your principles led to Scepticism.

Hyl. For the present I am, if not entirely convinced, at least silenced.

Phil. I would fain know what more you would require in order to a perfect conviction. Have you not had the liberty of explaining yourself all manner of ways? Were any little slips in discourse laid hold and insisted on? Or were you not allowed to retract or reinforce anything you had offered, as best served your purpose? Hath not everything you could say been heard and examined with all the fairness imaginable? In a word, have you not in every point been convinced out of your own mouth? And, if you can at present discover any flaw in any of your former concessions, or think of any remaining subterfuge, any new distinction, colour, or comment whatsoever, why do you not produce it?

Hyl. A little patience, Philonous. I am at present so amazed to see myself ensnared, and as it were imprisoned in the labyrinths you have drawn me into, that on the sudden it cannot be expected I should find my way out. You must give me time to look about me and recollect myself.

Phil. Hark; is not this the college bell?

Hyl. It rings for prayers.

Phil. We will go in then, if you please, and meet here again to-morrow morning. In the meantime, you may employ your thoughts on this morning's discourse, and try if you can find any fallacy in it, or invent any new means to extricate yourself.

Hyl. Agreed.

The Second Dialogue

Hylas. I beg your pardon, Philonous, for not meeting you sooner. All this morning my head was so filled with our late conversation that I had not leisure to think of the time of the day, or indeed of anything else.

Philonous. I am glad you were so intent upon it, in hopes if there were any mistakes in your concessions, or fallacies in my reasonings from them, you will now discover them to me.

Hyl. I assure you I have done nothing ever since I saw you but search after mistakes and fallacies, and, with that view, have minutely examined the whole series of yesterday's discourse: but all in vain, for the notions it led me into, upon review, appear still more clear and evident; and, the more I consider them, the more irresistibly do they force my assent.

Phil. And is not this, think you, a sign that they are genuine, that they proceed from nature, and are conformable to right reason? Truth and beauty are in this alike, that the strictest survey sets them both off to advantage; while the false lustre of error and disguise cannot endure being reviewed, or too nearly inspected.

Hyl. I own there is a great deal in what you say. Nor can any one be more entirely satisfied of the truth of those odd consequences, so long as I have in view the reasonings that lead to them. But, when these are out of my thoughts, there seems, on the other hand, something so satisfactory, so natural and intelligible, in the modern way of explaining things that, I profess, I know not how to reject it.

Phil. I know not what way you mean.

Hyl. I mean the way of accounting for our sensations or ideas.

Phil. How is that?

Hyl. It is supposed the soul makes her residence in some part of the brain, from which the nerves take their rise, and are thence extended to all parts of the body; and that outward objects, by the different impressions they make on the organs of sense, communicate certain vibrative motions to the nerves; and these being filled with spirits propagate them to the brain or seat of the soul, which, according to the various impressions or traces thereby made in the brain, is variously affected with ideas.

Phil. And call you this an explication of the manner whereby we are affected with ideas?

Hyl. Why not, Philonous? Have you anything to object against it?

Phil. I would first know whether I rightly understood your hypothesis. You make certain traces in the brain to be the causes or occasions of our ideas. Pray tell me whether by the *brain* you mean any sensible thing.

Hyl. What else think you I could mean?

Phil. Sensible things are all immediately perceivable; and those things which are immediately perceivable are ideas; and these exist only in the mind. Thus much you have, if I mistake not, long since agreed to.

Hyl. I do not deny it.

Phil. The brain therefore you speak of, being a sensible thing, exists only in the mind. Now, I would fain know whether you think it reasonable to suppose that one idea or thing existing in the mind occasions all other ideas. And, if you think so, pray how do you account for the origin of that primary idea or brain itself?

Hyl. I do not explain the origin of our ideas by that brain which is perceivable to sense—this being itself only a combination of sensible ideas—but by another which I imagine.

Phil. But are not things imagined as truly *in the mind* as things perceived?

Hyl. I must confess they are.

Phil. It comes, therefore, to the same thing; and you have been all this while accounting for ideas by certain motions or impressions of the brain; that is, by some alterations in an idea, whether sensible or imaginable it matters not.

Hyl. I begin to suspect my hypothesis.

Phil. Besides spirits, all that we know or conceive are our own ideas. When, therefore, you say all ideas are occasioned by impressions in the brain, do you conceive this brain or no? If you do, then you talk of ideas imprinted in an idea causing that same idea, which is absurd. If you do not conceive it, you talk unintelligibly, instead of forming a reasonable hypothesis.

Hyl. I now clearly see it was a mere dream. There is nothing in it.

Phil. You need not be much concerned at it; for after all, this way of explaining things, as you called it, could never have satisfied any reasonable man. What connexion is there between a motion in the nerves, and the sensations of sound or colour in the mind? Or how is it possible these should be the effect of that?

Hyl. But I could never think it had so little in it as now it seems to have.

Phil. Well then, are you at length satisfied that no sensible things have a real existence; and that you are in truth an arrant sceptic?

Hyl. It is too plain to be denied.

Phil. Look! are not the fields covered with a delightful verdure? Is there not something in the woods and groves, in the rivers and clear springs, that soothes, that delights, that transports the soul? At the prospect of the wide and deep ocean, or some huge mountain whose top is lost in the clouds, or of an old gloomy forest, are not our minds filled with a pleasing horror? Even in rocks and deserts is there not an agreeable wildness? How sincere a pleasure is it to behold the natural beauties of the earth! To preserve and renew our relish for them, is not the veil of night alternately drawn over her face, and doth she not change her dress with the seasons? How aptly are the elements disposed! What variety and use in the meanest productions of nature! What delicacy, what beauty, what contrivance, in animal and vegetable bodies! How exquisitely are all things suited, as well to their particular ends, as to constitute opposite parts of the whole! And, while they mutually aid and support, do they not also set off and illustrate each other? Raise now your thoughts from this ball of earth to all those glorious luminaries that adorn the high arch of heaven. The motion and situation of the planets, are they not admirable for use and order? Were those (miscalled *erratic*) globes ever known to stray, in their repeated journeys through the pathless void? Do they not measure areas round the sun ever proportioned to the times? So fixed, so immutable are the laws by which the unseen Author of nature actuates the universe. How vivid and radiant is the lustre of the fixed stars! How magnificent and rich that negligent profusion with which they appear to be scattered throughout the whole azure vault! Yet, if you take the telescope, it brings into your sight a new host of stars that escape the naked eye. Here they seem contiguous and minute, but to a nearer view immense orbs of light are various distances, far sunk in the abyss of space. Now you must call imagination to your aid. The feeble narrow sense cannot descry innumerable worlds revolving round the central fires; and in those worlds the energy of an all-perfect Mind displayed in endless forms. But, neither sense nor imagination are big enough to comprehend the boundless extent, with all its glittering furniture. Though the labouring mind exert and strain each power to its utmost reach, there still stands out ungrasped a surplusage immeasurable. Yet all the vast bodies that compose this mighty frame, how distant and remote soever, are by some secret mechanism, some Divine art and force, linked in a mutual dependence and intercourse with each other; even with this earth, which was almost slipt from my thoughts and lost in the crowd of worlds. Is not the whole system immense, beautiful, glorious beyond expression and beyond thought! What treatment, then, do those philosophers deserve, who would deprive these noble and delightful scenes of all *reality*? How should those Principles be entertained that lead us to think all the visible beauty of the creation a false imaginary glare? To be plain, can you expect this Scepticism of yours will not be thought extravagantly absurd by all men of sense?

Hyl. Other men may think as they please; but for your part you have nothing to reproach me with. My comfort is, you are as much a sceptic as I am.

Phil. There, Hylas, I must beg leave to differ from you.

Hyl. What! Have you all along agreed to the premises, and do you now deny the conclusion, and leave me to maintain those paradoxes by myself which you led me into? This surely is not fair.

Phil. I deny that I agreed with you in those notions that led to Scepticism. You indeed said the *reality* of sensible things consisted in an *absolute existence out of the minds of spirits,* or distinct from their being perceived. And pursuant to this notion of reality, *you* are obliged to deny sensible things any real existence: that is, according to your own definition, you profess yourself a sceptic. But I neither said nor thought the reality of sensible things was to be defined after that manner. To me it is evident, for the reasons you allow, that sensible things cannot exist otherwise than in a mind or spirit. Whence I conclude, not that they have no real existence, but that, seeing they depend not on my thought, and have an existence distinct from being perceived by me, *there must be some other Mind wherein they exist.* As sure, therefore, as the sensible world really exists, so sure is there an infinite omnipresent Spirit who contains and supports it.

Hyl. What! This is no more than I and all Christians hold; nay, and all others too who believe there is a God, and that He knows and comprehends all things.

Phil. Aye, but here lies the difference. Men commonly believe that all things are known or perceived by God, because they believe the being of a God; whereas I, on the other side, immediately and necessarily conclude the being of a God, because all sensible things must be perceived by Him.

Hyl. But, so long as we all believe the same thing, what matter is it how we come by that belief?

Phil. But neither do we agree in the same opinion. For philosophers, though they acknowledge all corporeal beings to be perceived by God, yet they attribute to them an absolute subsistence distinct from their being perceived by any mind whatever; which I do not. Besides, is there no difference between saying, *There is a God, therefore He perceives all things;* and saying, *Sensible things do really exist; and, if they really exist, they are necessarily perceived by an infinite Mind: therefore there is an infinite Mind, or God?* This furnishes you with a direct and immediate demonstration, from a most evident principle, of the *being of a God.* Divines and philosophers had proved beyond all controversy, from the beauty and usefulness of the several parts of the creation, that it was the workmanship of God. But that—setting aside all help of astronomy and natural philosophy, all contemplation of the contrivance, order, and adjustment of things—an infinite Mind should be necessarily inferred from the bare *existence of the sensible world,* is an advantage to them only who have made this easy reflexion: That the sensible world is that which we perceive by our several senses; and that nothing is perceived by the senses beside ideas; and that no idea or archetype of an idea can exist otherwise than in a mind. You may now, without any laborious search into the sciences, without any subtlety of reason, or tedious length of discourse, oppose and baffle the most strenuous advocate for Atheism.

Those miserable refuges, whether in an eternal succession of unthinking causes and effects, or in a fortuitous concourse of atoms; those wild imaginations of Vanini, Hobbes, and Spinoza: in a word, the whole system of Atheism, is it not entirely overthrown, by this single reflexion on the repugnancy included in supposing the whole, or any part, even the most rude and shapeless, of the visible world, to exist without a Mind? Let any one of those abettors of impiety but look into his own thoughts, and there try if he can conceive how so much as a rock, a desert, a chaos, or confused jumble of atoms; how anything at all, either sensible or imaginable, can exist independent of a Mind, and he need go no farther to be convinced of his folly. Can anything be fairer than to put a dispute on such an issue, and leave it to a man himself to see if he can conceive, even in thought, what he holds to be true in fact, and from a notional to allow it a real existence?

Hyl. It cannot be denied there is something highly serviceable to religion in what you advance. But do you not think it looks very like a notion entertained by some eminent moderns,[1] of *seeing all things in God?*

Phil. I would gladly know that opinion: pray explain it to me.

Hyl. They conceive that the soul, being immaterial, is incapable of being united with material things, so as to perceive them in themselves; but that she perceives them by her union with the substance of God, which, being spiritual, is therefore purely intelligible, or capable of being the immediate object of a spirit's thought. Besides, the Divine essence contains in it perfections correspondent to each created being; and which are, for that reason, proper to exhibit or represent them to the mind.

Phil. I do not understand how our ideas, which are things altogether passive and inert, can be the essence, or any part (or like any part) of the essence or substance of God, who is an impassive, indivisible, pure, active being. Many more difficulties and objections there are which occur at first view against this hypothesis; but I shall only add, that it is liable to all the absurdities of the common hypothesis, in making a created world exist otherwise than in the mind of a Spirit. Beside all which it hath this peculiar to itself; that it makes

[1] [Malebranche.—Ed.]

that material world serve to no purpose. And, if it pass for a good argument against other hypotheses in the sciences, that they suppose Nature, or the Divine wisdom, to make something in vain, or do that by tedious roundabout methods which might have been performed in a much more easy and compendious way, what shall we think of that hypothesis which supposes the whole world made in vain?

Hyl. But what say you? Are not you too of opinion that we see all things in God? If I mistake not, what you advance comes near it.

Phil. Few men think; yet all have opinions. Hence men's opinions are superficial and confused. It is nothing strange that tenets which in themselves are ever so different, should nevertheless be confounded with each other, by those who do not consider them attentively. I shall not therefore be surprised if some men imagine that I run into the enthusiasm of Malebranche; though in truth I am very remote from it. He builds on the most abstract general ideas, which I entirely disclaim. He asserts an absolute external world, which I deny. He maintains that we are deceived by our senses, and know not the real natures or the true forms and figures of extended beings; of all which I hold the direct contrary. So that upon the whole there are no Principles more fundamentally opposite than his and mine. It must be owned that I entirely agree with what the holy Scripture saith, "That in God we live and move and have our being." But that we see things in His essence, after the manner above set forth, I am far from believing. Take here in brief my meaning:—It is evident that the things I perceive are my own ideas, and that no idea can exist unless it be in a mind: nor is it less plain that these ideas or things by me perceived, either themselves or their archetypes, exist independently of *my* mind, since I know myself not to be their author, it being out of my power to determine at pleasure what particular ideas I shall be affected with upon opening my eyes or ears: they must therefore exist in some other Mind, whose Will it is they should be exhibited to me. The things, I say, immediately perceived are ideas or sensations, call them which you will. But how can any idea or sensation exist in, or be produced by, anything but a mind or spirit? This indeed is inconceivable. And to assert that which is inconceivable is to talk nonsense: is it not?

Hyl. Without doubt.

Phil. But, on the other hand, it is very conceivable that they should exist in and be produced by a Spirit; since this is no more than I daily experience in myself, inasmuch as I perceive numberless ideas; and, by an act of my will, can form a great variety of them, and raise them up in my imagination: though, it must be confessed, these creatures of the fancy are not altogether so distinct, so strong, vivid, and permanent, as those perceived by my senses—which latter are called *real things*. From all which I conclude, *there is a Mind which affects me every moment with all the sensible impressions I perceive*. And, from the variety, order, and manner of these, I conclude *the Author of them to be wise, powerful, and good, beyond comprehension*. Mark it well; I do not say, I see things by perceiving that which represents them in the intelligible Substance of God. This I do not understand; but I say, the things by me perceived are known by the understanding, and produced by the will of an infinite Spirit. And is not all this most plain and evident? Is there any more in it than what a little observation in our own minds, and that which passeth in them, not only enables us to conceive, but also obliges us to acknowledge?

Hyl. I think I understand you very clearly; and own the proof you give of a Deity seems no less evident than it is surprising. But, allowing that God is the supreme and universal Cause of all things, yet, may there not be still a Third Nature besides Spirits and Ideas? May we not admit a subordinate and limited cause of our ideas? In a word, may there not for all that be *Matter?*

Phil. How often must I inculcate the same thing? You allow the things immediately perceived by sense to exist nowhere without the mind; but there is nothing perceived by sense which is not perceived immediately: therefore there is nothing sensible that exists without the mind. The Matter, therefore, which you still insist on is something intelligible, I suppose; something that may be discovered by reason, and not by sense.

Hyl. You are in the right.

Phil. Pray let me know what reasoning your belief of Matter is grounded on; and what this Matter is, in your present sense of it.

Hyl. I find myself affected with various ideas, whereof I know I am not the cause; neither are they the cause of themselves, or of one another, or capable of subsisting by themselves, as being altogether inactive, fleeting, dependent beings. They have therefore *some* cause distinct from me and them: of which I pretend to know no more than that it is the *cause of my ideas*. And this thing, whatever it be, I can Matter.

Phil. Tell me, Hylas, hath every one a liberty to change the current proper signification attached to a common name in any language? For example, suppose a traveller should tell you that in a certain country men pass unhurt through the fire; and, upon explaining himself, you found he meant by the word *fire* that which others call *water*. Or, if he should assert that there are trees that walk upon two legs, meaning men by the term *trees*. Would you think this reasonable?

Hyl. No; I should think it very absurd. Common custom is the standard of propriety in language. And for any man to affect speaking improperly is to pervert the use of speech, and can never serve to a better purpose than to protract and multiply disputes where there is no difference in opinion.

Phil. And doth not *Matter*, in the common current acceptation of the word, signify an extended, solid, moveable, unthinking, inactive Substance?

Hyl. It doth.

Phil. And, hath it not been made evident that no *such* substance can possibly exist? And, though it should be allowed to exist, yet how can that which is *inactive* be a *cause;* or that which is *unthinking* be a *cause of thought?* You may, indeed, if you please, annex to the word *Matter* a contrary meaning to what is vulgarly received; and tell me you understand by it, an unextended, thinking, active being, which is the cause of our ideas. But what else is this than to play with words, and run into that very fault you just now condemned with so much reason? I do by no means find fault with your reasoning, in that you collect *a* cause from the *phenomena:* but I deny that *the* cause deducible by reason can properly be termed Matter.

Hyl. There is indeed something in what you say. But I am afraid you do not thoroughly comprehend my meaning. I would by no means be thought to deny that God, or an infinite Spirit, is the Supreme Cause of all things. All I contend for is, that, subordinate to the Supreme Agent, there is a cause of a limited and inferior nature, which *concurs* in the production of our ideas, not by any act of will, or spiritual efficiency, but by that kind of action which belongs to Matter, viz. *motion*.

Phil. I find you are at every turn relapsing into your old exploded conceit, of a moveable, and consequently an extended, substance, existing without the mind. What! Have you already forgotten you were convinced; or are you willing I should repeat what has been said on that head? In truth this is not fair dealing in you, still to suppose the being of that which you have so often acknowledged to have no being. But, not to insist farther on what has been so largely handled, I ask whether all your ideas are not perfectly passive and inert, including nothing of action in them.

Hyl. They are.

Phil. And are sensible qualities anything else but ideas?

Hyl. How often have I acknowledged that they are not.

Phil. But is not *motion* a sensible quality?

Hyl. It is.

Phil. Consequently it is no action?

Hyl. I agree with you. And indeed it is very plain that when I stir my finger, it remains passive; but my will which produced the motion is active.

Phil. Now, I desire to know, in the first place, whether, motion being allowed to be no action, you can conceive any action besides volition: and, in the second place, whether to say something and conceive nothing be not to talk nonsense: and, lastly, whether, having considered the premises, you do not perceive that to suppose any efficient or active Cause of our ideas, other than *Spirit*, is highly absurd and unreasonable?

Hyl. I give up the point entirely. But, though Matter may not be a cause, yet what hinders its being an *instrument*, subservient to the supreme Agent in the production of our ideas?

Phil. An instrument say you; pray what may be the figure, springs, wheels, and motions, of that instrument?

Hyl. Those I pretend to determine nothing of, both the substance and its qualities being entirely unknown to me.

Phil. What? You are then of opinion it is made up of unknown parts, that it hath unknown motions, and an unknown shape?

Hyl. I do not believe that it hath any figure or motion at all, being already convinced, that no sensible qualities can exist in an unperceiving substance.

Phil. But what notion is it possible to frame of an instrument void of all sensible qualities, even extension itself?

Hyl. I do not pretend to have any notion of it.

Phil. And what reason have you to think this unknown, this inconceivable Somewhat doth exist? Is it that you imagine God cannot act as well without it; or that you find by experience the use of some such thing, when you form ideas in your own mind?

Hyl. You are always teasing me for reasons of my belief. Pray what reasons have you not to believe it?

Phil. It is to me a sufficient reason not to believe the existence of anything, if I see no reason for believing it. But, not to insist on reasons for believing, you will not so much as let me know *what it is* you would have me believe; since you say you have no manner of notion of it. After all, let me entreat you to consider whether it be like a philosopher, or even like a man of common sense, to pretend to believe you know not what, and you know not why.

Hyl. Hold, Philonous. When I tell you Matter is an *instrument,* I do not mean altogether nothing. It is true I know not the particular kind of instrument; but, however, I have some notion of *instrument in general,* which I apply to it.

Phil. But what if it should prove that there is something, even in the most general notion of *instrument,* as taken in a distinct sense from *cause,* which makes the use of it inconsistent with the Divine attributes?

Hyl. Make that appear and I shall give up the point.

Phil. What mean you by the general nature or notion of *instrument?*

Hyl. That which is common to all particular instruments composeth the general notion.

Phil. Is it not common to all instruments, that they are applied to the doing those things only which cannot be performed by the mere act of our wills? Thus, for instance, I never use an instrument to move my finger, because it is done by a volition. But I should use one if I were to remove part of a rock, or tear up a tree by the roots. Are you of the same mind? Or, can you shew any example where an instrument is made use of in producing an effect *immediately* depending on the will of the agent?

Hyl. I own I cannot.

Phil. How therefore can you suppose that an All-perfect

Spirit, on whose Will all things have an absolute and immediate dependence, should need an instrument in his operations, or, not needing it, make use of it? Thus it seems to me that you are obliged to own the use of a lifeless inactive instrument to be incompatible with the infinite perfection of God; that is, by your own confession, to give up the point.

Hyl. It doth not readily occur what I can answer you.

Phil. But, methinks you should be ready to own the truth, when it has been fairly proved to you. We indeed, who are beings of finite powers, are forced to make use of instruments. And the use of an instrument sheweth the agent to be limited by rules of another's prescription, and that he cannot obtain his end but in such a way, and by such conditions. Whence it seems a clear consequence, that the supreme unlimited Agent useth no tool or instrument at all. The will of an Omnipotent Spirit is no sooner exerted than executed, without the application of means; which, if they are employed by inferior agents, it is not upon account of any real efficacy that is in them, or necessary aptitude to produce any effect, but merely in compliance with the laws of nature, or those conditions prescribed to them by the First Cause, who is Himself above all limitation or prescription whatsoever.

Hyl. I will no longer maintain that Matter is an instrument. However, I would not be understood to give up its existence neither; since, notwithstanding what hath been said, it may still be an *occasion*.

Phil. How many shapes is your Matter to take? Or, how often must it be proved not to exist, before you are content to part with it? But, to say no more of this (though by all the laws of disputation I may justly blame you for so frequently changing the signification of the principal term)—I would fain know what you mean by affirming that matter is an occasion, having already denied it to be a cause. And, when you have shewn in what sense you understand *occasion*, pray, in the next place, be pleased to shew me what reason induceth you to believe there is such an occasion of our ideas?

Hyl. As to the first point: by *occasion* I mean an inactive unthinking being, at the presence whereof God excites ideas in our minds.

Phil. And what may be the nature of that inactive unthinking being?

Hyl. *I* know nothing of its nature.

Phil. Proceed then to the second point, and assign some

reason why we should allow an existence to this inactive, unthinking, unknown thing.

Hyl. When we see ideas produced in our minds, after an orderly and constant manner, it is natural to think they have some fixed and regular occasions, at the presence of which they are excited.

Phil. You acknowledge then God alone to be the cause of our ideas, and that He causes them at the presence of those occasions?

Hyl. That is my opinion.

Phil. Those things which you say are present to God, without doubt He perceives.

Hyl. Certainly; otherwise they could not be to Him an occasion of acting.

Phil. Not to insist now on your making sense of this hypothesis, or answering all the puzzling questions and difficulties it is liable to: I only ask whether the order and regularity observable in the series of our ideas, or the course of nature, be not sufficiently accounted for by the wisdom and power of God; and whether it doth not derogate from those attributes, to suppose He is influenced, directed, or put in mind, when and what He is to act, by an unthinking substance? And, lastly, whether, in case I granted all you contend for, it would make anything to your purpose; it not being easy to conceive how the external or absolute existence of an unthinking substance, distinct from its being perceived, can be inferred from my allowing that there are certain things perceived by the mind of God, which are to Him the occasion of producing ideas in us?

Hyl. I am perfectly at a loss what to think, this notion of *occasion* seeming now altogether as groundless as the rest.

Phil. Do you not at length perceive that in all these different acceptations of *Matter,* you have been only supposing you know not what, for no manner of reason, and to no kind of use?

Hyl. I freely own myself less fond of my notions since they have been so accurately examined. But still, methinks, I have some confused perception that there is such a thing as *Matter.*

Phil. Either you perceive the being of Matter immediately or mediately. If immediately, pray inform me by which of the senses you perceive it. If mediately, let me know by what reasoning it is inferred from those things which you perceive immediately. So much for the perception. Then for the Matter itself, I ask whether it is object, *substratum,* cause, instrument, or occasion? You have already pleaded for each of these, shifting your notions, and making Matter to appear sometimes in one shape, then in another. And what you have offered hath been disapproved and rejected by yourself. If you have anything new to advance I would gladly hear it.

Hyl. I think I have already offered all I had to say on those heads. I am at a loss what more to urge.

Phil. And yet you are loath to part with your old prejudice. But, to make you quit it more easily, I desire that, beside what has been hitherto suggested, you will farther consider whether, upon supposition that Matter exists, you can possibly conceive how you should be affected by it. Or, supposing it did not exist, whether it be not evident you might for all that be affected with the same ideas you now are, and consequently have the very same reasons to believe its existence that you now can have.

Hyl. I acknowledge it is possible we might perceive all things just as we do now, though there was no Matter in the world; neither can I conceive, if there be Matter, how it should produce any idea in our minds. And, I do farther grant you have entirely satisfied me that it is impossible there should be such a thing as Matter in any of the foregoing acceptations. But still I cannot help supposing that there is *Matter* in some sense or other. *What that is* I do not indeed pretend to determine.

Phil. I do not expect you should define exactly the nature of that unknown being. Only be pleased to tell me whether it is a Substance; and if so, whether you can suppose a Substance without accidents; or, in case you suppose it to have accidents or qualities, I desire you will let me know what those qualities are, at least what is meant by Matter's supporting them?

Hyl. We have already argued on those points. I have no more to say to them. But, to prevent any farther questions, let me tell you I at present understand by *Matter* neither substance nor accident, thinking nor extended being, neither cause, instrument, nor occasion, but Something entirely unknown, distinct from all these.

Phil. It seems then you include in your present notion of Matter nothing but the general abstract idea of *entity.*

Hyl. Nothing else; save only that I superadd to this general idea the negation of all those particular things, qualities, or ideas, that I perceive, imagine, or in anywise apprehend.

Phil. Pray where do you suppose this unknown Matter to exist?

Hyl. Oh Philonous! now you think you have entangled me; for, if I say it exists in place, then you will infer that it exists in the mind, since it is agreed that place or extension exists only in the mind. But I am not ashamed to own my ignorance. I know not where it exists; only I am sure it exists not in place. There is a negative answer for you. And you must expect no other to all the questions you put for the future about Matter.

Phil. Since you will not tell me where it exists, be pleased to inform me after what manner you suppose it to exist, or what you mean by its *existence?*

Hyl. It neither thinks nor acts, neither perceives nor is perceived.

Phil. But what is there positive in your abstracted notion of its existence?

Hyl. Upon a nice observation, I do not find I have any positive notion or meaning at all. I tell you again, I am not ashamed to own my ignorance. I know not what is meant by its *existence,* or how it exists.

Phil. Continue, good Hylas, to act the same ingenuous part, and tell me sincerely whether you can frame a distinct idea of Entity in general, prescinded from and exclusive of all thinking and corporeal beings, all particular things whatsoever.

Hyl. Hold, let me think a little——I profess, Philonous, I do not find that I can. At first glance, methought I had some dilute and airy notion of Pure Entity in abstract; but, upon closer attention, it hath quite vanished out of sight. The more I think on it, the more am I confirmed in my prudent resolution of giving none but negative answers, and not pretending to the least degree of any positive knowledge or conception of Matter, its *where,* its *how,* its *entity,* or anything belonging to it.

Phil. When, therefore, you speak of the existence of Matter, you have not any notion in your mind?

Hyl. None at all

Phil. Pray tell me if the case stands not thus:——At first, from a belief of material substance, you would have it that the immediate objects existed without the mind; then that they are archetypes; then causes; next instruments; then occasions: lastly, *something in general,* which being interpreted proves *nothing.* So Matter comes to nothing. What think you, Hylas, is not this a fair summary of your whole proceeding?

Hyl. Be that as it will, yet I still insist upon it, that *our* not being able to conceive a thing is no argument against its existence.

Phil. That from a cause, effect, operation, sign, or other circumstance, there may reasonably be inferred the existence of a thing not immediately perceived; and that it were absurd for any man to argue against the existence of that thing, from his having no direct and positive notion of it, I freely own. But, where there is nothing of all this; where neither reason nor revelation induces us to believe the existence of a thing; where we have not even a relative notion of it; where an abstraction is made from perceiving and being perceived, from Spirit and idea: lastly, where there is not so much as the most inadequate or faint idea pretended to—I will not indeed thence conclude against the reality of any notion, or existence of anything; but my inference shall be, that you mean nothing at all; that you employ words to no manner of purpose, without any design or signification whatsoever. And I leave it to you to consider how mere jargon should be treated.

Hyl. To deal frankly with you, Philonous, your arguments seem in themselves unanswerable; but they have not so great an effect on me as to produce that entire conviction, that hearty acquiescence, which attends demonstration. I find myself still relapsing into an obscure surmise of I know not what, *matter.*

Phil. But, are you not sensible, Hylas, that two things must concur to take away all scruple, and work a plenary assent in the mind? Let a visible object be set in never so clear a light, yet, if there is any imperfection in the sight, or if the eye is not directed towards it, it will not be distinctly seen. And though a demonstration be never so well grounded and fairly proposed, yet, if there is withal a stain of prejudice, or a wrong bias on the understanding, can it be expected on a sudden to perceive clearly, and adhere firmly to the truth? No; there is need of time and pains: the attention must be awakened and detained by a frequent repetition of the same thing placed oft in the same, oft in different lights. I have said it already, and find I must still repeat and inculcate, that it is an unaccountable license you take, in pretending to maintain you know not what, for you know not what reason, to you know not what purpose. Can this be paralleled in any art of science, any sect or profession of men? Or is there anything so barefacedly groundless and unreasonable to be met with even in the lowest of common conversation? But, perhaps you will still say, Matter may exist; though at the same time you neither know *what is meant* by *Matter*, or by its *existence*. This indeed is surprising, and the more so because it is altogether voluntary, you not being led to it by any one reason; for I challenge you to shew me that thing in nature which needs Matter to explain or account for it.

Hyl. The *reality* of things cannot be maintained without supposing the existence of Matter. And is not this, think you, a good reason why I should be earnest in its defence?

Phil. The reality of things! What things? sensible or intelligible?

Hyl. Sensible things.

Phil. My glove for example?

Hyl. That, or any other thing perceived by the senses.

Phil. But to fix on some particular thing. Is it not a sufficient evidence to me of the existence of this *glove*, that I see it, and feel, and wear it? Or, if this will not do, how is it possible I should be assured of the reality of this thing, which I actually see in this place, by supposing that some unknown thing, which I never did or can see, exists after an unknown manner, in an unknown place, or in no place at all? How can the supposed reality of that which is intangible be a proof that anything tangible really exists? Or, of that which is invisible, that any visible thing, or, in general of anything which is imperceptible, that a perceptible exists? Do but explain this and I shall think nothing too hard for you.

Hyl. Upon the whole, I am content to own the existence of Matter is highly improbable; but the direct and absolute impossibility of it does not appear to me.

Phil. But granting Matter to be possible, yet, upon that account merely, it can have no more claim to existence than a golden mountain, or a centaur.

Hyl. I acknowledge it; but still you do not deny it is possible; and that which is possible, for aught you know, may actually exist.

Phil. I deny it to be possible; and have, if I mistake not, evidently proved, from your own concessions, that it is not. In the common sense of the word *Matter*, is there any more implied than an extended, solid, figured, moveable substance, existing without the mind? And have not you acknowledged, over and over, that you have seen evident reason for denying the possibility of such a substance?

Hyl. True, but that is only one sense of the term *Matter*.

Phil. But is it not the only proper genuine received sense? And, if Matter, in such a sense, be proved impossible, may it not be thought with good grounds absolutely impossible? Else how could anything be proved impossible? Or, indeed, how could there be any proof at all one way or other, to a man who takes the liberty to unsettle and change the common signification of words?

Hyl. I thought philosophers might be allowed to speak more accurately than the vulgar, and were not always confined to the common acceptation of a term.

Phil. But this now mentioned is the common received sense among philosophers themselves. But, not to insist on that, have you not been allowed to take Matter in what sense you pleased? And have you not used this privilege in the utmost extent; sometimes entirely changing, at others leaving out, or putting into the definition of it whatever, for the present, best served your design, contrary to all the known rules of reason and logic? And hath not this shifting, unfair method of yours spun out our dispute to an unnecessary length; Matter having been particularly examined, and by your own confession refuted in each of those senses? And can any more be required to prove the absolute impossibilty of a thing, than the proving it impossible in every particular sense that either you or any one else understands it in?

Hyl. But I am not so thoroughly satisfied that you have proved the impossibility of Matter, in the last most obscure abstracted and indefinite sense.

Phil. When is a thing shewn to be impossible?

Hyl. When a repugnancy is demonstrated between the ideas comprehended in its definition.

Phil. But where there are no ideas, there no repugnancy can be demonstrated between ideas?

Hyl. I agree with you.

Phil. Now, in that which you call the obscure indefinite sense of the word *Matter*, it is plain, by your own confession, there was included no idea at all, no sense except an unknown sense; which is the same thing as none. You are not, therefore, to expect I should prove a repugnancy between ideas, where there are no ideas; or the impossibility of Matter taken in an *unknown* sense, that is, no sense at all. My business was only to shew you meant *nothing;* and this you were brought to own. So that, in all your various senses, you have been shewed either to mean nothing at all, or, if anything, an absurdity. And if this be not sufficient to prove the impossibility of a thing, I desire you will let me know what is.

Hyl. I acknowledge you have proved that Matter is impossible; nor do I see what more can be said in defence of it. But, at the same time that I give up this, I suspect all my other notions. For surely none could be more seemingly evident than this once was: and yet it now seems as false and absurd as ever it did true before. But I think we have discussed the point sufficiently for the present. The remaining part of the day I would willingly spend in running over in my thoughts the several heads of this morning's conversation, and tomorrow shall be glad to meet you here again about the same time.

Phil. I will not fail to attend you.

The Third Dialogue

Philonous. Tell me, Hylas, what are the fruits of yesterday's meditation? Has it confirmed you in the same mind you were in at parting? or have you since seen cause to change your opinion?

Hylas. Truly my opinion is that all our opinions are alike vain and uncertain. What we approve to-day, we condemn to-morrow. We keep a stir about knowledge, and spend our lives in the pursuit of it, when, alas! we know nothing all the while: nor do I think it possible for us ever to know anything in this life. Our faculties are too narrow and too few. Nature certainly never intended us for speculation.

Phil. What! Say you we can know nothing, Hylas?

Hyl. There is not that single thing in the world whereof we can know the real nature, or what it is in itself.

Phil. Will you tell me I do not really know what fire or water is?

Hyl. You may indeed know that fire appears hot, and water

fluid; but this is no more than knowing what sensations are produced in your own mind, upon the application of fire and water to your organs of sense. Their internal constitution, their true and real nature, you are utterly in the dark as to *that*.

Phil. Do I not know this to be a real stone that I stand on, and that which I see before my eyes to be a real tree?

Hyl. Know? No, it is impossible you or any man alive should know it. All you know is, that you have such a certain idea or appearance in your own mind. But what is this to the real tree or stone? I tell you that colour, figure, and hardness, which you perceive, are not the real natures of those things, or in the least like them. The same may be said of all other real things, or corporeal substances, which compose the world. They have none of them anything of themselves, like those sensible qualities by us perceived. We should not therefore pretend to affirm or know anything of them, as they are in their own nature.

Phil. But surely, Hylas, I can distinguish gold, for example, from iron: and how could this be, if I knew not what either truly was?

Hyl. Believe me, Philonous, you can only distinguish between your own ideas. That yellowness, that weight, and other sensible qualities, think you they are really in the gold? They are only relative to the senses, and have no absolute existence in nature. And in pretending to distinguish the species of real things, by the appearances in your mind, you may perhaps act as wisely as he that should conclude two men were of a different species, because their clothes were not of the same colour.

Phil. It seems, then, we are altogether put off with the appearance of things, and those false ones too. The very meat I eat, and the cloth I wear, have nothing in them like what I see and feel.

Hyl. Even so.

Phil. But is it not strange the whole world should be thus imposed on, and so foolish as to believe their senses? And yet I know not how it is, but men eat, and drink, and sleep, and perform all the offices of life, as comfortably and conveniently as if they really knew the things they are conversant about.

Hyl. They do so: but you know ordinary practice does not require a nicety of speculative knowledge. Hence the vulgar retain their mistakes, and for all that make a shift to bustle through the affairs of life. But philosophers know better things.

Phil. You mean, they *know* that they *know nothing.*

Hyl. That is the very top and perfection of human knowledge.

Phil. But are you all this while in earnest, Hylas; and are you seriously persuaded that you know nothing real in the world? Suppose you are going to write, would you not call for pen, ink, and paper, like another man; and do you not know what it is you call for?

Hyl. How often must I tell you, that I know not the real nature of any one thing in the universe? I may indeed upon occasion make use of pen, ink, and paper. But what any one of them is in its own true nature, I declare positively I know not. And the same is true with regard to every other corporeal thing. And, what is more, we are not only ignorant of the true and real nature of things, but even of their existence. It cannot be denied that we perceive such certain appearances or ideas; but it cannot be concluded from thence that bodies really exist. Nay, now I think on it, I must, agreeably to my former concessions, farther declare that it is impossible any *real* corporeal thing could exist in nature.

Phil. You amaze me. Was ever anything more wild and extravagant than the notions you now maintain: and is it not evident you are led into all these extravagances by the belief of *material substance?* This makes you dream of those unknown natures in everything. It is this occasions your distinguishing between the reality and sensible appearances of things. It is to this you are indebted for being ignorant of what everybody else knows perfectly well. Nor is this all: you are not only ignorant of the true nature of everything, but you know not whether anything really exists, or whether there are any natures at all; forasmuch as you attribute to your material beings an absolute or external existence, wherein you suppose their reality consists. And, as you are forced in the end to acknowledge such an existence means either a direct repugnancy, or nothing at all, it follows that you are obliged to pull down your own hypothesis of material Substance, and positively to deny the real existence of any part of the universe. And so you are plunged into the deepest and most deplorable scepticism that ever man was. Tell me, Hylas, is it not as I say?

Hyl. I agree with you. *Material substance* was no more

than an hypothesis; and a false and groundless one too. I will no longer spend my breath in defence of it. But whatever hypothesis you advance, or whatsoever scheme of things you introduce in its stead, I doubt not it will appear every whit as false: let me but be allowed to question you upon it. That is, suffer me to serve you in your own kind, and I warrant it shall conduct you through as many perplexities and contradictions, to the very same state of scepticism that I myself am in at present.

Phil. I assure you, Hylas, I do not pretend to frame any hypothesis at all. I am of a vulgar cast, simple enough to believe my senses, and leave things as I find them. To be plain, it is my opinion that the real things are those very things I see, and feel, and perceive by my senses. These I know; and, finding they answer all the necessities and purposes of life, have no reason to be solicitous about any other unknown beings. A piece of sensible bread, for instance, would stay my stomach better than ten thousand times as much of that insensible, unintelligible, real bread you speak of. It is likewise my opinion that colours and other sensible qualities are on the objects. I cannot for my life help thinking that snow is white, and fire hot. You indeed, who by *snow* and *fire* mean certain external, unperceived, unperceiving substances, are in the right to deny whiteness or heat to be affections inherent in *them*. But I, who understand by those words the things I see and feel, am obliged to think like other folks. And, as I am no sceptic with regard to the nature of things, so neither am I as to their existence. That a thing should be really perceived by my senses, and at the same time not really exist, is to me a plain contradiction; since I cannot prescind or abstract, even in thought, the existence of a sensible thing from its being perceived. Wood, stones, fire, water, flesh, iron, and the like things, which I name and discourse of, are things that I know. And I should not have known them but that I perceived them by my senses; and things perceived by the senses are immediately perceived; and things immediately perceived are ideas; and ideas cannot exist without the mind; their existence therefore consists in being perceived; when, therefore, they are actually perceived there can be no doubt of their existence. Away then with all that scepticism, all those ridiculous philosophical doubts. What a jest is it for a philosopher to question the existence of sensible things, till he hath it proved to him from the veracity of God; or to pretend our knowledge in this point falls short of intuition or demonstration! I might as well doubt of my own being, as of the being of those things I actually see and feel.

Hyl. Not so fast, Philonous: you say you cannot conceive how sensible things should exist without the mind. Do you not?

Phil. I do.

Hyl. Supposing you were annihilated, cannot you conceive it possible that things perceivable by sense may still exist?

Phil. I can; but then it must be in another mind. When I deny sensible things an existence out of the mind, I do not mean my mind in particular, but all minds. Now, it is plain they have an existence exterior to my mind; since I find them by experience to be independent of it. There is therefore some other Mind wherein they exist, during the intervals between the times of my perceiving them: as likewise they did before my birth, and would do after my supposed annihilation. And, as the same is true with regard to all other finite created spirits, it necessarily follows there is an *omnipresent eternal Mind,* which knows and comprehends all things, and exhibits them to our view in such a manner, and according to such rules, as He Himself hath ordained, and are by us termed the *laws of nature.*

Hyl. Answer me, Philonous. Are all our ideas perfectly inert beings? Or have they any agency included in them?

Phil. They are altogether passive and inert.

Hyl. And is not God an agent, a being purely active?

Phil. I acknowledge it.

Hyl. No idea therefore can be like unto, or represent the nature of God?

Phil. It cannot.

Hyl. Since therefore you have no *idea* of the mind of God, how can you conceive it possible that things should exist in His mind? Or, if you can conceive the mind of God, without having an idea of it, why may not I be allowed to conceive the existence of Matter, notwithstanding I have no idea of it?

Phil. As to your first question: I own I have properly no *idea,* either of God or any other spirit; for these being active, cannot be represented by things perfectly inert, as our ideas are. I do nevertheless know that I, who am a spirit or thinking substance, exist as certainly as I know my ideas exist. Farther,

I know what I mean by the terms *I* and *myself;* and I know this immediately or intuitively, though I do not perceive it as I perceive a triangle, a colour, or a sound. The Mind, Spirit, or Soul is that indivisible unextended thing which thinks, acts, and perceives. I say *indivisible,* because unextended; and *unextended,* because extended, figured, moveable things are ideas; and that which perceives ideas, which thinks and wills, is plainly itself no idea, nor like an idea. Ideas are things inactive, and perceived. And Spirits a sort of beings altogether different from them. I do not therefore say my soul is an idea, or like an idea. However, taking the word *idea* in a large sense, my soul may be said to furnish me with an idea, that is, an image or likeness of God—though indeed extremely inadequate. For, all the notion I have of God is obtained by reflecting on my own soul, heightening its powers, and removing its imperfections. I have, therefore, though not an inactive idea, yet in *myself* some sort of an active thinking image of the Deity. And, though I perceive Him not by sense, yet I have a notion of Him, or know Him by reflexion and reasoning. My own mind and my own ideas I have an immediate knowledge of; and, by the help of these, do mediately apprehend the possibility of the existence of other spirits and ideas. Farther, from my own being, and from the dependency I find in myself and my ideas, I do, by an act of reason, necessarily infer the existence of a God, and of all created things in the mind of God. So much for your first question. For the second: I suppose by this time you can answer it yourself. For you neither perceive Matter objectively, as you do an inactive being or idea; nor know it, as you do yourself, by a reflex act; neither do you mediately apprehend it by similitude of the one or the other; nor yet collect it by reasoning from that which you know immediately. All which makes the case of *Matter* widely different from that of the *Deity.*

[1] [*Hyl.* You say your own soul supplies you with some sort of an idea or image of God. But, at the same time, you acknowledge you have, properly speaking, no *idea* of your own soul. You even affirm that spirits are a sort of being altogether different from ideas. Consequently that no idea can be like a spirit. We have therefore no idea of any spirit. You admit nevertheless that there is spiritual Substance, although you

[1] [Added in the third edition.—Ed.]

have no idea of it; while you deny there can be such a thing as material Substance, because you have no notion or idea of it. Is this fair dealing? To act consistently, you must either admit Matter or reject Spirit. What say you to this?

Phil. I say, in the first place, that I do not deny the existence of material substance, merely because I have no notion of it, but because the notion of it is inconsistent; or, in other words, because it is repugnant that there should be a notion of it. Many things, for aught I know, may exist, whereof neither I nor any other man hath or can have any idea or notion whatsoever. But then those things must be possible, that is, nothing inconsistent must be included in their definition. I say, secondly, that, although we believe things to exist which we do not perceive, yet we may not believe that any particular thing exists, without some reason for such belief: but I have no reason for believing the existence of Matter. I have no immediate intuition thereof: neither can I immediately from my sensations, ideas, notions, actions, or passions, infer an unthinking, unperceiving, inactive Substance—either by probable deduction, or necessary consequence. Whereas the being of my Self, that is, my own soul, mind, or thinking principle, I evidently know by reflexion. You will forgive me if I repeat the same things in answer to the same objections. In the very notion or definition of *material Substance*, there is included a manifest repugnance and inconsistency. But this cannot be said of the notion of Spirit. That ideas should exist in what doth not perceive, or be produced by what doth not act, is repugnant. But, it is no repugnancy to say that a perceiving thing should be the subject of ideas, or an active thing the cause of them. It is granted we have neither an immediate evidence nor a demonstrative knowledge of the existence of other finite spirits; but it will not thence follow that such spirits are on a foot with material substances: if to suppose the one be inconsistent, and it be not inconsistent to suppose the other; if the one can be inferred by no argument, and there is a probability for the other; if we see signs and effects indicating distinct finite agents like ourselves, and see no sign or symptom whatever that leads to a rational belief of Matter. I say, lastly, that I have a notion of Spirit, though I have not, strictly speaking, an idea of it. I do not perceive it as an idea, or by means of an idea, but know it by reflexion.

Hyl. Notwithstanding all you have said, to me it seems that, according to your own way of thinking, and in consequence of your own principles, it should follow that *you* are only a system of floating ideas, without any substance to support them. Words are not to be used without a meaning. And, as there is no more meaning in *spiritual Substance* than in *material Substance*, the one is to be exploded as well as the other.

Phil. How often must I repeat, that I know or am conscious of my own being; and that *I myself* am not my ideas, but somewhat else, a thinking, active principle that perceives, knows, wills, and operates about ideas. I know that I, one and the same self, perceive both colours and sounds: that a colour cannot perceive a sound, nor a sound a colour: that I am therefore one individual principle, distinct from colour and sound; and, for the same reason, from all other sensible things and inert ideas. But, I am not in like manner conscious either of the existence or essense of Matter. On the contrary, I know that nothing inconsistent can exist, and that the existence of Matter implies an inconsistency. Farther, I know what I mean when I affirm that there is a spiritual substance or support of ideas, that is, that a spirit knows and perceives ideas. But, I do not know what is meant when it is said that an unperceiving substance hath inherent in it and supports either ideas or the archetypes of ideas. There is therefore upon the whole no parity of case between Spirit and Matter.]

Hyl. I own myself satisfied in this point. But, do you in earnest think the real existence of sensible things consists in their being actually perceived? If so; how comes it that all mankind distinguish between them? Ask the first man you meet, and he shall tell you, *to be perceived* is one thing, and *to exist* is another.

Phil. I am content, Hylas, to appeal to the common sense of the world for the truth of my notion. Ask the gardener why he thinks yonder cherry-tree exists in the garden, and he shall tell you, because he sees and feels it; in a word, because he perceives it by his senses. Ask him why he thinks an orange-tree not to be there, and he shall tell you, because he does not perceive it. What he perceives by sense, that he terms a real being, and saith it *is* or *exists;* but, that which is not perceivable, the same, he saith, hath no being.

Hyl. Yes, Philonous, I grant the existence of a sensible thing consists in being perceivable, but not in being actually perceived.

Phil. And what is perceivable but an idea? And can an idea exist without being actually perceived? These are points long since agreed between us.

Hyl. But, be your opinion never so true, yet surely you will not deny it is shocking, and contrary to the common sense of men. Ask the fellow whether yonder tree hath an existence out of his mind: what answer think you he would make?

Phil. The same that I should myself, to wit, that it doth exist out of his mind. But then to a Christian it cannot surely be shocking to say, the real tree, existing without his mind, is truly known and comprehended by (that is *exists in*) the infinite mind of God. Probably he may not at first glance be aware of the direct and immediate proof there is of this; inasmuch as the very being of a tree, or any other sensible thing, implies a mind wherein it is. But the point itself he cannot deny. The question between the Materialists and me is not, whether things have a *real* existence out of the mind of this or that person, but, whether they have an *absolute* existence, distinct from being perceived by God, and exterior to *all* minds. This indeed some heathens and philosophers have affirmed, but whoever entertains notions of the Deity suitable to the Holy Scriptures will be of another opinion.

Hyl. But, according to your notions, what difference is there between real things, and chimeras formed by the imagination, or the visions of a dream—since they are all equally in the mind?

Phil. The ideas formed by the imagination are faint and indistinct; they have, besides, an entire dependence on the will. But the ideas perceived by sense, that is, real things, are more vivid and clear; and, being imprinted on the mind by a spirit distinct from us, have not the like dependence on our will. There is therefore no danger of confounding these with the foregoing: and there is as little of confounding them with the visions of a dream, which are dim, irregular, and confused. And, though they should happen to be never so lively and natural, yet, by their not being connected, and of a piece with the preceding and subsequent transactions of our lives, they might easily be distinguished from realities. In short, by whatever method you distinguish *things* from *chimeras* on your scheme, the same, it is evident, will hold also upon mine. For, it must be, I presume, by some perceived difference; and I am not for depriving you of any one thing that you perceive.

Hyl. But still, Philonous, you hold, there is nothing in the world but spirits and ideas. And this, you must needs acknowledge, sounds very oddly.

Phil. I own the word *idea,* not being commonly used for *thing,* sounds something out of the way. My reason for using it was, because a necessary relation to the mind is understood to be implied by that term; and it is now commonly used by philosophers to denote the immediate objects of the understanding. But, however oddly the proposition may sound in words, yet it includes nothing so very strange or shocking in its sense; which in effect amounts to no more than this, to wit, that there are only things perceiving, and things perceived; or that every unthinking being is necessarily, and from the very nature of its existence, perceived by some mind; if not by a finite created mind, yet certainly by the infinite mind of God, in whom 'we live, and move, and have our being.' Is this as strange as to say, the sensible qualities are not on the objects: or that we cannot be sure of the existence of things, or know anything of their real natures—though we both see and feel them, and perceive them by all our senses?

Hyl. And, in consequence of this, must we not think there are no such things as physical or corporeal causes; but that a Spirit is the immediate cause of all the phenomena in nature? Can there be anything more extravagant than this?

Phil. Yes, it is infinitely more extravagant to say—a thing which is inert operates on the mind, and which is unperceiving is the cause of our perceptions, [without any regard either to consistency, or the old known axiom, *Nothing can give to another that which it hath not itself*].[2] Besides, that which to you, I know not for what reason, seems so extravagant is no more than the Holy Scriptures assert in a hundred places. In them God is represented as the sole and immediate Author of all those effects which some heathens and philosophers are wont to ascribe to Nature, Matter, Fate, or the like unthinking principle. This is so much the constant language of Scripture that it were needless to confirm it by citations.

Hyl. You are not aware, Philonous, that, in making God the immediate Author of all the motions in nature, you make Him the Author of murder, sacrilege, adultery, and the like heinous sins.

[2] [Omitted in the third edition.—Ed.]

Phil. In answer to that, I observe, first, that the imputation of guilt is the same, whether a person commits an action with or without an instrument. In case therefore you suppose God to act by the mediation of an instrument, or occasion, called *Matter,* you as truly make Him the author of sin as I, who think Him the immediate agent in all those operations vulgarly ascribed to Nature. I farther observe that sin or moral turpitude doth not consist in the outward physical action, or motion, but in the internal deviation of the will from the laws of reason and religion. This is plain, in that the killing an enemy in a battle, or putting a criminal legally to death, is not thought sinful; though the outward act be the very same with that in the case of murder. Since, therefore, sin doth not consist in the physical action, the making God an immediate cause of all such actions is not making Him the Author of sin. Lastly, I have nowhere said that God is the only agent who produces all the motions in bodies. It is true I have denied there are any other agents besides spirits; but this is very consistent with allowing to thinking rational beings, in the production of motions, the use of limited powers, ultimately indeed derived from God, but immediately under the direction of their own wills, which is sufficient to entitle them to all the guilt of their actions.

Hyl. But the denying Matter, Philonous, or corporeal Substance; there is the point. You can never persuade me that this is not repugnant to the universal sense of mankind. Were our dispute to be determined by most voices, I am confident you would give up the point, without gathering the votes.

Phil. I wish both our opinions were fairly stated and submitted to the judgment of men who had plain common sense, without the prejudices of a learned education. Let me be represented as one who trusts his senses, who thinks he knows the things he sees and feels, and entertains no doubts of their existence; and you fairly set forth with all your doubts, your paradoxes, and your scepticism about you, and I shall willingly acquiesce in the determination of any indifferent person. That there is no substance wherein ideas can exist beside spirit is to me evident. And that the objects immediately perceived are ideas, is on all hands agreed. And that sensible qualities are objects immediately perceived no one can deny. It is therefore evident there can be no *substratum* of those qualities but spirit; *in* which they exist, not by way of mode or property, but as a thing perceived in that which perceives it. I deny therefore that there is any unthinking *substratum* of the objects of sense, and *in that acceptation* that there is any material substance. But if by *material substance* is meant only *sensible body*—that which is seen and felt (and the unphilosophical part of the world, I dare say, mean no more)—then I am more certain of matter's existence than you or any other philosopher pretend to be. If there be anything which makes the generality of mankind averse from the notions I espouse: it is a misapprehension that I deny the reality of sensible things. But, as it is you who are guilty of that, and not I, it follows that in truth their aversion is against your notions and not mine. I do therefore assert that I am as certain as of my own being, that there are bodies or corporeal substances (meaning the things I perceive by my senses); and that, granting this, the bulk of mankind will take no thought about, nor think themselves at all concerned in the fate of those unknown natures, and philosophical quiddities, which some men are so fond of.

Hyl. What say you to this? Since, according to you, men judge of the reality of things by their senses, how can a man be mistaken in thinking the moon a plain lucid surface, about a foot in diameter; or a square tower, seen at a distance, round; or an oar, with one end in the water, crooked?

Phil. He is not mistaken with regard to the ideas he actually perceives, but in the inferences he makes from his present perceptions. Thus, in the case of the oar, what he immediately perceives by sight is certainly crooked; and so far he is in the right. But if he thence conclude that upon taking the oar out of the water he shall perceive the same crookedness; or that it would affect his touch as crooked things are wont to do: in that he is mistaken. In like manner, if he shall conclude from what he perceives in one station, that, in case he advances towards the moon or tower, he should still be affected with the like ideas, he is mistaken. But his mistake lies not in what he perceives immediately, and at present, (it being a manifest contradiction to suppose he should err in respect of that) but in the wrong judgment he makes concerning the ideas he apprehends to be connected with those immediately perceived; or, concerning the ideas that, from what he perceives at present, he imagines would be perceived in other circumstances. The case is the same with regard to the Copernican system. We do not here perceive any motion of the earth: but it were erroneous thence to conclude, that, in case we were placed at as great a distance from that as we are now from the other planets, we should not then perceive its motion.

Hyl. I understand you; and must needs own you say things plausible enough. But, give me leave to put you in mind of one thing. Pray, Philonous, were you not formerly as positive that Matter existed, as you are now that it does not?

Phil. I was. But here lies the difference. Before, my positiveness was founded, without examination, upon prejudice; but now, after inquiry, upon evidence.

Hyl. After all, it seems our dispute is rather about words than things. We agree in the thing, but differ in the name. That we are affected with ideas *from without* is evident; and it is no less evident that there must be (I will not say archetypes, but) Powers without the mind, corresponding to those ideas. And, as these Powers cannot subsist by themselves, there is some subject of them necessarily to be admitted; which I call *Matter*, and you call *Spirit*. This is all the difference.

Phil. Pray, Hylas, is that powerful Being, or subject of powers, extended?

Hyl. It hath not extension; but it hath the power to raise in you the idea of extension.

Phil. It is therefore itself unextended?

Hyl. I grant it.

Phil. Is it not also active?

Hyl. Without doubt. Otherwise, how could we attribute powers to it?

Phil. Now let me ask you two questions: First, Whether it be agreeable to the usage either of philosophers or others to give the name *Matter* to an unextended active being? And, *Secondly*, Whether it be not ridiculously absurd to misapply names contrary to the common use of language?

Hyl. Well then, let it not be called Matter, since you will have it so, but some *Third Nature* distinct from Matter and Spirit. For what reason is there why you should call it Spirit? Does not the notion of spirit imply that it is thinking, as well as active and unextended?

Phil. My reason is this: because I have a mind to have some notion of meaning in what I say: but I have no notion of any action distinct from volition, neither can I conceive volition to be anywhere but in a spirit: therefore, when I speak of an active being, I am obliged to mean a Spirit. Beside, what can be plainer than that a thing which hath no ideas in itself cannot impart them to me; and, if it hath ideas, surely it must be a Spirit. To make you comprehend the point still more clearly if it be possible. I assert as well as you that, since we are affected from without, we must allow Powers to be without, in a Being distinct from ourselves. So far we are agreed. But then we differ as to the kind of this powerful Being. I will have it to be Spirit, you Matter, or I know not what (I may add too, you know not what) Third Nature. Thus I prove it to be Spirit. From the effects I see produced, I conclude there are actions; and, because actions, volitions; and, because there are volitions, there must be a *will*. Again, the things I perceive must have an existence, they or their archetypes, out of *my* mind: but, being ideas, neither they nor their archetypes can exist otherwise than in an understanding; there is therefore an *understanding*. But will and understanding constitute in the strictest sense a mind or spirit. The powerful cause, therefore, of my ideas is in strict propriety of speech a *Spirit*.

Hyl. And now I warrant you think you have made the point very clear, little suspecting that what you advance leads directly to a contradiction. Is it not an absurdity to imagine any imperfection in God?

Phil. Without a doubt.

Hyl. To suffer pain is an imperfection?

Phil. It is.

Hyl. Are we not sometimes affected with pain and uneasiness by some other Being?

Phil. We are.

Hyl. And have you not said that Being is a Spirit, and is not that Spirit God?

Phil. I grant it.

Hyl. But you have asserted that whatever ideas we perceive from without are in the mind which affects us. The ideas, therefore, of pain and uneasiness are in God; or, in other words, God suffers pain: that is to say, there is an imperfection in the Divine nature: which, you acknowledged, was absurd. So you are caught in a plain contradiction.

Phil. That God knows or understands all things, that He knows, among other things, what pain is, even every sort of painful sensation, and what it is for His creatures to suffer pain, I make no question. But, that God, though He knows and sometimes causes painful sensations in us, can Himself suffer pain, I positively deny. We, who are limited and dependent spirits, are liable to impressions of sense, the effects of an external Agent, which, being produced against our wills, are sometimes painful and uneasy. But God, whom no external being can affect, who perceives nothing by sense as we do; whose will is absolute and independent, causing all things, and liable to be thwarted or resisted by nothing: it is evident, such a Being as this can suffer nothing, nor be affected with any painful sensation, or indeed any sensation at all. We are chained to a body: that is to say, our perceptions are connected with corporeal motions. By the law of our nature, we are affected upon every alteration in the nervous parts of our sensible body; which sensible body, rightly considered, is nothing but a complexion of such qualities or ideas as have no existence distinct from being perceived by a mind. So that this connexion of sensations with corporeal motions means no more than a correspondence in the order of nature, between two sets of ideas, or things immediately perceivable. But God is a Pure Spirit, disengaged from all such sympathy, or natural ties. No corporeal motions are attended with the sensations of pain or pleasure in His mind. To know everything knowable, is certainly a perfection; but to endure, or suffer, or feel anything by sense, is an imperfection. The former, I say, agrees to God, but not the latter. God knows, or hath ideas; but His ideas are not conveyed to Him by sense, as ours are. Your not distinguishing, where there is so manifest a difference, makes you fancy you see an absurdity where there is none.

Hyl. But, all this while you have not considered that the quantity of Matter has been demonstrated to be proportioned to the gravity of bodies. And what can withstand demonstration?

Phil. Let me see how you demonstrate that point.

Hyl. I lay it down for a principle, that the moments or quantities of motion in bodies are in a direct compounded reason of the velocities and quantities of Matter contained in them. Hence, where the velocities are equal, it follows the moments are directly as the quantity of Matter in each. But it is found by experience that all bodies (bating the small inequalities, arising from the resistance of the air) descend with an equal velocity; the motion therefore of descending bodies, and consequently their gravity, which is the cause or principle of that motion, is proportional to the quantity of Matter; which was to be demonstrated.

Phil. You lay it down as a self-evident principle that the quantity of motion in any body is proportional to the velocity and *Matter* taken together; and this is made use of to prove a proposition from whence the existence of *Matter* is inferred. Pray is not this arguing in a circle?

Hyl. In the premise I only mean that the motion is proportional to the velocity, jointly with the extension and solidity.

Phil. But, allowing this to be true, yet it will not thence follow that gravity is proportional to *Matter,* in your philosophic sense of the word; except you take it for granted that unknown *substratum,* or whatever else you call it, is proportional to those sensible qualities; which to suppose is plainly begging the question. That there is magnitude and solidity, or resistance, perceived by sense, I readily grant; as likewise, that gravity may be proportional to those qualities I will not dispute. But that either these qualities as perceived by us, or the powers producing them, do exist in a *material substratum;* this is what I deny, and you indeed affirm, but, notwithstanding your demonstration, have not yet proved.

Hyl. I shall insist no longer on that point. Do you think, however, you shall persuade me the natural philosophers have been dreaming all this while? Pray what becomes of all their hypotheses and explications of the phenomena, which suppose the existence of Matter?

Phil. What mean you, Hylas, by the *phenomena?*

Hyl. I mean the appearances which I perceive by my senses.

Phil. And the appearances perceived by sense, are they not ideas?

Hyl. I have told you so a hundred times.

Phil. Therefore, to explain the phenomena is, to shew how we come to be affected with ideas, in that manner and order wherein they are imprinted on our senses. Is it not?

Hyl. It is.

Phil. Now, if you can prove that any philosopher has explained the production of any one idea in our minds by the help of *Matter,* I shall for ever acquiesce, and look on all that hath been said against it as nothing; but, if you cannot, it is vain to urge the explication of phenomena. That a Being endowed with knowledge and will should produce or exhibit ideas is easily understood. But that a Being which is utterly destitute of these faculties should be able to produce ideas, or in any sort to affect an intelligence, this I can never understand. This I say, though we had some positive conception of Matter, though we knew its qualities, and could comprehend its existence, would yet be so far from explaining things, that it is itself the most inexplicable thing in the world. And yet, for all this, it will not follow that philosophers have been doing nothing; for, by observing and reasoning upon the connexion of ideas, they discover the laws and methods of nature, which is a part of knowledge both useful and entertaining.

Hyl. After all, can it be supposed God would deceive all mankind? Do you imagine He would have induced the whole world to believe the being of Matter, if there was no such thing?

Phil. That every epidemical opinion, arising from prejudice, or passion, or thoughtlessness, may be imputed to God, as the Author of it, I believe you will not affirm. Whatsoever opinion we father on Him, it must be either because He has discovered it to us by supernatural revelation; or because it is so evident to our natural faculties, which were framed and given us by God, that it is impossible we should withhold our assent from it. But where is the revelation? or where is the evidence that extorts the belief of Matter? Nay, how does it appear, that Matter, *taken for something distinct from what we perceive by our senses,* is thought to exist by all mankind; or, indeed, by any except a few philosophers, who do not know what they would be at? Your question supposes these points are clear; and, when you have cleared them, I shall think myself obliged to give you another answer. In the meantime, let it suffice that I tell you, I do not suppose God has deceived mankind at all.

Hyl. But the novelty, Philonous, the novelty! There lies the danger. New notions should always be discountenanced; they unsettle men's minds, and nobody knows where they will end.

Phil. Why the rejecting a notion that has no foundation, either in sense, or in reason, or in Divine authority, should be thought to unsettle the belief of such opinions as are grounded on all or any of these, I cannot imagine. That innovations in government and religion are dangerous, and ought to be discountenanced, I freely own. But is there the like reason why they should be discouraged in philosophy? The making anything known which was unknown before is an innovation in knowledge: and, if all such innovations had been forbidden, men would not have made a notable progress in the arts and sciences. But it is none of my business to plead for novelties and paradoxes. That the qualities we perceive are not on the objects: that we must not believe our senses: that we know nothing of the real nature of things, and can never be assured even of their existence: that real colours and sounds are nothing but certain unknown figures and motions: that motions are in themselves neither swift nor slow: that there are in bodies absolute extensions, without any particular magnitude or figure: that a thing stupid, thoughtless, and inactive, operates on a spirit: that the least particle of a body contains innumerable extended parts:—these are the novelties, these are the strange notions which shock the genuine uncorrupted judgment of all mankind; and being once admitted, embarrass the mind with endless doubts and difficulties. And it is against these and the like innovations I endeavour to vindicate Common Sense. It is true, in doing this, I may perhaps be obliged to use some *ambages*, and ways of speech not common. But, if my notions are once thoroughly understood, that which is most singular in them will, in effect, be found to amount to no more than this:—that it is absolutely impossible, and a plain contradiction, to suppose any unthinking Being should exist without being perceived by a Mind. And, if this notion be singular, it is a shame it should be so, at this time of day, and in a Christian country.

Hyl. As for the difficulties other opinions may be liable to, those are out of the question. It is your business to defend your own opinion. Can anything be plainer than that you are for changing all things into ideas? You, I say, who are not ashamed to charge me with *scepticism*. This is so plain, there is no denying it.

Phil. You mistake me. I am not for changing things into ideas, but rather ideas into things, since those immediate objects of perception, which, according to you, are only appearances of things, I take to be the real things themselves.

Hyl. Things! You may pretend what you please; but it is certain you leave us nothing but the empty forms of things, the outside only which strikes the senses.

Phil. What you call the empty forms and outside of things seem to me the very things themselves. Nor are they empty or incomplete, otherwise than upon your supposition—that Matter is an essential part of all corporeal things. We both, therefore, agree in this, that we perceive only sensible forms: but herein we differ—you will have them to be empty appearances, I real beings. In short, you do not trust your senses, I do.

Hyl. You say you believe your senses; and seem to applaud yourself that in this you agree with the vulgar. According to you, therefore, the true nature of a thing is discovered by the senses. If so, whence comes that disagreement? Why is not the same figure, and other sensible qualities, perceived all manner of ways? and why should we use a microscope the better to discover the true nature of a body, if it were discoverable to the naked eye?

Phil. Strictly speaking, Hylas, we do not see the same object that we feel; neither is the same object perceived by the microscope which was by the naked eye. But, in case every variation was thought sufficient to constitute a new kind or individual, the endless number or confusion of names would render language impracticable. Therefore, to avoid this, as well as other inconveniences which are obvious upon a little thought, men combine together several ideas, apprehended by divers senses, or by the same sense at different times, or in different circumstances, but observed, however, to have some connexion in nature, either with respect to co-existence or succession; all which they refer to one name, and consider as one thing. Hence it follows that when I examine, by my other senses, a thing I have seen, it is not in order to understand better the same object which I had perceived by sight, the object of one sense not being perceived by the other senses. And, when I look through a microscope, it is not that I may perceive more clearly what I perceived already with my bare eyes; the object perceived by the glass being quite different from the former. But, in both cases, my aim is only to know what ideas are connected together; and the more a man knows of the connexion of ideas, the more he is said to know of the nature of things. What, therefore, if our ideas are variable; what if our senses are not in all circumstances affected with the same appearances? It will not thence follow they are not to be trusted; or that they are inconsistent either with themselves or anything else: except it be with your preconceived notion of (I know not what) one single, unchanged, unperceivable, real Nature, marked by each name. Which prejudice seems to have taken its rise from not rightly understanding the common language of men, speaking of several distinct ideas as united into one thing by the mind. And, indeed, there is cause to suspect several erroneous conceits of the philosophers are owing to the same original: while they began to build their schemes not so much on notions as on words, which were framed by the vulgar, merely for conveniency and dispatch in the common actions of life, without any regard to speculation.

Hyl. Methinks I apprehend your meaning.

Phil. It is your opinion the ideas we perceive by our senses are not real things, but images or copies of them. Our knowledge, therefore, is no farther real than as our ideas are the true *representations* of those *originals*. But, as the supposed originals are in themselves unknown, it is impossible to know how far our ideas resemble them; or whether they resemble them at all. We cannot, therefore, be sure we have any real knowledge. Farther, as our ideas are perpetually varied, without any change in the supposed real things, it necessarily follows they cannot all be true copies of them: or, if some are and others are not, it is impossible to distinguish the former from the latter. And this plunges us yet deeper in uncertainty. Again, when we consider the point, we cannot conceive how any idea, or anything like an idea, should have an absolute existence out of a mind: nor consequently, according to you, how there should be any real thing in nature. The result of all which is that we are thrown into the most hopeless and abandoned scepticism. Now, give me leave to ask you, First, Whether your referring ideas to certain absolutely existing unperceived substances, as their originals, be not the source of all this scepticism? Secondly, whether you are informed, either by sense or reason, of the existence of those unknown originals? And, in case you are not, whether it be not absurd to suppose them? Thirdly, Whether, upon inquiry, you find there is anything distinctly conceived or meant by the *absolute or external existence of unperceiving substances?* Lastly, Whether, the premises considered, it be not the wisest way to follow nature, trust your senses, and, laying aside all anxious thought about unknown natures or substances, admit with the vulgar those for real things which are perceived by the senses?

Hyl. For the present, I have no inclination to the answering part. I would much rather see how you can get over what follows. Pray are not the objects perceived by the *senses* of one, likewise perceivable to others present? If there were a hundred more here, they would all see the garden, the trees, and flowers, as I see them. But they are not in the same manner affected with the ideas I frame in my *imagination*. Does not this make a difference between the former sort of objects and the latter?

Phil. I grant it does. Nor have I ever denied a difference between the objects of sense and those of imagination. But what would you infer from thence? You cannot say that sensible objects exist unperceived, because they are perceived by many.

Hyl. I own I can make nothing of that objection: but it hath led me into another. Is it not your opinion that by our senses we perceive only the ideas existing in our minds?

Phil. It is.

Hyl. But the *same* idea which is in my mind cannot be in yours, or in any other mind. Doth it not therefore follow, from your principles, that no two can see the same thing? And is not this highly absurd?

Phil. If the term *same* be taken in the vulgar acceptation, it is certain (and not at all repugnant to the principles I maintain) that different persons may perceive the same thing; or the same thing or idea exist in different minds. Words are of arbitrary imposition; and, since men are used to apply the word *same* where no distinction or variety is perceived, and I do not pretend to alter their perceptions, it follows that, as men have said before, *several saw the same thing,* so they may, upon like occasions, still continue to use the same phrase, without any deviation either from propriety of language, or the truth of things. But, if the term *same* be used in the acceptation of philosophers, who pretend to an abstracted notion of identity, then, according to their sundry definitions of this notion (for it is not yet agreed wherein that philosophic identity consists), it may or may not be possible for divers persons to perceive the same thing. But whether philosophers shall think fit to *call* a thing the *same* or no, is, I conceive, of small importance. Let us suppose several men together, all endued with the same faculties, and consequently affected in like sort by their senses, and who had yet never known the use of language; they would, without question, agree in their perceptions. Though perhaps, when they came to the use of speech, some regarding the uniformness of what was perceived, might call it the *same* thing: others, especially regarding the diversity of persons who perceived, might choose the denomination of *different* things. But who sees not that all the dispute is about a word? to wit, whether what is perceived by different persons may yet have the term *same* applied to it? Or, suppose a house, whose walls or outward shell remaining unaltered, the chambers are all pulled down, and new ones built in their place; and that you should call this the *same*, and I should say it was not the *same* house:—would we not, for all this, perfectly agree in our thoughts of the house, considered in itself? And would not all the difference consist in a sound? If you should say, We differed in our notions; for that you superadded to your idea of the house the simple abstracted idea of identity, whereas I did not; I would tell you, I know not what you mean by the *abstracted idea of identity;* and should desire you to look into your own thoughts, and be sure you understood yourself.—Why so silent, Hylas? Are you not yet satisfied men may dispute about identity and diversity, without any real difference in their thoughts and opinions, abstracted from names? Take this farther reflexion with you—that whether Matter be allowed to exist or no, the case is exactly the same as to the point in hand. For the Materialists themselves acknowledge what we immediately perceive by our senses to be our own ideas. Your difficulty, therefore, that no two see the same thing, makes equally against the Materialists and me.

Hyl. But they suppose an external archetype, to which referring their several ideas they may truly be said to perceive the same thing.

Phil. And (not to mention your having discarded those archetypes) so may you suppose an external archetype on my principles;—*external, I mean, to your own mind:* though indeed it must be supposed to exist in that Mind which comprehends all things; but then, this serves all the ends of *identity*, as well as if it existed out of a mind. And I am sure you yourself will not say it is less intelligible.

Hyl. You have indeed clearly satisfied me—either that there is no difficulty at bottom in this point; or, if there be, that it makes equally against both opinions.

Phil. But that which makes equally against two contradictory opinions can be a proof against neither.

Hyl. I acknowledge it.

But, after all, Philonous, when I consider the substance of what you advance against *Scepticism*, it amounts to no more than this:—We are sure that we really see, hear, feel; in a word, that we are affected with sensible impressions.

Phil. And how are *we* concerned any farther? I see this cherry, I feel it, I taste it: and I am sure *nothing* cannot be seen, or felt, or tasted: it is therefore *real*. Take away the sensations of softness, moisture, redness, tartness, and you take away the cherry, since it is not a being distinct from sensations. A cherry, I say, is nothing but a congeries of sensible impressions, or ideas perceived by various senses: which ideas are united into one thing (or have one name given them) by the mind, because they are observed to attend each other. Thus, when the palate is affected with such a particular taste, the sight is affected with a red colour, the touch with roundness, softness, &c. Hence, when I see, and feel, and taste, in sundry certain manners, I am sure the cherry exists, or is real; its reality being in my opinion nothing abstracted from those sensations. But if by the word *cherry* you mean an unknown nature, distinct from all those sensible qualities, and by its *existence* something distinct from its being perceived; then, indeed, I own, neither you nor I, nor any one else, can be sure it exists.

Hyl. But, what would you say, Philonous, if I should bring the very same reasons against the existence of sensible things *in a mind*, which you have offered against their existing *in a material substratum*?

Phil. When I see your reasons, you shall hear what I have to say to them.

Hyl. Is the mind extended or unextended?

Phil. Unextended, without doubt.

Hyl. Do you say the things you perceive are in your mind?

Phil. They are.

Hyl. Again, have I not heard you speak of sensible impressions?

Phil. I believe you may.

Hyl. Explain to me now, O Philonous! how it is possible there should be room for all those trees and houses to exist in your mind. Can extended things be contained in that which is unextended? Or, are we to imagine impressions made on a thing void of all solidity? You cannot say objects are in your mind, as books in your study: or that things are imprinted on it, as the figure of a seal upon wax. In what sense, therefore, are we to understand those expressions? Explain me this if you can: and I shall then be able to answer all those queries you formerly put to me about my *substratum*.

Phil. Look you, Hylas, when I speak of objects as existing in the mind, or imprinted on the senses, I would not be understood in the gross literal sense; as when bodies are said to exist in a place, or a seal to make an impression upon wax. My meaning is only that the mind comprehends or perceives them; and that it is affected from without, or by some being distinct from itself. This is my explication of your difficulty; and how it can serve to make your tenet of an unperceiving material *substratum* intelligible, I would fain know.

Hyl. Nay, if that be all, I confess I do not see what use can be made of it. But are you not guilty of some abuse of language in this?

Phil. None at all. It is no more than common custom, which you know is the rule of language, hath authorised: nothing being more usual, than for philosophers to speak of the immediate objects of the understanding as things existing in the mind. Nor is there anything in this but what is comformable to the general analogy of language; most part of the mental operations being signified by words borrowed from sensible things; as is plain in the terms *comprehend, reflect, discourse, &c.*, which, being applied to the mind, must not be taken in their gross, original sense.

Hyl. You have, I own, satisfied me in this point. But there still remains one great difficulty, which I know not how you will get over. And, indeed, it is of such importance that if you could solve all others, without being able to find a solu-

tion for this, you must never expect to make me a proselyte
to your principles.

Phil. Let me know this mighty difficulty.

Hyl. The Scripture account of the creation is what appears
to me utterly irreconcilable with your notions. Moses tells
us of a creation: a creation of what? of ideas? No, certainly,
but of things, of real things, solid corporeal substances. Bring
your principles to agree with this, and I shall perhaps agree
with you.

Phil. Moses mentions the sun, moon, and stars, earth
and sea, plants and animals. That all these do really exist,
and were in the beginning created by God, I make no
question. If by *ideas* you mean fictions and fancies of the
mind, then these are no ideas. If by *ideas* you mean immediate objects of the understanding, or sensible things,
which cannot exist unperceived, or out of a mind, then
these things are ideas. But whether you do or do not call
them *ideas,* it matters little. The difference is only about a
name. And, whether that name be retained or rejected, the
sense, the truth, and reality of things continues the same. In
common talk, the objects of our senses are not termed *ideas,*
but *things.* Call them so still: provided you do not attribute
to them any absolute external existence, and I shall never
quarrel with you for a word. The creation, therefore, I allow
to have been a creation of things, of *real* things. Neither is
this in the least inconsistent with my principles, as is evident
from what I have now said; and would have been evident to
you without this, if you had not forgotten what had been
so often said before. But as for solid corporeal substances,
I desire you to shew where Moses makes any mention of
them; and, if they should be mentioned by him, or any other
inspired writer, it would still be incumbent on you to shew
those words were not taken in the vulgar acceptation, for
things falling under our senses, but in the philosophic acceptation, for Matter, or *an unknown quiddity, with an
absolute existence.* When you have proved these points, then
(and not till then) may you bring the authority of Moses into
our dispute.

Hyl. It is in vain to dispute about a point so clear. I am
content to refer it to your own conscience. Are you not
satisfied there is some peculiar repugnancy between the
Mosaic account of the creation and your notions?

Phil. If all possible sense which can be put on the first chapter of Genesis may be conceived as consistently with my principles as any other, then it has no peculiar repugnancy with them. But there is no sense you may not as well conceive, believing as I do. Since, besides spirits, all you conceive are ideas; and the existence of these I do not deny. Neither do you pretend they exist without the mind.

Hyl. Pray let me see any sense you can understand it in.

Phil. Why, I imagine that if I had been present at the creation, I should have seen things produced into being— that is become perceptible—in the order prescribed by the sacred historian. I ever before believed the Mosaic account of the creation, and now find no alteration in my manner of believing it. When things are said to begin or end their existence, we do not mean this with regard to God, but His creatures. All objects are eternally known by God, or, which is the same thing, have an eternal existence in His mind: but when things, before imperceptible to creatures, are, by a decree of God, perceptible to them, then are they said to begin a relative existence, with respect to created minds. Upon reading therefore the Mosaic account of the creation, I understand that the several parts of the world became gradually perceivable to finite spirits, endowed with proper faculties; so that, whoever such were present, they were in truth perceived by them. This is the literal obvious sense suggested to me by the words of the Holy Scripture: in which is included no mention, or no thought, either of *substratum*, instrument, occasion, or absolute existence. And, upon inquiry, I doubt not it will be found that most plain honest men, who believe the creation, never think of those things any more than I. What metaphysical sense you may understand it in, you only can tell.

Hyl. But, Philonous, you do not seem to be aware that you allow created things, in the beginning, only a relative, and consequently hypothetical being: that is to say, upon supposition there were *men* to perceive them; without which they have no actuality of absolute existence, wherein creation might terminate. Is it not, therefore, according to you, plainly impossible the creation of any inanimate creatures should precede that of man? And is not this directly contrary to the Mosaic account?

Phil. In answer to that, I say, first, created beings might begin to exist in the mind of other created intelligences, beside men. You will not therefore be able to prove any contradiction between Moses and my notions, unless you first shew there was no other order of finite created spirits in being, before man. I say, farther, in case we conceive the creation, as we should at this time, a parcel of plants or vegetables of all sorts produced, by an invisible Power, in a desert where nobody was present—that this way of explaining or conceiving it is consistent with my principles, since they deprive you of nothing, either sensible or imaginable; that it exactly suits with the common, natural, and undebauched notions of mankind; that it manifests the dependence of all things on God; and consequently hath all the good effect or influence, which it is possible that important article of our faith should have in making men humble, thankful, and resigned to their Creator. I say, moreover, that, in this naked conception of things, divested of words, there will not be found any notion of what you call the *actuality of absolute existence*. You may indeed raise a dust with those terms, and so lengthen our dispute to no purpose. But I entreat you calmly to look into your own thoughts, and then tell me if they are not a useless and unintelligible jargon.

Hyl. I own I have no very clear notion annexed to them. But what say you to this? Do you not make the existence of sensible things consist in their being in a mind? And were not all things eternally in the mind of God? Did they not therefore exist from all eternity, according to you? And how could that which was eternal be created in time? Can anything be clearer or better connected than this?

Phil. And are not you too of opinion, that God knew all things from eternity?

Hyl. I am.

Phil. Consequently they always had a being in the Divine intellect.

Hyl. This I acknowledge.

Phil. By your own confession, therefore, nothing is new, or begins to be, in respect of the mind of God. So we are agreed in that point.

Hyl. What shall we make then of the creation?

Phil. May we not understand it to have been entirely in respect of finite spirits; so that things, with regard to us, may properly be said to begin their existence, or be created, when God decreed they should become perceptible to intelligent creatures, in that order and manner which He then established, and we now call the laws of nature? You may call this a *relative*, or *hypothetical existence* if you please. But, so long as it supplies us with the most natural, obvious, and literal sense of the Mosaic history of the creation; so long as it answers all the religious ends of that great article; in a word, so long as you can assign no other sense or meaning in its stead; why should we reject this? Is it to comply with a ridiculous sceptical humour of making everything nonsense and unintelligible? I am sure you cannot say it is for the glory of God: For, allowing it to be a thing possible and conceivable that the corporeal world should have an absolute existence extrinsical to the mind of God, as well as to the minds of all created spirits; yet how could this set forth either the immensity or omniscience of the Deity, or the necessary and immediate dependence of all things on Him? Nay, would it not rather seem to derogate from those attributes?

Hyl. Well, but as to this decree of God's, for making things perceptible, what say you, Philonous? Is it not plain, God did either execute that decree from all eternity, or at some certain time began to will what He had not actually willed before, but only designed to will? If the former, then there could be no creation, or beginning of existence, in finite things. If the latter, then we must acknowledge something new to befall the Deity; which implies a sort of change: and all change argues imperfection.

Phil. Pray consider what you are doing. Is it not evident this objection concludes equally against a creation in any sense; nay, against every other act of the Deity, discoverable by the light of nature? None of which can *we* conceive, otherwise than as performed in time, and having a beginning. God is a Being of transcendent and unlimited perfections: His nature, therefore, is incomprehensible to finite spirits. It is not, therefore, to be expected, that any man, whether Materialist or Immaterialist, should have exactly just notions of the Deity, His attributes, and ways of operation. If then you would infer anything against me, your difficulty must not be drawn from the inadequacies of our conceptions of the Divine nature, which is unavoidable on any scheme; but from the denial of Matter, of which there is not one word, directly or indirectly, in what you have now objected.

Hyl. I must acknowledge the difficulties you are concerned to clear are such only as arise from the nonexistence of Matter, and are peculiar to that notion. So far you are in the right. But I cannot by any means bring myself to think there is no such peculiar repugnancy between the creation and your opinion; though indeed where to fix it, I do not distinctly know.

Phil. What would you have? Do I not acknowledge a twofold state of things—the one ectypal or natural, the other archetypal and eternal? The former was created in time; the latter existed from everlasting in the mind of God. Is not this agreeable to the common notions of divines? or, is any more than this necessary in order to conceive the creation? But you suspect some peculiar repugnancy, though you know not where it lies. To take away all possibility of scruple in the case, do but consider this one point. Either you are not able to conceive the creation on any hypothesis whatsoever; and, if so, there is no ground for dislike or complaint against any particular opinion on that score: or you are able to conceive it; and, if so, why not on my Principles, since thereby nothing conceivable is taken away? You have all along been allowed the full scope of sense, imagination, and reason. Whatever, therefore, you could before apprehend, either immediately or mediately by your senses, or by ratiocination from your senses; whatever you could perceive, imagine, or understand, remains still with you. If, therefore, the notion you have of the creation by other Principles be intelligible, you have it still upon mine; if it be not intelligible, I conceive it to be no notion at all; and so there is no loss of it. And indeed it seems to me very plain that the supposition of Matter, that is a thing perfectly unknown and inconceivable, cannot serve to make us conceive anything. And, I hope it need not be proved to you that if the existence of Matter doth not make the creation conceivable, the creation's being without it inconceivable can be no objection against its non-existence.

Hyl. I confess, Philonous, you have almost satisfied me in this point of the creation.

Phil. I would fain know why you are not quite satisfied. You tell me indeed of a repugnancy between the Mosaic history and Immaterialism: but you know not where it lies. Is this reasonable, Hylas? Can you expect I should solve a difficulty without knowing what it is? But, to pass by all that, would not a man think you were assured there is no repugnancy between the received notions of Materialists and the inspired writings?

Hyl. And so I am.

Phil. Ought the historical part of Scripture to be understood in a plain obvious sense, or in a sense which is metaphysical and out of the way?

Hyl. In the plain sense, doubtless.

Phil. When Moses speaks of herbs, earth, water, &c. as having been created by God; think you not the sensible things commonly signified by those words are suggested to every unphilosophical reader?

Hyl. I cannot help thinking so.

Phil. And are not all ideas, or things perceived by sense, to be denied a real existence by the doctrine of the Materialist?

Hyl. This I have already acknowledged.

Phil. The creation, therefore, according to them, was not the creation of things sensible, which have only a relative being, but of certain unknown natures, which have an absolute being, wherein creation might terminate?

Hyl. True.

Phil. Is it not therefore evident the assertors of Matter destroy the plain obvious sense of Moses, with which their notions are utterly inconsistent; and instead of it obtrude on us I know not what; something equally unintelligible to themselves and me?

Hyl. I cannot contradict you.

Phil. Moses tells us of a creation. A creation of what? of unknown quiddities, of occasions, or *substratum?* No, certainly; but of things obvious to the senses. You must first reconcile this with your notions, if you expect I should be reconciled to them.

Hyl. I see you can assault me with my own weapons.

Phil. Then as to *absolute existence;* was there ever known a more jejune notion than that? Something it is so abstracted and unintelligible that you have frankly owned you could not conceive it, much less explain anything by it. But allowing Matter to exist, and the notion of absolute existence to be as clear as light; yet, was this ever known to make the creation more credible? Nay, hath it not furnished the atheists and infidels of all ages with the most plausible arguments against a creation? That a corporeal substance, which hath an absolute existence without the minds of spirits, should be produced out of nothing, by the mere will of a Spirit, hath been looked upon as a thing so contrary to all reason, so impossible and absurd, that not only the most celebrated among the ancients, but even divers modern and Christian philosophers have thought Matter co-eternal with the Deity. Lay these things together, and then judge you whether Materialism disposes men to believe the creation of things.

Hyl. I own, Philonous, I think it does not. This of the *creation* is the last objection I can think of; and I must needs own it hath been sufficiently answered as well as the rest. Nothing now remains to be overcome but a sort of unaccountable backwardness that I find in myself towards your notions.

Phil. When a man is swayed, he knows not why, to one side of the question, can this, think you, be anything else but the effect of prejudice, which never fails to attend old and rooted notions? And indeed in this respect I cannot deny the belief of Matter to have very much the advantage over the contrary opinion, with men of a learned education.

Hyl. I confess it seems to be as you say.

Phil. As a balance, therefore, to this weight of prejudice, let us throw into the scale the great advantages that arise from the belief of Immaterialism, both in regard to religion and human learning. The being of a God, and incorruptibility of the soul, those great articles of religion, are they not proved with the clearest and most immediate evidence? When I say the being of a God, I do not mean an obscure general Cause of things, whereof we have no conception, but God, in the strict and proper sense of the word. A Being whose spirituality, omnipresence, providence, omniscience, infinite power and goodness, are as conspicuous as the existence of sensible things, of which (notwithstanding the fallacious pretences and affected scruples of Sceptics) there is no more reason to doubt than of our own being.—Then, with relation to human sciences. In Natural Philosophy, what intricacies, what obscurities, what contradictions hath the belief of Matter led men into! To say nothing of the numberless disputes about its extent, continuity, homogeneity, gravity, divisibility, &c.— do they not pretend to explain all things by bodies operating on bodies, according to the laws of motion? and yet, are they able to comprehend how one body should move another? Nay, admitting there was no difficulty in reconciling the notion of an inert being with a cause, or in conceiving how an accident might pass from one body to another; yet, by all their strained thoughts and extravagant suppositions, have they been able to reach the *mechanical* production of any one animal or vegetable body? Can they account, by the laws of motion, for sounds, tastes, smells, or colours; or for the regular course of things? Have they accounted, by physical principles, for the aptitude and contrivance even of the most inconsiderable parts of the universe? But, laying aside Matter and corporeal causes, and admitting only the efficiency of an All-perfect Mind, are not all the effects of nature easy and intelligible? If the *phenomena* are nothing else but *ideas;* God is a *spirit,* but Matter an unintelligent, unperceiving being. If they demonstrate an unlimited power in their cause; God is active and omnipotent, but Matter an inert mass. If the order, regularity, and usefulness of them can never be sufficiently admired; God is infinitely wise and provident, but Matter destitute of all contrivance and design. These surely are great advantages in *Physics.* Not to mention that the apprehension of a distant Deity naturally disposes men to a negligence in their moral actions; which they would be more cautious of, in case they thought Him immediately present, and acting on their minds, without the interposition of Matter, or unthinking second causes.—Then in *Metaphysics:* what difficulties concerning entity in abstract, substantial forms, hylarchic principles, plastic natures, substance and accident, principle of individuation, possibility of Matter's thinking, origin of ideas, the manner how two independent substances so widely different as *Spirit* and *Matter,* should mutually operate on each other? what difficulties, I say, and endless disquisitions, concerning these and innumerable other the like points, do we escape, by supposing only Spirits and ideas?— Even the *Mathematics* themselves, if we take away the absolute existence of extended things, becomes much more clear and easy; the most shocking paradoxes and intricate speculations in those sciences depending on the infinite divisibility of finite extension; which depends on that supposition.—But what need is there to insist on the particular sciences? Is not that opposition to all science whatsoever, that frenzy of the ancient and modern Sceptics, built on the same foundation? Or can you produce so much as one argument against the reality of corporeal things, or in behalf of that avowed utter ignorance of their natures, which doth not suppose their reality to consist in an external absolute existence? Upon this supposition, indeed, the objections from the change of colours in a pigeon's neck, or the appearance of the broken oar in the water, must be allowed to have weight. But these and the like objections vanish, if we do not maintain the being of absolute external originals, but place the reality of things in ideas, fleeting indeed, and changeable;—however, not changed at random, but according to the fixed order of nature. For, herein consists that constancy and truth of things which secures all the concerns of life, and distinguishes that which is *real* from the *irregular visions* of the fancy.

Hyl. I agree to all you have now said, and must own that nothing can incline me to embrace your opinion more than the advantages I see it is attended with. I am by nature lazy; and this would be a mighty abridgment in knowledge. What doubts, what hypotheses, what labyrinths of amusement, what fields of disputation, what an ocean of false learning, may be avoided by that single notion of *Immaterialism!*

Phil. After all, is there anything farther remaining to be done? You may remember you promised to embrace that opinion which upon examination should appear most agreeable to Common Sense and remote from Scepticism. This, by your own confession, is that which denies Matter, or the *absolute* existence of corporeal things. Nor is this all; the same notion has been proved several ways, viewed in different lights, pursued in its consequences, and all objections against it cleared. Can there be a greater evidence of its truth? or is it possible it should have all the marks of a true opinion and yet be false?

Hyl. I own myself entirely satisfied for the present in all respects. But, what security can I have that I shall still continue the same full assent to your opinion, and that no unthought-of objection or difficulty will occur hereafter?

Phil. Pray, Hylas, do you in other cases, when a point is once evidently proved, withhold your consent on account of objections or difficulties it may be liable to? Are the difficulties that attend the doctrine of incommensurable quantities, of the angle of contact, of the asymptotes to curves, or the like, sufficient to make you hold out against mathematical demonstration? Or will you disbelieve the Providence of God, because there may be some particular things which *you* know not how to reconcile with it? If there are difficulties attending *Immaterialism*, there are at the same time direct and evident proofs of it. But for the existence of Matter there is not one proof, and far more numerous and insurmountable objections lie againt it. But where are those mighty difficulties you insist on? Alas! you know not where or what they are; something which may possibly occur hereafter. If this be a sufficient pretence for withholding your full assent, you should never yield it to any proposition, how free soever from exceptions, how clearly and solidly soever demonstrated.

Hyl. You have satisfied me, Philonous.

Phil. But, to arm you against all future objections, do but consider: That which bears equally hard on two contradictory opinions can be proof against neither. Whenever, therefore, any difficulty occurs, try if you can find a solution for it on the hypothesis of the *Materialists*. Be not deceived by words; but sound your own thoughts. And in case you cannot conceive it easier by the help of *Materialism*, it is plain it can be no objection against *Immaterialism*. Had you proceeded all along by this rule, you would probably have spared yourself abundance of trouble in objecting; since of all your difficulties I challenge you to shew one that is explained by Matter: nay, which is not more unintelligible with than without that supposition; and consequently makes rather *against* than *for* it. You should consider, in each particular, whether the difficulty arises from the *non-existence of Matter*. If it doth not, you might as well argue from the infinite divisibility of extension against the Divine prescience, as from such a difficulty against *Immaterialism*. And yet, upon recollection, I believe you will find this to have been often, if not always, the case. You should likewise take heed not to argue on a *petitio principii*. One is apt to say— The unknown substances ought to be esteemed real things, rather than the ideas in our minds: and who can tell but the unthinking external substance may concur, as a cause or instrument, in the production of our ideas? But is not this proceeding on a supposition that there are such external substances? And to suppose this, is it not begging the question? But, above all things, you should beware of imposing on yourself by that vulgar sophism which is called *ignoratio elenchi*. You talked often as if you thought I maintained the nonexistence of Sensible Things. Whereas in truth no one can be more thoroughly assured of their existence than I am. And it is you who doubt; I should have said, positively deny it. Everything that is seen, felt, heard, or any way perceived by the senses, is, on the principles I embrace, a real being; but not on yours. Remember, the Matter you contend for is an Unknown Somewhat (if indeed it may be termed *somewhat*), which is quite stripped of all sensible qualities, and can neither be perceived by sense, nor apprehended by the mind. Remember, I say, that it is not any object which is hard or soft, hot or cold, blue or white, round or square, &c. For all these things I affirm do exist. Though indeed I deny they have an existence distinct from being perceived; or that they exist out of all minds whatsoever. Think on these points; let them be attentively considered and still kept in view. Otherwise you will not comprehend the state of the question; without which your objections will always be wide of the mark, and, instead of mine, may possibly be directed (as more than once they have been) against your own notions.

Hyl. I must needs own, Philonous, nothing seems to have kept me from agreeing with you more than this same *mistaking the question*. In denying Matter, at first glimpse I am tempted to imagine you deny the things we see and feel: but, upon reflexion, find there is no ground for it. What think you, therefore, of retaining the name *Matter*, and applying it to *sensible things*? This may be done without any change in your sentiments: and, believe me, it would be a means of reconciling them to some persons who may be more shocked at an innovation in words than in opinion.

Phil. With all my heart: retain the word *Matter*, and apply it to the objects of sense, if you please; provided you do not attribute to them any subsistence distinct from their being perceived. I shall never quarrel with you for an expression. *Matter*, or *material substance*, are terms introduced by philosophers; and, as used by them, imply a sort of independency, or a subsistence distinct from being perceived by a mind: but are never used by common people; or, if ever, it is to signify the immediate objects of sense. One would think, therefore, so long as the names of all particular things, with the terms *sensible, substance, body, stuff,* and the like, are retained, the word *Matter* should be never missed in common talk. And in philosophical discourses it seems the best way to leave it quite out: since there is not, perhaps, any one thing that hath more favoured and strengthened the depraved bent of the mind toward Atheism than the use of that general confused term.

Hyl. Well but, Philonous, since I am content to give up the notion of an unthinking substance exterior to the mind, I think you ought not to deny me the privilege of using the word *Matter* as I please, and annexing it to a collection of sensible qualities subsisting only in the mind. I freely own there is no other substance, in a strict sense, than *Spirit.* But I have been so long accustomed to the *term Matter* that I know not how to part with it: to say, there is no *Matter* in the world, is still shocking to me. Whereas to say—There is no *Matter,* if by that term be meant an unthinking substance existing without the mind; but if by *Matter* is meant some sensible thing, whose existence consists in being perceived, then there is *Matter:*—this distinction gives it quite another term; and men will come into your notions with small difficulty, when they are proposed in that manner. For, after all, the controversy about *Matter* in the strict acceptation of it, lies altogether between you and the philosophers: whose principles, I acknowledge, are not near so natural, or so agreeable to the common sense of mankind, and Holy Scripture, as yours. There is nothing we either desire or shun but as it makes, or is apprehended to make, some part of our happiness or misery. But what hath happiness or misery, joy or grief, pleasure or pain, to do with Absolute Existence; or with unknown entities, *abstracted from all relation to us?* It is evident, things regard us only as they are pleasing or displeasing: and they can please or displease only so far forth as they are perceived. Farther, therefore, we are not concerned; and thus far you leave things as you found them. Yet still there is something new in this doctrine. It is plain, I do not now think with the philosophers; nor yet altogether with the vulgar. I would know how the case stands in that respect; precisely, what you have added to, or altered in my former notions.

Phil. I do not pretend to be a setter-up of new notions. My endeavours tend only to unite, and place in a clearer light, that truth which was before shared between the vulgar and the philosophers:—the former being of opinion, that *those things they immediately perceive are the real things;* and the latter, that *the things immediately perceived are ideas, which exist only in the mind*. Which two notions put together, do, in effect, constitute the substance of what I advance.

Hyl. I have been a long time distrusting my senses: methought I saw things by a dim light and through false glasses. Now the glasses are removed and a new light breaks in upon my understanding. I am clearly convinced that I see things in their native forms, and am no longer in pain about their *unknown natures* or *absolute existence*. This is the state I find myself in at present; though, indeed, the course that brought me to it I do not yet thoroughly comprehend. You set out upon the same principles that Academics, Cartesians, and the like sects usually do; and for a long time it looked as if you were advancing their philosophical Scepticism: but, in the end, your conclusions are directly opposite to theirs.

Phil. You see, Hylas, the water of yonder fountain, how it is forced upwards, in a round column, to a certain height; at which it breaks, and falls back into the basin from whence it rose: its ascent, as well as descent, proceeding from the same uniform law or principle of gravitation. Just so, the same Principles which, at first view, lead to Scepticism, pursued to a certain point, bring men back to Common Sense.

Philosophical Correspondence with Samuel Johnson

THE SAMUEL JOHNSON with whom Berkeley corresponded is not the great Doctor. Berkeley's correspondent is known to cataloguers as Samuel Johnson, D.D. to distinguish him from Samuel Johnson, LL.D. (Both were honorary degrees bestowed by Oxford University.) He was educated at Yale, was a tutor there for some years, and later became the first President of King's College, New York, now Columbia University. He is regarded as the father of American philosophy, and he was deeply influenced by Berkeley. The letters that follow were exchanged in 1729-30, and were part of a longer philosophical correspondence that has not survived. Johnson was at that time living at Stratford, Connecticut, and Berkeley was at Newport, Rhode Island, having come to America to pursue his scheme for a college in the Bermudas.

Johnson's two letters are of the greatest interest (Berkeley's replies are a trifle perfunctory) and show a good contemporary mind, sympathetic to what Berkeley has to say, nevertheless pressing him shrewdly on a number of difficult points in Berkeley's system: Cause, Space and Time, Spirits and Unobserved Objects.

The correspondence is reprinted here by kind permission of Columbia University Press.

I Johnson to Berkeley

Stratford, Sept. 10, 1729.

Rev'd Sir:—

The kind invitation you gave me to lay before you any difficulties that should occur to me in reading those excellent books which you was pleased to order into my hands, is all the apology I shall offer for the trouble I now presume to give you. But nothing could encourage me to expose to your view my low and mean way of thinking and writing, but my hopes of an interest in that candor and tenderness which are so conspicuous both in your writings and conversation.

These books (for which I stand humbly obliged to you) contain speculations the most surprisingly ingenious I have ever met with; and I must confess that the reading of them has almost convinced me that matter as it has been commonly defined for an unknown Quiddity is but a mere non-entity. That it is a strong presumption against the existence of it, that there never could be conceived any manner of connection between it and our ideas. That the *esse* of things is only their *percipi;* and that the rescuing us from the absurdities of abstract ideas and the gross notion of matter that have so much obtained, deserves well of the learned world, in that it clears away very many difficulties and perplexities in the sciences.

And I am of opinion that this way of thinking can't fail of prevailing in the world, because it is likely to prevail very much among us in these parts, several ingenious men having entirely come in to it. But there are many others on the other hand that cannot be reconciled to it; tho' of these there are some who have a very good opinion of it and plainly see many happy consequences attending it, on account of which they are well inclined to embrace it, but think they find some difficulties in their way which they can't get over, and some objections not sufficiently answered to their satisfaction. And since you have condescended to give me leave to do so, I will make bold to lay before you sundry things, which yet remain in the dark either to myself or to others, and which I can't account for either to my own, or at least to their satisfaction.

1. The great prejudice that lies against it with some is its repugnancy to and subversion of Sir I. Newton's philosophy in sundry points; to which they have been so much attached that they can't suffer themselves in the least to call it in question in any instance, but indeed it does not appear to me so inconsistent therewith as at first blush it did, for the laws of nature which he so happily explains are the same whether matter be supposed or not. However, let Sir Isaac Newton, or any other man, be heard only so far as his opinion is supported by reason:—but after all I confess I have so great a regard for the philosophy of that great man, that I would gladly see as much of it as may be, to obtain in this ideal scheme.

2. The objection, that it takes away all subordinate natural causes, and accounts for all appearances merely by the immediate will of the supreme spirit, does not seem to many to be answered to their satisfaction. It is readily granted that our ideas are inert, and can't cause one another, and are truly only signs one of another. For instance my idea of fire is not the cause of my idea of burning and of ashes. But inasmuch as these ideas are so connected as that they seem necessarily to point out to us the relations of cause and effect, we can't help thinking that our ideas are pictures of things without our minds at least, tho' not without the Great Mind, and which are their archetypes, between which these relations do obtain. I kindle a fire and leave it, no created mind beholds it; I return again and find a great alteration in the fuel; has there not been in my absence all the while that gradual alteration making in the archetype of my idea of wood which I should have had the idea of if I had been present? And is there not some archetype of my idea of the fire, which under the agency of the Divine Will has gradually caused this alteration? And so in all other instances, our ideas are so connected, that they seem necessarily to refer our minds to some originals which are properly (tho' subordinate) causes and effects one of another; insomuch that unless they be so, we can't help thinking ourselves under a perpetual delusion.

3. That all the phenomena of nature, must ultimately be referred to the will of the Infinite Spirit, is what must be allowed; but to suppose his immediate energy in the production of every effect, does not seem to impress so lively and great a sense of his power and wisdom upon our minds, as to suppose a subordination of causes and effects among the

archetypes of our ideas, as he that should make a watch or clock of ever so beautiful an appearance and that should measure the time ever so exactly yet if he should be obliged to stand by it and influence and direct all its motions, he would seem but very deficient in both his ability and skill in comparison with him who should be able to make one that would regularly keep on its motion and measure the time for a considerable while without the intervention of any immediate force of its author or any one else impressed upon it.

4. And as this tenet seems thus to abate our sense of the wisdom and power of God, so there are some that cannot be persuaded that it is sufficiently cleared from bearing hard on his holiness; those who suppose that the corrupt affections of our souls and evil practices consequent to them, are occasioned by certain irregular mechanical motions of our bodies, and that these motions come to have an habitual irregular bias and tendency by means of our own voluntary indulgence to them, which we might have governed to better purpose, do in this way of thinking, sufficiently bring the guilt of those ill habits and actions upon ourselves; but if in an habitual sinner, every object and motion be but an idea, and every wicked appetite the effect of such a set of ideas, and these ideas, the immediate effect of the Almighty upon his mind; it seems to follow, that the immediate cause of such ideas must be the cause of those immoral appetites and actions; because he is borne down before them seemingly, even in spite of himself. At first indeed they were only occasions, which might be withstood, and so, proper means of trial, but now they become causes of his immoralities. When therefore a person is under the power of a vicious habit, and it can't but be foreseen that the suggestion of such and such ideas will unavoidably produce those immoralities, how can it consist with the holiness of God to suggest them?

5. It is, after all that has been said on that head, still something shocking to many to think that there should be nothing but a mere show in all the art and contrivance appearing in the structure (for instance) of a human body, particularly of the organs of sense. The curious structure of the eye, what can it be more than merely a fine show, if there be no connection more than you admit of, between that and vision? It seems from the make of it to be designed for an instrument or means of conveying the images of external things to the perceptive faculty within; and if it be

not so, if it be really of no use in conveying visible objects to our minds, and if our visible ideas are immediately created in them by the will of the Almighty, why should it be made to seem to be an instrument or medium as much as if indeed it really were so? It is evident, from the conveying of images into a dark room thro' a lens, that the eye is a lens, and that the images of things are painted on the bottom of it. But to what purpose is all this, if there be no connection between this fine apparatus and the act of vision; can it be thought a sufficient argument that there is no connection between them because we can't discover it, or conceive how it should be?

6. There are some who say, that if our sensations don't depend on any bodily organs—they don't see how death can be supposed to make any alteration in the manner of our perception, or indeed how there should be (properly speaking) any separate state of the soul at all. For if our bodies are nothing but ideas, and if our having ideas in this present state does not depend upon what are thought to be the organs of sense, and lastly, if we are supposed (as doubtless we must) to have ideas in that state; it should seem that immediately upon our remove from our present situation, we should still be attended with the same ideas of bodies as we have now, and consequently with the same bodies or at least with bodies however different, and if so, what room is there left for any resurrection, properly so-called? So that while this tenet delivers us from the embarrassments that attend the doctrine of a material resurrection, it seems to have no place for any resurrection at all, at least in the sense that word seems to bear in St. John 5; 28, 29.

7. Some of us are at a loss to understand your meaning when you speak of archetypes. You say the beings of things consists in their being perceived. And that things are nothing but ideas, that our ideas have no unperceived archetypes, but yet you allow archetypes to our ideas when things are not perceived by our minds; they exist in, *i.e.*, are perceived by, some other mind. Now I understand you, that there is a twofold existence of things or ideas, one in the divine mind, and the other in created minds; the one archetypal, and the other ectypal; that, therefore, the real original and permanent existence of things is archetypal, being ideas in *mente Divinâ*, and that our ideas are copies of them, and so far forth real things as they are correspondent to their archetypes and ex-

hibited to us, or begotten in us by the will of the Almighty, in such measure and degrees and by such stated laws and rules as He is pleased to observe; that, therefore, there is no unperceived substance intervening between the divine ideas and ours as a medium, occasion or instrument by which He begets our ideas in us, but that which was thought to be the material existence of things is in truth only ideal in the divine mind. Do I understand you right? Is it not therefore your meaning, that the existence of our ideas (*i.e.,* the ectypal things) depends upon our perceiving them, yet there are external to any created mind, in the all-comprehending Spirit, real and permanent archetypes (as stable and permanent as ever matter was thought to be), to which these ideas of ours are correspondent, and so that (tho' our visible and tangible ideas are *toto coelo* different and distinct things, yet) there may be said to be external to my mind, in the divine mind, an archetype (for instance of the candle that is before me) in which the originals of both my visible and tangible ideas, light, heat, whiteness, softness, etc., under such a particular cylindrical figure, are united, so that it may be properly said to be the same thing that I both see and feel?

8. If this, or something like it might be understood to be your meaning, it would seem less shocking to say that we don't see and feel the same thing, because we can't dispossess our minds of the notion of an external world, and would be allowed to conceive that, tho' there were no intelligent creature before Adam to be a spectator of it, yet the world was really six days in *archetypo,* gradually proceeding from an informal chaotic state into that beautiful show wherein it first appeared to his mind, and that the comet that appeared in 1680 (for instance) has now, tho' no created mind beholds it, a real existence in the all-comprehending spirit, and is making its prodigious tour through the vast fields of ether, and lastly that the whole vast congeries of heaven and earth, the mighty systems of worlds with all their furniture, have a real being in the eternal mind antecedent to and independent of the perception of created spirit, and that when we see and feel, etc., that that almighty mind, by his immediate *fiat,* begets in our minds (*pro nostro modulo*) ideas correspondent to them, and which may be imagined in some degree resemblances of them.

9. But if there be archetypes to our ideas, will it not follow

that there is external space, extention, figure and motion, as being archetypes of our ideas, to which we give these names. And indeed for my part I cannot disengage my mind from the persuasion that there is external space; when I have been trying ever so much to conceive of space as being nothing but an idea in my mind, it will return upon me even in spite of my utmost efforts, certainly there must be, there can't but be, external space. The length, breadth, and thickness of any idea, it's true, are but ideas; the distance between two trees in my mind is but an idea, but if there are archetypes to the ideas of the trees, there must be an archetype to the idea of the distance betweeen them. Nor can I see how it follows that there is no external absolute height, bigness, or distance of things, because they appear greater or less to us according as we are nearer or remote from them, or see them with our naked eyes, or with glasses; any more than it follows that a man, for instance, is not really absolutely six foot high measured by a two foot rule applied to his body, because divers pictures of him may be drawn some six, some four, some two foot long according to the same measure. Nobody ever imagined that the idea of distance is without the mind, but does it therefore follow that there is no external distance to which the idea is correspondent, for instance, between Rhode Island and Stratford? Truly I wish it were not so great, that I might be so happy as to have a more easy access to you, and more nearly enjoy the advantages of your instructions.

10. You allow spirits to have a real existence external to one another. Methinks, if so, there must be distance between them, and space wherein they exist, or else they must all exist in one individual spot or point, and as it were coincide one with another. I can't see how external space and duration are any more abstract ideas than spirits. As we have (properly speaking) no ideas of spirits, so, indeed, neither have we of external space and duration. But it seems to me that the existence of these must unavoidably follow from the existence of those, insomuch that I can no more conceive of their not being, than I can conceive of the non-existence of the infinite and eternal mind. They seem as necessarily existent independent of any created mind as the Deity Himself. Or must we say there is nothing in Dr. Clarke's argument *a priori*, in his demonstration of the being and attributes of God, or in

what Sir Isaac Newton says about the infinity and eternity of God in his *Scholium Generale* to his *Principia?* I should be glad to know your sense of what those two authors say upon this subject.

11. You will forgive the confusedness of my thoughts and not wonder at my writing like a man something bewildered, since I am, as it were, got into a new world amazed at everything about me. These ideas of ours, what are they? Is the substance of the mind the *substratum* to its ideas? Is it proper to call them modifications of our minds? Or impressions upon them? Or what? Truly I can't tell what to make of them, any more than of matter itself. What is the *esse* of spirits?—you seem to think it impossible to abstract their existence from their thinking. *Princ.* p. 143. sec. 98. Is then the *esse* of minds nothing else but *percipere,* as the *esse* of ideas is *percipi?* Certainly, methinks there must be an unknown somewhat that thinks and acts, as difficult to be conceived of as matter, and the creation of which, as much beyond us as the creation of matter. Can actions be the *esse* of any thing? Can they exist or be exerted without some being who is the agent? And may not that being be easily imagined to exist without acting, *e.g.,* without thinking? And consequently (for you are there speaking of duration) may he not be said *durare, etsi non cogitet,* to persist in being, tho' thinking were intermitted for a while? And is not this sometimes fact? The duration of the eternal mind, must certainly imply something besides an eternal succession of ideas. May I not then conceive that, tho' I get my idea of duration by observing the succession of ideas in my mind, yet there is a *perseverare in existendo,* a duration of my being, and of the being of other spirits distinct from, and independent of, this succession of ideas.

But, Sir, I doubt I have more than tired your patience with so many (and I fear you will think them impertinent) questions; for tho' they are difficulties with me, or at least with some in my neighborhood, for whose sake, in part, I write, yet I don't imagine they can appear such to you, who have so perfectly digested your thoughts upon this subject. And perhaps they may vanish before me upon a more mature consideration of it. However, I should be very thankful for your assistance, if it were not a pity you should waste your time (which would be employed to much better purposes) in writing to a person so obscure and so unworthy of such a favor as I am. But I shall live with some impatience till I see the second part of your design accomplished, wherein I hope to see these (if they can be thought such) or any other objections, that may have occurred to you since your writing the first part, obviated; and the usefulness of this doctrine more particularly displayed in the further application of it to the arts and sciences. May we not hope to see logic, mathematics, and natural philosophy, pneumatology, theology and morality, all in their order, appearing with a new lustre under the advantages they may receive from it? You have at least given us to hope for a geometry cleared of many perplexities that render that sort of study troublesome, which I shall be very glad of, who have found that science more irksome to me than any other, tho', indeed, I am but very little versed in any of them. But I will not trespass any further upon your patience. My very humble service to Mr. James and Mr. Dalton, and I am with the greatest veneration,

  Rev'd Sir,
   your most obliged
    and most obedient
     humble servant
     Samuel Johnson

II Berkeley to Johnson

Nov. 25, 1729.

Rev. Sir:—

The ingenious letter you favored me with found me very much indisposed with a gathering or imposthumation in my head, which confined me several weeks, and is now, I thank God, relieved. The objections of a candid thinking man to what I have written will always be welcome, and I shall not fail to give all the satisfaction I am able, not without hopes either of convincing or being convinced. It is a common fault for men to hate opposition, and be too much wedded to their own opinions. I am so sensible of this in others that I could not pardon it to myself, if I considered mine any further than they seem to me to be true, which I shall the better be able to judge of when they have passed the scrutiny of persons so well qualified to examine them as you and your friends appear to be, to whom my illness must be an apology for not sending this answer sooner.

1. The true use and end of natural philosophy is to explain the phenomena of nature, which is done by discovering the laws of nature, and reducing particular appearances to them. This is Sir Isaac Newton's method; and such method or design is not in the least inconsistent with the principles I lay down. This mechanical philosophy doth not assign or suppose any one natural efficient cause in the strict and proper sense; nor is it, as to its use, concerned about *matter;* nor is matter connected therewith; nor doth it infer the being of matter. It must be owned, indeed, that the mechanical philosophers do suppose (though unnecessarily) the being of matter. They do even pretend to demonstrate that matter is proportional to gravity, which, if they could, this indeed would furnish an unanswerable objection. But let us examine their demonstration—it is laid down in the first place, that the momentum of any body is the product of its quantity by its velocity, *moles in celeritatem ducta.* If, therefore, the velocity is given, the momentum will be as its quantity. But it is observed that bodies of all kinds descend *in vacuo* with the same velocity; therefore, the momentum of descending bodies is as the quantity of moles, *i.e.,* gravity is as matter. But this argument concludes nothing, and is a mere circle. For, I ask, when it is premised that the momentum is equal to the *moles in celeritatem ducta,* how the moles or quantity of matter is estimated. If you say, by extent, the proposition is not true; if by weight, then you suppose that the quantity of matter is proportional to matter: *i.e.,* the conclusion is taken for granted in one of the premises. As for absolute space and motion, which are also supposed without any necessity or use, I refer you to what I have already published; particularly in a Latin treatise, *De Motu,* which I shall take care to send you.

2. Cause is taken in different senses. A proper active efficient cause I can conceive none but spirit; nor any action, strictly speaking, but where there is will. But this doth not hinder the allowing occasional causes (which are in truth but signs), and more is not requisite in the best physics, *i.e.,* the mechanical philosophy. Neither doth it hinder the admitting other causes besides God; such as spirits of different orders, which may be termed active causes, as acting indeed,

though by limited and derivative powers. But as for an unthinking agent, no point of physics is explained by it, nor is it conceivable.

3. Those who have all along contended for a material world, have yet acknowledged that *natura naturans* (to use the language of the Schoolmen) is God; and that the divine conservation of things is equipollent to, and in fact, the same thing with a continued repeated creation; in a word, that conservation and creation differ only in the *terminus a quo*. These are the common opinions of the Schoolmen; and Durandus, who held the world to be a machine like a clock, made and put in motion by God, but afterwards continuing to go of itself, was therein particular and had few followers. The very poets teach a doctrine not unlike the schools,— *Mens agitat molem.* (Virg. Aenid VI.) The Stoics and Platonists are everywhere full of the same notion. I am not therefore singular in this point itself, so much as in my way of proving it. Further, it seems to me that the power and wisdom of God are as worthily set forth by supposing Him to act immediately as an omnipresent, infinitely active spirit, as by supposing Him to act by the mediation of subordinate causes, in preserving and governing the natural world. A clock may indeed go independent of its maker or artificer, inasmuch as the gravitation of its pendulum proceeds from another cause, and that the artificer is not the adequate cause of the clock; so that the analogy would not be just to suppose a clock is in respect of its artist what the world is in respect of its creator. For aught I can see, it is no disparagement to the perfection of God to say that all things necessarily depend on Him as their conservator as well as creator, and that all nature would shrink to nothing, if not upheld and preserved in being by the same force that first created it. This, I am sure, is agreeable to Holy Scripture, as well as to the writings of the most esteemed philosophers; and if it is to be considered that men make use of tools and machines to supply defect of power in themselves, we shall think it no honor to the divinity to attribute such things to him.

4. As to guilt, it is the same thing whether I kill a man with my hands or an instrument; whether I do it myself or make use of a ruffian. The imputation therefore upon the sanctity of God is equal, whether we suppose our sensations to be produced immediately by God, or by the mediation of

instruments and subordinate causes, all which are his creatures, and moved by his laws. This theological consideration,
therefore, may be waived, as leading besides the question;
for such I hold are points to be which bear equally hard
on both sides of it. Difficulties about the principle of moral
actions will cease, if we consider that all guilt is in the will,
and that our ideas, from whatever cause they are produced,
are alike inert.

5. As to the art and contrivance in the parts of animals,
etc., I have considered that matter in the *Principles of Human
Knowledge*, and, if I mistake not, sufficiently shown the wisdom and use thereof, considered as signs and means of information. I do not indeed wonder that on first reading what
I have written, men are not thoroughly convinced. On the
contrary, I should very much wonder if prejudices, which
have been many years taking root, should be extirpated in a
few hours' reading. I had no inclination to trouble the world
with large volumes. What I have done was rather with a view
of giving hints to thinking men, who have leisure and curiosity to go to the bottom of things, and pursue them in their
own minds. Two or three times reading these small tracts,
and making what is read the occasion of thinking, would,
I believe, render the whole familiar and easy to the mind,
and take off that shocking appearance which hath often been
observed to attend speculative truths.

6. I see no difficulty in conceiving a change of state, such
as is vulgarly called death, as well without as with material
substance. It is sufficient for that purpose that we allow
sensible bodies, *i.e.*, such as are immediately perceived by
sight and touch; the existence of which I am so far from
questioning (as philosophers are used to do) that I establish
it, I think, upon evident principles. Now, it seems very easy
to conceive the soul to exist in a separate state (*i.e.* divested
from those limits and laws of motion and perception with
which she is embarrassed here), and to exercise herself on
new ideas, without the intervention of these tangible things
we call bodies. It is even very possible to apprehend how
the soul may have ideas of color without an eye, or of sounds
without an ear. . . .

And now, Sir, I submit these hints (which I have hastily
thrown together as soon as my illness gave me leave) to your
own maturer thoughts, which after all you will find the best

instructors. What you have seen of mine was published when I was very young, and without doubt hath many defects. For though the notions should be true (as I verily think they are), yet it is difficult to express them clearly and consistently, language being framed to common use and received prejudices. I do not therefore pretend that my books can teach truth. All I hope for is that they may be an occasion to inquisitive men of discovering truth by consulting their own minds and looking into their own thoughts. As to the second part of my treatise concerning the principles of human knowledge, the fact is that I had made a considerable progress in it, but the manuscript was lost about fourteen years ago during my travels in Italy; and I never had leisure since to do so disagreeable a thing as writing twice on the same subject.

Objections passing through your hands have their full force and clearness. I like them the better. This intercourse with a man of parts and a philosophic genius is very agreeable. I sincerely wish we were nearer neighbors. In the meantime whenever either you or your friends favor me with your thoughts, you may be sure of a punctual correspondence on my part. Before I have done I will venture to recommend three points: 1. To consider well the answers I have already given in my books to several objections. 2. To consider whether any new objection that shall occur doth not suppose the doctrine of abstract general ideas. 3. Whether the difficulties proposed in objection to my scheme can be solved by the contrary, for if they cannot, it is plain they can be no objection to mine.

I know not whether you have got my treatise concerning the principles of human knowledge. I intend to send it with my tract *De Motu*. If you know of a safe hand favor me with a line, and I will make use of that opportunity to send them. My humble service to your friends, to whom I understand myself indebted for some part of your letter.

I am, your very faithful, humble servant,

Geor. Berkeley

III Johnson to Berkeley

Rev'd Sir:—   Feb. 5, 1730.
Yours of November 25th, I received not till January 17th,

and this being the first convenient opportunity I now return you my humblest thanks for it.

I am very sorry to understand that you have labored under the illness you mention, but am exceeding glad and thankful for your recovery; I pray God preserve your life and health, that you may have opportunity to perfect these great and good designs for the advancement of learning and religion wherewith your mind labors.

I am very much obliged to you for the favorable opinion you are pleased to express at what I made bold to write to you and that you have so kindly vouchsafed so large and particular an answer to it. But you have done me too great an honor in putting any value on my judgment; for it is impossible my thoughts on this subject should be of any consequence, who have been bred up under the greatest disadvantages, and have had so little ability and opportunity to be instructed in things of this nature. And therefore I should be very vain to pretend any thing else but to be a learner; 'tis merely with this view that I give you this trouble.

I am sensible that the greatest part of what I wrote was owing to not sufficiently attending to those three important considerations you suggest at the end of your letter. And I hope a little more time and a more careful attention to and application of them, will clear up what difficulties yet lie in the way of our entirely coming into your sentiments. Indeed I had not had opportunity sufficiently to digest your books; for no sooner had I just read them over, but they were greedily demanded by my friends, who live much scattered up and down, and who expected I would bring them home with me, because I had told them before that if the books were to be had in Boston, I intended to purchase a set of them; and indeed they have not yet quite finished their tour. The *Theory of Vision* is still at New York and the *Dialogues* just gone to Long Island. But I am the better content to want them because I know they are doing good.

For my part I am content to give up the cause of matter, glad to get rid of the absurdities thereon depending if it be defensible, I am sure, at least, it is not in my power to defend it. And being spoiled of that sandy foundation, I only want now to be more thoroughly taught how and where to set down my foot again and make out a clear and consistent scheme without it. And of all the particulars I troubled you with before, there remain only these that I have difficulty about, *viz.*, archetypes, space and duration, and the *esse* of spirits. And indeed these were the chief of my difficulties before. Most of the rest were such objections as I found by conversation among my acquaintance, did not appear to them sufficiently answered. But I believe upon a more mature consideration of the matter, and especially of this kind reply, they will see reason to be better satisfied. They that have seen it (especially my friend Mr. Wetmore) join with me in thankfully acknowledging your kindness, and return their very humble service to you.

1. As to those difficulties that yet remain with me, I believe all my hesitation about the first of them (and very likely the rest) is owing to my dullness and want of attention so as not rightly to apprehend your meaning. I believe I expressed myself unworthily about archetypes in my 7th and 8th articles, but upon looking back upon your *Dialogues,* and comparing again three or four passages, I can't think I meant any thing different from what you intended.

You allow, *Dial.* p. 74, "That things have an existence distinct from being perceived by us" (*i.e.*, any created spirits), "and that they exist in, *i.e.*, are perceived by, the infinite and omnipresent mind who contains and supports this sensible world as being perceived by him." And p. 109, "That things have an existence exterior to our minds, and that during the intervals of their being perceived by us, they exist in another (*i.e.*, the infinite) mind"; from whence you justly and excellently infer the certainty of his existence, "who knows and comprehends all things and exhibits them to our view in such manner and according to such rules as he himself has ordained." And p. 113, "That, *e.g.*, a tree when we don't perceive it, exists without our minds in the infinite mind of God." And this exterior existence of things (if I understand you right) is what you call the archetypal state of things. p. 150.

From these and the like expressions, I gathered what I said about the archetypes of our ideas, and thence inferred that there is exterior to us, in the divine mind, a system of universal nature, whereof the ideas we have are in such a degree resemblances as the Almighty is pleased to communicate to us. And I cannot yet see but my inference was just; because according to you, the idea we see is not in the divine mind, but in our own. When, therefore, you say sensible things exist in, as understood by, the infinite mind I humbly conceive you must be understood that the originals or archetypes of our sensible things or ideas exist independent of us in the infinite mind, or that sensible things exist *in archetypo* in the divine mind. The divine idea, therefore, of a tree suppose (or a tree in the divine mind), must be the original or archetype of ours, and ours a copy or image of His (our ideas images of His, in the same sense as our souls are images of Him) of which there may be several, in several created minds, like so many several pictures of the same original to which they are all to be referred.

When therefore, several people are said to see the same tree or star, etc., whether at the same or at so many several distances from it, it is (if I understand you) *unum et idem in Archetypo*, tho' *multiplex et diversum in Ectypo*, for it is as evident that your idea is not mine nor mine yours when we say we both look on the same tree, as that you are not I nor I you. But in having each our idea being dependent upon and impressed upon by the same almighty mind, wherein you say this tree exists, while we shut our eyes (and doubtless you mean the same also, while they are open), our several trees must, I think be so many pictures (if I may so call them) of the one original, the tree in the infinite mind, and so of all other things. Thus I understand you not indeed that our ideas are in any measure adequate resemblances of the system in the divine mind, but however that they are just and true resemblances or copies of it, so far as He is pleased to communicate His mind to us.

2. As to space and duration, I do not pretend to have any other notion of their exterior existence than what is necessarily implied in the notion we have of God; I do not suppose they are any thing distinct from, or exterior to, the infinite and external mind; for I conclude with you that there is nothing exterior to my mind but God and other spirits with the attributes or properties belonging to them and ideas contained in them.

External space and duration therefore I take to be those properties or attributes in God, to which our ideas, which we signify by those names, are correspondent, and of which they are the faint shadows. This I take to be Sir Isaac Newton's meaning when he says, *Schol. General. Deus—durat semper et adest ubique et existendo semper et ubique, durationem et spacium, etèrnitatem et infinitatem constituit.* And in his *Optics* calls space *as it were God's boundless sensorium,* nor can I think you have a different notion of these attributes from that great philosopher, tho' you may differ in your ways of expressing or explaining yourselves. However it be, when you call the Deity infinite and eternal, and in that most beautiful and charming description, *Dial.* p. 71. etc., when you speak of the *abyss of space and boundless extent beyond thought* and imagination, I don't know how to understand you any otherwise than I understood Sir Isaac, when he uses the like expressions. The truth is we have no proper ideas of God or His attributes, and conceive of them only by analogy from what we find in ourselves; and so, I think we conceive His immensity and eternity to be what in Him are correspondent to our space and duration.

As for the *punctum stans* of the Schools, and the τὸ νῦν of the Platonists, they are notions too fine for my gross thoughts; I can't tell what to make of those words, they don't seem to convey any ideas or notions to my mind, and whatever the matter is, the longer I think of them, the more they disappear, and seem to dwindle away into nothing. Indeed they seem to me very much like abstract ideas, but I doubt the reason is because I never rightly understood them. I don't see why the term *punctum stans* may not as well, at least, be applied to the immortality as the eternity of God; for the word *punctum* is more commonly used in relation to extension or space than duration; and to say that a being is immense, and yet that it is but a point, and that its duration is perpetual without beginning or end, and yet that it is but a τὸ νῦν , look to me like a contradiction.

I can't therefore understand the term τὸ νῦν, unless it be designed to adumbrate the divine omnisciency or the perfection of the divine knowledge, by the more perfect notion we have of things present than of things past; and in this sense it would imply that all things past, present and to come are always at every point of duration equally perfectly known or present to God's mind (tho' in a manner infinitely more perfect), as the things that are known to us are present to our minds at any point of our duration which we call *now*. So that with respect to His equally perfect knowledge of things past, present or to come, it is in effect always now with Him. To this purpose it seems well applied and intelligible enough, but His duration I take to be a different thing from this, as that point of our duration which we call *now*, is a different thing from our actual knowledge of things, as distinguished from our remembrance. And it may as well be said that God's immensity consists in His knowing at once what is, and is transacted in all places (*e.g.*, China, Jupiter, Saturn, all the systems of fixed stars, etc.) everywhere, however so remote from us (tho' in a manner infinitely more perfect), as we know what is, and is transacted in us and about us just at hand; as that His eternity consists in this τò νῦν as above explained, *i.e.*, in His knowing things present. past and to come, however so remote, all at once or equally perfectly as we know the things that are present to us *now*.

In short our ideas expressed by the terms immensity and eternity are only space and duration considered as boundless or with the negation of any limits, and I can't help thinking there is something analogous to them without us, being in and belonging to, or attributes of, that glorious mind, whom for that reason we call immense and eternal, in whom we and all other spirits, *live, move and have their being,* not all in a point, but in so many different points, places or *alicubis*, and variously situated with respect one to another, or else as I said before, it seems as if we should all coincide one with another.

I conclude, if I am wrong in my notion of eternal space, and duration, it is owing to the rivetted prejudices of abstract ideas; but really when I have thought it over and over again in my feeble way of thinking, I can't see any connection between them (as I understand them) and that doctrine. They don't seem to be any more abstract ideas than spirits, for, as I said, I take them to be attributes of the necessarily existing spirit; and consequently the same reasons that convince me of His existence, bring with them the existence of these attributes. So that of the ways of coming to the knowledge of things that you mention, it is that of inference or deduction by which I seem to know that there is external infinite space and duration because there is without me a mind infinite and eternal.

3. As to the *esse* of spirits, I know Descartes held the soul always thinks, but I thought Mr. Locke had sufficiently confuted this notion, which he seems to have entertained only to serve an hypothesis. The Schoolmen, it is true, call the

soul *Actus* and God *Actus purus;* but I confess I could never well understand their meaning perhaps because I never had opportunity to be much versed in their writings. I should have thought the schoolmen to be of all sorts of writers the most unlikely to have had recourse to for the understanding of your sentiments, because they of all others, deal the most in abstract ideas; tho' to place the very being of spirits in the mere act of thinking, seems to me very much like making abstract ideas of them.

There is certainly something passive in our souls, we are purely passive in the reception of our ideas; and reasoning and willing are actions of something that reasons and wills, and therefore must be only modalities of that something. Nor does it seem to me that when I say [something] I mean an abstract idea. It is true I have no idea of it, but I feel it; I feel that it is, because I feel or am conscious of the exertions of it; but the exertions of it are not the thing but the modalities of it distinguished from it as actions from an agent, which seems to me distinguishable without having recourse to abstract ideas.

And, therefore, when I suppose the existence of a spirit while it does not actually think, it does not appear to me that I do it by supposing an abstract idea of existence, and another of absolute time. The existence of John asleep by me, without so much as a dream is not an abstract idea. Nor is the time passing the while an abstract idea, they are only partial considerations of him. *Perseverare in existendo* in general, without reflecting on any particular thing existing, I take to be what is called an abstract idea of time or duration; but the *perseverare in existendo* of John is, if I mistake not, a partial consideration of him. And I think it is as easy to conceive of him as continuing to exist without thinking as without seeing.

Has a child no soul till it actually perceives? And is there not such a thing as sleeping without dreaming, or being in a *deliquium* without a thought? If there be, and yet at the same time the *esse* of a spirit be nothing else but its actual thinking, the soul must be dead during those intervals; and if ceasing or intermitting to think be the ceasing to be, or death of the soul, it is many times and easily put to death. According to this tenet, it seems to me the soul may sleep on to the resurrection, or rather may wake up in the resurrection state, the next moment after death. Nay I don't see upon what we can build any natural argument for the soul's immortality. I think I once heard you allow a principle of perception and spontaneous motion in beasts. Now if their *esse* as well as ours consists in perceiving, upon what is the natural immortality of our souls founded that will not equally conclude in in favor of them? I mention this last consideration because I am at a loss to understand how you state the argument for the soul's natural immortality; for the argument from thinking to immaterial and from thence to indivisible, and from thence to immortal don't seem to obtain in your way of thinking.

If *esse* be only *percipere*, upon what is our consciousness founded? I perceived yesterday, and I perceive now, but last night between my yesterday's and today's perception there has been an intermission when I perceived nothing. It seems to me there must be some principle common to these perceptions, whose *esse* don't depend on them, but in which they are, as it were, connected, and on which they depend, whereby I am and continue conscious of them.

Lastly, Mr. Locke's argument (B. 2. Ch. 19. Sec. 4.) from the intention and remission of thought, appears to me very considerable; according to which, upon this supposition the soul must exist more or have a greater degree of being at one time than at another, according as it thinks more intensely or more remissly.

I own I said very wrong when I said I did not know what to make of ideas more than of matter. My meaning was, in effect, the same as I expressed afterwards about the substance of the soul's being a somewhat as unknown as matter. And what I intended by those questions was whether our ideas are not the substance of the soul itself, under so many various modifications, according to that saying (if I understand it right) *Intellectus intelligendo fit omnia?* It is true, those expressions (modifications, impressions, etc.) are metaphorical, and it seems to me to be no less so, to say that ideas exist in the mind, and I am under some doubt whether this last way of speaking don't carry us further from the thing, than to say ideas are the mind variously modified; but as you observe, it is scarce possible to speak of the mind without a metaphor.

Thus Sir, your goodness has tempted me to presume again to trouble you once more; and I submit the whole to your correction; but I can't conclude without saying that I am so much persuaded that your books teach truth, indeed the most excellent truths, and that in the most excellent manner, that I can't but express myself again very solicitously desirous that the noble design you have begun may be yet further pursued in the second part. And everybody that has seen the first is earnestly with me in this request. In hopes of which I will not desire you to waste your time in writing to me (tho' otherwise I should esteem it the greatest favor), at least till I have endeavored further to gain satisfaction by another perusal of the books I have, with the other pieces you are so kind as to offer, which I will thankfully accept, for I had not *The Principles* of my own, it was a borrowed one I used.

The bearer hereof, Capt. Gorham, is a coaster bound now to Boston, which trade he constantly uses (except that it has been now long interrupted by the winter). But he always touches at Newport, and will wait on the Rev'd Mr. Honyman both going and returning, by whom you will have opportunity to send those books.

I am, Rev'd Sir,

> with the greatest gratitude,
> your most devoted humble servant,
> S. Johnson

Stratford, Feb. 5, 1729/30

IV Berkeley to Johnson

March 24, 1730.

Rev. Sir:—

Yours of Feb. 5th came not to my hands before yesterday; and this afternoon being informed that a sloop is ready to sail towards your town, I would not let slip the opportunity of returning you an answer, though wrote in a hurry.

1. I have no objection against calling the ideas in the mind of God, archetypes of ours. But I object against those archetypes by philosophers supposed to be real things, and to have an absolute rational existence distinct from their being perceived by any mind whatsoever, it being the opinion

of all materialists that an ideal existence in the divine mind is one thing, and the real existence of material things another.

2. As to space, I have no notion of any but that which is relative. I know some late philosophers have attributed extension to God, particularly mathematicians; one of whom, in a treatise *de Spacio reali*, pretends to find out fifteen of the incommunicable attributes of God in space. But it seems to me, that they being all negative, he might as well have found them in nothing; and that it would have been as justly inferred from space being impassive, uncreated, indivisible, etc., that it was nothing, as that it was God.

Sir Isaac Newton supposeth an absolute space different from relative, and consequent thereto, absolute motion different from relative motion; and with all other mathematicians, he supposeth the infinite divisibility of the finite parts of this absolute space; he also supposeth material bodies to drift therein. Now, though I do acknowledge Sir Isaac to have been an extraordinary man and most profound mathematician, yet I cannot agree with him in these particulars. I make no scruple to use the word space, as well as other words in common use, but I do not mean thereby a distinct absolute being. For my meaning I refer you to what I have published.

By the τὸ νῦν I suppose to be implied that all things past and to come are actually present to the mind of God, and that there is in Him no change, variation, or succession—a succession of ideas I take to constitute time and not to be only the sensible measure thereof, as Mr. Locke and others think. But in these matters every man is to think for himself, and speak as he finds. One of my earliest inquiries was about time, which led me into several paradoxes that I did not think fit or necessary to publish, particularly into the notion that the resurrection follows next moment to death. We are confounded and perplexed about time. (1) Supposing a succession in God. (2) Conceiving that we have an abstract idea of time. (3) Supposing that the time in one mind is to be measured by the succession of ideas in another. (4) Not considering the true use and ends of words, which as often terminate in the will as the understanding, being employed rather to excite influence, and direct action than to produce clear and distinct ideas.

3. That the soul of man is passive as well as active I make

no doubt. Abstract general ideas was a notion that Mr. Locke held in common with the Schoolmen, and I think all other philosophers; it runs through his whole book *Of Human Understanding*. He holds an abstract idea of existence exclusive of perceiving and being perceived. I cannot find I have any such idea, and this is my reason against it. Descartes proceeds upon other principles. One square foot of snow is as white as one thousand yards; one single perception is as truly a perception as one hundred. Now any degree of perception being sufficient to existence, it will not follow that we should say one existed more at one time than another, any more than we should say one thousand yards of snow are whiter than one yard. But after all, this comes to a verbal dispute. I think it might prevent a good deal of obscurity and dispute to examine well what I have said about abstraction, and about the true use of sense and significancy of words, in several parts of these things that I have published, though much remains to be said on that subject.

You say you agree with me that there is nothing within your mind but God and other spirits, with the attributes or properties belonging to them, and the ideas contained in them. This is a principle or main point from which, and from what I had laid down about abstract ideas, much may be deduced. But if in every inference we should not agree, so long as the main points are settled and well understood, I should be less solicitous about particular conjectures. I could wish that all the things I have published on these philosophical subjects were read in the order wherein I published them, once to take the design and connection of them, and a second time with a critical eye, adding your own thought and observation upon every part as you went along. I send you herewith ten bound books and one unbound. You will take yourself what you have not already. You will give *The Principles, The Theory, The Dialogue*, one of each, with my service to the gentleman who is Fellow of New Haven College, whose compliments you brought me. What remains you will give as you please.

If at any time your affairs should draw you into these parts, you shall be very welcome to pass as many days as you can spend at my house. Four or five days' conversation would set several things in a fuller and clearer light than writing could do in as many months. In the meantime I shall

be glad to hear from you or your friends when ever you
please to favor,

> Rev. Sir,
>> Your very humble servant,
>>> Geor. Berkeley.

Pray let me know whether they would admit the writings of
Hooker and Chillingworth into the library of the College in
New Haven.

De Motu (Of Motion)

or

The Principle and Nature of Motion

and the Cause of the Communication

of Motions

BERKELEY PUBLISHED *De Motu* in 1721. The essay was submitted for a prize offered by the Royal Academy of Sciences at Paris, but was unsuccessful. It may profitably be read as a supplement to Berkeley's discussion of natural science in the *Principles of Human Knowledge,* Sections 101-17. (See Part 4 of the Introduction to this volume: "Berkeley's Philosophy of Science." The translation from the Latin is by A. A. Luce, one of the leading students of Berkeley in our age, and is reprinted here by kind permission of Thomas Nelson and Sons Ltd.

1. In the pursuit of truth we must beware of being misled by terms which we do not rightly understand. That is the chief point. Almost all philosophers utter the caution; few observe it. Yet it is not so difficult to observe, where sense, experience, and geometrical reasoning obtain, as is especially the case in physics. Laying aside, then, as far as possible, all prejudice, whether rooted in linguistic usage or in philosophical authority, let us fix our gaze on the very nature of things. For no one's authority ought to rank so high as to set a value on his words and terms unless they are found to be based on clear and certain fact.

2. The consideration of motion greatly troubled the minds of the ancient philosophers, giving rise to various exceedingly difficult opinions (not to say absurd) which have almost entirely gone out of fashion, and not being worth a detailed discussion need not delay us long. In works on motion by the more recent and sober thinkers of our age, not a few terms of somewhat abstract and obscure signification are used, such as *solicitation of gravity, urge, dead forces,* etc., terms which darken writings in other respects very learned, and beget opinions at variance with truth and the commonsense of men. These terms must be examined with great care, not from a desire to prove other people wrong, but in the interest of truth.

3. *Solicitation* and *effort* or *conation* belong properly to animate beings alone. When they are attributed to other things, they must be taken in a metaphorical sense; but a philosopher should abstain from metaphor. Besides, anyone who has seriously considered the matter will agree that those terms have no clear and distinct meaning apart from all affection of the mind and motion of the body.

4. While we support heavy bodies we feel in ourselves effort, fatigue, and discomfort. We perceive also in heavy bodies falling an accelerated motion towards the centre of the earth; and that is all the senses tell us. By reason, however, we infer that there is some cause or principle of the phenomena, and that is popularly called *gravity*. But since the cause of the fall of heavy bodies is unseen and unknown,

gravity in that usage cannot properly be styled a sensible quality. It is, therefore, an occult quality. But what an occult quality is, or how any quality can act or do anything, we can scarcely conceive—indeed we cannot conceive. And so men would do better to let the occult quality go, and attend only to be sensible effects. Abstract terms (however useful they may be in argument) should be discarded in meditation, and the mind should be fixed on the particular and the concrete, that is, on the things themselves.

5. *Force* likewise is attributed to bodies; and that word is used as if it meant a known quality, and one distinct from motion, figure, and every other sensible thing and also from every affection of the living thing. But examine the matter more carefully and you will agree that such force is nothing but an occult quality. Animal effort and corporeal motion are commonly regarded as symptoms and measures of this occult quality.

6. Obviously then it is idle to lay down gravity or force as the principle of motion; for how could that principle be known more clearly by being styled an occult quality? What is itself occult explains nothing. And I need not say that an unknown acting cause could be more correctly styled substance than quality. Again, *force, gravity,* and terms of that sort are more often used in the concrete (and rightly so) so as to connote the body in motion, the effort of resisting, etc. But when they are used by philosophers to signify certain natures carved out and abstracted from all these things, natures which are not objects of sense, nor can be grasped by any force of intellect, nor pictured by the imagination, then indeed they breed errors and confusion.

7. About general and abstract terms many men make mistakes; they see their value in argument, but they do not appreciate their purpose. In part the terms have been invented by common habit to abbreviate speech, and in part they have been thought out by philosophers for instructional purposes, not that they are adapted to the natures of things which are in fact singulars and concrete, but they come in useful for handing on received opinions by making the notions or at least the propositions universal.

8. We generally suppose that corporeal force is something easy to conceive. Those, however, who have studied the matter more carefully are of a different opinion, as appears

from the strange obscurity of their language when they try to explain it. Torricelli says that force and impetus are abstract and subtle things and quintessences which are included in corporeal substance as in the magic vase of Circe.[1] Leibniz likewise in explaining the nature of force says this "Active primitive force which is ἐντελέχεια ἡ πρώτη corresponds to the soul or substantial form." See *Acta Erudit. Lips.* Thus even the greatest men when they give way to abstractions are bound to pursue terms which have no certain significance and are mere shadows of scholastic things. Other passages in plenty from the writings of the younger men could be produced which give abundant proof that metaphysical abstractions have not in all quarters given place to mechanical science and experiment, but still make useless trouble for philosophers.

9. From that source derive various absurdities, such as that dictum: "The force of percussion, however small, is infinitely great"—which indeed supposes that gravity is a certain real quality different from all others, and that gravitation is, as it were, an act of this quality, really distinct from motion. But a very small percussion produces a greater effect than the greatest gravitation without motion. The former gives out some motion indeed, the latter none. Whence it follows that the force of percussion exceeds the force of gravitation by an infinite ratio, *i.e.* is infinitely great. See the experiments of Galileo, and the writings of Torricelli, Borelli, and others on the definite force of percussion.

10. We must, however, admit that no force is immediately felt by itself, nor known or measured otherwise than by its effect; but of a dead force or of simple gravitation in a body at rest, no change taking place, there is no effect; of percussion there is some effect. Since, then, forces are proportional to effects, we may conclude that there is no dead force, but we must not on that account infer that the force of percussion is infinite; for we cannot regard as infinite any positive quantity on the ground that it exceeds by an infinite ratio a zero-quantity or nothing.

[1] Matter is nothing else than a magic vase of Circe, which serves as a receptacle of force and of the moments of the impetus. Force and the impetus are such subtle abstractions and such volatile quintessences that they cannot be shut up in any vessel except in the innermost substance of natural solids. See *Academic Lectures.*

11. The force of gravitation is not to be separated from momentum; but there is no momentum without velocity, since it is mass multiplied by velocity; again, velocity cannot be understood without motion, and the same holds therefore of the force of gravitation. Then no force makes itself known except through action, and through action it is measured; but we are not able to separate the action of a body from its motion; therefore as long as a heavy body changes the shape of a piece of lead put under it, or of a cord, so long is it moved; but when it is at rest, it does nothing, or (which is the same thing) it is prevented from acting. In brief, those terms *dead force* and *gravitation* by the aid of metaphysical abstraction are supposed to mean something different from moving, moved, motion, and rest, but, in point of fact, the supposed difference in meaning amounts to nothing at all.

12. If anyone were to say that a weight hung or placed on the cord acts on it, since it prevents it from restoring itself by elastic force, I reply that by parity of reasoning any lower body acts on the higher body which rests on it, since it prevents it from coming down. But for one body to prevent another from existing in that space which *it* occupies cannot be styled the action of that body.

13. We feel at times the pressure of a gravitating body. But that unpleasant sensation arises from the motion of the heavy body communicated to the fibres and nerves of our body and changing their situation, and therefore it ought to be referred to percussion. In these matters we are afflicted by a number of serious prejudices, which should be subdued, or rather entirely exorcised by keen and continued reflection.

14. In order to prove that any quantity is infinite, we have to show that some, finite, homogeneous part is contained in it an infinite number of times. But dead force is to the force of percussion, not as part to the whole, but as the point to the line, according to the very writers who maintain the infinite force of percussion. Much might be added on this matter, but I am afraid of being prolix.

15. By the foregoing principles famous controversies which have greatly exercised the minds of learned men can be solved; for instance, that controversy about the proportion of forces. One side conceding that momenta, motions, and impetus, given the mass, are simply as the velocities, affirms

that the forces are as the squares of the velocities. Everyone sees that this opinion supposes that the force of the body is distinguished from momentum, motion, and impetus, and without that supposition it collapses.

16. To make it still clearer that a certain strange confusion has been introduced into the theory of motion by metaphysical abstractions, let us watch the conflict of opinion about force and impetus among famous men. Leibniz confuses impetus with motion. According to Newton impetus is in fact the same as the force of inertia. Borelli asserts that impetus is only the degree of velocity. Some would make impetus and effort different, others identical. Most regard the motive force as proportional to the motion; but a few prefer to suppose some other force besides the motive, to be measured differently, for instance by the squares of the velocities into the masses. But it would be an endless task to follow out this line of thought.

17. *Force, gravity, attraction,* and terms of this sort are useful for reasonings and reckonings about motion and bodies in motion, but not for understanding the simple nature of motion itself or for indicating so many distinct qualities. As for attraction, it was certainly introduced by Newton, not as a true, physical quality, but only as a mathematical hypothesis. Indeed Leibniz when distinguishing elementary effort or solicitation from impetus, admits that those entities are not really found in nature, but have to be formed by abstraction.

18. A similar account must be given of the composition and resolution of any direct forces into any oblique ones by means of the diagonal and sides of the parallelogram. They serve the purpose of mechanical science and reckoning; but to be of service to reckoning and mathematical demonstrations is one thing, to set forth the nature of things is another.

19. Of the moderns many are of the opinion that motion is neither destroyed nor generated anew, but that the quantity of motion remains for ever constant. Aristotle indeed propounded that problem long ago, Does motion come into being and pass away, or is it eternal? *Phys.* Bk. 8. That sensible motion perishes is clear to the senses, but apparently they will have it that the same impetus and effort remains, or the same sum of forces. Borelli affirms that force in percussion is not lessened, but expanded, that even contrary impetus are received and retained in the same body. Likewise Leibniz con-

tends that effort exists everywhere and always in matter, and that it is understood by reason where it is not evident to the senses. But these points, we must admit, are too abstract and obscure, and of much the same sort as substantial forms and entelechies.

20. All those who, to explain the cause and origin of motion, make use of the hylarchic principle, or of a nature's want or appetite, or indeed of a natural instinct, are to be considered as having said something, rather than thought it. And from these they [2] are not far removed who have supposed "that the parts of the earth are self-moving, or even that spirits are implanted in them like a form" in order to assign the cause of the acceleration of heavy bodies falling. So too with him [3] who said "that in the body besides solid extension, there must be something posited to serve as starting-point for the consideration of forces." All these indeed either say nothing particular and determinate, or if there is anything in what they say, it will be as difficult to explain as that very thing it was brought forward to explain.

21. To throw light on nature it is idle to adduce things which are neither evident to the senses, nor intelligible to reason. Let us see then what sense and experience tell us, and reason that rests upon them. There are two supreme classes of things, body and soul. By the help of sense we know the extended thing, solid, mobile, figured, and endowed with other qualities which meet the senses, but the sentient, percipient, thinking thing we know by a certain internal consciousness. Further we see that those things are plainly different from one another, and quite heterogeneous. I speak of things known; for of the unknown it is profitless to speak.

22. All that which we know to which we have given the name *body* contains nothing in itself which could be the principle of motion or its efficient cause; for impenetrability, extension, and figure neither include nor connote any power of producing motion; nay, on the contrary, if we review singly those qualities of body, and whatever other qualities there may be, we shall see that they are all in fact passive and that there is nothing active in them which can in any way be understood as the source and principle of motion. As for gravity we have already shown above that by that term is

[2] Borelli.
[3] Leibniz.

meant nothing we know, nothing other than the sensible effect, the cause of which we seek. And indeed when we call a body heavy we understand nothing else except that it is borne downwards, and we are not thinking at all about the cause of this sensible effect.

23. And so about body we can boldly state as established fact that it is not the principle of motion. But if anyone maintains that the term *body* covers in its meaning occult quality, virtue, form, and essence, besides solid extension and its modes, we must just leave him to his useless disputation with no ideas behind it, and to his abuse of names which express nothing distinctly. But the sounder philosophical method, it would seem, abstains as far as possible from abstract and general notions (if *notions* is the right term for things which cannot be understood).

24. The contents of the idea of body we know; but what we know in body is agreed not to be the principle of motion. But those who as well maintain something unknown in body of which they have no idea and which they call the principle of motion, are in fact simply stating that the principle of motion is unknown, and one would be ashamed to linger long on subtleties of this sort.

25. Besides corporeal things there is the other class, *viz.* thinking things, and that there is in them the power of moving bodies we have learned by personal experience, since our mind at will can stir and stay the movements of our limbs, whatever be the ultimate explanation of the fact. This is certain that bodies are moved at the will of the mind, and accordingly the mind can be called, correctly enough, a principle of motion, a particular and subordinate principle indeed, and one which itself depends on the first and universal principle.

26. Heavy bodies are borne downwards, although they are not affected by any apparent impulse; but we must not think on that account that the principle of motion is contained in them. Aristotle gives this account of the matter, "Heavy and light things are not moved by themselves; for that would be a characteristic of life, and they would be able to stop themselves." All heavy things by one and the same certain and constant law seek the centre of the earth, and we do not observe in them a principle or any faculty of halting that motion, of diminishing it or increasing it except in fixed proportion, or finally of altering it in any way. They behave

quite passively. Again, in strict and accurate speech, the same must be said of percussive bodies. Those bodies as long as they are being moved, as also in the very moment of percussion, behave passively, exactly as when they are at rest. Inert body so acts as body moved acts, if the truth be told. Newton recognizes that fact when he says that the force of inertia is the same as impetus. But body, inert and at rest, does nothing; therefore body moved does nothing.

27. Body in fact persists equally in either state, whether of motion or of rest. Its existence is not called its action; nor should its persistence be called its action. Persistence is only continuance in the same way of existing which cannot properly be called action. Resistance which we experience in stopping a body in motion we falsely imagine to be its action, deluded by empty appearance. For that resistance which we feel is in fact passion in ourselves, and does not prove that body acts, but that we are affected; it is quite certain that we should be affected in the same way, whether that body were to be moved by itself, or impelled by another principle.

28. Action and reaction are said to be in bodies, and that way of speaking suits the purposes of mechanical demonstrations; but we must not on that account suppose that there is some real virtue in them which is the cause or principle of motion. For those terms are to be understood in the same way as the term *attraction;* and just as attraction is only a mathematical hypothesis, and not a physical quality, the same must be understood also about action and reaction, and for the same reason. For in mechanical philosophy the truth and the use of theorems about the mutual attraction of bodies remain firm, as founded solely in the motion of bodies, whether that motion be supposed to be caused by the action of bodies mutually attracting each other, or by the action of some agent different from the bodies, impelling and controlling them. Similarly the traditional formulations of rules and laws of motions, along with the theorems thence deduced remain unshaken, provided that sensible effects and the reasonings grounded in them are granted, whether we suppose the action itself or the force that causes these effects to be in the body or in the incorporeal agent.

29. Take away from the idea of body extension, solidity, and figure, and nothing will remain. But those qualities are indifferent to motion, nor do they contain anything which

could be called the principle of motion. This is clear from our very ideas. If therefore by the term *body* be meant that which we conceive, obviously the principle of motion cannot be sought therein, that is, no part or attribute thereof is the true, efficient cause of the production of motion. But to employ a term, and conceive nothing by it is quite unworthy of a philosopher.

30. A thinking, active thing is given which we experience as the principle of motion in ourselves. This we call *soul*, *mind*, and *spirit*. Extended thing also is given, inert, impenetrable, moveable, totally different from the former and constituting a new genus. Anaxagoras, wisest of men, was the first to grasp the great difference between thinking things and extended things, and he asserted that the mind has nothing in common with bodies, as is established from the first book of Aristotle's *De Anima*. Of the moderns Descartes has put the same point most forcibly. What was left clear by him others have rendered involved and difficult by their obscure terms.

31. From what has been said it is clear that those who affirm that active force, action, and the principle of motion are really in bodies are adopting an opinion not based on experience, are supporting it with obscure and general terms, and do not well understand their own meaning. On the contrary those who will have mind to be the principle of motion are advancing an opinion fortified by personal experience, and one approved by the suffrages of the most learned men in every age.

32. Anaxagoras was the first to introduce *nous* to impress motion on inert matter. Aristotle, too, approves that opinion and confirms it in many ways, openly stating that the first mover is immoveable, indivisible, and has no magnitude. And he rightly notes that to say that every mover must be moveable is the same as to say that every builder must be capable of being built. *Phys*. Bk. 8. Plato, moreover, in the Timaeus records that this corporeal machine, or visible world, is moved and animated by mind which eludes all sense. To-day indeed Cartesian philosophers recognize God as the principle of natural motions. And Newton everywhere frankly intimates that not only did motion originate from God, but that still the mundane system is moved by the same actus. This is agreeable to Holy Scripture; this is approved by the opinion of the

schoolmen; for though the Peripatetics tell us that nature is the principle of motion and rest, yet they interpret *natura naturans* to be God. They understand of course that all the bodies of this mundane system are moved by Almighty Mind according to certain and constant reason.

33. But those who attribute a vital principle to bodies are imagining an obscure notion and one ill suited to the facts. For what is meant by being endowed with the vital principle, except to live? And to live, what is it but to move oneself, to stop, and to change one's state? But the most learned philosophers of this age lay it down for an indubitable principle that every body persists in its own state, whether of rest or of uniform movement in a straight line, except in so far as it is compelled from without to alter that state. The contrary is the case with mind; we feel it as a faculty of altering both our own state and that of other things, and that is properly called vital, and puts a wide distinction between soul and bodies.

34. Modern thinkers consider motion and rest in bodies as two states of existence in either of which every body, without pressure from external force, would naturally remain passive; whence one might gather that the cause of the existence of bodies is also the cause of their motion and rest. For no other cause of the successive existence of the body in different parts of space should be sought, it would seem, than that cause whence is derived the successive existence of the same body in different parts of time. But to treat of the good and great God, creator and preserver of all things, and to show how all things depend on supreme and true being, although it is the most excellent part of human knowledge, is, however, rather the province of first philosophy or metaphysics and theology than of natural philosophy which to-day is almost entirely confined to experiments and mechanics. And so natural philosophy either presupposes the knowledge of God or borrows it from some superior science. Although it is most true that the investigation of nature everywhere supplies the higher sciences with notable arguments to illustrate and prove the wisdom, the goodness, and the power of God.

35. The imperfect understanding of this situation has caused some to make the mistake of rejecting the mathematical principles of physics on the ground that they do not assign

the efficient causes of things. It is not, however, in fact the business of physics or mechanics to establish efficient causes, but only the rules of impulsions or attractions, and, in a word, the laws of motions, and from the established laws to assign the solution, not the efficient cause, of particular phenomena.

36. It will be of great importance to consider what properly a principle is, and how that term is to be understood by philosophers. The true, efficient and conserving cause of all things by supreme right is called their fount and principle. But the principles of experimental philosophy are properly to be called foundations and springs, not of their existence but of our knowledge of corporeal things, both knowledge by sense and knowledge by experience, foundations on which that knowledge rests and springs from which it flows. Similarly in mechanical philosophy those are to be called principles, in which the whole discipline is grounded and contained, those primary laws of motions which have been proved by experiments, elaborated by reason and rendered universal. These laws of motion are conveniently called principles, since from them are derived both general mechanical theorems and particular explanations of the phenomena.

37. A thing can be said to be explained mechanically then indeed when it is reduced to those most simple and universal principles, and shown by accurate reasoning to be in agreement and connection with them. For once the laws of nature have been found out, then it is the philosopher's task to show that each phenomenon is in constant conformity with those laws, that is, necessarily follows from those principles. In that consist the explanation and solution of phenomena and the assigning their cause, *i.e.* the reason why they take place.

38. The human mind delights in extending and expanding its knowledge; and for this purpose general notions and propositions have to be formed in which particular propositions and cognitions are in some way comprised, which then, and not till then, are believed to be understood. Geometers know this well. In mechanics also notions are premised, *i.e.*, definitions and first and general statements about motion from which afterwards by mathematical method conclusions more remote and less general are deduced. And just as by the application of geometrical theorems, the sizes of particular bodies are measured, so also by the application of the universal theorems of mechanics, the movements of any parts of the

mundane system, and the phenomena thereon depending, become known and are determined. And that is the sole mark at which the physicist must aim.

39. And just as geometers for the sake of their art make use of many devices which they themselves cannot describe nor find in the nature of things, even so the mechanician makes use of certain abstract and general terms, imagining in bodies force, action, attraction, solicitation, etc. which are of first utility for theories and formulations, as also for computations about motion, even if in the truth of things, and in bodies actually existing, they would be looked for in vain, just like the geometers' fictions made by mathematical abstraction.

40. We actually perceive by the aid of the senses nothing except the effects or sensible qualities and corporeal things entirely passive, whether in motion or at rest; and reason and experience advise us that there is nothing active except mind or soul. Whatever else is imagined must be considered to be of a kind with other hypotheses and mathematical abstractions. This ought to be laid to heart; otherwise we are in danger of sliding back into the obscure subtlety of the schoolmen, which for so many ages like some dread plague, has corrupted philosophy.

41. Mechanical principles and universal laws of motions or of nature, happy discoveries of the last century, treated and applied by aid of geometry, have thrown a remarkable light upon philosophy. But metaphysical principles and real efficient causes of the motion and existence of bodies or of corporeal attributes in no way belong to mechanics or experiment, nor throw light on them, except in so far as by being known beforehand they may serve to define the limits of physics, and in that way to remove imported difficulties and problems.

42. Those who derive the principle of motion from spirits mean by *spirit* either a corporeal thing or an incorporeal; if a corporeal thing, however tenuous, yet the difficulty recurs; if an incorporeal thing, however true it may be, yet it does not properly belong to physics. But if anyone were to extend natural philosophy beyond the limits of experiments and mechanics, so as to cover a knowledge of incorporeal and inextended things, that broader interpretation of the term permits a discussion of soul, mind, or vital principle. But it will be more convenient to follow the usage which is fairly well accepted, and so to distinguish between the sciences as to

confine each to its own bounds; thus the natural philosopher should concern himself entirely with experiments, laws of motions, mechanical principles, and reasonings thence deduced; but if he shall advance views on other matters, let him refer them for acceptance to some superior science. For from the known laws of nature very elegant theories and mechanical devices of practical utility follow; but from the knowledge of the Author of nature Himself by far the most excellent considerations arise, but they are metaphysical, theological, and moral.

43. So far about principles; now we must speak of the nature of motion. Motion though it is clearly perceived by the senses has been rendered obscure rather by the learned comments of philosophers than by its own nature. Motion never meets our senses apart from corporeal mass, space, and time. There are indeed those who desire to contemplate motion as a certain simple and abstract idea, and separated from all other things. But that very fine-drawn and subtle idea eludes the keen edge of intellect, as anyone can find for himself by meditation. Hence arise great difficulties about the nature of motion, and definitions far more obscure than the thing they are meant to illustrate. Such are those definitions of Aristotle and the school-men, who say that motion is the act "of the moveable in so far as it is moveable, or the act of a being in potentiality in so far as it is in potentiality." Such is the saying of a famous man [4] of modern times, who asserts that "there is nothing real in motion except that momentary thing which must be constituted when a force is striving towards a change." Again, it is agreed that the authors of these and similar definitions had it in mind to explain the abstract nature of motion, apart from every consideration of time and space; but how that abstract quintessence, so to speak, of motion, can be understood I do not see.

44. Not content with this they go further and divide and separate from one another the parts of motion itself, of which parts they try to make distinct ideas, as if of entities in fact distinct. For there are those who distinguish movement from motion, looking on the movement as an instantaneous element in the motion. Moreover, they would have velocity, conation, force, and impetus to be so many things differing in essence,

[4] [Leibniz.—Ed.]

each of which is presented to the intellect through its own abstract idea separated from all the rest. But we need not spend any more time on these discussions if the principles laid down above hold good.

45. Many also define motion by *passage*, forgetting indeed that passage itself cannot be understood without motion, and through motion ought to be defined. So very true is it that definitions throw light on some things, and darkness again on others. And certainly hardly anyone could by defining them make clearer or better known the things we perceive by sense. Enticed by the vain hope of doing so, philosophers have rendered easy things very difficult, and have ensnared their own minds in difficulties which for the most part they themselves produced. From this desire of defining and abstracting many very subtle questions both about motion and other things take their rise. Those useless questions have tortured the minds of men to no purpose; so that Aristotle often actually confesses that motion is "a certain act difficult to know," and some of the ancients became such pastmasters in trifling as to deny the existence of motion altogether.

46. But one is ashamed to linger on minutiæ of this sort; let it suffice to have indicated the sources of the solutions; but this, too, I must add. The traditional mathematical doctrines of the infinite divison of time and space have, from the very nature of the case, introduced paradoxes and thorny theories (as are all those that involve the infinite) into speculations about motion. All such difficulties motion shares with space and time, or rather has taken them over from that source.

47. Too much abstraction, on the one hand, or the division of things truly inseparable, and on the other hand composition or rather confusion of very different things have perplexed the nature of motion. For it has become usual to confuse motion with the efficient cause of motion. Whence it comes about that motion appears, as it were, in two forms, presenting one aspect to the senses, and keeping the other aspect covered in dark night. Thence obscurity, confusion, and various paradoxes of motion · take their rise, while what belongs in truth to the cause alone is falsely attributed to the effect.

48. This is the source of the opinion that the same quantity of motion is always conserved; anyone will easily satisfy himself of its falsity unless it be understood of the force and

power of the cause, whether that cause be called nature or *nous*, or whatever be the ultimate agent. Aristotle indeed (*Phys*. Bk. 8) when he asks whether motion be generated and destroyed, or is truly present in all things from eternity like life immortal, seems to have understood the vital principle rather than the external effect or change of place.

49. Hence it is that many suspect that motion is not mere passivity in bodies. But if we understand by it that which in the movement of a body is an object to the senses, no one can doubt that it is entirely passive. For what is there in the successive existence of body in different places which could relate to action, or be other than bare, lifeless effect?

50. The Peripatetics who say that motion is the one act of both the mover and the moved do not sufficiently divide cause from effect. Similarly those who imagine effort or conation in motion, or think that the same body at the same time is borne in opposite directions, seem to be the sport of the same confusion of ideas, and the same ambiguity of terms.

51. Diligent attention in grasping the concepts of others and in formulating one's own is of great service in the science of motion as in all other things; and unless there had been a failing in this respect I do not think that matter for dispute could have come from the query, Whether a body is indifferent to motion and to rest, or not. For since experience shows that it is a primary law of nature that a body persists exactly in "a state of motion and rest as long as nothing happens from elsewhere to change that state," and on that account it is inferred that the force of inertia is under different aspects either resistance or impetus, in this sense assuredly a body can be called indifferent in its own nature to motion or rest. Of course it is as difficult to induce rest in a moving body as motion in a resting body; but since the body conserves equally either state, why should it not be said to be indifferent to both?

52. The Peripatetics used to distinguish various kinds of motion corresponding to the variety of changes which a thing could undergo. To-day those who discuss motion understand by the term only local motion. But local motion cannot be understood without understanding the meaning of *locus*. Now *locus* is defined by moderns as "the part of space which a body occupies," whence it is divided into relative and absolute corresponding to space. For they distinguish between

absolute or true space and relative or apparent space. That is they postulate space on all sides measureless, immoveable, insensible, permeating and containing all bodies, which they ·call absolute space. But space comprehended or defined by bodies, and therefore an object of sense, is called relative, apparent, vulgar space.

53. And so let us suppose that all bodies were destroyed and brought to nothing. What is left they call absolute space, all relation arising from the situation and distances of bodies being removed together with the bodies. Again, that space is infinite, immoveable, indivisible, insensible, without relation and without distinction. That is, all its attributes are privative or negative. It seems therefore to be mere nothing. The only slight difficulty arising is that it is extended, and extension is a positive quality. But what sort of extension, I ask, is that which cannot be divided nor measured, no part of which can be perceived by sense or pictured by the imagination? For nothing enters the imagination which from the nature of the thing cannot be perceived by sense, since indeed the imagination is nothing else than the faculty which represents sensible things either actually existing or at least possible. Pure intellect, too, knows nothing of absolute space. That faculty is concerned only with spiritual and inextended things, such as our minds, their states, passions, virtues, and such like. From absolute space then let us take away now the words of the name, and nothing will remain in sense, imagination, or intellect. Nothing else then is denoted by those words than pure privation or negation, *i.e* mere nothing.

54. It must be admitted that in this matter we are in the grip of serious prejudices, and to win free we must exert the whole force of our minds. For many, so far from regarding absolute space as nothing, regard it as the only thing (God excepted) which cannot be annihilated; and they lay down that it necessarily exists of its own nature, that it is eternal and uncreated, and is actually a participant in the divine attributes. But in very truth since it is most certain that all things which we designate by names are known by qualities or relations, at least in part (for it would be stupid, to use words to which nothing known, no notion, idea or concept, were attached), let us diligently inquire whether it is possible to form any idea of that pure, real, and absolute space continuing to exist after the annihilation of all bodies. Such an idea, more-

over, when I watch it somewhat more intently, I find to be the purest idea of nothing, if indeed it can be called an idea. This I myself have found on giving the matter my closest attention; this, I think, others will find on doing likewise.

55. We are sometimes deceived by the fact that when we imagine the removal of all other bodies, yet we suppose our own body to remain. On this supposition we imagine the movement of our limbs fully free on every side; but motion without space cannot be conceived. None the less if we consider the matter again we shall find, 1st, relative space conceived defined by the parts of our body; 2nd, a fully free power of moving our limbs obstructed by no obstacle; and besides these two things nothing. It is false to believe that some third thing really exists, *viz.* immense space which confers on us the free power of moving our body; for this purpose the absence of other bodies is sufficient. And we must admit that this absence or privation of bodies is nothing positive.[5]

56. But unless a man has examined these points with a free and keen mind, words and terms avail little. To one who meditates, however, and reflects, it will be manifest, I think, that predications about pure and absolute space can all be predicated about nothing. By this argument the human mind is easily freed from great difficulties, and at the same time from the absurdity of attributing necessary existence to any being except to the good and great God alone.

57. It would be easy to confirm our opinion by arguments drawn, as they say *a posteriori,* by proposing questions about absolute space, *e.g.* Is it substance or accidents? Is it created or uncreated? and showing the absurdities which follow from either answer. But I must be brief. I must not omit, however, to state that Democritus of old supported this opinion with his vote. Aristotle is our authority for the statement, *Phys.* Bk. 1, where he has these words, "Democritus lays down as principles the solid and the void, of which the one, he says, is as what is, the other as what is not." That the distinction between absolute and relative space has been used by philosophers of great name, and that on it as on a foundation many fine theorems have been built, may make us scruple to accept

---

[5] See the arguments against absolute space in my book on *The Principles of Human Knowledge* in the English tongue published ten years ago [1710—Ed.]

the argument, but those are empty scruples as will appear from what follows.

58. From the foregoing it is clear that we ought not to define the true place of the body as the part of absolute space which the body occupies, and true or absolute motion as the change of true or absolute place; for all place is relative just as all motion is relative. But to make this appear more clearly we must point out that no motion can be understood without some determination or directon, which in turn cannot be understood unless besides the body in motion our own body also, or some other body, be understood to exist at the same time. For *up, down, left,* and *right* and all places and regions are founded in some relation, and necessarily connote and suppose a body different from the body moved. So that if we suppose the other bodies were annihilated and, for example, a globe were to exist alone, no motion could be conceived in it; so necessary is it that another body should be given by whose situation the motion should be understood to be determined. The truth of this opinion will be very clearly seen if we shall have carried out thoroughly the supposed annihilation of all bodies, our own and that of others, except that solitary globe.

59. Then let two globes be conceived to exist and nothing corporeal besides them. Let forces then be conceived to be applied in some way; whatever we may understand by the application of forces, a circular motion of the two globes round a common centre cannot be conceived by the imagination. Then let us suppose that the sky of the fixed stars is created; suddenly from the conception of the approach of the globes to different parts of that sky the motion will be conceived. That is to say that since motion is relative in its own nature, it could not be conceived before the correlated bodies were given. Similarly no other relation can be conceived without correlates.

60. As regards circular motion many think that, as motion truly circular increases, the body necessarily tends ever more and more away from its axis. This belief arises from the fact that circular motion can be seen taking its origin, as it were, at every moment from two directions, one along the radius and the other along the tangent, and if in this latter direction only the impetus be increased, then the body in motion will retire from the centre, and its orbit will cease to be circular.

But if the forces be increased equally in both directions the motion will remain circular though accelerated—which will not argue an increase in the forces of retirement from the axis, any more than in the forces of approach to it. Therefore we must say that the water forced round in the bucket rises to the sides of the vessel, because when new forces are applied in the direction of the tangent to any particle of water, in the same instant new equal centripetal forces are not applied. From which experiment it in no way follows that absolute circular motion is necessarily recognized by the forces of retirement from the axis of motion. Again, how those terms *corporeal forces* and *conation* are to be understood is more than sufficiently shown in the foregoing discussion.

61. A curve can be considered as consisting of an infinite number of straight lines, though in fact it does not consist of them. That hypothesis is useful in geometry; and just so circular motion can be regarded as arising from an infinite number of rectilinear directions—which supposition is useful in mechanics. Not, however, on that account must it be affirmed that it is impossible that the centre of gravity of each body should exist successively in single points of the circular periphery, no account being taken of any rectilineal direction in the tangent or the radius.

62. We must not omit to point out that the motion of a stone in a sling or of water in a whirled bucket cannot be called truly circular motion as that term is conceived by those who define the true places of bodies by the parts of absolute space, since it is strangely compounded of the motions, not alone of bucket or sling, but also of the daily motion of the earth round her own axis, of her monthly motion round the common centre of gravity of earth and moon, and of her annual motion round the sun. And on that account each particle of the stone or the water describes a line far removed from circular. Nor in fact does that supposed axifugal conation exist, since it is not concerned with some one axis in relation to absolute space, supposing that such a space exists; accordingly I do not see how that can be called a single conation to which a truly circular motion corresponds as to its proper and adequate effect.

63. No motion can be recognized or measured, unless through sensible things. Since then absolute space in no way affects the senses, it must necessarily be quite useless for the

distinguishing of motions. Besides, determination or direction is essential to motion; but that consists in relation. Therefore it is impossible that absolute motion should be conceived.

64. Further, since the motion of the same body may vary with the diversity of relative place, nay actually since a thing can be said in one respect to be in motion and in another respect to be at rest, to determine true motion and true rest, for the removal of ambiguity and for the furtherance of the mechanics of these philosophers who take the wider view of the system of things, it would be enough to bring in, instead of absolute space, relative space as confined to the heavens of the fixed stars, considered as at rest. But motion and rest marked out by such relative space can conveniently be substituted in place of the absolutes, which cannot be distinguished from them by any mark. For however forces may be impressed, whatever conations there are, let us grant that motion is distinguished by actions exerted on bodies; never, however, will it follow that that space, absolute place, exists, and that change in it is true place.

65. The laws of motions and the effects, and theorems containing the proportions and calculations of the same for the different configurations of the paths, likewise for accelerations and different directions, and for mediums resisting in greater or less degree, all these hold without bringing absolute motion into account. As is plain from this that since according to the principles of those who introduce absolute motion we cannot know by any indication whether the whole frame of things is at rest, or is moved uniformly in a direction, clearly we cannot know the absolute motion of any body.

66. From the foregoing it is clear that the following rules will be of great service in determining the true nature of motion: (1) to distinguish mathematical hypotheses from the natures of things; (2) to beware of abstractions; (3) to consider motion as something sensible, or at least imaginable; and to be content with relative measures. If we do so, all the famous theorems of the mechanical philosophy by which the secrets of nature are unlocked, and by which the system of the world is reduced to human calculation, will remain untouched; and the study of motion will be freed from a thousand minutiæ, subtleties, and abstract ideas. And let these words suffice about the nature of motion.

67. It remains to discuss the cause of the communication

of motions. Most people think that the force impressed on the moveable body is the cause of motion in it. However that they do not assign a known cause of motion, and one distinct from the body and the motion is clear from the preceding argument. It is clear, moreover, that force is not a thing certain and determinate, from the fact that great men advance very different opinions, even contrary opinions, about it, and yet in their results attain the truth. For Newton says that impressed force consists in action alone, and is the action exerted on the body to change its state, and does not remain after the action. Torricelli contends that a certain heap or aggregate of forces impressed by percussion is received into the mobile body, and there remains and constitutes impetus. Borelli and others say much the same. But although Newton and Torricelli seem to be disagreeing with one another, they each advance consistent views, and the thing is sufficiently well explained by both. For all forces attributed to bodies are mathematical hypotheses just as are attractive forces in planets and sun. But mathematical entities have no stable essence in the nature of things; and they depend on the notion of the definer. Whence the same thing can be explained in different ways.

68. Let us lay down that the new motion in the body struck is conserved either by the natural force by reason of which any body persists in its own uniform state of motion or of rest, or by the impressed force, received (while the percussion lasts) into the body struck, and there remaining; it will be the same in fact, the difference existing only in name. Similarly when the striking moveable body loses motion, and the struck body acquires it, it is not worth disputing whether the acquired motion is numerically the same as the motion lost; the discussion would lead into metaphysical and even verbal minutiæ about identity. And so it comes to the same thing whether we say that motion passes from the striker to the struck, or that motion is generated *de novo* in the struck, and is destroyed in the striker. In either case it is understood that one body loses motion, the other acquires it, and besides that, nothing.

69. That the Mind which moves and contains this universal, bodily mass, and is the true efficient cause of motion, is the same cause, properly and strictly speaking, of the communication thereof I would not deny. In physical philosophy,

however, we must seek the causes and solutions of phenomena among mechanical principles. Physically, therefore, a thing is explained not by assigning its truly active and incorporeal cause, but by showing its connection with mechanical principles, such as *action and reaction are always opposite and equal*. From such laws as from the source and primary principle, those rules for the communication of motions are drawn, which by the moderns for the great good of the sciences have been already found and demonstrated.

70. I, for my part, will content myself with hinting that that principle could have been set forth in another way. For if the true nature of things, rather than abstract mathematics, be regarded, it will seem more correct to say that in attraction or percussion, the passion of bodies, rather than their action, is equal on both sides. For example, the stone tied by a rope to a horse is dragged towards the horse just as much as the horse towards the stone; for the body in motion impinging on a quiescent body suffers the same change as the quiescent body. And as regards real effect, the striker is just as the struck, and the struck as the striker. And that change on both sides, both in the body of the horse and in the stone, both in the moved and in the resting, is mere passivity. It is not established that there is force, virtue, or bodily action truly and properly causing such effects. The body in motion impinges on the quiescent body; we speak, however, in terms of action and say that it impels this; and it is correct to do so in mechanics where mathematical ideas, rather than the true natures of things, are regarded.

71. In physics sense and experience which reach only to apparent effects hold sway; in mechanics the abstract notions of mathematicians are admitted. In first philosophy or metaphysics we are concerned with incorporeal things, with causes, truth, and the existence of things. The physicist studies the series or successions of sensible things, noting by what laws they are connected, and in what order, what precedes as cause, and what follows as effect. And on this method we say that the body in motion is the cause of motion in the other, and impresses motion on it, draws it also or impels it. In this sense second corporeal causes ought to be understood, no account being taken of the actual seat of the forces or of the active powers or of the real cause in which they are. Further, besides body, figure, and motion, even the primary axioms

of mechanical science can be called causes or mechanical principles, being regarded as the causes of the consequences.

72. Only by meditation and reasoning can truly active causes be rescued from the surrounding darkness and be to some extent known. To deal with them is the business of first philosophy or metaphysics. Allot to each science its own province; assign it bounds; accurately distinguish the principles and objects belonging to each. Thus it will be possible to treat them with greater ease and clarity.

An Essay Towards a New Theory of Vision

The *New Theory of Vision* was published in 1709, when Berkeley was twenty-four or twenty-five. It was well received, and quickly ran to a second edition. In modern times it has tended to be neglected by philosophers, who are perhaps repelled by some of the optical and psychological detail. It is nevertheless well worth philosophical attention. The student is advised to omit Sections 29-40 on a first reading, and to concentrate particularly on Sections 2-28 and 41-51. The main conclusions of the essay are stated in 41-51. (See Part 3 of the Introduction to this volume: "Berkeley's Theory of Vision.")

To the Rt. Hon. Sir John Percivale, Bart.[1]

One of Her Majesty's Most Honourable Privy Council

In the Kingdom of Ireland.

SIR,

I COULD not, without doing violence to myself, forbear upon this occasion to give some public testimony of the great and well-grounded esteem I have conceived for you, ever since I had the honour and happiness of your acquaintance. The outward advantages of fortune, and the early honours with which you are adorned, together with the reputation you are known to have amongst the best and most considerable men, may well imprint veneration and esteem on the minds of those who behold you from a distance. But these are not the chief motives that inspire me with the respect I bear you. A nearer approach has given me the view of something in your person infinitely beyond the external ornaments of honour and estate. I mean, an intrinsic stock of virtue and good sense, a true concern for religion, and disinterested love of your country. Add to these an uncommon proficiency in the best and most useful parts of knowledge; together with (what in my mind is a perfection of the first rank) a surpassing goodness of nature. All which I have collected, not from the uncertain reports of fame, but from my own experience. Within these few months that I have the honour to be known unto you, the many delightful hours I have passed in your agreeable and improving conversation have afforded me the opportunity of discovering in you many excellent qualities, which at once fill me with admiration and esteem. That one at those years, and in those circumstances of wealth and greatness, should continue proof against the charms of luxury and those criminal pleasures so fashionable and predominant in the age we live in; that he should pre-

---

[1] [Omitted from the final edition.—Ed.]

serve a sweet and modest behaviour, free from that insolent and assuming air so familiar to those who are placed above the ordinary rank of men; that he should manage a great fortune with that prudence and inspection, and at the same time expend it with that generosity and nobleness of mind, as to shew himself equally remote from a sordid parsimony and a lavish inconsiderate profusion of the good things he is intrusted with—this, surely, were admirable and praiseworthy. But, that he should, moreover, by an impartial exercise of his reason, and constant perusal of the sacred Scriptures, endeavour to attain a right notion of the principles of natural and revealed religion; that he should with the concern of a true patriot have the interest of the public at heart, and omit no means of informing himself what may be prejudicial or advantageous to his country, in order to prevent the one and promote the other; in fine, that, by a constant application to the most severe and useful studies, by a strict observation of the rules of honour and virtue, by frequent and serious reflections on the mistaken measures of the world, and the true end and happiness of mankind, he should in all respects qualify himself bravely to run the race that is set before him, to deserve the character of great and good in this life, and be ever happy hereafter—this were amazing and almost incredible. Yet all this, and more than this, SIR, might I justly say of you, did either your modesty permit, or your character stand in need of it. I know it might deservedly be thought a vanity in me to imagine that anything coming from so obscure a hand as mine could add a lustre to your reputation. But, I am withal sensible how far I advance the interest of my own, by laying hold on this opportunity to make it known that I am admitted into some degree of intimacy with a person of your exquisite judgment. And, with that view, I have ventured to make you an address of this nature, which the goodness I have ever experienced in you inclines me to hope will meet with a favourable reception at your hands. Though I must own I have your pardon to ask, for touching on what may possibly be offensive to a virtue you are possessed of in a very distinguishing degree. Excuse me, SIR, if it was out of my power to mention the name of SIR JOHN PERCIVALE without paying some tribute to that extraordinary and surprising merit whereof I have so clear and affecting an idea, and which, I am sure, cannot be exposed in too full a light for the imitation of others.

Of late I have been agreeably employed in considering the most noble, pleasant, and comprehensive of all the senses. The fruit of that (labour shall I call it or) diversion is what I now present you with, in hopes it may give some entertainment to one who, in the midst of business and vulgar enjoyments, preserves a relish for the more refined pleasures of thought and reflexion. My thoughts concerning Vision have led me into some notions so far out of the common road that it had been improper to address them to one of a narrow and contracted genius. But, you, SIR, being master of a large and free understanding, raised above the power of those prejudices that enslave the far greater part of mankind, may deservedly be thought a proper patron for an attempt of this kind. Add to this, that you are no less disposed to forgive than qualified to discern whatever faults may occur in it. Nor do I think you defective in any one point necessary to form an exact judgment on the most abstract and difficult things, so much as in a just confidence of your own abilities. And, in this one instance, give me leave to say, you shew a manifest weakness of judgment. With relation to the following *Essay*, I shall only add that I beg your pardon for laying a trifle of that nature in your way, at a time when you are engaged in the important affairs of the nation, and desire you to think that I am, with all sincerity and respect,

SIR,

Your most faithful and most humble servant,

GEORGE BERKELEY.

Contents

137. The same idea of motion not common to sight and touch.
138. The way wherein we apprehend motion by sight easily collected from what hath been said.
139. *Ques.* How visible and tangible ideas came to have the same name, if not of the same kind.
140. This accounted for without supposing them of the same kind.
141. *Obj.* That a tangible square is liker to a visible square than to a visible circle.
142. *Ans.* That a visible square is fitter than a visible circle to represent a tangible square.
143. But it doth not hence follow that a visible square is like a tangible square.
144. Why we are more apt to confound visible with tangible ideas, than other signs with the things signified.
145. Several other reasons hereof assigned.
146. Reluctancy in rejecting any opinion no argument of its truth.

147. Proper objects of Vision [the Language of Nature.] [1]
148. In it there is much admirable and deserving our attention.

149. Question proposed concerning the object of geometry.

150. At first view we are apt to think visible extension the object of geometry.
151. Visible extension shewn not to be the object of geometry.
152. Words may as well be thought the object of geometry as visible extension.
153. It is proposed to inquire, what progress an intelligence that could see, but not feel, might make in geometry.
154. He cannot understand those parts which relate to solids, and their surfaces, and lines generated by their section.
155. Nor even the elements of plane geometry.
156. The proper objects of sight incapable of being managed as geometrical figures.

[1] [Altered in the third edition to "the language of the Author of Nature." Cf. Sec. 147.—Ed.]

157. The opinion of those who hold plane figures to be the immediate objects of sight considered.
158. Planes no more the immediate objects of sight than solids.
159. Difficult to enter precisely into the thoughts of the above-mentioned intelligence.

An Essay

Towards

a New Theory of Vision

1. My design is to shew the manner wherein we perceive by Sight the Distance, Magnitude, and Situation of objects: also to consider the difference there is betwixt the ideas of Sight and Touch, and whether there be any idea common to both senses.

2. It is, I think, agreed by all that Distance, of itself and immediately, cannot be seen. For, distance being a line directed endwise to the eye, it projects only one point in the fund of the eye, which point remains invariably the same, whether the distance be longer or shorter.

3. I find it also acknowledged that the estimate we make of the distance of objects considerably remote is rather an act of judgment grounded on experience than of sense. For example, when I perceive a great number of intermediate objects, such as houses, fields, rivers, and the like, which I have experienced to take up a considerable space, I thence form a judgment or conclusion, that the object I see beyond them is at a great distance. Again, when an object appears faint and small which at a near distance I have experienced to make a vigorous and large appearance, I instantly conclude it to be far off. And this, it is evident, is the result of experience; without which, from the faintness and littleness, I should not have inferred anything concerning the distance of objects.

4. But, when an object is placed at so near a distance as that the interval between the eyes bears any sensible proportion to it, the opinion of speculative men is, that the two optic axes (the fancy that we see only with one eye at once being exploded), concurring at the object, do there make an angle, by means of which, according as it is greater or lesser, the object is perceived to be nearer or farther off.[1]

5. Betwixt which and the foregoing manner of estimating

[1] [See what Descartes and others have written on this subject. —Ed.]

distance there is this remarkable difference:—that, whereas there was no apparent *necessary* connexion between small distance and a large and strong appearance, or between great distance and a little and faint appearance, there appears a very *necessary* connexion between an obtuse angle and near distance, and an acute angle and farther distance. It does not in the least depend upon experience, but may be evidently known by any one before he had experienced it, that the nearer the concurrence of the optic axes the greater the angle, and the remoter their concurrence is, the lesser will be the angle comprehended by them.

6. There is another way, mentioned by optic writers, whereby they will have us judge of those distances in respect of which the breadth of the pupil hath any sensible bigness. And that is the greater or lesser divergency of the rays which, issuing from the visible point, do fall on the pupil—that point being judged nearest which is seen by most diverging rays, and that remoter which is seen by less diverging rays, and so on; the apparent distance still increasing, as the divergency of the rays decreases, till at length it becomes infinite, when the rays that fall on the pupil are to sense parallel. And after this manner it is said we perceive distance when we look only with one eye.

7. In this case also it is plain we are not beholden to experience: it being a certain necessary truth that, the nearer the direct rays falling on the eye approach to a parallelism, the farther off is the point of their intersection, or the visible point from whence they flow.

8. Now, though the accounts here given of perceiving *near* distance by sight are received for true, and accordingly made use of in determining the apparent places of objects, they do nevertheless seem to me very unsatisfactory, and that for these following reasons:—

9. It is evident that, when the mind perceives any idea not immediately and of itself, it must be by the means of some other idea. Thus, for instance, the passions which are in the mind of another are of themselves to me invisible. I may nevertheless perceive them by sight; though not immediately, yet by means of the colours they produce in the countenance. We often see shame or fear in the looks of a man, by perceiving the changes of his countenance to red or pale.

10. Moreover, it is evident that no idea which is not itself perceived can be to me the means of perceiving any other idea. If I do not perceive the redness or paleness of a man's face themselves, it is impossible I should perceive by them the passions which are in his mind.

11. Now, from sect. ii., it is plain that distance is in its own nature imperceptible, and yet it is perceived by sight. It remains, therefore, that it be brought into view by means of some other idea, that is itself immediately perceived in the act of vision.

12. But those lines and angles, by means whereof some men pretend to explain the perception of distance, are themselves not at all perceived; nor are they in truth ever thought of by those unskilful in optics. I appeal to any one's experience, whether, upon sight of an object, he computes its distance by the bigness of the angle made by the meeting of the two optic axes? or whether he ever thinks of the greater or lesser divergency of the rays which arrive from any point to his pupil? nay, whether it be not perfectly impossible for him to perceive by sense the various angles wherewith the rays, according to their greater or lesser divergence, do fall on the eye? Every one is himself the best judge of what he perceives, and what not. In vain shall any man tell me, that I perceive certain lines and angles, which introduce into my mind the various ideas of distance, so long as I myself am conscious of no such thing.

13. Since therefore those angles and lines are not themselves perceived by sight, it follows, from sect. x., that the mind does not by them judge of the distance of objects.

14. The truth of this assertion will be yet farther evident to any one that considers those lines and angles have no real existence in nature, being only an hypothesis framed by the mathematicians, and by them introduced into optics, that they might treat of that science in a geometrical way.

15. The last reason I shall give for rejecting that doctrine is, that though we should grant the real existence of those optic angles, &c., and that it was possible for the mind to perceive them, yet these principles would not be found sufficient to explain the phenomena of distance, as shall be shewn hereafter.

16. Now it being already shewn that distance is *suggested* to the mind, by the mediation of some other idea which is itself perceived in the act of seeing, it remains that we inquire,

what ideas or sensations there be that attend vision, unto which we may suppose the ideas of distance are connected, and by which they are introduced into the mind.

And, *first,* it is certain by experience, that when we look at a near object with both eyes, according as it approaches or recedes from us, we alter the disposition of our eyes, by lessening or widening the interval between the pupils. This disposition or turn of the eyes is attended with a sensation, which seems to me to be that which in this case brings the idea of greater or lesser distance into the mind.

17. Not that there is any natural or necessary connexion between the sensation we perceive by the turn of the eyes and greater or lesser distance. But—because the mind has, by constant experience, found the different sensations corresponding to the different dispositions of the eyes to be attended each with a different degree of distance in the object— there has grown an habitual or customary connexion between those two sorts of ideas: so that the mind no sooner perceives the sensation arising from the different turn it gives the eyes, in order to bring the pupils nearer or farther asunder, but it withal perceives the different idea of distance which was wont to be connected with that sensation. Just as, upon hearing a certain sound, the idea is immediately suggested to the understanding which custom had united with it.

18. Nor do I see how I can easily be mistaken in this matter. I know evidently that distance is not perceived of itself; that, by consequence, it must be perceived by means of some other idea, which is immediately perceived, and varies with the different degree of distance. I know also that the sensation arising from the turn of the eyes is of itself immediately perceived; and various degrees thereof are connected with different distances, which never fail to accompany them into my mind, when I view an object distinctly with both eyes whose distance is so small that in respect of it the interval between the eyes has any considerable magnitude.

19. I know it is a received opinion that, by altering the disposition of the eyes, the mind perceives whether the angle of the optic axes, or the lateral angles comprehended between the interval of the eyes or the optic axes, are made greater or lesser; and that, accordingly, by a kind of natural geometry, it judges the point of their intersection to be nearer

or farther off. But that this is not true I am convinced by my own experience; since I am not conscious that I make any such use of the perception I have by the turn of my eyes. And for me to make those judgments and draw those conclusions from it, without knowing that I do so, seems altogether incomprehensible.

20. From all which it follows, that the judgment we make of the distance of an object viewed with both eyes is entirely the result of experience. If we had not constantly found certain sensations, arising from the various dispositions of the eyes, attended with certain degrees of distance, we should never make those sudden judgments from them concerning the distance of objects; no more than we would pretend to judge of a man's thoughts by his pronouncing words we had never heard before.

21. *Secondly,* an object placed at a certain distance from the eye, to which the breadth of the pupil bears a considerable proportion, being made to approach, is seen more confusedly. And the nearer it is brought the more confused appearance it makes. And this being found constantly to be so, there arises in the mind an habitual connexion between the several degrees of confusion and distance; the greater confusion still implying the lesser distance, and the lesser confusion the greater distance of the object.

22. This confused appearance of the object doth therefore seem to be the medium whereby the mind judges of distance, in those cases wherein the most approved writers of optics will have it judge by the different divergency with which the rays flowing from the radiating point fall on the pupil. No man, I believe, will pretend to see or feel those imaginary angles that the rays are supposed to form, according to their various inclinations on his eye. But he cannot choose seeing whether the object appear more or less confused. It is therefore a manifest consequence from what has been demonstrated that, instead of the greater or lesser divergency of the rays, the mind makes use of the greater or lesser confusedness of the appearance, thereby to determine the apparent place of an object.

23. Nor doth it avail to say there is not any necessary connexion between confused vision and distance great or small. For I ask any man what necessary connexion he sees between the redness of a blush and shame? And yet no sooner shall

he behold that colour to arise in the face of another but it brings into his mind the idea of that passion which hath been observed to accompany it.

24. What seems to have misled the writers of optics in this matter is, that they imagine men judge of distance as they do of a conclusion in mathematics; betwixt which and the premises it is indeed absolutely requisite there be an apparent necessary connexion. But it is far otherwise in the sudden judgments men make of distance. We are not to think that brutes and children, or even grown reasonable men, whenever they perceive an object to approach or depart from them, do it by virtue of geometry and demonstration.

25. That one idea may suggest another to the mind, it will suffice that they have been observed to go together, without any demonstration of the *necessity* of their coexistence, or without so much as knowing what it is that makes them so to coexist. Of this there are innumerable instances, of which no one can be ignorant.

26. Thus, greater confusion having been constantly attended with nearer distance, no sooner is the former idea perceived but it suggests the latter to our thoughts. And, if it had been the ordinary course of nature that the farther off an object were placed the more confused it should appear, it is certain the very same perception that now makes us think an object approaches would then have made us to imagine it went farther off, that perception, abstracting from custom and experience, being equally fitted to produce the idea of great distance, or small distance, or no distance at all.

27. *Thirdly*, an object being placed at the distance above specified, and brought nearer to the eye, we may nevertheless prevent, at least for some time, the appearance's growing more confused, by straining the eye. In which case that sensation supplies the place of confused vision, in aiding the mind to judge of the distance of the object; it being esteemed so much the nearer by how much the effort or straining of the eye in order to distinct vision is greater.

28. I have here set down those sensations or ideas that seem to be the constant and general occasions of introducing into the mind the different ideas of near distance. It is true, in most cases, that divers other circumstances contribute to frame our idea of distance, viz. the particular number, size, kind, &c. of the things seen. Concerning which, as well as all

other the forementioned occasions which suggest distance, I shall only observe, they have none of them, in their own nature, any relation or connexion with it: nor is it possible they should ever signify the various degrees thereof, otherwise than as by experience they have been found to be connected with them.

29. I shall proceed upon these principles to account for a phenomenon which has hitherto strangely puzzled the writers of optics, and is so far from being accounted for by any of their theories of vision, that it is, by their own confession, plainly repugnant to them; and of consequence, if nothing else could be objected, were alone sufficient to bring their credit in question. The whole difficulty I shall lay before you in the words of the learned Doctor Barrow, with which he concludes his *Optic Lectures:*—

"Hæc sunt, quæ circa partem opticæ præcipue mathematicam dicenda mihi suggessit meditatio. Circa reliquas (quæ φυσικώτεραι sunt, adeoque sæpiuscule pro certis principiis plausibiles conjecturas venditare necessum habent) nihil fere quicquam admodum verisimile succurrit, a pervulgatis (ab iis, inquam, quæ Keplerus, Scheinerus, Cartesius, et post illos alii tradiderunt) alienum aut diversum. Atqui tacere malo, quam toties oblatam crambem reponere. Proinde receptui cano; nec ita tamen ut prorsus discedam, anteaquam improbam quandam difficultatem (pro sinceritate quam et vobis et veritati debeo minime dissimulandam) in medium protulero, quæ doctrinæ nostræ, hactenus inculcatæ, se objicit adversam, ab ea saltem nullam admittit solutionem. Illa, breviter, talis est. Lenti vel speculo cavo *EBF* exponatur punctum visibile *A*, ita distans, ut radii ex *A* manantes ex inflectione versus axem *AB* cogantur. Sitque radiationis limes (seu puncti *A* imago, qualem supra passim statuimus) punctum *Z*. Inter hoc autem et inflectentis verticem *B* uspiam positus concipiatur oculus. Quæri jam potest, ubi loci debeat punctum *A* apparere? Retrorsum ad punctum *Z* videri non fert natura (cum omnis impressio sensum afficiens proveniat a partibus *A*) ac experientia reclamat. Nostris autem e placitis consequi videtur, ipsum ad partes anticas apparens, ab intervallo longissime dissito (quod et maximum sensibile quodvis intervallum quodammodo exsuperet), apparere. Cum enim quo radiis minus divergentibus attingitur objectum, eo (seclusis utique prænotionibus et præjudiciis) longius abesse sentiatur; et quod parallelos ad oculum radios projicit, remotissime positum æstimetur: exigere ratio videtur, ut quod convergentibus radiis apprehenditur, adhuc magis, si fieri posset, quoad apparentiam elongetur. Quin et circa casum hunc generatim inquiri possit, quidnam omnino sit, quod apparentem puncti *A* locum determinet, faciatque quod constanti ratione nunc propius, nunc remotius appareat? Cui itidem dubio nihil quicquam ex hactenus dictorum analogia responderi posse videtur, nisi debere punctum *A* perpetuo longissime remotum videri. Verum experientia secus attestatur, illud pro diversa oculi inter puncta *B, Z*, positione varie distans, nunquam fere (si unquam) longinquius ipso *A* libere spectato, subinde vero multo propinquius adparere; quinimo, quo oculum appellentes radii magis convergunt, eo speciem objecti propius accedere. Nempe, si puncto *B* admoveatur oculus, suo (ad lentem) fere nativo in loco conspicitur punc-

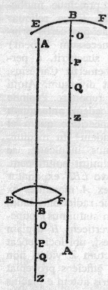

tum *A* (vel æque distans, ad speculum); ad *O* reductos oculus ejusce speciem appropinquantem cernit; ad *P* adhuc vicinius ipsum existimat; ac ita sensim, donec alicubi tandem, velut ad *Q*, constituto oculo, objectum summe propinquum apparens in meram confusionem incipiat evanescere. Quæ sane cuncta rationibus atque decretis nostris repugnare videntur, aut cum iis saltem parum amice conspirant. Neque nostram tantum sententiam pulsat hoc experimentum, at ex æquo cæteras quas norim omnes: veterem imprimis ac vulgatam, nostræ præ reliquis affinem, ita convellere videtur, ut ejus vi coactus doctissimus *A.* Tacquetus isti principio (cui pene soli totam inædificaverat *Catoptricam suam*) ceu infido ac inconstanti renunciarit, adeoque suam ipse doctrinam labefactarit? id tamen, opinor, minime facturus, si rem totam inspexissit penitius, atque difficultatis fundum attigissit. Apud me vero non ita pollet hæc, nec eousque præpollebit ulla difficultas, ut ab iis quæ manifeste rationi consentanea video, discedam; præsertim quum, ut hic accidit, ejusmodi difficultas in singularis cujuspiam casus disparitate fundetur. Nimirum in præsente casu peculiare quiddam, naturæ subtilitati involutum, delitescit, ægre fortassis, nisi perfectius explorato videndi modo, detergendum. Circa quod nil, fateor, hactenus excogitare potui, quod adblandiretur animo meo, nedum plane satisfaceret. Vobis itaque nodum hunc, utinam felicore conatu, resolvendum committo."

In English as follows:

"I have here delivered what my thoughts have suggested to me concerning that part of optics which is more properly mathematical. As for the other parts of that science (which, being rather physical, do consequently abound with plausible conjectures instead of certain principles), there has in them scarce anything occurred to my observation different from what has been already said by Kepler, Scheinerus, Descartes, &c. And methinks I had better say nothing at all than repeat that which has been so often said by others. I think it therefore high time to take my leave of this subject. But, before I quit it for good and all, the fair and ingenuous dealing that I owe both to you and to truth obliges me to acquaint you with a certain untoward difficulty, which seems directly opposite to the doctrine I have been hitherto inculcating, at least admits of no solution from it. In short it is this. Before the double convex glass or concave speculum *EBF*, let the point *A* be placed at such a distance that the rays proceeding from *A*, after refraction or reflection, be brought to unite somewhere in the axis *AB*. And suppose the point of union (*i.e.* the image of the point *A*, as hath been already set forth) to be *Z*; between which and *B*, the vertex of the glass or speculum, conceive the eye to be anywhere placed. The question now is, where the point *A* ought to appear. Experience shews that it doth not appear behind at the point *Z*; and it were contrary to nature that it should; since all the impression which affects the sense comes from towards *A*. But, from our tenets it should seem to follow that it would appear before the eye at a vast distance off, so great as should in some sort surpass all sensible distance. For since, if we exclude all anticipations and prejudices, every object appears by so much the farther off by how much the rays it sends to the eye are less diverging; and that object is thought to be most remote from which parallel rays proceed unto the eye; reason would make one think that object should appear at yet a greater distance which is seen by converging rays. Moreover, it may in general be asked concerning this case, what it is that determines the apparent place of the point *A*, and maketh it to appear after a constant manner, sometimes nearer, at other times farther off? To which doubt I see nothing that can be answered agreeable to the principles we have laid down, except only that the point *A* ought always to appear extremely remote. But, on the contrary, we are assured by experience, that the point *A* appears variously distant, according to the different situations of the eye between the points *B* and *Z*. And that it doth almost never (if at all) seem farther off than it would if it were beheld by the naked eye; but, on the contrary, it doth sometimes appear much nearer. Nay, it is even certain that by how much the rays falling on the eye do more converge, by so much the nearer does the object seem to approach. For, the eye being placed close to the point *B*, the object *A* appears nearly in its own natural place, if the point *B* is taken in the glass, or at the same distance, if in the speculum. The eye being brought back to *O*, the object seems to draw near; and, being come to *P*, it beholds it still nearer: and so on by little and little, till at length the eye being placed somewhere, suppose at *Q*, the object appearing extremely near begins to vanish into mere confusion. All which doth seem repugnant to our principles; at least, not rightly to agree with them. Nor is our tenet alone struck at by this experiment, but likewise all others that ever came to my knowledge are every whit as much endangered by it. The ancient one especially (which is most commonly received, and comes nearest to mine) seems to be so effectually overthrown thereby that the most learned Tacquet has been forced to reject that principle, as false and uncertain, on which alone he had built almost his whole *Catoptrics*, and consequently, by taking away the foundation, hath himself pulled down the superstructure he had raised on it. Which, nevertheless, I do not believe he would have done, had he but considered the whole matter more thoroughly, and examined the difficulty to the bottom. But as for me, neither this nor any other difficulty shall have so great an influence on me, as to make me renounce that which I know to be manifestly agreeable to reason. Especially when, as it here falls out, the difficulty is founded in the peculiar nature of a certain odd and particular case. For, in the present case something peculiar lies hid, which, being involved in the subtilty of nature, will perhaps hardly be discovered till such time as the manner of vision is more perfectly made known. Concerning which, I must own I have hitherto been able to find out nothing that has the least show of probability, not to mention certainty. I shall therefore leave this knot to be untied by you, wishing you may have better success in it than I have had."

30. The ancient and received principle, which Dr. Barrow here mentions as the main foundation of Tacquet's *Catoptrics*, is, that every "visible point seen by reflection from a speculum shall appear placed at the intersection of the reflected ray and the perpendicular of incidence." Which intersection in the present case happening to be behind the eye, it greatly shakes the authority of that principle whereon the aforementioned author proceeds throughout his whole *Catoptrics*, in determining the apparent place of objects seen by reflection from any kind of speculum.

31. Let us now see how this phenomenon agrees with our tenets. The eye, the nearer it is placed to the point B in the above figures, the more distinct is the appearance of the object: but, as it recedes to O, the appearance grows more confused; and at P it sees the object yet more confused; and so on, till the eye, being brought back to Z, sees the object in the greatest confusion of all. Wherefore, by sect. 21, the object should seem to approach the eye gradually, as it recedes from the point B; that is, at O it should (in consequence of the principle I have laid down in the aforesaid section) seem nearer than it did at B, and at P nearer than at O, and at Q nearer than at P, and so on, till it quite vanishes at Z. Which is the very matter of fact, as any one that pleases may easily satisfy himself by experiment.

32. This case is much the same as if we should suppose an Englishman to meet a foreigner who used the same words with the English, but in a direct contrary signification. The Englishman would not fail to make a wrong judgment of the ideas annexed to those sounds, in the mind of him that used them. Just so in the present case, the object speaks (if I may so say) with words that the eye is well acquainted with, that is, confusions of appearance; but, whereas heretofore the greatest confusions were always wont to signify nearer distances, they have in this case a direct contrary signification, being connected with the greater distances. Whence it follows

that the eye must unavoidably be mistaken, since it will take the confusions in the sense it has been used to, which is directly opposed to the true.

33. This phenomenon, as it entirely subverts the opinion of those who will have us judge of distance by lines and angles, on which supposition it is altogether inexplicable, so it seems to me no small confirmation of the truth of that principle whereby it is explained. But, in order to a more full explication of this point, and to shew how far the hypothesis of the mind's judging by the various divergency of rays may be of use in determining the apparent place of an object, it will be necessary to premise some few things, which are already well known to those who have any skill in Dioptrics.

34. *First*, Any radiating point is then distinctly seen when the rays proceeding from it are, by the refractive power of the crystalline, accurately reunited in the retina or fund of the eye. But if they are reunited either before they arrive at the retina, or after they have passed it, then there is confused vision.

35. *Secondly*, Suppose, in the adjacent figures, *NP* represent an eye duly framed, and retaining its natural figure. In fig. 1 the rays falling nearly parallel on the eye, are, by the crystalline *AB*, refracted, so as their focus, or point of union *F*, falls exactly on the retina. But, if the rays fall sensibly diverging on the eye, as in fig. 2, then their focus falls beyond the retina; or, if the rays are made to converge by the lens *QS*, before they come at the eye, as in fig. 3, their focus *F* will fall before the retina. In which two last cases it is evident, from the foregoing section, that the appearance of the point *Z* is confused. And, by how much the greater is the convergency or divergency of the rays falling on the pupil, by so much the farther will the point of their reunion be from the retina, either before or behind it, and consequently the point *Z* will appear by so much the more confused. And this, by the bye, may shew us the difference between confused and faint vision. Confused vision is, when the rays proceeding from each distinct point of the object are not accurately re-collected in one corresponding point on the retina, but take up some space thereon—so that rays from different points become mixed and confused together. This is opposed to a distinct vision, and attends near objects. Faint vision is when, by reason of the distance of the object, or grossness of the inter-

jacent medium, few rays arrive from the object to the eye. This is opposed to vigorous or clear vision, and attends remote objects. But to return.

36. The eye, or (to speak truly) the mind, perceiving only the confusion itself, without ever considering the cause from which it proceeds, doth constantly annex the same degree of distance to the same degree of confusion. Whether that confusion be occasioned by converging or diverging rays it matters not. Whence it follows that the eye, viewing the object Z through the glass QS (which by refraction causeth the rays ZQ, ZS, &c. to converge), should judge it to be at such a nearness, at which, if it were placed, it would

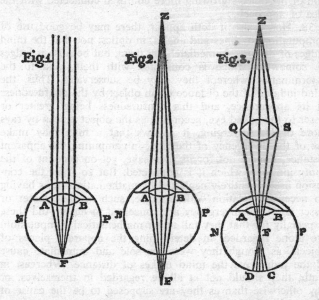

radiate on the eye, with rays diverging to that degree as would produce the same confusion which is now produced by converging rays, i.e. would cover a portion of the retina equal to DC. (Vid. fig. 3, sup.) But then this must be understood (to use Dr. Barrow's phrase) "seclusis prænotionibus et præjudiciis," in case we abstract from all other circumstances of vision, such as the figure, size, faintness, &c. of the visible objects—all which do ordinarily concur to form our idea of distance, the mind having, by frequent experience, observed their several sorts or degrees to be connected with various distances.

37. It plainly follows from what has been said, that a person perfectly purblind (*i.e.* that could not see an object distinctly but when placed close to his eye) would not make the same wrong judgment that others do in the foxementioned case. For, to him, greater confusions constantly suggesting greater distances, he must, as he recedes from the glass, and the object grows more confused, judge it to be at a farther distance; contrary to what they do who have had the perception of the objects growing more confused connected with the idea of approach.

38. Hence also it doth appear, there may be good use of computation, by lines and angles, in optics; not that the mind judges of distance immediately by them, but because it judges by somewhat which is connected with them, and to the determination whereof they may be subservient. Thus, the mind judging of the distance of an object by the confusedness of its appearance, and this confusedness being greater or lesser to the naked eye, according as the object is seen by rays more or less diverging, it follows that a man may make use of the divergency of the rays, in computing the apparent distance, though not for its own sake, yet on account of the confusion with which it is connected. But so it is, the confusion itself is entirely neglected by mathematicians, as having no necessary relation with distance, such as the greater or lesser angles of divergency are conceived to have. And these (especially for that they fall under mathematical computation) are alone regarded, in determining the apparent places of objects, as though they were the sole and immediate cause of the judgments the mind makes of distance. Whereas, in truth, they should not at all be regarded in themselves, or any otherwise than as they are supposed to be the cause of confused vision.

39. The not considering of this has been a fundamental and perplexing oversight. For proof whereof, we need go no farther than the case before us. It having been observed that the most diverging rays brought into the mind the idea of nearest distance, and that still as the divergency decreased the distance increased, and it being thought the connexion

between the various degrees of divergency and distance was immediate—this naturally leads one to conclude, from an ill-grounded analogy, that converging rays shall make an object appear at an immense distance, and that, as the convergency increases, the distance (if it were possible) should do so likewise. That this was the cause of Dr. Barrow's mistake is evident from his own words which we have quoted. Whereas had the learned Doctor observed that diverging and converging rays, how opposite soever they may seem, do nevertheless agree in producing the same effect, to wit, confusedness of vision, greater degrees whereof are produced indifferently, either as the divergency or convergency of the rays increaseth; and that it is by this effect, which is the same in both, that either the divergency or convergency is perceived by the eye—I say, had he but considered this, it is certain he would have made a quite contrary judgment, and rightly concluded that those rays which fall on the eye with greater degrees of convergency should make the object from whence they proceed appear by so much the nearer. But it is plain it was impossible for any man to attain to a right notion of this matter so long as he had regard only to lines and angles, and did not apprehend the true nature of vision, and how far it was of mathematical consideration.

40. Before we dismiss this subject, it is fit we take notice of a query relating thereto, proposed by the ingenious Mr. Molyneux, in his *Treatise of Dioptrics* (par. i. prop. 31. sec. 9), where, speaking of the difficulty we have been explaining, he has these words: "And so he (*i.e.* Dr. Barrow) leaves this difficulty to the solution of others, which I (after so great an example) shall do likewise; but with the resolution of the same admirable author, of not quitting the evident doctrine which we have before laid down, for determining the *locus objecti,* on account of being pressed by one difficulty, which seems inexplicable till a more intimate knowledge of the visive faculty be obtained by mortals. In the meantime I propose it to the consideration of the ingenious, whether the *locus apparens* of an object placed as in this ninth section be not as much before the eye as the distinct base is behind the eye?" To which query we may venture to answer in the negative. For, in the present case, the rule for determining the distance of the distinct base, or respective focus from the glass is this: *As the difference between the distance of the*

object and focus is to the focus or focal length, so the distance of the object from the glass is to the distance of the respective focus or distinct base from the glass. (Molyneux, *Dioptr.*, par. i. prop. 5.) Let us now suppose the object to be placed at the distance of the focal length, and one-half of the focal length from the glass, and the eye close to the glass. Hence it will follow, by the rule, that the distance of the distinct base behind the eye is double the true distance of the object before the eye. If, therefore, Mr. Molyneux's conjecture held good, it would follow that the eye should see the object twice as far off as it really is; and in other cases at three or four times its due distance, or more. But this manifestly contradicts experience, the object never appearing, at farthest, beyond its due distance. Whatever, therefore, is built on this supposition (vid. corol. i. prop. 57. ibid.) comes to the ground along with it.

41. From what hath been premised, it is a manifest consequence, that a man born blind, being made to see, would at first have no idea of distance by sight: the sun and stars, the remotest objects as well as the nearer, would all seem to be in his eye, or rather in his mind. The objects intromitted by sight would seem to him (as in truth they are) no other than a new set of thoughts or sensations, each whereof is as near to him as the perceptions of pain or pleasure, or the most inward passions of his soul. For, our judging objects perceived by sight to be at any distance, or without the mind, is (vid. sect. xxviii.) entirely the effect of experience; which one in those circumstances could not yet have attained to.

42. It is indeed otherwise upon the common supposition—that men judge of distance by the angle of the optic axes, just as one in the dark, or a blind man by the angle comprehended by two sticks, one whereof he held in each hand. For, if this were true, it would follow that one blind from his birth, being made to see, should stand in need of no new experience, in order to perceive distance by sight. But that this is false has, I think, been sufficiently demonstrated.

43. And perhaps, upon a strict inquiry, we shall not find that even those who from their birth have grown up in a continued habit of seeing are irrecoverably prejudiced on the other side, to wit, in thinking what they see to be at a

distance from them. For, at this time it seems agreed on all hands, by those who have had any thoughts of that matter, that colours, which are the proper and immediate object of sight, are not without the mind.—But then, it would be said, by sight we have also the ideas of extension, and figure, and motion; all which may well be thought without and at some distance from the mind, though colour should not. In answer to this, I appeal to any man's experience, whether the visible extension of any object do not appear as near to him as the colour of that object; nay, whether they do not both seem to be in the very same place. Is not the extension we see coloured, and is it possible for us, so much as in thought, to separate and abstract colour from extension? Now, where the extension is, there surely is the figure, and there the motion too. I speak of those which are perceived by sight.

44. But for a fuller explication of this point, and to shew that the immediate objects of sight are not so much as the ideas or resemblances of things placed at a distance, it is requisite that we look nearer into the matter, and carefully observe what is meant in common discourse when one says, that which he sees is at a distance from him. Suppose, for example, that looking at the moon I should say it were fifty or sixty semidiameters of the earth distant from me. Let us see what moon this is spoken of. It is plain it cannot be the visible moon, or anything like the visible moon, or that which I see—which is only a round luminous plain, of about thirty visible points in diameter. For, in case I am carried from the place where I stand directly towards the moon, it is manifest the object varies still as I go on; and, by the time that I am advanced fifty or sixty semidiameters of the earth, I shall be so far from being near a small, round, luminous flat that I shall perceive nothing like it—this object having long since disappeared, and, if I would recover it, it must be by going back to the earth from whence I set out. Again, suppose I perceive by sight the faint and obscure idea of something, which I doubt whether it be a man, or a tree, or a tower, but judge it to be at the distance of about a mile. It is plain I cannot mean that what I see is a mile off, or that it is the image or likeness of anything which is a mile off; since that every step I take towards it the appearance alters, and from being obscure, small, and faint, grows clear, large,

and vigorous. And when I come to the mile's end, that which I saw first is quite lost, neither do I find anything in the likeness of it.

45. In these and the like instances, the truth of the matter, I find, stands thus:—Having of a long time experienced certain ideas perceivable by touch—as distance, tangible figure, and solidity—to have been connected with certain ideas of sight, I do, upon perceiving these ideas of sight, forthwith conclude what tangible ideas are, by the wonted ordinary course of nature, like to follow. Looking at an object, I perceive a certain visible figure and colour, with some degree of faintness and other circumstances, which, from what I have formerly observed, determine me to think that if I advance forward so many paces, miles, &c., I shall be affected with such and such ideas of touch. So that, in truth and strictness of speech, I neither see distance itself, nor anything that I take to be at a distance. I say, neither distance nor things placed at a distance are themselves, or their ideas, truly perceived by sight. This I am persuaded of, as to what concerns myself. And I believe whoever will look narrowly into his own thoughts, and examine what he means by saying he sees this or that thing at a distance, will agree with me, that what he sees only suggests to his understanding that, after having passed a certain distance, to be measured by the motion of his body, which is perceivable by touch, he shall come to perceive such and such tangible ideas, which have been usually connected with such and such visible ideas. But, that one might be deceived by these suggestions of sense, and that there is no necessary connexion between visible and tangible ideas suggested by them, we need go no farther than the next looking-glass or picture to be convinced. Note that, when I speak of tangible ideas, I take the word idea for any immediate object of sense, or understanding—in which large signification it is commonly used by the moderns.

46. From what we have shewn, it is a manifest consequence that the ideas of space, outness, and things placed at a distance are not, strictly speaking, the object of sight; they are not otherwise perceived by the eye than by the ear. Sitting in my study I hear a coach drive along the street; I look through the casement and see it; I walk out and enter into it. Thus, common speech would incline one to think I heard, saw, and touched the same thing, to wit, the coach. It is

nevertheless certain the ideas intromitted by each sense are widely different, and distinct from each other; but, having been observed constantly to go together, they are spoken of as one and the same thing. By the variation of the noise, I perceive the different distances of the coach, and know that it approaches before I look out. Thus, by the ear I perceive distance just after the same manner as I do by the eye.

47. I do not nevertheless say I hear distance, in like manner as I say that I see it—the ideas perceived by hearing not being so apt to be confounded with the ideas of touch as those of sight are. So likewise a man is easily convinced that bodies and external things are not properly the object of hearing, but only sounds, by the mediation whereof the idea of this or that body, or distance, is suggested to his thoughts. But then one is with more difficulty brought to discern the difference there is betwixt the ideas of sight and touch: though it be certain, a man no more sees and feels the same thing, than he hears and feels the same thing.

48. One reason of which seems to be this. It is thought a great absurdity to imagine that one and the same thing should have any more than one extension and one figure. But, the extension and figure of a body being let into the mind two ways, and that differently, either by sight or touch, it seems to follow that we see the same extension and the same figure which we feel.

49. But, if we take a close and accurate view of the matter, it must be acknowledged that we never see and feel one and the same object. That which is seen is one thing, and that which is felt is another. If the visible figure and extension be not the same with the tangible figure and extension, we are not to infer that one and the same thing has divers extensions. The true consequence is that the objects of sight and touch are two distinct things. It may perhaps require some thought rightly to conceive this distinction. And the difficulty seems not a little increased, because the combination of visible ideas hath constantly the same name as the combination of tangible ideas wherewith it is connected—which doth of necessity arise from the use and end of language.

50. In order, therefore, to treat accurately and unconfusedly of vision, we must bear in mind that there are two sorts of objects apprehended by the eye—the one primarily and immediately, the other secondarily and by intervention

of the former. Those of the first sort neither are nor appear to be without the mind, or at any distance off. They may, indeed, grow greater or smaller, more confused, or more clear, or more faint. But they do not, cannot approach, or recede from us. Whenever we say an object is at a distance, whenever we say it draws near, or goes farther off, we must always mean it of the latter sort, which properly belong to the touch, and are not so truly perceived as suggested by the eye, in like manner as thoughts by the ear.

51. No sooner do we hear the words of a familiar language pronounced in our ears but the ideas corresponding thereto present themselves to our minds: in the very same instant the sound and the meaning enter the understanding: so closely are they united that it is not in our power to keep out the one except we exclude the other also. We even act in all respects as if we heard the very thoughts themselves. So likewise the secondary objects, or those which are only suggested by sight, do often more strongly affect us, and are more regarded, than the proper objects of that sense; along with which they enter into the mind, and with which they have a far more strict connexion than ideas have with words. Hence it is we find it so difficult to discriminate between the immediate and mediate objects of sight, and are so prone to attribute to the former what belongs only to the latter. They are, as it were, most closely twisted, blended, and incorporated together. And the prejudice is confirmed and riveted in our thoughts by a long tract of time, by the use of language, and want of reflection. However, I doubt not but any one that shall attentively consider what we have already said, and shall say upon this subject before we have done (especially if he pursue it in his own thoughts), may be able to deliver himself from that prejudice. Sure I am, it is worth some attention to whoever would understand the true nature of vision.

52. I have now done with Distance, and proceed to shew how it is that we perceive by sight the Magnitude of objects. It is the opinion of some that we do it by angles, or by angles in conjunction with distance. But, neither angles nor distance being perceivable by sight, and the things we see being in truth at no distance from us, it follows that, as we have shewn lines and angles not to be the medium the mind makes use of in apprehending the apparent place, so neither are they

the medium whereby it apprehends the apparent magnitude of objects.

53. It is well known that the same extension at a near distance shall subtend a greater angle, and at a farther distance a lesser angle. And by this principle (we are told) the mind estimates the magnitude of an object, comparing the angle under which it is seen with its distance, and thence inferring the magnitude thereof. What inclines men to this mistake (beside the humour of making one see by geometry) is, that the same perceptions or ideas which suggest distance do also suggest magnitude. But, if we examine it, we shall find they suggest the latter as immediately as the former. I say, they do not first suggest distance and then leave it to the judgment to use that as a medium whereby to collect the magnitude; but they have as close and immediate a connexion with the magnitude as with the distance; and suggest magnitude as independently of distance, as they do distance independently of magnitude. All which will be evident to whoever considers what has been already said and what follows.

54. It has been shewn there are two sorts of objects apprehended by sight, each whereof has its distinct magnitude, or extension—the one, properly tangible, *i.e.* to be perceived and measured by touch, and not immediately falling under the sense of seeing; the other, properly and immediately visible, by mediation of which the former is brought in view. Each of these magnitudes are greater or lesser, according as they contain in them more or fewer points, they being made up of points or minimums. For, whatever may be said of extension in abstract, it is certain sensible extension is not infinitely divisible. There is a *minimum tangibile*, and a *minimum visibile*, beyond which sense cannot perceive. This every one's experience will inform him.

55. The magnitude of the object which exists without the mind, and is at a distance, continues always invariably the same: but, the visible object still changing as you approach to or recede from the tangible object, it hath no fixed and determinate greatness. Whenever therefore we speak of the magnitude of any thing, for instance a tree or a house, we must mean the tangible magnitude; otherwise there can be nothing steady and free from ambiguity spoken of it. Now, though the tangible and visible magnitude do in truth belong to two distinct objects, I shall nevertheless (especially since those objects are called by the same name, and are observed

to coexist), to avoid tediousness and singularity of speech, sometimes speak of them as belonging to one and the same thing.

56. Now, in order to discover by what means the magnitude of tangible objects is perceived by sight, I need only reflect on what passes in my own mind, and observe what those things be which introduce the ideas of greater or lesser into my thoughts when I look on any object. And these I find to be, *first,* the magnitude or extension of the visible object, which, being immediately perceived by sight, is connected with that other which is tangible and placed at a distance: *secondly,* the confusion or distinctness: and *thirdly,* the vigorousness or faintness of the aforesaid visible appearance. *Cæteris paribus,* by how much the greater or lesser the visible object is, by so much the greater or lesser do I conclude the tangible object to be. But, be the idea immediately perceived by sight never so large, yet, if it be withal confused, I judge the magnitude of the thing to be but small. If it be distinct and clear, I judge it greater. And, if it be faint, I apprehend it to be yet greater. What is here meant by confusion and faintness has been explained in sect. 35.

57. Moreover, the judgments we make of greatness do, in like manner as those of distance, depend on the disposition of the eye; also on the figure, number, and situation of objects, and other circumstances that have been observed to attend great or small tangible magnitudes. Thus, for instance, the very same quantity of visible extension which in the figure of a tower doth suggest the idea of great magnitude shall in the figure of a man suggest the idea of much smaller magnitude. That this is owing to the experience we have had of the usual bigness of a tower and a man, no one, I suppose, need be told.

58. It is also evident that confusion or faintness have no more a necessary connexion with little or great magnitude than they have with little or great distance. As they suggest the latter, so they suggest the former to our minds. And, by consequence, if it were not for experience, we should no more judge a faint or confused appearance to be connected with great or little magnitude than we should that it was connected with great or little distance.

59. Nor will it be found that great or small visible magnitude hath any necessary relation to great or small tangible

magnitude—so that the one may certainly and infallibly be inferred from the other. But, before we come to the proof of this, it is fit we consider the difference there is betwixt the extension and figure which is the proper object of touch, and that other which is termed visible; and how the former is principally, though not immediately, taken notice of when we look at any object. This has been before mentioned, but we shall here inquire into the cause thereof. We regard the objects that environ us in proportion as they are adapted to benefit or injure our own bodies, and thereby produce in our minds the sensations of pleasure or pain. Now, bodies operating on our organs by an immediate application, and the hurt or advantage arising therefrom depending altogether on the tangible, and not at all on the visible, qualities of any object —this is a plain reason why those should be regarded by us much more than these. And for this end the visive sense seems to have been bestowed on animals, to wit, that, by the perception of visible ideas (which in themselves are not capable of affecting or anywise altering the frame of their bodies), they may be able to foresee (from the experience they have had what tangible ideas are connected with such and such visible ideas) the damage or benefit which is like to ensue upon the application of their own bodies to this or that body which is at a distance. Which foresight, how necessary it is to the preservation of an animal, every one's experience can inform him. Hence it is that, when we look at an object, the tangible figure and extension thereof are principally attended to; whilst there is small heed taken of the visible figure and magnitude, which, though more immediately perceived, do less concern us, and are not fitted to produce any alteration in our bodies.

60. That the matter of fact is true will be evident to any one who considers that a man placed at ten foot distance is thought as great as if he were placed at the distance only of five foot; which is true, not with relation to the visible, but tangible greatness of the object: the visible magnitude being far greater at one station than it is at the other.

61. Inches, feet, &c. are settled, stated lengths, whereby we measure objects and estimate their magnitude. We say, for example, an object appears to be six inches, or six foot long. Now, that this cannot be meant of visible inches, &c. is evident, because a visible inch is itself no constant de-

terminate magnitude, and cannot therefore serve to mark out and determine the magnitude of any other thing. Take an inch marked upon a ruler; view it successively, at the distance of half a foot, a foot, a foot and a half, &c. from the eye: at each of which, and at all the intermediate distances, the inch shall have a different visible extension, *i.e.* there shall be more or fewer points discerned in it. Now, I ask which of all these various extensions is that stated determinate one that is agreed on for a common measure of other magnitudes? No reason can be assigned why we should pitch on one more than another. And, except there be some invariable determinate extension fixed on to be marked by the word inch, it is plain it can be used to little purpose; and to say a thing contains this or that number of inches shall imply no more than that it is extended, without bringing any particular idea of that extension into the mind. Farther, an inch and a foot, from different distances, shall both exhibit the same visible magnitude, and yet at the same time you shall say that one seems several times greater than the other. From all which it is manifest, that the judgments we make of the magnitude of objects by sight are altogether in reference to their tangible extension. Whenever we say an object is great or small, of this or that determinate measure, I say, it must be meant of the tangible and not the visible extension, which, though immediately perceived, is nevertheless little taken notice of.

62. Now, that there is no necessary connexion between these two distinct extensions is evident from hence—because our eyes might have been framed in such a manner as to be able to see nothing but what were less than the *minimum tangibile*. In which case it is not impossible we might have perceived all the immediate objects of sight the very same that we do now; but unto those visible appearances there would not be connected those different tangible magnitudes that are now. Which shews the judgments we make of the magnitude of things placed at a distance, from the various greatness of the immediate objects of sight, do arise not from any essential or necessary, but only a customary, tie which has been observed betwixt them.

63. Moreover, it is not only certain that any idea of sight might not have been connected with this or that idea of touch we now observe to accompany it, but also that the greater visible magnitudes might have been connected with and intro-

duced into our minds lesser tangible magnitudes, and the lesser visible magnitudes greater tangible magnitudes. Nay, that it actually is so, we have daily experience—that object which makes a strong and large appearance not seeming near so great as another the visible magnitude whereof is much less, but more faint, and the appearance upper, or which is the same thing, painted lower on the retina, which faintness and situation suggest both greater magnitude and greater distance.

64. From which, and from sects. 57 and 58, it is manifest that, as we do not perceive the magnitude of objects immediately by sight, so neither do we perceive them by the mediation of anything which has a necessary connexion with them. Those ideas that now suggest unto us the various magnitudes of external objects before we touch them might possibly have suggested no such thing; or they might have signified them in a direct contrary manner, so that the very same ideas on the perception whereof we judge an object to be small might as well have served to make us conclude it great; —those ideas being in their own nature equally fitted to bring into our minds the idea of small or great, or no size at all, of outward objects, just as the words of any language are in their own nature indifferent to signify this or that thing, or nothing at all.

65. As we see distance so we see magnitude. And we see both in the same way that we see shame or anger in the looks of a man. Those passions are themselves invisible; they are nevertheless let in by the eye along with colours and alterations of countenance which are the immediate object of vision, and which signify them for no other reason than barely because they have been observed to accompany them. Without which experience we should no more have taken blushing for a sign of shame than of gladness.

66. We are nevertheless exceedingly prone to imagine those things which are perceived only by the mediation of others to be themselves the immediate objects of sight, or at least to have in their own nature a fitness to be suggested by them before ever they had been experienced to co-exist with them. From which prejudice every one perhaps will not find it easy to emancipate himself, by any the clearest convictions of reason. And there are some grounds to think that, if there was one only invariable and universal language in the world,

and that men were born with the faculty of speaking it, it would be the opinion of many, that the ideas in other men's minds were properly perceived by the ear, or had at least a necessary and inseparable tie with the sounds that were affixed to them. All which seems to arise from want of a due application of our discerning faculty, thereby to discriminate between the ideas that are in our understandings, and consider them apart from each other; which would preserve us from confounding those that are different, and make us see what ideas do, and what do not, include or imply this or that other idea.

67. There is a celebrated phenomenon the solution whereof I shall attempt to give, by the principles that have been laid down, in reference to the manner wherein we apprehend by sight the magnitude of objects.—The apparent magnitude of the moon, when placed in the horizon, is much greater than when it is in the meridian, though the angle under which the diameter of the moon is seen be not observed greater in the former case than in the latter; and the horizontal moon doth not constantly appear of the same bigness, but at some times seemeth far greater than at others.

68. Now, in order to explain the reason of the moon's appearing greater than ordinary in the horizon, it must be observed that the particles which compose our atmosphere do intercept the rays of light proceeding from any object to the eye; and, by how much the greater is the portion of atmosphere interjacent between the object and the eye, by so much the more are the rays intercepted, and, by consequence, the appearance of the object rendered more faint—every object appearing more vigorous or more faint in proportion as it sendeth more or fewer rays into the eye. Now, between the eye and the moon when situated in the horizon there lies a far greater quantity of atmosphere than there does when the moon is in the meridian. Whence it comes to pass, that the appearance of the horizontal moon is fainter, and therefore, by sect. 56, it should be thought bigger in that situation than in the meridian, or in any other elevation above the horizon.

69. Farther, the air being variously impregnated, sometimes more and sometimes less, with vapours and exhalations fitted to retund and intercept the rays of light, it follows that the appearance of the horizontal moon hath not always an

equal faintness, and, by consequence, that luminary, though in the very same situation, is at one time judged greater than at another.

70. That we have here given the true account of the phenomena of the horizontal moon, will, I suppose, be farther evident to any one from the following considerations:—*First*, it is plain, that which in this case suggests the idea of greater magnitude, must be something which is itself perceived; for, that which is unperceived cannot suggest to our perception any other thing. *Secondly*, it must be something that does not constantly remain the same, but is subject to some change or variation; since the appearance of the horizontal moon varies, being at one time greater than at another. And yet, *thirdly*, it cannot be the visible figure or magnitude; since that remains the same, or is rather lesser, by how much the moon is nearer to the horizon. It remains therefore, that the true cause is that affection or alteration of the visible appearance, which proceeds from the greater paucity of rays arriving at the eye, and which I term faintness: since this answers all the forementioned conditions, and I am not conscious of any other perception that does.

71. Add to this that in misty weather it is a common observation, that the appearance of the horizontal moon is far larger than usual, which greatly conspires with and strengthens our opinion. Neither would it prove in the least irreconcilable with what we have said, if the horizontal moon should chance sometimes to seem enlarged beyond its usual extent, even in more serene weather. For, we must not only have regard to the mist which happens to be in the place where we stand; we ought also to take into our thoughts the whole sum of vapours and exhalations which lie betwixt the eye and the moon: all which co-operating to render the appearance of the moon more faint, and thereby increase its magnitude, it may chance to appear greater than it usually does even in the horizontal position, at a time when, though there be no extraordinary fog or haziness just in the place where we stand, yet the air between the eye and the moon, taken altogether, may be loaded with a greater quantity of interspersed vapours and exhalations than at other times.

72. It may be objected that, in consequence of our principles, the interposition of a body in some degree opaque, which may intercept a great part of the rays of light, should

render the appearance of the moon in the meridian as large as when it is viewed in the horizon. To which I answer, it is not faintness anyhow applied that suggests greater magnitude; there being no necessary, but only an experimental, connexion between those two things. It follows that the faintness which enlarges the appearance must be applied in such sort, and with such circumstances, as have been observed to attend the vision of great magnitudes. When from a distance we behold great objects, the particles of the intermediate air and vapours, which are themselves unperceivable, do interrupt the rays of light, and thereby render the appearance less strong and vivid. Now, faintness of appearance, caused in this sort, hath been experienced to co-exist with great magnitude. But when it is caused by the interposition of an opaque sensible body, this circumstance alters the case; so that a faint appearance this way caused does not suggest greater magnitude, because it hath not been experienced to coexist with it.

73. Faintness, as well as all other ideas or perceptions which suggest magnitude or distance, does it in the same way that words suggest the notions to which they are annexed. Now, it is known a word pronounced with certain circumstances, or in a certain context with other words, hath not always the same import and signification that it hath when pronounced in some other circumstances, or different context of words. The very same visible appearance, as to faintness and all other respects, if placed on high, shall not suggest the same magnitude that it would if it were seen at an equal distance on a level with the eye. The reason whereof is, that we are rarely accustomed to view objects at a great height; our concerns lie among things situated rather before than above us; and accordingly our eyes are not placed on the top of our heads, but in such a position as is most convenient for us to see distant objects standing in our way. And, this situation of them being a circumstance which usually attends the vision of distant objects, we may from hence account for (what is commonly observed) an object's appearing of different magnitude, even with respect to its horizontal extension, on the top of a steeple, *e.g.* a hundred feet high, to one standing below, from what it would if placed at a hundred feet distance, on a level with his eye. For, it hath been shewn that the judgment we make on the magnitude of a thing depends not on the visible appearance only, but also on divers

other circumstances, any one of which being omitted or varied may suffice to make some alteration in our judgment. Hence, the circumstance of viewing a distant object in such a situation as is usual and suits with the ordinary posture of the head and eyes, being omitted, and instead thereof a different situation of the object, which requires a different posture of the head, taking place—it is not to be wondered at if the magnitude be judged different. But it will be demanded, why a high object should constantly appear less than an equidistant low object of the same dimensions; for so it is observed to be. It may indeed be granted that the variation of some circumstances may vary the judgment made on the magnitude of high objects, which we are less used to look at; but it does not hence appear why they should be judged less rather than greater? I answer, that in case the magnitude of distant objects was suggested by the extent of their visible appearance alone, and thought proportional thereto, it is certain they would then be judged much less than now they seem to be. (Vid. sect. 79.) But, several circumstances concurring to form the judgment we make on the magnitude of distant objects, by means of which they appear far larger than others whose visible appearance hath an equal or even greater extension, it follows that upon the change or omission of any of those circumstances which are wont to attend the vision of distant objects, and so come to influence the judgments made on their magnitude, they shall proportionably appear less than otherwise they would. For, any of those things that caused an object to be thought greater than in proportion to its visible extension being either omitted, or applied without the usual circumstances, the judgment depends more entirely on the visible extension; and consequently the object must be judged less. Thus, in the present case the situation of the thing seen being different from what it usually is in those objects we have occasion to view, and whose magnitude we observe, it follows that the very same object being a hundred feet high, should seem less than if it was a hundred feet off, on (or nearly on) a level with the eye. What has been here set forth seems to me to have no small share in contributing to magnify the appearance of the horizontal moon, and deserves not to be passed over in the explication of it.

74. If we attentively consider the phenomenon before us, we shall find the not discerning between the mediate and

immediate objects of sight to be the chief cause of the difficulty that occurs in the explication of it. The magnitude of the visible moon, or that which is the proper and immediate object of vision, is no greater when the moon is in the horizon than when it is in the meridian. How comes it, therefore, to seem greater in one situation than the other? What is it can put this cheat on the understanding? It has no other perception of the moon than what it gets by sight. And that which is seen is of the same extent—I say, the visible appearance hath the same, or rather a less, magnitude, when the moon is viewed in the horizontal than when in the meridional position. And yet it is esteemed greater in the former than in the latter. Herein consists the difficulty; which doth vanish and admit of the most easy solution, if we consider that as the visible moon is not greater in the horizon than in the meridian, so neither is it thought to be so. It hath been already shewn that, in any act of vision, the visible object absolutely, or in itself, is little taken notice of—the mind still carrying its view from that to some tangible ideas, which have been observed to be connected with it, and by that means come to be suggested by it. So that when a thing is said to appear great or small, or whatever estimate be made of the magnitude of any thing, this is meant not of the visible but of the tangible object. This duly considered, it will be no hard matter to reconcile the seeming contradiction there is, that the moon should appear of a different bigness, the visible magnitude thereof remaining still the same. For, by sect. 56, the very same visible extension, with a different faintness, shall suggest a different tangible extension. When therefore the horizontal moon is said to appear greater than the meridional moon, this must be understood, not of a greater visible extension, but of a greater tangible or real extension, which, by reason of the more than ordinary faintness of the visible appearance, is suggested to the mind along with it.

75. Many attempts have been made by learned men to account for this appearance. Gassendus, Descartes, Hobbes, and several others have employed their thoughts on that subject; but how fruitless and unsatisfactory their endeavours have been is sufficiently shewn in the *Philosophical Transactions* (Numb. 187, p. 314), where you may see their several opinions at large set forth and confuted, not without some surprise at the gross blunders that ingenious men have been forced into by endeavouring to reconcile this appearance

with the ordinary principles of optics. Since the writing of which there hath been published in the *Transactions* (Numb. 187, p. 323) another paper relating to the same affair, by the celebrated Dr. Wallis, wherein he attempts to account for that phenomenon; which, though it seems not to contain anything new, or different from what had been said before by others, I shall nevertheless consider in this place.

76. His opinion, in short, is this:—We judge not of the magnitude of an object by the visual angle alone, but by the visual angle in conjunction with the distance. Hence, though the angle remain the same, or even become less, yet, if withal the distance seem to have been increased, the object shall appear greater. Now, one way whereby we estimate the distance of anything is by the number and extent of the intermediate objects. When therefore the moon is seen in the horizon, the variety of fields, houses, &c. together with the large prospect of the wide extended land or sea that lies between the eye and the utmost limb of the horizon, suggest unto the mind the idea of greater distance, and consequently magnify the appearance. And this, according to Dr. Wallis, is the true account of the extraordinary largeness attributed by the mind to the horizontal moon, at a time when the angle subtended by its diameter is not one jot greater than it used to be.

77. With reference to this opinion, not to repeat what has been already said concerning distance, I shall only observe, *first,* that if the prospect of interjacent objects be that which suggests the idea of farther distance, and this idea of farther distance be the cause that brings into the mind the idea of greater magnitude, it should hence follow that if one looked at the horizontal moon from behind a wall, it would appear no bigger than ordinary. For, in that case, the wall interposing cuts off all that prospect of sea and land, &c. which might otherwise increase the apparent distance, and thereby the apparent magnitude of the moon. Nor will it suffice to say, the memory doth even then suggest all that extent of land, &c. which lies within the horizon, which suggestion occasions a sudden judgment of sense, that the moon is farther off and larger than usual. For, ask any man who from such a station beholding the horizontal moon shall think her greater than usual, whether he hath at that time in his mind any idea of the intermediate objects, or long tract of land that lies between his eye and the extreme edge of the horizon? and whether it be that idea which is the cause of his making the

aforementioned judgment? He will, without doubt, reply in the negative, and declare the horizontal moon shall appear greater than the meridional, though he never thinks of all or any of those things that lie between him and it. *Secondly,* it seems impossible, by this hypothesis, to account for the moon's appearing, in the very same situation, at one time greater than at another; which, nevertheless, has been shewn to be very agreeable to the principles we have laid down, and receives a most easy and natural explication from them. For the further clearing up of this point, it is to be observed, that what we immediately and properly see are only lights and colours in sundry situations and shades, and degrees of faintness and clearness, confusion and distinctness. All which visible objects are only in the mind; nor do they suggest aught external, whether distance or magnitude, otherwise than by habitual connexion, as words do things. We are also to remark, that beside the straining of the eyes, and beside the vivid and faint, the distinct and confused appearances (which, bearing some proportion to lines and angles, have been substituted instead of them in the foregoing part of this Treatise), there are other means which suggest both distance and magnitude—particularly the situation of visible points or objects, as upper or lower; the former suggesting a farther distance and greater magnitude, the latter a nearer distance and lesser magnitude—all which is an effect only of custom and experience, there being really nothing intermediate in the line of distance between the uppermost and the lowermost, which are both equidistant, or rather at no distance from the eye; as there is also nothing in upper or lower which by necessary connexion should suggest greater or lesser magnitude. Now, as these customary experimental means of suggesting distance do likewise suggest magnitude, so they suggest the one as immediately as the other. I say, they do not (vide sect. 53) first suggest distance, and then leave the mind from thence to infer or compute magnitude, but suggest magnitude as immediately and directly as they suggest distance.

78. This phenomenon of the horizontal moon is a clear instance of the insufficiency of lines and angles for explaining the way wherein the mind perceives and estimates the magnitude of outward objects. There is, nevertheless, a use of computation by them—in order to determine the apparent magnitude of things, so far as they have a connexion with

and are proportional to those other ideas or perceptions which are the true and immediate occasions that suggest to the mind the apparent magnitude of things. But this in general may, I think, be observed concerning mathematical computation in optics—that it can never be very precise and exact, since the judgments we make of the magnitude of external things do often depend on several circumstances which are not proportional to or capable of being defined by lines and angles.

79. From what has been said, we may safely deduce this consequence, to wit, that a man born blind, and made to see, would, at first opening of his eyes, make a very different judgment of the magnitude of objects intromitted by them from what others do. He would not consider the ideas of sight with reference to, or as having any connexion with, the ideas of touch. His view of them being entirely terminated within themselves, he can no otherwise judge them great or small than as they contain a greater or lesser number of visible points. Now, it being certain that any visible point can cover or exclude from view only one other visible point, it follows that whatever object intercepts the view of another hath an equal number of visible points with it; and consequently, they shall both be thought by him to have the same magnitude. Hence, it is evident one in those circumstances would judge his thumb, with which he might hide a tower, or hinder its being seen, equal to that tower; or his hand, the interposition whereof might conceal the firmament from his view, equal to the firmament: how great an inequality soever there may, in our apprehensions, seem to be betwixt those two things, because of the customary and close connexion that has grown up in our minds between the objects of sight and touch, whereby the very different and distinct ideas of those two senses are so blended and confounded together as to be mistaken for one and the same thing—out of which prejudice we cannot easily extricate ourselves.

80. For the better explaining the nature of vision, and setting the manner wherein we perceive magnitudes in a due light, I shall proceed to make some observations concerning matters relating thereto, whereof the want of reflection, and duly separating between tangible and visible ideas, is apt to create in us mistaken and confused notions. And, *first*, I shall observe, that the *minimum visibile* is exactly equal in all beings

whatsoever that are endowed with the visive faculty. No exquisite formation of the eye, no peculiar sharpness of sight, can make it less in one creature than in another; for, it not being distinguishable into parts, nor in anywise consisting of them, it must necessarily be the same to all. For, suppose it otherwise, and that the *minimum visibile* of a mite, for instance, be less than the *minimum visibile* of a man; the latter therefore may, by detraction of some part, be made equal to the former. It doth therefore consist of parts, which is inconsistent with the notion of a *minimum visibile* or point.

81. It will, perhaps, be objected, that the *minimum visibile* of a man doth really and in itself contain parts whereby it surpasses that of a mite, though they are not perceivable by the man. To which I answer, the *minimum visibile* having (in like manner as all other the proper and immediate objects of sight) been shewn not to have any existence without the mind of him who sees it, it follows there cannot be any part of it that is not actually perceived and therefore visible. Now, for any object to contain several distinct visible parts, and at the same time to be a *minimum visibile,* is a manifest contradiction.

82. Of these visible points we see at all times an equal number. It is every whit as great when our view is contracted and bounded by near objects as when it is extended to larger and remoter ones. For, it being impossible that one *minimum visibile* should obscure or keep out of sight more than one other, it is a plain consequence that, when my view is on all sides bounded by the walls of my study, I see just as many visible points as I could in case that, by the removal of the study-walls and all other obstructions, I had a full prospect of the circumjacent fields, mountains, sea, and open firmament. For, so long as I am shut up within the walls, by their interposition every point of the external objects is covered from my view. But, each point that is seen being able to cover or exclude from sight one only other corresponding point, it follows that, whilst my sight is confined to those narrow walls, I see as many points, or *minima visibilia,* as I should were those walls away, by looking on all the external objects whose prospect is intercepted by them. Whenever, therefore, we are said to have a greater prospect at one time than another, this must be understood with relation, not to the proper and immediate, but the secondary and mediate

objects of vision—which, as hath been shewn, do properly belong to the touch.

83. The visive faculty, considered with reference to its immediate objects, may be found to labour of two defects. *First,* in respect of the extent or number of visible points that are at once perceivable by it, which is narrow and limited to a certain degree. It can take in at one view but a certain determinate number of *minima visibilia,* beyond which it cannot extend its prospect. *Secondly,* our sight is defective in that its view is not only narrow, but also for the most part confused. Of those things that we take in at one prospect, we can see but a few at once clearly and unconfusedly; and the more we fix our sight on any one object, by so much the darker and more indistinct shall the rest appear.

84. Corresponding to these two defects of sight, we may imagine as many perfections, to wit, 1st. That of comprehending in one view a greater number of visible points; 2dly, of being able to view them all equally and at once, with the utmost clearness and distinction. That those perfections are not actually in some intelligences of a different order and capacity from ours, it is impossible for us to know.

85. In neither of those two ways do microscopes contribute to the improvement of sight. For, when we look through a microscope, we neither see more visible points, nor are the collateral points more distinct, than when we look with the naked eye at objects placed at a due distance. A microscope brings us, as it were, into a new world. It presents us with a new scene of visible objects, quite different from what we behold with the naked eye. But herein consists the most remarkable difference, to wit, that whereas the objects perceived by the eye alone have a certain connexion with tangible objects, whereby we are taught to foresee what will ensue upon the approach or application of distant objects to the parts of our own body—which much conduceth to its preservation—there is not the like connexion between things tangible and those visible objects that are perceived by help of a fine microscope.

86. Hence, it is evident that, were our eyes turned into the nature of microscopes, we should not be much benefitted by the change. We should be deprived of the forementioned advantage we at present received by the visive faculty, and have left us only the empty amusement of seeing, without

any other benefit arising from it. But, in that case, it will perhaps be said, our sight would be endued with a far greater sharpness and penetration than it now hath. But it is certain, from what we have already shewn, that the *minimum visibile* is never greater or lesser, but in all cases constantly the same. And in the case of microscopical eyes, I see only this difference, to wit, that upon the ceasing of a certain observable connexion betwixt the divers perceptions of sight and touch, which before enabled us to regulate our actions by the eye, it would now be rendered utterly unserviceable to that purpose.

87. Upon the whole, it seems that if we consider the use and end of sight, together with the present state and circumstances of our being, we shall not find any great cause to complain of any defect or imperfection in it, or easily conceive how it could be mended. With such admirable wisdom is that faculty contrived, both for the pleasure and convenience of life.

88. Having finished what I intended to say concerning the Distance and Magnitude of objects, I come now to treat of the manner wherein the mind perceives by sight their Situation. Among the discoveries of the last age, it is reputed none of the least, that the manner of vision has been more clearly explained than ever it had been before. There is, at this day, no one ignorant that the pictures of external objects are painted on the retina or fund of the eye; that we can see nothing which is not so painted; and that, according as the picture is more distinct or confused, so also is the perception we have of the object. But then, in this explication of vision, there occurs one mighty difficulty, viz. the objects are painted in an inverted order on the bottom of the eye: the upper part of any object being painted on the lower part of the eye, and the lower part of the object on the upper part of the eye; and so also as to right and left. Since therefore the pictures are thus inverted, it is demanded, how it comes to pass that we see the objects erect and in their natural posture?

89. In answer to this difficulty, we are told that the mind, perceiving an impulse of a ray of light on the upper part of the eye, considers this ray as coming in a direct line from the lower part of the object; and, in like manner, tracing the ray that strikes on the lower part of the eye, it is directed

to the upper part of the object. Thus, in the adjacent figure, *C*, the lower point of the object *ABC*, is projected on *c* the upper part of the eye. So likewise, the highest point *A* is projected on *a* the lowest part of the eye; which makes the representation *cba* inverted. But the mind—considering the stroke that is made on *c* as coming in the straight line *Cc* from the lower end of the object; and the stroke or impulse on *a*, as coming in the line *Aa* from the upper end of the object—is directed to make a right judgment of the situation

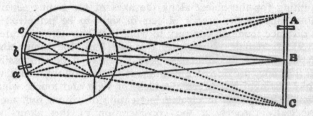

of the object *ABC*, notwithstanding the picture of it be inverted. Moreover, this is illustrated by conceiving a blind man, who, holding in his hands two sticks that cross each other, doth with them touch the extremities of an object, placed in a perpendicular situation. It is certain this man will judge that to be the upper part of the object which he touches with the stick held in the undermost hand, and that to be the lower part of the object which he touches with the stick in his uppermost hand. This is the common explication of the erect appearance of objects, which is generally received and acquiesced in, being (as Mr. Molyneux tells us, *Diopt*. part ii. ch. vii. p. 289) "allowed by all men as satisfactory."

90. But this account to me does not seem in any degree true. Did I perceive those impulses, decussations, and directions of the rays of light, in like manner as hath been set forth, then, indeed, it would not at first view be altogether void of probability. And there might be some pretence for the comparison of the blind man and his cross sticks. But the case is far otherwise. I know very well that I perceive no such thing. And, of consequence, I cannot thereby make an estimate of the situation of objects. Moreover, I appeal to any one's experience, whether he be conscious to himself that he thinks on the intersection made by the radius pencils,

or pursues the impulses they give in right lines, whenever he perceives by sight the position of any object? To me it seems evident that crossing and tracing of the rays, &c. is never thought on by children, idiots, or, in truth, by any other, save only those who have applied themselves to the study of optics. And for the mind to judge of the situation of objects by those things without perceiving them, or to perceive them without knowing it, take which you please, it is perfectly beyond my comprehension. Add to this, that the explaining the manner of vision by the example of cross sticks, and hunting for the object along the axes of the radius pencils, doth suppose the proper objects of sight to be perceived at a distance from us, contrary to what hath been demonstrated.

91. It remains, therefore, that we look for some other explication of this difficulty. And I believe it not impossible to find one, provided we examine it to the bottom, and carefully distinguish between the ideas of sight and touch; which cannot be too oft inculcated in treating of vision. But, more especially throughout the consideration of this affair, we ought to carry that distinction in our thoughts; for that from want of a right understanding thereof, the difficulty of explaining erect vision seems chiefly to arise.

92. In order to disentangle our minds from whatever prejudices we may entertain with relation to the subject in hand, nothing seems more apposite than the taking into our thoughts the case of one born blind, and afterwards, when grown up, made to see. And—though perhaps it may not be a task altogether easy and familiar to us, to divest ourselves entirely of the experiences received from sight, so as to be able to put our thoughts exactly in the posture of such a one's—we must, nevertheless, as far as possible, endeavour to frame true conceptions of what might reasonably be supposed to pass in his mind.

93. It is certain that a man actually blind, and who had continued so from his birth, would, by the sense of feeling, attain to have ideas of upper and lower. By the motion of his hand, he might discern the situation of any tangible object placed within his reach. That part on which he felt himself supported, or towards which he perceived his body to gravitate, he would term *lower,* and the contrary to this *upper;* and accordingly denominate whatsoever objects he touched.

94. But then, whatever judgments he makes concerning the situation of objects are confined to those only that are

perceivable by touch. All those things that are intangible, and of a spiritual nature—his thoughts and desires, his passions, and in general all the modifications of his soul—to these he would never apply the terms upper and lower, except only in a metaphorical sense. He may perhaps, by way of allusion, speak of high or low thoughts: but those terms, in their proper signification, would never be applied to anything that was not conceived to exist without the mind. For, a man born blind, and remaining in the same state, could mean nothing else by the words higher and lower than a greater or lesser distance from the earth; which distance he would measure by the motion or application of his hand, or some other part of his body. It is, therefore, evident that all those things which, in respect of each other, would by him be thought higher or lower, must be such as were conceived to exist without his mind, in the ambient space.[2]

95. Whence it plainly follows, that such a one, if we suppose him made to see, would not at first sight think that anything he saw was high or low, erect or inverted. For, it hath been already demonstrated, in sect. 41, that he would not think the things he perceived by sight to be at any distance from him, or without his mind. The objects to which he had hitherto been used to apply the terms up and down, high and low, were such only as affected, or were some way perceived by his touch. But the proper objects of vision make a new set of ideas, perfectly distinct and different from the former, and which can in no sort make themselves perceived by touch. There is, therefore, nothing at all that could induce him to think those terms applicable to them. Nor would he ever think it, till such time as he had observed their connexion with tangible objects, and the same prejudice began to insinuate itself into his understanding, which, from their infancy, had grown up in the understandings of other men.

96. To set this matter in a clearer light, I shall make use of an example. Suppose the above-mentioned blind person, by his touch, perceives a man to stand erect. Let us inquire into the manner of this. By the application of his hand to the several parts of a human body, he had perceived different tangible ideas; which being collected into sundry complex ones have distinct names annexed to them. Thus, one combi-

[2] [Cf. *Principles*, Secs. 43-44, for comment on this statement. —Ed.]

nation of a certain tangible figure, bulk, and consistency of parts is called the head; another the hand; a third the foot, and so of the rest—all which complex ideas could, in his understanding, be made up only of ideas perceivable by touch. He had also, by his touch, obtained an idea of earth or ground, towards which he perceives the parts of his body to have a natural tendency. Now—by *erect* nothing more being meant than that perpendicular position of a man wherein his feet are nearest to the earth—if the blind person, by moving his hand over the parts of the man who stands before him, do perceive the tangible ideas that compose the head to be farthest from, and those that compose the feet to be nearest to, that other combination of tangible ideas which he calls earth, he will denominate that man erect. But, if we suppose him on a sudden to receive his sight, and that he behold a man standing before him, it is evident, in that case, he would neither judge the man he sees to be erect nor inverted; for he, never having known those terms applied to any other save tangible things, or which existed in the space without him, and what he sees neither being tangible, nor perceived as existing without, he could not know that, in propriety of language, they were applicable to it.

97. Afterwards, when, upon turning his head or eyes up and down to the right and left, he shall observe the visible objects to change, and shall also attain to know that they are called by the same names, and connected with the objects perceived by touch; then, indeed, he will come to speak of them and their situation in the same terms that he has been used to apply to tangible things: and those that he perceives by turning up his eyes he will call upper, and those that by turning down his eyes he will call lower.

98. And this seems to me the true reason why he should think those objects uppermost that are painted on the lower part of his eye. For, by turning the eye up they shall be distinctly seen; as likewise they that are painted on the highest part of the eye shall be distinctly seen by turning the eye down, and are for that reason esteemed lowest. For we have shewn that to the immediate objects of sight, considered in themselves, he would not attribute the terms high and low. It must therefore be on account of some circumstances which are observed to attend them. And these, it is plain, are the actions of turning the eye up and down, which suggest a very obvious reason why the mind should denominate the

objects of sight accordingly high or low. And, without this motion of the eye—this turning it up and down in order to discern different objects—doubtless *erect, inverse,* and other the like terms relating to the position of tangible objects, would never have been transferred, or in any degree apprehended to belong to the ideas of sight, the mere act of seeing including nothing in it to that purpose; whereas the different situations of the eye naturally direct the mind to make a suitable judgment of the situation of objects intromitted by it.

99. Farther, when he has by experience learned the connexion there is between the several ideas of sight and touch, he will be able, by the perception he has of the situation of visible things in respect of one another, to make a sudden and true estimate of the situation of outward, tangible things corresponding to them. And thus it is he shall perceive by sight the situation of external objects, which do not properly fall under that sense.

100. I know we are very prone to think that, if just made to see, we should judge of the situation of visible things as we do now. But, we are also as prone to think that, at first sight, we should in the same way apprehend the distance and magnitude of objects, as we do now; which hath been shewn to be a false and groundless persuasion. And, for the like reasons, the same censure may be passed on the positive assurance that most men, before they have thought sufficiently of the matter, might have of their being able to determine by the eye, at first view, whether objects were erect or inverse.

101. It will perhaps be objected to our opinion, that a man, for instance, being thought erect when his feet are next the earth, and inverted when his head is next the earth, it doth hence follow that, by the mere act of vision, without any experience or altering the situation of the eye, we should have determined whether he were erect or inverted. For both the earth itself, and the limbs of the man who stands thereon, being equally perceived by sight, one cannot choose seeing what part of the man is nearest the earth, and what part farthest from it, *i.e.* whether he be erect or inverted.

102. To which I answer, the ideas which constitute the tangible earth and man are entirely different from those which constitute the visible earth and man. Nor was it possible, by virtue of the visive faculty alone, without superadding any experience of touch, or altering the position of the eye, ever to have known, or so much as suspected, there had been any

relation or connexion between them. Hence, a man at first view would not denominate anything he saw, *earth*, or *head*, or *foot;* and consequently, he could not tell, by the mere act of vision, whether the head or feet were nearest the earth. Nor, indeed, would we have thereby any thought of earth or man, erect or inverse, at all—which will be made yet more evident, if we nicely observe, and make a particular comparison between, the ideas of both senses.

103. That which I see is only variety of light and colours. That which I feel is hard or soft, hot or cold, rough or smooth. What similitude, what connexion, have those ideas with these? Or, how is it possible that any one should see reason to give one and the same name to combinations of ideas so very different, before he had experienced their coexistence? We do not find there is any necessary connexion betwixt this or that tangible quality, and any colour whatsoever. And we may sometimes perceive colours, where there is nothing to be felt. All which doth make it manifest that no man, at first receiving of his sight, would know there was any agreement between this or that particular object of his sight and any object of touch he had been already acquainted with. The colours therefore of the head would to him no more suggest the idea of head than they would the idea of feet.

104. Farther, we have at large shewn (vid. sect. 63 and 64) there is no discoverable necessary connexion between any given visible magnitude and any one particular tangible magnitude; but that it is entirely the result of custom and experience, and depends on foreign and accidental circumstances, that we can, by the perception of visible extension, inform ourselves what may be the extension of any tangible object connected with it. Hence, it is certain, that neither the visible magnitude of head or foot would bring along with them into the mind, at first opening of the eyes, the respective tangible magnitudes of those parts.

105. By the foregoing section, it is plain the visible figure of any part of the body hath no necessary connexion with the tangible figure thereof, so as at first sight to suggest it to the mind. For, figure is the termination of magnitude. Whence it follows that no visible magnitude having in its own nature an aptness to suggest any one particular tangible magnitude, so neither can any visible figure be inseparably connected with its corresponding tangible figure, so as of itself, and in a

way prior to experience, it might suggest it to the under-standing. This will be farther evident, if we consider that what seems smooth and round to the touch may to sight, if viewed through a microscope, seem quite otherwise.

106. From all which, laid together and duly considered, we may clearly deduce this inference:—In the first act of vision, no idea entering by the eye would have a perceivable connexion with the ideas to which the names earth, man, head, foot, &c. were annexed in the understanding of a person blind from his birth; so as in any sort to introduce them into his mind, or make themselves be called by the same names, and reputed the same things with them, as afterwards they come to be.

107. There doth, nevertheless, remain one difficulty, which perhaps may seem to press hard on our opinion, and deserve not to be passed over. For, though it be granted that neither the colour, size, nor figure of the visible feet have any neces-sary connexion with the ideas that compose the tangible feet, so as to bring them at first sight into my mind, or make me in danger of confounding them, before I had been used to and for some time experienced their connexion; yet thus much seems undeniable, namely, that the number of the visible feet being the same with that of the tangible feet, I may from hence, without any experience of sight, reasonably conclude that they represent or are connected with the feet rather than the head. I say, it seems the idea of two visible feet will sooner suggest to the mind the idea of two tangible feet than of one head—so that the blind man, upon first reception of the visive faculty, might know which were the feet or two, and which the head or one.

108. In order to get clear of this seeming difficulty, we need only observe that diversity of visible objects does not necessarily infer diversity of tangible objects corresponding to them. A picture painted with great variety of colours affects the touch in one uniform manner; it is therefore evident that I do not, by any necessary consecution, independent of experi-ence, judge of the number of things tangible from the number of things visible. I should not therefore at first opening my eyes conclude that because I see two I shall feel two. How, therefore, can I, before experience teaches me, know that the visible legs, because two, are connected with the tangible legs; or the visible head, because one, is connected with the

tangible head? The truth is, the things I see are so very different and heterogeneous from the things I feel that the perception of the one would never have suggested the other to my thoughts, or enabled me to pass the least judgment thereon, until I had experienced their connexion.

109. But, for a fuller illustration of this matter, it ought to be considered, that number (however some may reckon it amongst the primary qualities) is nothing fixed and settled, really existing in things themselves. It is entirely the creature of the mind, considering either an idea by itself, or any combination of ideas to which it gives one name, and so makes it pass for a unit. According as the mind variously combines its ideas, the unit varies; and as the unit, so the number, which is only a collection of units, doth also vary. We call a window one, a chimney one; and yet a house, in which there are many windows and many chimneys, has an equal right to be called one; and many houses go to the making of one city. In these and the like instances, it is evident the *unit* constantly relates to the particular draughts the mind makes of its ideas, to which it affixes names, and wherein it includes more or less, as best suits its own ends and purposes. Whatever therefore the mind considers as one, that is an unit. Every combination of ideas is considered as one thing by the mind, and in token thereof is marked by one name. Now, this naming and combining together of ideas is perfectly arbitrary, and done by the mind in such sort as experience shews it to be most convenient—without which our ideas had never been collected into such sundry distinct combinations as they now are.

110. Hence, it follows that a man born blind, and afterwards, when grown up, made to see, would not, in the first act of vision, parcel out the ideas of sight into the same distinct collections that others do who have experienced which do regularly co-exist and are proper to be bundled up together under one name. He would not, for example, make into one complex idea and thereby esteem and unite all those particular ideas which constitute the visible head or foot. For, there can be no reason assigned why he should do so, barely upon his seeing a man stand upright before him. There crowd into his mind the ideas which compose the visible man, in company with all the other ideas of sight perceived at the same time. But, all these ideas offered at once to his view he

would not distribute into sundry distinct combinations, till such time as, by observing the motion of the parts of the man and other experiences, he comes to know which are to be separated and which to be collected together.

111. From what hath been premised, it is plain the objects of sight and touch make, if I may so say, two sets of ideas, which are widely different from each other. To objects of either kind we indifferently attribute the terms high and low, right and left, and such like, denoting the position or situation of things; but then we must well observe that the position of any object is determined with respect only to objects of the same sense. We say any object of touch is high or low, according as it is more or less distant from the tangible earth: and in like manner we denominate any object of sight high or low, in proportion as it is more or less distant from the visible earth. But, to define the situation of visible things with relation to the distance they bear from any tangible thing, or *vice versa*, this were absurd and perfectly unintelligible. For all visible things are equally in the mind, and take up no part of the external space; and consequently are equidistant from any tangible thing which exists without the mind.[3]

112. Or rather, to speak truly, the proper objects of sight are at no distance, neither near nor far from any tangible thing. For, if we inquire narrowly into the matter, we shall find that those things only are compared together in respect of distance which exist after the same manner, or appertain unto the same sense. For, by the distance between any two points, nothing more is meant than the number of intermediate points. If the given points are visible, the distance between them is marked out by the number of the interjacent visible points; if they are tangible, the distance between them is a line consisting of tangible points; but, if they are one tangible and the other visible, the distance between them doth neither consist of points perceivable by sight nor by touch, *i.e.* it is utterly inconceivable. This, perhaps, will not find an easy admission into all men's understanding. However, I should gladly be informed whether it be not true, by any one who will be at the pains to reflect a little, and apply it home to his thoughts.

[3] [Cf. *Principles*, Secs. 43-44, for comment on this statement. —Ed.]

113. The not observing what has been delivered in the two last sections, seems to have occasioned no small part of the difficulty that occurs in the business of direct appearances. The head, which is painted nearest the earth, seems to be farthest from it; and on the other hand, the feet, which are painted farthest from the earth, are thought nearest to it. Herein lies the difficulty, which vanishes if we express the thing more clearly and free from ambiguity, thus:—How comes it that, to the eye, the visible head, which is nearest the tangible earth, seems farthest from the earth; and the visible feet, which are farthest from the tangible earth, seem nearest the earth? The question being thus proposed, who sees not the difficulty is founded on a supposition that the eye or visive faculty, or rather the soul by means thereof, should judge of the situation of visible objects with reference to their distance from the tangible earth? Whereas, it is evident the tangible earth is not perceived by sight. And it hath been shewn, in the two last preceding sections, that the location of visible objects is determined only by the distance they bear from one another, and that it is nonsense to talk of distance, far or near, between a visible and tangible thing.

114. If we confine our thoughts to the proper objects of sight, the whole is plain and easy. The head is painted farthest from, and the feet nearest to, the visible earth; and so they appear to be. What is there strange or unaccountable in this? Let us suppose the pictures in the fund of the eye to be the immediate objects of sight. The consequence is that things should appear in the same posture they are painted in; and is it not so? The head which is seen seems farthest from the earth which is seen; and the feet which are seen seem nearest to the earth which is seen. And just so they are painted.

115. But, say you, the picture of the man is inverted, and yet the appearance is erect. I ask, what mean you by the picture of the man, or, which is the same thing, the visible man's being inverted? You tell me it is inverted, because the heels are uppermost and the head undermost? Explain me this. You say that by the head's being undermost, you mean that it is nearest to the earth; and, by the heels being uppermost, that they are farthest from the earth. I ask again, what earth you mean? You cannot mean the earth that is painted on the eye or the visible earth—for the picture of the head is farthest from the picture of the earth, and the picture

of the feet nearest to the picture of the earth; and accordingly the visible head is farthest from the visible earth, and the visible feet nearest to it. It remains, therefore, that you mean the tangible earth; and so determine the situation of visible things with respect to tangible things—contrary to what hath been demonstrated in sect. 111 and 112. The two distinct provinces of sight and touch should be considered apart, and as though their objects had no intercourse, no manner of relation to one another, in point of distance or position.

116. Farther, what greatly contributes to make us mistake in this matter is that, when we think of the pictures in the fund of the eye, we imagine ourselves looking on the fund of another's eye, or another looking on the fund of our own eye, and beholding the pictures painted thereon. Suppose two eyes, A and B. A from some distance looking on the pictures in B sees them inverted, and for that reason concludes they are inverted in B. But this is wrong. There are projected in little on the bottom of A the images of the pictures of, suppose, man, earth, &c., which are painted on B. And, besides these, the eye B itself, and the objects which environ it, together with another earth, are projected in a larger size on A. Now, by the eye A these larger images are deemed the true objects and the lesser only pictures in miniature. And it is with respect to those greater images that it determines the situation of the smaller images; so that, comparing the little man with the great earth, A judges him inverted, or that the feet are farthest from and the head nearest to the great earth. Whereas, if A compare the little man with the little earth, then he will appear erect, i.e., his head shall seem farthest from and his feet nearest to the little earth. But we must consider that B does not see two earths as A does. It sees only what is represented by the little pictures in A, and consequently shall judge the man erect. For, in truth, the man in B is not inverted, for there the feet are next the earth; but it is the representation of it in A which is inverted, for there the head of the representation of the picture of the man in B is next the earth, and the feet farthest from the earth—meaning the earth which is without the representation of the pictures in B. For, if you take the little images of the pictures in B, and consider them by themselves, and with respect only to one another, they are all erect and in their natural posture.

117. Farther, there lies a mistake in our imagining that

the pictures of external objects are painted on the bottom of the eye. It has been shewn there is no resemblance between the ideas of sight and things tangible. It hath likewise been demonstrated, that the proper objects of sight do not exist without the mind. Whence it clearly follows that the pictures painted on the bottom of the eye are not the pictures of external objects. Let any one consult his own thoughts, and then tell me, what affinity, what likeness, there is between that certain variety and disposition of colours which constitute the visible man, or picture of a man, and that other combination of far different ideas, sensible by touch, which compose the tangible man. But, if this be the case, how come they to be accounted pictures or images, since that supposes them to copy or represent some originals or other?

118. To which I answer—In the forementioned instance, the eye *A* takes the little images, included within the representation of the other eye *B*, to be pictures or copies, whereof the archetypes are not things existing without, but the larger pictures projected on its own fund; and which by *A* are not thought pictures, but the originals or true things themselves. Though if we suppose a third eye *C*, from a due distance, to behold the fund of *A*, then indeed the things projected thereon shall, to *C*, seem pictures or images, in the same sense that those projected on *B* do to *A*.

119. Rightly to conceive the business in hand, we must carefully distinguish between the ideas of sight and touch, between the visible and tangible eye; for certainly on the tangible eye nothing either is or seems to be painted. Again, the visible eye, as well as all other visible objects, hath been shewn to exist only in the mind; which, perceiving its own ideas, and comparing them together, does call some pictures in respect to others. What hath been said, being rightly comprehended and laid together, does, I think, afford a full and genuine explication of the erect appearance of objects—which phenomenon, I must confess, I do not see how it can be explained by any theories of vision hitherto made public.

120. In treating of these things, the use of language is apt to occasion some obscurity and confusion, and create in us wrong ideas. For, language being accommodated to the common notions and prejudices of men, it is scarce possible to deliver the naked and precise truth, without great circumlocution, impropriety, and (to an unwary reader) seeming contradictions. I do, therefore, once for all, desire whoever

shall think it worth his while to understand what I have written concerning vision, that he would not stick in this or that phrase or manner of expression, but candidly collect my meaning from the whole sum and tenor of my discourse, and, laying aside the words as much as possible, consider the bare notions themselves, and then judge whether they are agreeable to truth and his own experience or no.

121. We have shewn the way wherein the mind, by mediation of visible ideas, doth perceive or apprehend the distance, magnitude, and situation of tangible objects. I come now to inquire more particularly concerning the difference between the ideas of sight and touch which are called by the same names, and see whether there be any idea common to both senses. From what we have at large set forth and demonstrated in the foregoing parts of this treatise, it is plain there is no one self-same numerical extension, perceived both by sight and touch; but that the particular figures and extensions perceived by sight, however they may be called by the same names, and reputed the same things with those perceived by touch, are nevertheless different, and have an existence very distinct and separate from them. So that the question is not now concerning the same numerical ideas, but whether there be any one and the same sort or species of ideas equally perceivable to both senses? or, in other words, whether extension, figure, and motion perceived by sight, are not specifically distinct from extension, figure, and motion perceived by touch?

122. But, before I come more particularly to discuss this matter, I find it proper to take into my thoughts extension in abstract. For of this there is much talk; and I am apt to think that when men speak of extension as being an idea common to two senses, it is with a secret supposition that we can single out extension from all other tangible and visible qualities, and form thereof an abstract idea, which idea they will have common both to sight and touch. We are therefore to understand by extension in abstract, an idea of extension— for instance, a line or surface entirely stripped of all other sensible qualities and circumstances that might determine it to any particular existence; it is neither black, nor white, nor red, nor hath it any colour at all, or any tangible quality whatsoever, and consequently it is of no finite determinate

magnitude; for that which bounds or distinguishes one extension from another is some quality or circumstance wherein they disagree.

123. Now, I do not find that I can perceive, imagine, or anywise frame in my mind such an abstract idea as is here spoken of. A line or surface which is neither black, nor white, nor blue, nor yellow, &c.; nor long, nor short, nor rough, nor smooth, nor square, nor round, &c. is perfectly incomprehensible. This I am sure of as to myself; how far the faculties of other men may reach they best can tell.

124. It is commonly said that the object of geometry is abstract extension. But geometry centemplates figures: now, figure is the termination of magnitude; but we have shewn that extension in abstract hath no finite determinate magnitude; whence it clearly follows that it can have no figure, and consequently is not the object of geometry. It is indeed a tenet, as well of the modern as the ancient philosophers, that all general truths are concerning universal abstract ideas; without which, we are told, there could be no science, no demonstration of any general proposition in geometry. But it were no hard matter, did I think it necessary to my present purpose, to shew that propositions and demonstrations in geometry might be universal, though they who make them never think of abstract general ideas of triangles or circles.

125. After reiterated efforts and pangs of thought to apprehend the general idea of a triangle, I have found it altogether incomprehensible. And surely, if any one were able to let that idea into my mind, it must be the author of the *Essay concerning Human Understanding:* he, who has so far distinguished himself from the generality of writers, by the clearness and significancy of what he says. Let us therefore see how this celebrated author describes the general or abstract idea of a triangle. "It must be," says he, "neither oblique nor rectangle, neither equilateral, equicrural, nor scalenum; but all and none of these at once. In effect it is somewhat imperfect that cannot exist; an idea, wherein some parts of several different and inconsistent ideas are put together." (*Essay on Human Understanding,* B. iv. ch. 7. s. 9.) This is the idea which he thinks needful for the enlargement of knowledge, which is the subject of mathematical demonstration, and without which we could never come to know any general proposition concerning triangles. That author acknowledges it doth "require some pains and skill to form

this general idea of a triangle." (*Ibid.*) But, had he called to mind what he says in another place, to wit, "that ideas of mixed modes wherein any inconsistent ideas are put together, cannot so much as exist in the mind, *i.e.* be conceived," (vid. B. iii. ch. 10. s. 33, *ibid.*)—I say, had this occurred to his thoughts, it is not improbable he would have owned it above all the pains and skill he was master of, to form the above-mentioned idea of a triangle, which is made up of manifest staring contradictions. That a man who laid so great a stress on clear and determinate ideas, should nevertheless talk at this rate, seems very surprising. But the wonder will lessen, if it be considered that the source when this opinion flows is the prolific womb which has brought forth innumerable errors and difficulties, in all parts of philosophy, and in all the sciences. But this matter, taken in its full extent, were a subject too comprehensive to be insisted on in this place. And so much for extension in abstract.

126. Some, perhaps, may think pure space, vacuum, or trine dimension, to be equally the object of sight and touch. But, though we have a very great propension to think the ideas of outness and space to be the immediate object of sight, yet, if I mistake not, in the foregoing parts of this *Essay*, that hath been clearly demonstrated to be a mere delusion, arising from the quick and sudden suggestion of fancy, which so closely connects the idea of distance with those of sight, that we are apt to think it is itself a proper and immediate object of that sense, till reason corrects the mistake.

127. It having been shewn that there are no abstract ideas of figure, and that it is impossible for us, by any precision of thought, to frame an idea of extension separate from all other visible and tangible qualities, which shall be common both to sight and touch—the question now remaining is, whether the particular extensions, figures, and motions perceived by sight, be of the same kind with the particular extensions, figures, and motions perceived by touch? In answer to which I shall venture to lay down the following proposition:—*The extension, figures, and motions perceived by sight are specifically distinct from the ideas of touch, called by the same names; nor is there any such thing as one idea, or kind of idea, common to both senses.* This proposition may, without much difficulty, be collected from what hath been said in several places of this Essay. But, because it seems so remote

from, and contrary to the received notions and settled opinion of mankind, I shall attempt to demonstrate it more particularly and at large by the following arguments:—

128. When, upon perception of an idea, I range it under this or that sort, it is because it is perceived after the same manner, or because it has a likeness or conformity with, or affects me in the same way as the ideas of the sort I rank it under. In short, it must not be entirely new, but have something in it old and already perceived by me. It must, I say, have so much, at least, in common with the ideas I have before known and named, as to make me give it the same name with them. But, it has been, if I mistake not, clearly made out that a man born blind would not, at first reception of his sight, think the things he saw were of the same nature with the objects of touch, or had anything in common with them; but that they were a new set of ideas, perceived in a new manner, and entirely different from all he had ever perceived before. So that he would not call them by the same name, nor repute them to be of the same sort, with anything he had hitherto known.

129. *Secondly,* Light and colours are allowed by all to constitute a sort or species entirely different from the ideas of touch; nor will any man, I presume, say they can make themselves perceived by that sense. But there is no other immediate object of sight besides light and colours. It is therefore a direct consequence, that there is no idea common to both senses.

130. It is a prevailing opinion, even amongst those who have thought and writ most accurately concerning our ideas, and the ways whereby they enter into the understanding, that something more is perceived by sight than barely light and colours with their variations. Mr. Locke termeth sight "the most comprehensive of all our senses, conveying to our minds the ideas of light and colours, which are peculiar only to that sense; and also the far different ideas of space, figure, and motion." (*Essay on Human Understanding*, B. iii. ch. 9. s. 9.) Space or distance, we have shewn, is no otherwise the object of sight than of hearing. (Vid. sect. 46.) And, as for figure and extension, I leave it to any one that shall calmly attend to his own clear and distinct ideas to decide whether he has any idea intromitted immediately and properly by sight save only light and colours: or, whether it be possible for him to frame

in his mind a distinct abstract idea of visible extension, or figure, exclusive of all colour; and, on the other hand, whether he can conceive colour without visible extension? For my own part, I must confess, I am not able to attain so great a nicety of abstraction. I know very well that, in a strict sense, I see nothing but light and colours, with their several shades and variations. He who beside these doth also perceive by sight ideas far different and distinct from them, hath that faculty in a degree more perfect and comprehensive than I can pretend to. It must be owned, indeed, that, by the mediation of light and colours, other far different ideas are suggested to my mind. But so they are by hearing, which beside sounds which are peculiar to that sense, doth, by their mediation, suggest not only space, figure, and motion, but also all other ideas whatsoever that can be signified by words.

131. *Thirdly,* It is, I think, an axiom universally received, that "quantities of the same kind may be added together and make one entire sum." Mathematicians add lines together; but they do not add a line to a solid, or conceive it as making one sum with a surface. These three kinds of quantity being thought incapable of any such mutual addition, and consequently of being compared together in the several ways of proportion, are by them for that reason esteemed entirely disparate and heterogeneous. Now let any one try in his thoughts to add a visible line or surface to a tangible line or surface, so as to conceive them making one continued sum or whole. He that can do this may think them homogeneous; but he that cannot must, by the foregoing axiom, think them heterogeneous. A blue and a red line I can conceive added together into one sum and making one continued line; but, to make, in my thoughts, one continued line of a visible and tangible line added together, is, I find, a task far more difficult, and even insurmountable—and I leave it to the reflection and experience of every particular person to determine for himself.

132. A farther confirmation of our tenet may be drawn from the solution of Mr. Molyneux's problem, published by Mr. Locke in his *Essay:* which I shall set down as it there lies, together with Mr. Locke's opinion of it:—"Suppose a man born blind, and now adult, and taught by his touch to distinguish between a cube and a sphere of the same metal, and nighly of the same bigness, so as to tell when he felt

one and the other, which is the cube, and which the sphere. Suppose then the cube and sphere placed on a table, and the blind man made to see: Quære, Whether by his sight, before he touched them, he could now distinguish, and tell, which is the globe, which the cube. To which the acute and judicious proposer answers: Not. For, though he has obtained the experience of how a globe, how a cube affects his touch; yet he has not yet attained the experience, that what affects his touch so or so must affect his sight so or so: or that a protuberant angle in the cube, that pressed his hand unequally, shall appear to his eye as it doth in the cube. I agree with this thinking gentleman, whom I am proud to call my friend, in his answer to this his problem; and am of opinion that the blind man, at first sight, would not be able with certainty to say, which was the globe, which the cube whilst he only saw them." (*Essay on Human Understanding*, B. ii. ch. 9. s. 8.)

133. Now, if a square surface perceived by touch be of the same sort wth a square surface perceived by sight, it is certain the blind man here mentioned might know a square surface as soon as he saw it. It is no more but introducing into his mind, by a new inlet, an idea he has been already well acquainted with. Since therefore he is supposed to have known by his touch that a cube is a body terminated by square surfaces; and that a sphere is not terminated by square surfaces—upon the supposition that a visible and tangible square differ only *in numero*, it follows that he might know, by the unerring mark of the square surfaces, which was the cube, and which not, while he only saw them. We must therefore allow, either that visible extension and figures are specifically distinct from tangible extension and figures, or else, that the solution of this problem, given by those two thoughtful and ingenious men, is wrong.

134. Much more might be laid together in proof of the proposition I have advanced. But, what has been said is, if I mistake not, sufficient to convince any one that shall yield a reasonable attention. And, as for those that will not be at the pains of a little thought, no multiplication of words will ever suffice to make them understand the truth, or rightly conceive my meaning.

135. I cannot let go the above-mentioned problem without some reflection on it. It hath been made evident that a man

blind from his birth would not, at first sight, denominate any-thing he saw, by the names he had been used to appropriate to ideas of touch. (Vid. sect. 106.) Cube, sphere, table are words he has known applied to beings perceivable by touch, but to things perfectly intangible he never knew them applied. Those words, in their wonted application, always marked out to his mind bodies or solid things which were perceived by the resistance they gave. But there is no solidity, no resistance or protrusion, perceived by sight. In short, the ideas of sight are all new perceptions, to which there be no names annexed in his mind; he cannot therefore understand what is said to him concerning them. And, to ask of the two bodies he saw placed on the table, which was the sphere, which the cube, were to him a question downright bantering and unintelligible; nothing he sees being able to suggest to his thoughts the idea of body, distance, or, in general, of anything he had already known.

136. It is a mistake to think the same thing affects both sight and touch. If the same angle or square which is the object of touch be also the object of vision, what should hinder the blind man, at first sight, from knowing it? For, though the manner wherein it affects the sight be different from that wherein it affected his touch, yet, there being, beside this manner or circumstance, which is new and unknown, the angle or figure, which is old and known, he cannot choose but discern it.

137. Visible figure and extension having been demonstrated to be of a nature entirely different and heterogeneous from tangible figure and extension, it remains that we inquire con-cerning motion. Now, that visible motion is not of the same sort with tangible motion seems to need no farther proof; it being an evident corollary from what we have shewn concerning the difference there is betwixt visible and tangible extension. But, for a more full and express proof hereof, we need only observe that one who had not yet experienced vision would not at first sight know motion. Whence it clearly follows that motion perceivable by sight is of a sort distinct from motion perceivable by touch. The antecedent I prove thus—By touch he could not perceive any motion but what was up or down, to the right or left, nearer or farther from him; besides these, and their several varieties or complications, it is impossible he should have any idea of motion. He would not therefore

think anything to be motion, or give the name motion to any idea, which he could not range under some or other of those particular kinds thereof. But, from sect. 95, it is plain that, by the mere act of vision, he could not know motion upwards or downwards, to the right or left, or in any other possible direction. From which I conclude, he would not know motion at all at first sight. As for the idea of motion in abstract, I shall not waste paper about it, but leave it to my reader to make the best he can of it. To me it is perfectly unintelligible.

138. The consideration of motion may furnish a new field for inquiry. But, since the manner wherein the mind apprehends by sight the motion of tangible objects, with the various degrees thereof, may be easily collected from what has been said concerning the manner wherein that sense doth suggest their various distances, magnitudes, and situations, I shall not enlarge any farther on this subject, but proceed to inquire what may be alleged, with greatest appearance of reason, against the proposition we have demonstrated to be true; for, where there is so much prejudice to be encountered, a bare and naked demonstration of the truth will scarce suffice. We must also satisfy the scruples that men may start in favour of their preconceived notions, shew whence the mistake arises, how it came to spread, and carefully disclose and root out those false persuasions that an early prejudice might have implanted in the mind.

139. *First,* therefore, it will be demanded how visible extension and figures come to be called by the same name with tangible extension and figures, if they are not of the same kind with them? It must be something more than humour or accident that could occasion a custom so constant and universal as this, which has obtained in all ages and nations of the world, and amongst all ranks of men, the learned as well as the illiterate.

140. To which I answer, we can no more argue a visible and tangible square to be of the same species, from their being called by the same name, than we can that a tangible square, and the monosyllable consisting of six letters whereby it is marked, are of the same species, because they are both called by the same name. It is customary to call written words, and the things they signify, by the same name: for, words not being regarded in their own nature, or otherwise than as they are marks of things, it had been superfluous, and beside the design of language, to have given them names

distinct from those of the things marked by them. The same reason holds here also. Visible figures are the marks of tangible figures; and, from sect. 59, it is plain that in themselves they are little regarded, or upon any other score than for their connexion with tangible figures, which by nature they are ordained to signify. And, because this language of nature does not vary in different ages or nations, hence it is that in all times and places visible figures are called by the same names as the respective tangible figures suggested by them; and not because they are alike, or of the same sort with them.

141. But, say you, surely a tangible square is liker to a visible square than to a visible circle; it has four angles, and as many sides; so also has the visible square—but the visible circle has no such thing, being bounded by one uniform curve, without right lines or angles, which makes it unfit to represent the tangible square, but very fit to represent the tangible circle. Whence it clearly follows, that visible figures are patterns of, or of the same species with, the respective tangible figures represented by them; that they are like unto them, and of their own nature fitted to represent them, as being of the same sort; and that they are in no respect arbitrary signs, as words.

142. I answer, it must be acknowledged the visible square is fitter than the visible circle to represent the tangible square, but then it is not because it is liker, or more of a species with it; but, because the visible square contains in it several distinct parts, whereby to mark the several distinct corresponding parts of a tangible square, whereas the visible circle doth not. The square perceived by touch hath four distinct equal sides, so also hath it four distinct equal angles. It is therefore necessary that the visible figure which shall be most proper to mark it contain four distinct equal parts, corresponding to the four sides of the tangible square; as likewise four other distinct and equal parts, whereby to denote the four equal angles of the tangible square. And accordingly we see the visible figures contain in them distinct visible parts, answering to the distinct tangible parts of the figures signified or suggested by them.

143. But, it will not hence follow that any visible figure is like unto or of the same species with its corresponding tangible figure—unless it be also shewn that not only the number, but also the kind of the parts be the same in both. To illustrate this, I observe that visible figures represent tangible figures

much after the same manner that written words do sounds. Now, in this respect, words are not arbitrary; it not being indifferent what written word stands for any sound. But, it is requisite that each word contain in it as many distinct characters as there are variations in the sound it stands for. Thus, the single letter *a* is proper to mark one simple uniform sound; and the word *adultery* is accommodated to represent the sound annexed to it—in the formation whereof there being eight different collisions or modifications of the air by the organs of speech, each of which produces a difference of sound, it was fit the word representing it should consist of as many distinct characters, thereby to mark each particular difference or part of the whole sound. And yet nobody, I presume, will say the single letter *a,* or the word *adultery,* are alike unto or of the same species with the respective sounds by them represented. It is indeed arbitrary that, in general, letters of any language represent sounds at all; but, when that is once agreed, it is not arbitrary what combination of letters shall represent this or that particular sound. I leave this with the reader to pursue, and apply it in his own thoughts.

144. It must be confessed that we are not so apt to confound other signs with the things signified, or to think them of the same species, as we are visible and tangible ideas. But, a little consideration will shew us how this may well be, without our supposing them of a like nature. These signs are constant and universal; their connexion with tangible ideas has been learnt at our first entrance into the world; and ever since, almost every moment of our lives, it has been occurring to our thoughts, and fastening and striking deeper on our minds. When we observe that signs are variable, and of human institution; when we remember there was a time they were not connected in our minds with those things they now so readily suggest, but that their signification was learned by the slow steps of experience: this preserves us from confounding them. But, when we find the same signs suggest the same things all over the world; when we know they are not of human institution, and cannot remember that we ever learned their signification, but think that at first sight they would have suggested to us the same things they do now: all this persuades us they are of the same species as the things respectively represented by them, and that it is by a natural resemblance they suggest them to our minds.

145. Add to this that whenever we make a nice survey of any object, successively directing the optic axis to each point thereof, there are certain lines and figures, described by the motion of the head or eye, which, being in truth perceived by feeling, do nevertheless so mix themselves, as it were, with the ideas of sight that we can scarce think but they appertain to that sense. Again, the ideas of sight enter into the mind several at once, more distinct and unmingled than is usual in the other senses beside the touch. Sounds, for example, perceived at the same instant, are apt to coalesce, if I may so say, into one sound: but we can perceive, at the same time, great variety of visible objects, very separate and distinct from each other. Now, tangible extension being made up of several distinct co-existent parts, we may hence gather another reason that may dispose us to imagine a likeness or analogy between the immediate objects of sight and touch. But nothing, certainly, does more contribute to blend and confound them together, than the strict and close connexion they have with each other. We cannot open our eyes but the ideas of distance, bodies, and tangible figures are suggested by them. So swift, and sudden, and unperceived is the transit from visible to tangible ideas that we can scarce forbear thinking them equally the immediate object of vision.

146. The prejudice which is grounded on these, and whatever other causes may be assigned thereof, sticks so fast on our understandings, that it is impossible, without obstinate striving and labour of the mind, to get entirely clear of it. But then the reluctancy we find in rejecting any opinion can be no argument of its truth, to whoever considers what has been already shewn with regard to the prejudices we entertain concerning the distance, magnitude, and situation of objects; prejudices so familiar to our minds, so confirmed and inveterate, as they will hardly give way to the clearest demonstration.

147. Upon the whole, I think we may fairly conclude that the proper objects of Vision constitute [the Universal Language of Nature] [4]; whereby we are instructed how to regulate our actions, in order to attain those things that are necessary

[4] [Altered in the third edition to "an universal language of the Author of Nature."—Ed.]

to the preservation and well-being of our bodies, as also to avoid whatever may be hurtful and destructive of them. It is by their information that we are principally guided in all the transactions and concerns of life. And the manner wherein they signify and mark out unto us the objects which are at a distance is the same with that of languages and signs of human appointment; which do not suggest the things signified by any likeness or identity of nature, but only by an habitual connexion that experience has made us to observe between them.

148. Suppose one who had always continued blind be told by his guide that after he has advanced so many steps he shall come to the brink of a precipice, or be stopped by a wall; must not this to him seem very admirable and surprising? He cannot conceive how it is possible for mortals to frame such predictions as these, which to him would seem as strange and unaccountable as prophecy does to others. Even they who are blessed with the visive faculty may (though familiarity make it less observed) find therein sufficient cause of admiration. The wonderful art and contrivance wherewith it is adjusted to those ends and purposes for which it was apparently designed; the vast extent, number, and variety of objects that are at once, with so much ease, and quickness, and pleasure, suggested by it—all these afford subject for much and pleasing speculation, and may, if anything, give us some glimmering analogous prænotion of things, that are placed beyond the certain discovery and comprehension of our present state.

149. I do not design to trouble myself much with drawing corollaries from the doctrine I have hitherto laid down. If it bears the test, others may, so far as they shall think convenient, employ their thoughts in extending it farther, and applying it to whatever purposes it may be subservient to. Only, I cannot forbear making some inquiry concerning the object of geometry, which the subject we have been upon does naturally lead one to. We have shewn there is no such idea as that of extension in abstract; and that there are two kinds of sensible extension and figures, which are entirely distinct and heterogeneous from each other. Now, it is natural to inquire which of these is the object of geometry.

150. Some things there are which, at first sight, incline one to think geometry conversant about visible extension. The constant use of the eyes, both in the practical and speculative parts of that science, doth very much induce us thereto. It would, without doubt, seem odd to a mathematician to go about to convince him the diagrams he saw upon paper were not the figures, or even the likeness of the figures, which make the subject of the demonstration—the contrary being held an unquestionable truth, not only by mathematicians, but also by those who apply themselves more particularly to the study of logic; I mean who consider the nature of science, certainty, and demonstration; it being by them assigned as one reason of the extraordinary clearness and evidence of geometry, that in that science the reasonings are free from those inconveniences which attend the use of arbitrary signs, the very ideas themselves being copied out, and exposed to view upon paper. But, by the bye, how well this agrees with what they likewise assert of abstract ideas being the object of geometrical demonstration I leave to be considered.

151. To come to a resolution in this point, we need only observe what has been said in sect. 59, 60, 61, where it is shewn that visible extensions in themselves are little regarded, and have no settled determinate greatness, and that men measure altogether by the application of tangible extension to tangible extension. All which makes it evident that visible extension and figures are not the object of geometry.

152. It is therefore plain that visible figures are of the same use in geometry that words are. And the one may as well be accounted the object of that science as the other; neither of them being any otherwise concerned therein than as they represent or suggest to the mind the particular tangible figures connected with them. There is, indeed, this difference betwixt the signification of tangible figures by visible figures, and of ideas by words—that whereas the latter is variable and uncertain, depending altogether on the arbitrary appointment of men, the former is fixed, and, immutably the same in all times and places. A visible square, for instance, suggests to the mind the same tangible figure in Europe that it does in America. Hence it is, that [the voice of nature,] [5] which

---

[5] [Altered in the third edition to "the voice of the Author of Nature."—Ed.]

speaks to our eyes, is not liable to that misinterpretation and ambiguity that languages of human contrivance are unavoidably subject to.

153. Though what has been said may suffice to shew what ought to be determined with relation to the object of geometry, I shall, nevertheless, for the fuller illustration thereof, take into my thoughts the case of an intelligence or unbodied spirit, which is supposed to see perfectly well, *i.e.* to have a clear perception of the proper and immediate objects of sight, but to have no sense of touch. Whether there be any such being in nature or no, is beside my purpose to inquire; it suffices, that the supposition contains no contradiction in it. Let us now examine what proficiency such a one may be able to make in geometry. Which speculation will lead us more clearly to see whether the ideas of sight can possibly be the object of that science.

154. *First*, then, it is certain the aforesaid intelligence could have no idea of a solid or quantity of three dimensions, which follows from its not having any idea of distance. We, indeed, are prone to think that we have by sight the ideas of space and solids; which arises from our imagining that we do, strictly speaking, see distance, and some parts of an object at a greater distance than others; which has been demonstrated to be the effect of the experience we have had what ideas of touch are connected with such and such ideas attending vision. But the intelligence here spoken of is supposed to have no experience of touch. He would not, therefore, judge as we do, nor have any idea of distance, outness, or profundity, nor consequently of space or body, either immediately or by suggestion. Whence it is plain he can have no notion of those parts of geometry which relate to the mensuration of solids, and their convex or concave surfaces, and contemplate the properties of lines generated by the section of a solid. The conceiving of any part whereof is beyond the reach of his faculties.

155. *Farther*, he cannot comprehend the manner wherein geometers describe a right line or circle; the rule and compass, with their use, being things of which it is impossible he should have any notion. Nor is it an easier matter for him to conceive the placing of one plane or angle on another, in order to prove their equality; since that supposes some idea of distance, or external space. All which makes it evident our pure intelligence could never attain to know so much as the first

elements of plane geometry. And perhaps, upon a nice inquiry, it will be found he cannot even have an idea of plane figures any more than he can of solids; since some idea of distance is necessary to form the idea of a geometrical plane, as will appear to whoever shall reflect a little on it.

156. All that is properly perceived by the visive faculty amounts to no more than colours with their variations, and different proportions of light and shade—but the perpetual mutability and fleetingness of those immediate objects of sight render them incapable of being managed after the manner of geometrical figures; nor is it in any degree useful that they should. It is true there be divers of them perceived at once; and more of some, and less of others: but accurately to compute their magnitude, and assign precise determinate proportions between things so variable and inconstant, if we suppose it possible to be done, must yet be a very trifling and insignificant labour.

157. I must confess, it seems to be the opinion of some very ingenious men that flat or plane figures are immediate objects of sight, though they acknowledge solids are not. And this opinion of theirs is grounded on what is observed in painting, wherein (say they) the ideas immediately imprinted on the mind are only of planes variously coloured, which, by a sudden act of the judgment, are changed into solids: but, with a little attention, we shall find the planes here mentioned as the immediate objects of sight are not visible but tangible planes. For, when we say that pictures are planes, we mean thereby that they appear to the touch smooth and uniform. But then this smoothness and uniformity, or, in other words, this planeness of the picture is not perceived immediately by vision; for it appeareth to the eye various and multiform.

158. From all which we may conclude that planes are no more the immediate object of sight than solids. What we strictly see are not solids, nor yet planes variously coloured— they are only diversity of colours. And some of these suggest to the mind solids, and others plane figures; just as they have been experienced to be connected with the one or the other: so that we see planes in the same way that we see solids—both being equally suggested by the immediate objects of sight, which accordingly are themselves denominated planes and solids. But, though they are called by the same names with the things marked by them, they are, nevertheless, of a nature entirely different, as hath been demonstrated.

159. What has been said is, if I mistake not, sufficient to decide the question we proposed to examine, concerning the ability of a pure spirit, such as we have described, to know geometry. It is, indeed, no easy matter for us to enter precisely into the thoughts of such an intelligence; because we cannot, without great pains, cleverly separate and disentangle in our thoughts the proper objects of sight from those of touch which are connected with them. This, indeed, in a complete degree seems scarce possible to be performed; which will not seem strange to us, if we consider how hard it is for any one to hear the words of his native language pronounced in his ears without understanding them. Though he endeavour to disunite the meaning from the sound, it will nevertheless intrude into his thoughts, and he shall find it extreme difficult, if not impossible, to put himself exactly in the posture of a foreigner that never learnt the language, so as to be affected barely with the sounds themselves, and not perceive the signification annexed to them. By this time, I suppose, it is clear that neither abstract nor visible extension makes the object of geometry; the not discerning of which may, perhaps, have created some difficulty and useless labour in mathematics.

An Appendix[1]

THE CENSURES WHICH, I am informed, have been made on the foregoing *Essay* inclined me to think I had not been clear and express enough in some points; and, to prevent being misunderstood for the future, I was willing to make any necessary alterations or additions in what I had written. But that was impracticable, the present edition having been almost finished before I received this information. Wherefore, I think it proper to consider in this place the principal objections that are come to my notice.

In the *first* place, it is objected, that in the beginning of the Essay I argue either against all use of lines and angles in optics, and then what I say is false; or against those writers only who will have it that we can perceive by sense the optic axes, angles, &c., and then it is insignificant, this being an absurdity which no one ever held. To which I answer that I argue only against those who are of opinion that we perceive the distance of objects by lines and angles, or, as they term it, by a kind of innate geometry. And, to shew that this is not fighting with my own shadow, I shall here set down a passage from the celebrated Descartes:—[2]

"Distantiam præterea discimus, per mutuam quandam con-

---

[1] [Added in the second edition.—Ed.]

[2] [*Dioptrics*, VI, 13. Translated by D. W. Hamlyn as follows:
"Furthermore, we come to recognise distance, as a result of a certain mutual concord on the part of the eyes. For, consider our blind man, who is holding two sticks *AE* and *CE*, about the length of which he is uncertain, and who has found out by investigation only the interval between his hands *A* and *C*, together with the size of the angles *ACE* and *CAE;* he can know from that, as if by a certain Geometry inborn in everyone, where the point *E* is. In the same way, when both our eyes *RST* and *rst* are turned towards *X*, the size of the line *Ss* and that of the angles *XSs* and *XsS* make us aware of the position of the point *X*. And we can find out the same thing by means of either one of the eyes, by moving its position, so that if, keeping it always directed towards *X*, we stand first at point *S* and immediately afterwards at point *s*, this will be enough for the size of the line *Ss*, and that of the two angles *XSs* and *XsS*, to present themselves simultaneously to our imagination and inform us of the mind which, although it appears a simple judgment, involves nevertheless a certain process of reasoning, similar to that by means of which Geometers measure inaccessible places by taking up two different standpoints."]

spirationem oculorum. Ut enim cæcus noster duo bacilla tenens, *A E* et *C E*, de quorum longitudine incertus, solumque intervallum manuum *A* et *C*, cum magnitudine angulorum

A C E, et *C A E* exploratum habens, inde, ut ex Geometria quadam omnibus innata, scire potest ubi sit punctum *E*.

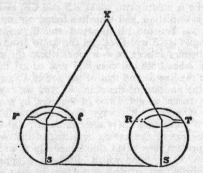

Sic quum nostri oculi *R S T* et *r s t* ambo, vertuntur ad *X*, magnitudo lineæ *S s*, et angulorum *X S s* et *X s S*, certos nos reddunt ubi sit punctum *X*. Et idem opera alterutrius possumus indagare, loco illum movendo, ut si versus *X* illum

semper dirigentes, primo sistamus in puncto *S*, et statim
post in puncto *s*, hoc sufficiet ut magnitudo lineæ *S s*, et
duorum angulorum *X S s* et *X s S* nostræ imaginationi simul
occurrant, et distantiam puncti *X* nos edoceant: idque per
actionem mentis, quæ licet simplex judicium esse videatur,
ratiocinationem tamen quandam involutam habet, similem
illi, qua Geometræ per duas stationes diversas, loca inaccessa
dimetiuntur."

I might amass togther citations from several authors to
the same purpose, but, this being so clear in the point, and
from an author of so great note, I shall not trouble the
reader with any more. What I have said on this head was
not for the sake of finding fault with other men; but, because
I judged it necessary to demonstrate in the first place that we
neither see distance *immediately,* nor yet perceive it by the
mediation of anything that hath (as lines and angles) a
necessary connexion with it. For on the demonstration of this
point the whole theory depends.

Secondly, it is objected, that the explication I give of the
appearance of the horizontal moon (which may also be
applied to the sun) is the same that Gassendus had given
before. I answer, there is indeed mention made of the grossness of the atmosphere in both; but then the methods wherein
it is applied to solve the phenomenon are widely different,
as will be evident to whoever shall compare what I have said
on this subject with the following words of Gassendus:—[3]

"Heinc dici posse videtur: solem humilem oculo specta-
tum ideo apparere majorem, quam dum altius egreditur, quia
dum vicinus est horizonti prolixa est series vaporum, atque

[3] [Translated by D. W. Hamlyn as follows:
"Hence it seems possible for it to be said that: the sun when
low-lying appears bigger when looked at by the eye than when it
ascends higher, for the reason that while it is near to the horizon
there is a wide-spread succession of vapours, and hence of atoms,
which so dull the rays of the sun, that the eye is less closed, and
the pupil, being as it were in the shade, is far more enlarged than
when, due to the sun's great height, fewer vapours intervene and
the sun itself is so bright that the pupil looking at it is made fully
contracted. This assuredly seems to be why a visible image leaving
the sun and admitted to the retina through the enlarged pupil
occupies a greater space on it, and so produces a larger appearance of the sun, than when, admitted to the same place, it passes
with effort through the contracted pupil." See Letter I, *On the
apparent size of the sun when low-lying and at its height,* p. 6.]

adeo corpusculorum quæ solis radios ita retundunt, ut oculus minus conniveat, et pupilla quasi umbrefacta longe magis amplificetur, quam dum sole multum elato rari vapores intercipiuntur, solque ipse ita splendescit, ut pupilla in ipsum spectans contractissima efficiatur. Nempe ex hoc esse videtur, cur visibilis species ex sole procedens, et per pupillam amplificatam intromissa in retinam, ampliorem in illa sedem occupet, majoremque proinde creet solis apparentiam, quam dum per contractam pupillam eodem intromissa contendit." Vid. *Epist.* I. *De Apparente Magnitudine Solis Humilis et Sublimis*, p. 6. This solution of Gassendus proceeds on a false principle, to wit, that the pupil's being enlarged augments the species or image on the fund of the eye.

Thirdly, against what is said in Sect. 80, it is objected, that the same thing which is so small as scarce to be discerned by a man, may appear like a mountain to some small insect; from which it follows that the *minimum visibile* is not equal in respect of all creatures. I answer, if this objection be sounded to the bottom, it will be found to mean no more than that the same particle of matter which is marked to a man by one *minimum visibile*, exhibits to an insect a great number of *minima visibilia*. But this does not prove that one *minimum visibile* of the insect is not equal to one *minimum visibile* of the man. The not distinguishing between the mediate and immediate objects of sight is, I suspect, a cause of misapprehension in this matter.

Some other misinterpretations and difficulties have been made, but, in the points they refer to, I have endeavoured to be so very plain that I know not how to express myself more clearly. All I shall add is, that if they who are pleased to criticise on my *Essay* would but read the whole over with some attention, they might be the better able to comprehend my meaning, and consequently to judge of my mistakes.

I am informed that, soon after the first edition of this treatise, a man somewhere near London was made to see, who had been born blind, and continued so for about twenty years. Such a one may be supposed a proper judge to decide how far some tenets laid down in several places of the foregoing Essay are agreeable to truth; and if any curious person hath the opportunity of making proper interrogatories to him thereon, I should gladly see my notions either amended or confirmed by experience.

The *Philosophical Commentaries* or Commonplace Book

In 1707–08 Berkeley filled two notebooks as a preliminary to writing the *Essay towards a New Theory of Vision* and the *Principles of Human Knowledge*. There are nearly nine hundred entries, some of the highest interest. The notebooks were originally referred to as Berkeley's *Commonplace Book,* but have been renamed by A. A. Luce the *Philosophical Commentaries*.

The present selections are an experiment. About a quarter of the entries have been ranged under a few headings, using the numbering of the Luce and Jessop edition. Occasionally, the same entry appears under two headings. The problems of the *New Theory of Vision* have not been represented, as being of less philosophical interest. The student must not think that every entry represents Berkeley's final view. We are shown Berkeley *thinking* about questions, not expounding a doctrine. But, with this caution, the notebooks are of the greatest value in studying Berkeley's philosophy.

Some of Berkeley's abbreviations have been expanded, spelling changed, and in a few cases extra punctuation has been introduced, to aid understanding.

Contents

1. *Physical objects cannot exist unperceived*

[In the entries, Berkeley's central contention that physical objects cannot exist unperceived is often referred to as the "Immaterial hypothesis" or the "New principle."]

19. In the immaterial hypothesis the wall is white, fire hot etc.

22. World without thought is *nec quid nec quantum nec quale* etc.

23. 'tis wondrous to contemplate the world emptied of intelligences.

24. Nothing properly but persons i.e. conscious things do exist, all other things are not so much existences as manners of the existence of persons.

79. Mem: that I take notice that I do not fall in with Sceptics Fardella etc, in that I make bodies to exist certainly, which they doubt of.

266. Mem: that I was distrustful at eight years old and consequently by nature disposed for these new Doctrines.

270. I wonder how men cannot see a truth so obvious, as that extension cannot exist without a thinking substance.

279. I wonder not at my sagacity in discovering the obvious though amazing truth, I rather wonder at my stupid inadvertency in not finding it out before. 'tis no witchcraft to see.

285. Ignorance in some sort requisite in the Person that should Discover the Principle.

291. The Principle easily proved by plenty of arguments *ad absurdum*.

304. The Reverse of the Principle introduced Scepticism.

349. Let my adversaries answer any one of mine I'll yield— If I don't answer every one of theirs I'll yield.

359. Our Eyes and Senses inform us not of the existence of Matter or ideas existing without the mind. They are not to be Blamed for the mistake.

377. An idea cannot exist unperceived.

379. N.B. Other arguments innumerable both *a priori* and *a posteriori* drawn from all the sciences, from the clearest plainest most obvious truths whereby to Demonstrate the Principle i.e. that neither our Ideas nor any thing like our ideas can possibly be in an unperceiving thing.

380. N.B. Not one argument, of any kind whatsoever, certain or probable, *a priori* or *a posteriori* from any art or science, from either sense or reason against it.

405. All things in the Scripture which side with the Vulgar against the Learned side with me also. I side in all things with the Mob.

406. I know there is a mighty sect of Men will oppose me, but yet I may expect to be supported by those whose minds are not so far overgrown with madness, these are far the greatest part of Mankind. Especially Moralists, Divines, Politicians, in a word all but Mathematicians and Natural Philosophers (I mean only the Hypothetical Gentlemen). Experimental Philosophers have nothing whereat to be offended in me.

407. Newton begs his Principle, I Demonstrate mine.

411. The Reverse of the Principle I take to have been the chief source of all that scepticism and folly all those contra-

dictions and inextricable puzzling absurdities, that have in all ages been a reproach to Human Reason, as well as of that Idolatry whether of Images or of Gold etc. that blinds the Greatest part of the World, as well as of that shameful immorality that turns us into Beasts.

427. We see the Horse itself, the Church itself it being an Idea and nothing more.

429. Existence is *percipi* or *percipere* ∧. the horse is in the stable, the Books are in the study as before.

429a.   ∧ or *velle* i.e. *agere*

430. In Physics I have a vast view of things soluble hereby but have not Leisure.

437. Impossible any thing Besides that which thinks and is thought on should exist.

444. I may say the pain is in my finger etc. according to my Doctrine.

491. Mem: Diligently to set forth how that many of the Ancient philosophers run into so great absurdities as even to deny the existence of motion and those other things they perceived actually by their senses. This sprung from their not knowing what existence was and wherein it consisted this the source of all their Folly, 'tis on the Discovering of the nature and meaning and import of Existence that I chiefly insist. This puts a wide difference betwixt the Sceptics and me. This I think wholly new. I am sure 'tis new to me.

563. I am the farthest from Scepticism of any man. I know with an intuitive knowledge the existence of other things as well as my own Soul. this is what Locke nor scarce any other Thinking Philosopher will pretend to.

573. Locke's very supposition that matter and motion should exist before thought is absurd, includes a manifest Contradiction.

585. Question: if there be any real Difference betwixt certain Ideas of Reflection and others of Sensation. e.g. 'twixt perception and white, black, sweet etc. wherein I pray you does the perception of white differ from white.

588. A good Proof that Existence is nothing without or distinct from Perception may be Drawn from Considering a Man put into the World without company.

589. There was a smell i.e. there was a smell perceived. Thus we see that common speech confirms my Doctrine.

593. Let it not be said that I take away Existence. I only declare the meaning of the Word so far as I can comprehend it.

597. But perhaps some man may say an inert thoughtless substance may exist though not extended, moved etc. but with other properties whereof we have no Idea. But even this I shall demonstrate to be Impossible when I come to treat more particularly of Existence.

604. I am persuaded would Men but examine what they mean by the Word Existence they would agree with me.

609. The Distinguishing betwixt an Idea and perception of the Idea has been one great cause of Imagining material substances.

625. Matter once allowed. I defy any man to prove that God is not matter.

670. Strange it is that Men should be at a loss to find their Idea of Existence since that (if such there be distinct from Perception) it is brought into the mind by all the Ways of Sensation and Reflection; methinks it should be most familiar to us and we best Acquainted with it.

671. This I am sure I have no such idea of Existence or annext to the Word Existence. and if others have that's nothing to me. they can Never make me sensible of it, simple Ideas being uncommunicable by Language.

686. Scripture and possibility are the only proofs with Malebranche add to these what he calls a great propension to think so. this perhaps may be questioned. perhaps men if they think before they speak will not be found so thoroughly persuaded of the Existence of Matter.

686a. On second thoughts I am on the other extreme, I am certain of that which Malebranche seems to doubt of. viz. the existence of Bodies.

689. The word thing as comprising or standing for Idea and volition useful. as standing for Idea and Archetype without the Mind Mischievous and useless.

740. We must with the Mob place certainty in the senses.

799. Opinion that existence was distinct from perception of Horrible Consequence it is the foundation of Hobbes' doctrine. etc.

824. My Doctrines rightly understood all that Philosophy of Epicurus, Hobbes, Spinoza etc. which has been a Declared Enemy of Religion Comes to the Ground.

832. The Philosophers Talk much of a distinction 'twixt absolute and relative things, or 'twixt things considered in their own natures, and the same things considered with respect to us. I know not what they mean by things considered in themselves. This is nonsense, Jargon.

2. *Primary and Secondary qualities*

20. Primary ideas proved not to exist in matter, after the same manner that secondary ones are proved not to exist therein.

57. Extension thought peculiarly inert because not accompanied with pleasure and pain; hence thought to exist in matter as also for that it was conceived common to two senses.

57a. as also the constant perception of them

78. Of solidity see Locke bk. 2 ch. 4 sec. 1, 5, 6. If any one ask what solidity is let him put a flint between his hands and he will know. Extension of Body is continuity of solid etc, extension of space is continuity of unsolid etc.

78a. Why may not I say visible extension is a continuity of visible points tangible extension is a Continuity of tangible points.

222. Men are in the right in judging their simple ideas to be in the things themselves, certainly Heat and colour is as much without the mind as figure, motion, time etc.

288a. The great argument to prove that Extension cannot be in an unthinking substance is that it cannot be conceived distinct from or without all tangible or visible quality.

325. Big, little and number are the works of the mind. How therefore can the extension you suppose in matter be big or little, how can it consist of any number of points?

392. There are men who say there are insensible extensions, there are others who say the Wall is not white, the fire is not hot etc. We Irish men cannot attain to these truths.

450a. Motion distinct from the thing moved is not Conceivable.

453. Ask a Cartesian whether he wont to imagine his globules without colour, pellucidness is a colour. The colour of ordinary light of the Sun is white. Newton in the right in assigning colours to the rays of light.

454. A man born Blind would not imagine Space as we do. we give it always some dilute or duskish or dark colour. in short we imagine it as visible or intromitted by the Eye which he would not do.

533. When you speak of the Corpuscularian Essences of Bodies mem: to reflect on sect: 11 and 12 bk. 4. ch. 3. Locke. Motion supposes not solidity a mere Coloured Extension may give us the Idea of motion.

711. Extension seems to be a Mode of some tangible or sensible quality according as it is seen or felt.

864. Certainly we should not see Motion if there was no diversity of Colours.

865. Motion is an abstract Idea i.e. there is no such Idea that Can be conceived by itself.

3. *Substance*

89. Material substance bantered by Locke bk. 2 ch. 13 sec. 19

512. Question: whether the substance of Body or any thing else, be any more than the Collection of Ideas included in that thing. Thus the substance of any particular Body is extension solidity figure. of General Body no idea.

517. I take not away substances. I ought not to be accused of discarding Substance out of the reasonable World. I only reject the Philosophic sense (which in effect is no sense) of the word substance. Ask a man never tainted with their jargon what he means by corporeal substance, or the substance of Body, He shall answer Bulk, Solidity and such like sensible qualities. These I retain. the Philosophic *nec quid nec quantum nec quale* whereof I have no idea I discard. if a man may be said to discard that which never had any being was never so much as imagined or conceived.

517a. N. B. I am more for reality than any other Philosophers, they make a thousand doubts and know not certainly but we may be deceived. I assert the direct Contrary.

518. In short be not angry you lose nothing. whether real or chimerical whatever you can in any wise conceive or imagine be it ever so wild so extravagant and absurd much good may it do you. you may enjoy it for me. I'll not deprive you of it.

601. Incongruous in Locke to fancy we want a sense proper to see substances withal.

724. There is a Philosopher who says we can get an idea of substance by no way of Sensation or Reflection. and seems to imagine that we want a sense proper for it. Truly if we had a new sense it could only give us a new Idea. now I suppose he will not say substance according to him is an Idea. for my part I own I have no Idea can stand for substance in his or the Schoolmen's sense of that word. But take it in the common vulgar sense and then we see and feel substance.

4. *We have no good reason to believe there are material objects lying beyond our ideas*

74. Allowing there be extended solid etc. substances without the mind 'tis impossible the mind should know or perceive them. the mind even according to the materialists perceiving only the impressions made upon its brain or rather the ideas attending those impressions.

476. The silliness of the Current Doctrine makes much for me. they commonly suppose a material world, figures, motions, bulks of various sizes etc. according to their own confession to no purpose, all our sensations may be and sometimes actually are without them. nor can men so much as conceive it possible they should concur in any wise to the production of them.

477. Ask a man I mean a Cartesian why he supposes this vast structure, this compages of Bodies. he shall be at a stand, he'll not have One word to say. which sufficiently shows the folly of the hypothesis:

477a. or rather why he supposes all this Matter, for bodies and their qualities I do allow to exist independently of Our mind.

606. The supposition that things are distinct from Ideas takes away all real Truth, and consequently brings in a Universal Scepticism, since all our knowledge and contemplation is confined barely to our own Ideas.

818. Say Descartes and Malebranche God hath given us strong inclinations to think our Ideas proceed from Bodies. or that Bodies do exist. Pray what mean they by this. Would they have it that the Ideas of imagination are images of and proceed from the Ideas of Sense. this is true but cannot be their meaning for they speak of Ideas of sense themselves as proceeding from being like unto I know not what.

5. *Ideas can only resemble ideas*

46. Question: what can be like a sensation but a sensation?

47. Question: Did ever any man see any other things besides his own ideas, that he should compare them to these and make these like unto them?

50. Nothing but ideas perceivable.

51. A man cannot compare two things together without perceiving them each, ergo he cannot say any thing which is not an idea is like or unlike an idea.

299. But say you the thought or perception I call extension is not itself in an unthinking thing or matter. But it is like something which is in matter. Well, says I, do you apprehend and conceive what you say extension is like unto or do you not. If the latter, how know you they are alike, how can you compare any things besides your own ideas. if the former it must be an idea i.e. perception thought, or sensation which to be in an unperceiving thing is a Contradiction.

438. That which is visible cannot be made up of invisible things.

861. What can an Idea be like but another Idea, we can compare it with Nothing else, a Sound like a sound, a Colour like a Colour.

862. Is it not nonsense to say a Smell is like a thing which cannot be smelt, a Colour is like a thing which cannot be seen.

6. *Causation*

71. By immateriality is solved the cohesion of bodies, or rather the dispute ceases.

109. What affects us must be a thinking thing for what thinks not cannot subsist.

131. No active power but the will, therefore matter if it exists affects us not.

155. We cannot possibly conceive any active power but the Will.

403. Trifling for the Philosophers to enquire the cause of Magnetical attractions etc. They only search after coexisting ideas.

433. One idea not the cause of another, one power not the cause of another. The cause of all natural things is only God. Hence trifling to enquire after second Causes. This Doctrine gives a most suitable idea of the Divinity.

461. The simple idea called Power seems obscure or rather none at all. but only the relation 'twixt cause and Effect. When I ask whether A can move B, if A be an intelligent thing, I mean no more than whether the volition of A that B move be attended with the motion of B, if A be senseless whether the impulse of A against B be followed by the motion of B.

486. Materialists must allow the Earth to be actually moved by the Attractive power of every stone that falls from the air. with many other the like absurdities.

498. Mem: much to Recommend and approve of Experimental Philosophy.

499. What means Cause as distinguished from Occasion? nothing but a Being which wills when the Effect follows the volition. Those things that happen from without we are not the Cause of, therefore there is some other Cause of them i.e. there is a being that wills these perceptions in us.

548. We move our Legs our selves. 'tis we that will their movement. Herein I differ from Malebranche.

754. Naturalists do not distinguish betwixt Cause and occasion. Useful to enquire after coexisting Ideas or occasions.

850. I say there are no Causes (properly speaking) but

Spiritual, nothing active but Spirit. Say you, this is only Verbal, 'tis only annexing a new sort of signification to the word Cause, and why may not others as well retain the old one, and call one Idea the Cause of another which always follows it. I answer, if you do so, I shall drive you into many absurdities. I say you cannot avoid running into opinions you'll be glad to disown if you stick firmly to that signification of the Word Cause.

855. We must carefully distinguish betwixt two sorts of Causes Physical and Spiritual;

856. Those may more properly be Called occasions yet (to comply) we may term them Causes. but then we must mean Causes that do nothing.

884. I think not that things fall out of necessity, the connexion of no two Ideas is necessary. 'tis all the result of freedom i.e. 'tis all Voluntary.

7. Unobserved objects

52. Bodies etc. do exist even when not perceived they being powers in the active Being.

98. The Trees are in the Park, that is, whether I will or no whether I imagine any thing about them or no, let me but go thither and open my Eyes by day and I shall not avoid seeing them.

185. Mem: to allow existence to colours in the dark, persons not thinking etc. but not an absolute actual existence. 'Tis prudent to correct men's mistakes without altering their language. This makes truth glide into their souls insensibly.

185a. Colours in the dark do exist really *i.e.* were there light or as soon as light comes we shall see them provided we open our eyes. and that whether we will or no.

436. How was light created before man? even so were Bodies created before man.

472. You ask me whether the books are in the study now when no one is there to see them. I answer yes. you ask me are we not in the wrong for imagining things to exist when they are not actually perceived by the senses. I answer no. the existence of our ideas consists in being perceived, imagined, thought on. whenever they are imagined or thought

on they do exist. Whenever they are mentioned or discoursed of they are imagined and thought on therefore you can at no time ask me whether they exist or no, but by reason of that very question they must necessarily exist.

473. But say you then a Chimera does exist. I answer it doth in one sense. *i.e.* it is imagined. but it must be well noted that existence is vulgarly restrained to actual perception. and that I use the word Existence in a larger sense than ordinary.

723. I may say earth, plants etc. were created before Man there being other intelligences to perceive them before Man was created.

8. *Appearance and Reality*

286. Thoughts do most properly signify or are mostly taken for the interior operations of the mind, wherein the mind is active, those that obey not the acts of Volition, and in which the mind is passive are more properly called sensations or perceptions, But that is all a case.

474. N. B. according to my Doctrine all things are *entia rationis* i.e. *solum habent esse in Intellectu.*

474a. according to my Doctrine all are not *entia rationis* the distinction between *ens rationis* and *ens reale* is kept up by it as well as any other Doctrine.

479. The grand, puzzling question whether I sleep or wake? easily solved.

535. Well say you according to this new Doctrine all is but mere Idea, there is nothing which not an *ens rationis*. I answer things are as real and exist *in rerum natura* as much as ever. the distinction betwixt *entia Realia* and *entia rationis* may be made as properly now as ever. Do but think before you speak. Endeavour rightly to comprehend my meaning and you'll agree with me in this.

550. Mem: again and again to mention and illustrate the Doctrine of the Reality of Things *Rerum Natura* etc.

582. The having Ideas is not the same thing with Perception. a Man may have Ideas when he only Imagines. But then this Imagination presupposeth Perception.

657a. properly speaking Idea is the picture of the Imagination's making, this is the likeness of and referred to the real Idea or (if you will) thing.

783. Cause of much error and Confusion that Men Knew not what was meant by Reality.

807. Say you, at this rate all's nothing but Idea mere phantasm. I answer every thing as real as ever. I hope to call a thing Idea makes it not the less real. truly I should perhaps have stuck to the word thing and not mentioned the Word Idea were it not for a Reason and I think a good one too which I shall give in the Second Book.

823. Ideas of Sense are the Real things or Archetypes. Ideas of Imagination, Dreams etc. are copies, images of these.

843. The distinction between Idea and Ideatum I cannot otherwise conceive than by making one the effect or consequence of Dream, rêverie, Imagination, the other of sense and the Constant laws of Nature.

9. *God*

41. Nothing corresponds to our primary ideas without but powers, hence a direct and brief demonstration of an active powerful being distinct from us on whom we depend. etc.

675. God May comprehend all Ideas even the Ideas which are painful and unpleasant without being in any degree pained thereby. Thus we ourselves can imagine the pain of a burn etc. without any misery or uneasiness at all.

782. Absurd to Argue the Existence of God from his Idea. we have no Idea of God. 'tis impossible!

830. Why may we not conceive it possible for God to create things out of Nothing. certainly we ourselves create in some wise whenever we imagine.

838. Every sensation of mine which happens in Consequence of the general, known Laws of nature and is from without *i.e.* independent of my Will demonstrates the Being of a God. *i.e.* of an unextended incorporeal Spirit which is omniscient, omnipotent etc.

10. *Spirits*

[The notebooks show us Berkeley in considerable doubt and difficulty on this topic. He changes his views a number of times. The nature of mind or spirit is the central internal problem in Berkeley's philosophy, but the entries here suggest that it was one that he never thought out fully or satisfactorily. This may explain why the projected Part II of the *Principles*, on spirits, was never published.]

24. Nothing properly but persons *i.e.* conscious things do exist, all other things are not so much existences as manners of the existence of persons.

25. Question: about the Soul or rather person whether it be not completely known.

44. Question: whether being might not be the substance of the soul. or (otherwise thus) whether being added to the faculties complete the real essence and adequate definition of the soul?

154. By Soul is meant only a Complex idea made up of existence, willing and perception in a large sense. therefore it is known and it may be defined

176. Speech metaphorical more than we imagine insensible things and their modes circumstances etc. being expressed for the most part by words borrowed from things sensible. the reason's plain. Hence Manifold Mistakes.

176a. The grand Mistake is that we think we have Ideas of the Operations of our Minds. certainly this Metaphorical dress is an argument we have not.

193. As well make tastes, smells, fear, shame wit, virtue, vice and all thoughts move with Local motion as immaterial spirit.

194. On account of my doctrine the identity of finite substances must consist in something else than continued existence, or relation to determined time and place of beginning to exist. the existence of our thoughts (which being combined make all substances) being frequently interrupted, and they having divers beginnings, and endings.

194a. Question: Whether Identity of Person consists not in the Will

200. Question: wherein consists identity of Person? not in actual consciousness, for then I'm not the same person I was this day twelvemonth, but while I think of what I then

did. Not in potential for then all persons may be the same for aught we know.

230. Absurd that men should know the soul by idea, ideas being inert, thoughtless, Hence Malebranche confuted.

478. Question: how is the soul distinguished from its ideas? certainly if there were no sensible ideas there could be no soul, no perception, remembrance, love, fear etc. no faculty could be exerted.

478a. The soul is the will properly speaking and, as it, is distinct from Ideas.

490. Question: whether it were not better not to call the operations of the mind ideas, confining this term to things sensible?

523. It seems improper and liable to difficulties to make the Word Person stand for an Idea, or to make ourselves Ideas or thinking things ideas.

576. We think we know not the Soul because we have no imaginable or sensible Idea annexed to that sound. This the Effect of prejudice.

577. The very existence of Ideas constitutes the soul.

579. Consult, ransack your Understanding what find you there besides several perceptions or thoughts. What mean you by the word mind. you must mean something that you perceive or that you do not perceive. a thing not perceived is a contradiction. to mean (also) a thing you do not perceive is a contradiction. We are in all this matter strangely abused by words.

580. Mind is a congeries of Perceptions. Take away Perceptions and you take away the Mind put the Perceptions and you put the mind.

581. Say you the Mind is not the Perceptions. but that thing which perceives. I answer you are abused by the words "that" and "thing" these are vague empty words without a meaning.

587. The Understanding seemeth not to differ from its perceptions or Ideas. Question: what must one think of the Will and passions.

614. the Understanding not distinct from particular perceptions or Ideas.

614a. The Understanding taken for a faculty is not really distinct from the Will.

615. The Will not distinct from Particular volitions.

615a. This altered hereafter

621. To say the Will is a power. Volition is an act. This *idem per idem*.

637. Say you there must be a thinking substance. Something unknown which perceives and supports and ties together the Ideas. Say I, make it appear there is any need of it and you shall have it for me. I care not to take away any thing I can see the least reason to think should exist.

643. The grand Cause of perplexity and darkness in treating of the Will, is that we Imagine it to be an object of thought (to speak with the vulgar), we think we may perceive, contemplate and view it like any of our Ideas whereas in truth 'tis no idea. Nor is there any Idea of it. 'tis *toto coelo* different from the Understanding *i.e.* from all our Ideas. If you say the will or rather a Volition is something I answer there is an Homonymy in the word thing when applied to Ideas and volitions and understanding and will. all ideas are passive, volitions active. . . .

644. Thing and Idea are much-what words of the same extent and meaning. why therefore do I not use the word thing? Answer: because thing is of greater latitude than Idea. Thing comprehends also volitions or actions. now these are no ideas.

650. Locke seems to be mistaken when he says thought is not essential to the mind.

651. Certainly the mind always and constantly thinks and we know this too In Sleep and trances the mind exists not there is no time no succession of Ideas.

652. To say the mind exists without thinking is a Contradiction, nonsense, nothing.

657. To ask have we an idea of the Will or volition is nonsense. an idea can resemble nothing but an idea.

663. I have no Idea of a Volition or act of the mind neither has any other Intelligence for that were a contradiction.

672. Say you the unknown substratum of Volitions and Ideas, is something whereof I have no Idea. I ask is there any other

Being which has or can have an Idea of it. if there be then it must be itself an Idea which you will think absurd.

684. An Idea being itself unactive cannot be the resemblance or image of an Active thing.

701. The substance of Body we know, the substance of Spirit we do not know it not being knowable. it being *purus actus*.

704. Locke's out. The case is different. we can have an Idea of Body without motion, but not of Soul without Thought.

706. No Perception according to Locke is active. Therefore no perception (*i.e.* no Idea) can be the image of or like unto that which is altogether active and not at all passive *i.e.* the Will.

708. The will and the Understanding may very well be thought two distinct beings.

712. The Spirit, the Active thing, that which is Soul and God, is the Will alone. The Ideas are effects impotent things.

713. The Concrete of the Will and understanding I must call Mind not person, lest offence be given, there being but one volition acknowledged to be God. Mem: Carefully to omit Defining of Person, or making much mention of it.

714. You ask do these volitions make one Will. what you ask is merely about a Word. Unite being no more.

715. N. B. To use utmost Caution not to give the least Handle of offence to the Church or Church-men.

738. *Cogito ergo sum*, Tautology, no mental Proposition answering thereto.

744. Question: what mean you by My perceptions, my Volitions? *Respondeo*, all the perceptions I perceive or conceive etc. are mine, all the Volitions I am Conscious to are mine.

788. We see no variety or difference betwixt the Volitions, only between their effects. 'Tis One Will one Act distinguished by the effects. This will, this Act is the Spirit, operative, Principle, Soul etc.

791. While I exist or have any Idea I am eternally, constantly willing, my acquiescing in the present State is willing.

792. The Existence of any thing imaginable is nothing dif-

ferent from Imagination or perception. Volition or Will which is not imaginable, regard must not be had to its existence at least in the first Book.

808. Idea is the object or Subject of thought; that I think on whatever it be, I call Idea. thought itself, or Thinking is no Idea 'tis an act i.e. Volition i.e. as contradistinguished to effects, the Will.

820. Question: may not there be an Understanding without a Will.

821. Understanding is in some sort an Action.

828. The Will is *purus actus* or rather pure Spirit not imaginable, not sensible, not intelligible, in no wise the object of the understanding, no wise perceivable.

829. Substance of a Spirit is that it acts, causes, wills, operates, or if you please (to avoid the quibble that may be made on the word it) to act, cause, will, operate. its substance is not knowable not being an Idea.

841. It seems to me that Will and understanding Volitions and ideas cannot be severed, that either cannot be possibly without the other.

842. Some Ideas or other I must have so long as I exist or Will. But no one Idea or sort of Ideas is essential.

847. But the Grand Mistake is that we know not what we mean by we or selves or mind etc. 'tis most sure and certain that our Ideas are distinct from the Mind i.e. the Will, the Spirit.

848. I must not Mention the Understanding as a faculty or part of the Mind, I must include Understanding and Will etc. in the word Spirit by which I mean all that is active. I must not say that the Understanding differs not from the particular Ideas, or the Will from particular Volitions.

849. The Spirit, the Mind, is neither a Volition nor an Idea.

854. Will, Understanding, desire, Hatred etc. so far forth as they are acts or active differ not, all their difference consists in their objects, circumstances etc.

863. Bodies exist without the Mind i.e. are not the Mind, but distinct from it. This I allow, the Mind being altogether different therefrom.

870. I must not give the Soul or Mind the Scholastic Name pure act, but rather pure Spirit or active Being.

871. I must not say the Will and Understanding are all one but that they are both Abstract Ideas *i.e.* none at all. they not being even *ratione* different from the Spirit, *Qua* faculties, or Active.

878. Extension tho' it exist only in the Mind, yet is no Property of the Mind, The Mind can exist without it tho' it cannot without the Mind. But in Book 2 I shall at large shew the difference there is betwixt the Soul and Body or Extended being:

882. I will grant you that extension, Colour etc. may be said to be without the Mind in a double respect *i.e.* as independent of our Will and as distinct from the Mind.

886. If a man with his Eyes shut Imagines to Himself the Sun and firmament you will not say he or his Mind is the Sun or Extended. tho' Neither sun or firmament be without his Mind.

887. 'Tis strange to find Philosophers doubting and disputing whether, they have Ideas of spiritual things or no. Surely 'tis easy to know.

11. *Abstract Ideas*

139. Preliminary discourse about singling and abstracting simple ideas.

318. Question. is it not impossible there should be General ideas? All ideas come from without, they are all particular. The mind, 'tis true, can consider one thing without another, but then considered asunder they make not two ideas. both together can make but one as for instance Colour and Visible extension.

497. Question: How can there be any abstract ideas of Colours? it seems not so easily as of tastes or sounds. But then all abstract ideas whatsoever are particular. I can by no means conceive a general idea. 'Tis one thing to abstract one idea from another of a different kind. and another thing to abstract an idea from all particulars of the same kind.

524. General Ideas Cause of much Trifling and Mistake.

552. The abstract Idea of Being or Existence is never thought

of by the Vulgar. they never use those words standing for abstract Ideas.

561. If men did not use words for Ideas they would never have thought of abstract ideas. certainly genera and species are not abstract general ideas. These include a contradiction in their nature v. Locke Bk. 4 Sec. 9 Ch. 7.

564. Doctrine of Abstraction of very evil consequence in all the Sciences. Mem: Bacon's remark. Entirely owing to Language.

566. Of great use and the last Importance to Contemplate a man put into the world alone with admirable abilities. and see how after long experience he would know without words. Such a one would never think of Genera and Species or abstract general Ideas.

567. Wonderful in Locke that he would when advanced in years see at all through a mist that had been so long a gathering and was consequently thick. This more to be admired than that he didn't see farther.

591. We are frequently puzzled and at a loss in obtaining clear and determined meanings of words commonly in use. and that because we imagine words stand for general Ideas which are altogether inconceivable.

594. If you take away abstraction, how do men differ from Beasts. I answer by shape. By Language rather by Degrees of more and less.

638. I affirm 'tis manifestly absurd. no excuse in the world can be given why a man should use a word without an idea. Certainly we shall find that whatever word we make use of in matter of pure reasoning has or ought to have a complete Idea annexed to it. *i.e.*: its meaning or the sense we take it in must be completely known.

667. 'Tis allowed that Particles stand not for Ideas and yet they are not said to be empty useless sounds. The truth on't is they stand for the operations of the mind *i.e.* volitions.

687. Mem: to bring the killing blow at the last v.g. in the matter of Abstraction to bring Locke's general triangle at the last.

688. They give good rules tho' perhaps they themselves do not always observe them. they speak much of clear and

distinct Ideas. tho' at the same they talk of General, abstract ideas etc. I'll instance in Locke's opinion of abstraction he being as clear a writer as I have met with. Such was the Candour of this great Man that I persuade my Self were he alive. he would not be offended that I differ from him seeing that even in so doing. I follow his advice viz. to use my own Judgment, see with my own eyes and not with an-others. Introd:

703. Abstract Ideas only to be had amongst the Learned. The Vulgar never think they have any such, nor truly do they find any want of them. Genera and Species and abstract Ideas are terms unknown to them.

772. Existence, Extension etc. are abstract *i.e.* no ideas. they are words unknown and useless to the Vulgar.

779. I approve of this axiom of the Schoolmen *nihil est in intellectu quod non prius fuit in sensu.* I wish they had stuck to it. it had never taught them the Doctrine of Abstract Ideas.

12. *Space*

36. When we imagine two bowls v.g. moving *in vacuo,* 'tis only conceiving a person affected with those sensations.

96. Space without any bodies being *in rerum natura,* would not be extended as not having parts in that parts are assigned to it with respect to body from whence also the notion of distance is taken, now without either parts or distance or mind how can there be space or anything beside one uniform nothing?

290. The great danger of making extension exist without the mind. in that if it does it must be acknowledged infinite immutable eternal etc. which will be to make either God extended (which I think dangerous) or an eternal, immutable, infinite, increate being beside God.

876. If there were only one Ball in the World it Could not be moved. there could be no variety of Appearance.

13. *Time*

[Like the question of Spirits, Time involves serious prob-lems within Berkeley's system, which are not discussed as they should be in his published writings. (See also the *Correspondence with Samuel Johnson,* in this volume.)]

3. Whether succession of ideas in the divine intellect?

4. Time train of ideas succeeding each other.

5. Duration not distinguished from existence.

7. Why time in pain, longer than time in pleasure?

9. The same "now" not common to all intelligences.

13. Time a sensation, therefore only in the mind.

14. Eternity is only a train of innumerable ideas. hence the immortality of the Soul easily conceived. or rather the immortality of the person, that of the soul not being necessary for aught we can see.

16. What if succession of ideas were swifter, what if slower?

39. In some dreams succession of ideas swifter than at other times.

48. The age of a fly for aught that we know may be as long as that of a man.

83. Men die or are in state of annihilation oft in a day.

92. Question: whether if succession of ideas in the Eternal mind, a day does not seem to God a thousand years rather than a thousand years a day?

590. No broken Intervals of Death or Annihilation. Those Intervals are nothing. Each Person's time being measured to him by his own Ideas.

651. Certainly the mind always and constantly thinks and we know this too In Sleep and trances the mind exists not there is no time no succession of Ideas.

Index

inquire which of these is the object of geometry.

Index

I

J

L

O

P

R

S

T

S

T

U

V

W